Death Sentences

DEATH SENTENCES

Styles of Dying in British Fiction

———————— □ ————————

Garrett Stewart

Harvard University Press
Cambridge, Massachusetts
London, England
1984

Copyright © 1984 by the President and Fellows of Harvard College
All rights reserved
Printed in the United States of America
10 9 8 7 6 5 4 3 2 1

Publication of this book has been aided by a grant from the
Andrew W. Mellon Foundation

This book is printed on acid-free paper, and its binding materials
have been chosen for strength and durability.

Library of Congress Cataloging in Publication Data
Stewart, Garrett.
Death sentences.
Includes bibliographical references and index.
1. English fiction—History and criticism.
2. Death in literature. I. Title.
PR830.D37S73 1984   823'.009'354   84-708
ISBN 0-674-19428-4 (alk. paper)

Page 392 constitutes an extension of the copyright page.

Illustration on title page
Death Staying the Hand of the Sculptor
by Daniel Chester French
Courtesy The Metropolitan Museum of Art,
Gift of a group of Trustees, 1926

Design by Marianne Perlak

For Nataša

Acknowledgments

A book on death has no less trouble getting born than any other, and accumulates no fewer debts in the arrival. The genesis of the present study was in the last paragraph of my earlier book, *Dickens and the Trials of Imagination*, where I suggested that by visionary wit alone certain Dickensian characters could face "the ultimate anonymity of death itself." That book was no sooner in print than I started seriously to wonder just what such a claim might really mean—why exactly death should in this way become the ultimate trial of the imagination.

When this embryonic question began shaping itself as a long-term topic of investigation, it had to develop from a mere subject into a manageable project. On the way, as with so many ideas, it became a grant application. For support at this stage I am pleased to record publicly my debt to J. Hillis Miller, John Rosenberg, Robert Scholes, and Mark Spilka. For the resulting year off during which to nurture the project into an argument, I thank the John Simon Guggenheim Memorial Foundation, and for grants in aid to start shaping the argument into chapters, the Faculty Senate of the University of California at Santa Barbara. I am grateful also to the research staffs of the Morgan Library, the Berg Collection of the New York Public Library, the British Library, and the Forster Collection of the Victoria and Albert Museum for their time and patience in facilitating my work with Dickens and Woolf manuscripts, and to Quentin Bell for permission to reproduce material from the latter.

At early stages of its gestation my thesis had the good fortune to begin testing itself on various reading and listening audiences. For the sometimes premature exercise of my ideas, none of them reprinted here in their original form, I am indebted both for space and advice to the editors of *Novel, ELH, The Missouri Review, PMLA, Dickens Studies Annual,* and the critical anthologies *Toward a Poetics of*

Fiction and *Philosophical Approaches to Literature.* A similar gratitude is extended to those responsive lecture audiences who helped question my provisional findings into firmer shape, both at the Davis and Santa Cruz campuses of the University of California and at Yale University, the latter a homecoming arranged through the unforgotten kindness of Marie Borroff.

Nor will I soon forget the friendship and hospitality of the several couples on both coasts who found themselves putting me up, and putting up with me, during research on this project. To Cindy and Paul Reggiardo, Kathleen and Leslie Langs, Betsy and Max Gitter, and especially to Sandra and Elliot Gilbert, who not only feasted me but helped diet my chapters, once again my thanks. So too to Gordon Stewart, who always kept a second home waiting for me—and a room to work.

Delivered now as a book after so much shared labor, these pages know that their afterlife will be partly owed not just to the faith but to the specific good works of others. I wish to thank in particular those first brave readers importuned by me, often to the tune of two chapters at a time, with rough drafts of my argument. Invaluable in those early anxious hours were Patrick McCarthy, David Neuman, Michael Ragussis, Muriel Zimmerman, and my superb research assistant Anthony Roche, who repeatedly turned sleuthing into collaboration. There too from the beginning was, as ever, Sharon Cameron.

Later versions of my chapters were eventually both chastened and graced by sets of readers as incisive as kind. The introductory pages, and I with them, have Timothy Gould, Donald Pearce, and Everett Zimmerman to thank; those on Dickens and the Victorians, Elliot and Sandra Gilbert and Linda Kauffman; on Conrad, Eloise Knapp Hay and Gary Karasik; on Lawrence and Woolf, Sandra again, Stephen Miko and Jan Bowman Swanson; and on Beckett and Nabokov, Porter Abbott and William Carroll. For at last making these chapters continuously legible, my thanks to the tireless and expert manuscript preparation, and wonderful good temper, of Kristina Nash.

Through it all (as she more than anyone else helped see me) my deepest gratitude is to the love and wit of Nataša Ďurovičová, the incomparable reader, translator, adviser, and friend to whom, with all love in return, this book is dedicated: a dedication which should rightly read "But for Nataša——."

Contents

Life has no end in the way our visual field has no limit

LUDWIG WITTGENSTEIN
Tractatus

It is a street of perishing blind houses, with their eyes stoned
out . . . and every door might be Death's Door.

CHARLES DICKENS
Bleak House

So she's at death's door, eh? Hope they can pull her through.

W. C. FIELDS
It's a Gift

For the approaches of Death are by illumination.

CHRISTOPHER SMART
Jubilate Agno

Points of Departure

The Drama, by Honoré Daumier
Courtesy Neue Pinakothek, Munich

In literature and in the theater . . . we find the plurality of
lives which we need. We die with the hero with whom we
have identified ourselves; yet we survive him, and are ready
to die again just as safely with another hero.

SIGMUND FREUD, "Thoughts for the
Times on War and Death"

1

Because we have neither hereditary nor direct
    knowledge of Death
It is the trigger of the literary man's biggest gun
And we are happy to equate it to any conceived calm.

    WILLIAM EMPSON, "Ignorance of Death"

Often beneath the wave, wide from this ledge
The dice of drowned men's bones he saw bequeath
An Embassy. Their numbers as he watched,
Beat on the dusty shore and were obscured.

And wrecks passed without sound of bells,
The calyx of death's bounty giving back
A scattered chapter, livid hieroglyph,
The portent wound in corridors of shells.

    HART CRANE, "At Melville's Tomb,"
    White Buildings

THIS IS A BOOK about terminals and boundaries, mortality and closure, the infinitesimals of style and the finite limits of representational language, about least and last things together. It is a book, to start with, about three vast and familiar facts of life and art: death, content, and form. Only by their particular triangulation in the genre of prose fiction do they mark out the hypothesis of the present study: that death in fiction is the fullest instance of form indexing content, is indeed the moment when content, comprising the imponderables of negation and vacancy, can be found dissolving to pure form. Death in narrative yields, by yielding to, sheer style.

In the life outside of novels, death often invites and defies imagination at once, terrifies and refutes our sense of identity and of the mortal language we would use to phrase its finish. What in everyday experience is there to say about—and what words for it—that sudden absence called death where a moment before there was a self? And how does the verbal artifice of fiction help to redeem our speechlessness in the face of such vacancy, to premeditate our sense of an ending?[1] Despite its brutal factuality as the close of life, dying is by nature the one inevitably fictional matter in prose fiction. Death for the self exists only as nonexistence, is not a topic so much as a voiding event, has no vocabulary native to it, would leave us mute before its impenetrable fact. In writers as divergent as the Victorians Dickens and Hardy, the modernists Conrad and Woolf, death as narrative moment must be approximated by a verbal style charged with elusive evocation in lieu of evidence, not just in the lack of such testimony but in the very space of its absence.

Even in the Vanitas mode in painting, with its looming death's-heads and skeletal forms, death is not finally a cogent abstraction. As in literature, the memento mori stands as an admonition based on no possible memory, motif without referent, a caveat with no accusative case in point except for the flayed structure of the once-living body. The literary abstraction of mortal closure must always come up against the referential blank of the impervious noun *death*,[2] the most rigid, ungiving, and empty of terms, what Hegel called that "single expressionless syllable."[3] A part of speech only, no piece of experience, the radical abstraction death is pure construct, pure language. Treacherous, excessive, the occasion of terror without being a renderable object of it, the notion lurking invisible in the name of death, waiting untamed beyond any representation, remains, for all its attendant anxiety, unthinkable; for all its tenacity, in the root sense *untenable*—refusing containment either of content or by form—becoming in itself just a form or figure of speech.

This is so even when an attempt is made to refigure, to objectify death as a concrete "thing" capable of attribution. Henry James is famously reported to have said, after suffering a stroke shortly before his death, that as he fell he thought to himself, "So here it has come at last—the Distinguished Thing."[4] In the etymological sense of *distinguished*, evoking what is apart from as well as above all else, death is the phenomenon absolutely distinct from others, the ultimate difference, antithesis taken to the limit. Only in this way can death be thought momentarily to elevate the self isolated by it to the central protagonist of the one universal plot. Exclusivity itself, death is pure distinction both constituted as well as bestowed. Despite the unsayable being discounted by James's irony to the honorifically modified noun *thing*, more generally it is the intransigent abstraction death that persists across literary history as a semantically unoccupied zone of utterance, at once linguistic horizon and void. Beckett's novel of an anonymous man dying is called *The Unnamable*, for instance, not only for its title character but for its title action. Once established as sheer term—whether as noun, adjective, or verb—the amorphous shape of death can manifest and ramify itself only by rhetorical ingenuity. More invention than evocation, death necessitates a mastery of "the Impossible" by style.[5] When the linguistic forms *death*, *dead*, and *die* are extrapolated from their own referential vacuum into anything like a subjective episode of narrated dying, language unfolds a definitive instance of pure story, unapproachable by report. Alternately void and fiction without ever emerging as cognitive event, death in the novel transforms human enigma to a paradigm of narrativity.

Death's consequent linguistic extremity—of vocabulary, syntax, and ellipsis—readily widens to a clarifying structural perspective on plot and closure. When the workings of prose edge near enough to death's essential void, the artifice of style's own inchings into or archings over the abyss is thrown into unprecedented relief against fatality's ground of negation. The death scene thereby becomes not just a sounding board of moral ultimates or psychological limits but an isolated field of entirely verbal energies and intersections. Death in fiction aspires beyond mimesis to an absolute poesis of the word. At the same time, the death scene inscribes an inevitable rehearsal of closure not only as inherent sense of limit but as ever-nearing end, the point where all utterance dissipates again to the fund of silence from which it comes.

As William Empson has it, death is the trigger of the writer's biggest gun. This is presumably because, in narrative prose for example, being pointed at one or more protagonists in any story, death is aimed always at the central component of plot, at character, and at the center of character: identity. But Empson would also respond to the delicate verbal mechanics by which that trigger must be engaged for its local dramatic aims, as well as to the enclosing structural motives for such an expenditure of narrative ammunition in the first place. Empson suggests in his poem "Ignorance of Death" that we may choose to "equate" death to "any conceived calm." We might take him in part to imply that this equation is often made to the structural calm of literary conception itself in the form of a closed story or text. In "The End" is thus our beginning. As resourceless, mute, or stupid as one may feel on the subject of death in the life beyond the confines of literature, so all the less can fiction afford, in either of Empson's typically ambiguous senses, to remain "ignorant" either of or about the human fact of dying in its shaping power over narrative. A novel, without seeking an unmediated knowledge of death, or any extraordinary wisdom on the subject, must nevertheless arrange to be informed by mortal boundaries, not just constrained by them. A mainstay of the novel from Dickens onward, the stylistically elaborated death scene is thus discovered time and again to enact its narrowly delineated "finis" (that loaded metatextual term in Conrad) under the aegis of, and as an allegory for, the novel's own acknowledgment of that rule of closure which dictates its whole plot. *A Tale of Two Cities* leads in his way through *Lord Jim* to *The Waves*, *The Newcomes* through *Jude the Obscure* to *Pale Fire*.

If we choose to consider as a definitive fact about the structure of prose fiction that it is a ranging of narrative material within the manifestations of bounding form, an order within a revealed border, then it may be a suggestive parallel that for most of its lexical life the substantive *mortality* meant not only the state of being mortal—that is, human—but also the death itself that lends its name to this condition: again both organic being and its organizing limits, human content and closural form. Around just such a dichotomy a further distinction begins to clarify itself: between stylistics and narratology. Because style is, as it were, the execution of death in fiction, it has to do not only with the inner functioning but with the far limit of narratability. Moreover, since at any point in a narrative, whether the scene is of death or not, there is an inevitable decentering—a chasm always yawning between word and world—the death scene locates and glosses a further convergence of issues: the narratological with the grammatological.

As narrative event, death is the ultimate form of closure plotted within the closure of form. Yet what fiction is closed off from in this sense is not just more of the same, more words; truncated by a formal necessity which an enacted death scene may simulate or predict, fiction as verbal act is also sealed off at every point from the universe it proposes to evoke. Long before the speculations of recent literary theory, such writers as Dickens and Thackeray, Conrad and Woolf sent into play a complementary sense of both modes of (en)closure, the terminal and the hermetic, the end-stopped and the referentially encased. In such writers death as narrative moment has a leverage on structural perceptions that is finally unmatched. At stake here is not just (as one might formulate a poststructuralist axiom) the fact that if the literary death scene is one kind of writing, all writing is another kind of death scene. The issue is broader than the confessed separation between putative presence and the absence that is never more than masked by inscription. Involved here are the full structural ramifications of the represented death moment. If all death is a kind of closure, then any death, at any point in a novel, coinciding with or anticipating "The End," may summon the sense, and suspended apprehension, of such a formal limit. The prose of the fictional death sentence may thus, at the circumscribed level of the stylistic microcosm, compact and so dramatize the very premises of representation that permit and condition it.

The polysemous ambiguities on which the vocabulary of the Victorian death scene thrives, and in a revised way its modern and postmodern offshoots, the vergings and retractions of the terms of eternity, motivating narrative continuity toward or across the point of mortal rupture—these strategies testify to the power of speech from moment to moment, postponing the void, deferring the effacements of the blank page, articulating the very field of meanings against which the idea of closure or closedness can alone come to definition. The stylistic close readings that guide my argument may thus display their own liminal status, being as close as reading itself can get to the indecipherable. Commissioned to monitor the approaching blank of death, the style of the death sentence contrives to hover over the eventuality of its own erasure or truncation. These verbal close calls with the unutterable grow commensurate in this way with the narrative act at large.

Two assumptions for the study of fictional techniques may well follow from such observations: first, that the novelistic representation of death necessitates a specialized rhetoric of figural and grammatical devices to approximate the evacuation of its very subject, devices that can be sorted out if not strictly codified; and second, that writers learn from each other's verbal experiments in this vein—that there is, in short, a literary legacy of the death scene not oblivious to but in some ways independent of historical drifts of faith or social ritual. It is a legacy, however, that one finds taking most overt form in the British novel well past its eighteenth-century origins. The prose death scene comes to the fore in the fiction generated out of the same metaphysical crisis and expressive license that spawned the Romantic revolution. Keats and Shelley prepare us for the elegiac and visionary Dickens at least as much as do Fielding and Smollett for the comic fabulator.

□   □   □

Some characters must die in any period of novel writing. As everyone allows, characters die more often, more slowly, and more vocally in the Victorian age than ever before or since. Yet to start this study from the escalating fascination with death in the novels of Dickens is a decision prompted by fictional genealogy rather than apologetics. As identity becomes with time a more problematic issue for fictional characterization, the death scene grows more prominent, whether the self in question suffers or merely oversees the moment of death. The typical Victorian death moment, dilated into novelistic set piece, has not only been underestimated by condescending criticism but summarily set aside as aberration from the main line of fictional innovation pressing on toward modernism. Under scrutiny, Victorian death scenes instead reveal themselves to be neither sentimental tangents, routine and egregious, nor passing symptoms of a cultural obsession too openly indulged. Furthermore, these scenes, as a formal expectation of narrative, are ironically modified rather than outmoded by modernist fiction. Long before this twentieth-century end of the heritage, the proliferation of dying moments in Victorian fiction also had an instructive prehistory, one that can help clarify death's demands upon stylistic invention as an address to questions of both identity and the limits of its textual presentation.

At roughly the historical turning point where Western culture gave up looking systematically beyond death for religious meaning, the novel emerged as a popular narrative form perfectly suited in its empirical leanings to the evaluation of death as an end in itself, a phenomenon of selfhood to be looked to rather than through. True to its origins in the material preoccupations of the bourgeoisie, the novel in the first century of its life, from Defoe through Austen, tended to relegate death to the wings of its drama, alluding to it only by rumor as an off-stage event. Before Dickens the psychology of death as an introspective moment—not only objectively enacted from without but subjectively transacted from within—was simply not crucial to the delineation of the fictional character as social creature; to be suddenly removed from the scene was a virtual definition of death in most of the eighteenth-century novelists besides Richardson in *Clarissa* and Sterne in the reflexive metaphysics of *Tristram Shandy*. Recasting the sense of self, and especially the literary self, the subsequent Romantic movement forced death's hand as not only the agent of identity's negation but at the same time its guarantor of being. If Blake never knew what was enough till he knew what was more than enough, the Romantic self never knew what it was to exist without exploring what it might be not to exist. To be and not to be: that was Romanticism's formulation of the Elizabethan dilemma.

Virginia Woolf notes about Defoe's early experiment in narrative prose, *Robinson Crusoe* (1719), that for all the killings and corpses, "there is no death,"[6] no conceptualization of dying as abstract inevitability, nor any portrayal of it as more than animal event. *Crusoe* in this sense anticipates the tabulated casualty lists and statistical charts of the subsequent *Journal of the Plague Year* (1722), where supernatural explanation is invoked without any metaphysical access by way of deathbed narration. In the same year, in *Moll Flanders*, Defoe repeatedly employs an idiom that would also appear more than once in Fielding's *Jonathan Wild* (1743), the allusion to the fact rather than act of death as the condition of having gone "out of this [or the] world."[7] This usage contrasts tellingly with the Victorian metaphoric treatment of death not as an irrevocable end but as a life-defining experience capable of being caught in the act. In the eighteenth-century novel, however, characters are more often feared or found gone than felt passing, whether on, over, or away. Thus, in Fielding's *Tom Jones* (1749) a natural extension of the picaresque motif characterizes death as a postmortem "journey," as later too, with more than ordinary biblical overtones, in Oliver Goldsmith's *Vicar of Wakefield* (1766), where the mortal "traveller" spies the "horizon" of "another abode."[8] In the majority of cases, though, dying is a journey "out of *this* world," neither explicitly directed nor closely mapped. Death registers as exit more than vector, requiring no demonstrative counterpart for the secular "this" nor (in contrast with Victorian practice) any internalizing of the "horizon" as psychological limit or closural self-definition. However analogized in these fictions, death emerges—rather, hovers—as either truth in prospect or fact in retrospect, rarely as a private transit portrayed. In Jane Austen's *Pride and Prejudice*, for example, just before the Romantic impact on British fiction, the patrilineal economics of the story may be "entailed" by death without plot at any point needing to entail the representation of a dying.

Romanticism calls all this to account, empowering not only the contemplation of death but attempting its mimesis from a perspective near or within the dying mind. Beyond such famous experiments in the symbolic assimilation of another's death as Wordsworth's in the Lucy poems or "The Boy of Winander," there are numerous short lyrics on mortality, most of them unabashedly titled "Death," by such later Romantic poets as Shelley, Byron, Hood, Darley, and Beddoes.[9] More important, there are extended closural death scenes, often allegorical of poetic aspiration itself and its reach beyond mortal limits, as in Keats's *Endymion* and *Lamia*, or Shelley's *Alastor* and *Epipsychidion*.[10] And at the very outset of Romanticism, in Blake's "The Book of Thel," there is the prolonged dying into the very possibility of death, where "this world" and "that" are ironically reversed. In Defoe, Fielding, Smollett, Austen, and others, following as they did the poetic practice of their age, death was, by being "out of this world," therefore out of the mimetic question altogether; by contrast, Romanticism recovered a central lyric and dramatic preoccupation of the seventeenth century, insisting that literature must, in both senses of the idiom, put death back in question, in all its human purport as well as its dubiety.

Fictional identity from Dickens forward is in multiple ways founded on death or figured by its extremity. The self of the nineteenth-century novel is conceived and nursed upon the irrational, whose chief deities are Eros and Thanatos. This post-Romantic era in prose does far more than sense how the death of God was the birth of a new mythology of dying, with death now on almost every count an end in itself. In conjunction with this agnostic shift there are also deflections mystic and erotic by which death is transferred to a metaphor for other human transitions. According to such transcendental or ecstatic analogues, death can bestow renewed identity on the self when it arrives in the regenerative guise of visionary trance or sexual oblivion, as well as when it appears in its familiar way to comment on a completed life. Romanticism thus curtails on the religious side, while extending on the secular, death's revelatory potential. Because of death's essentially amorphous nature, however, its actual moment must take form in fiction in a multiple relation to other narrative content. I shall label as *transposition* fiction's inherent need to account for death in idioms and metaphors drawn from life. When such an act of figural transference also serves to condense the particular identity whose individual terms it is so transposing, a character's psychology is then being summed up by the mechanism of abridgement or *epitome*, a special case of transposition. From this may ensue the dramatic and sometimes explicitly textual process of *displacement*, whereby identity epitomized by death can be deputized to an alter ego within the text or deflected by cathartic recognition onto a reader outside the perimeters of representation. The drama of death attended by a double can thus in itself enact the drama of reading about death when understood as a mortal encounter outlived and assimilated.

Transposition. Mortality must somehow utter itself in tongues out of its own final blank—brutal, cryptic, ambiguous, or sublime. For whether in the faltering and faint words of a deathbed valediction, for instance, or in the variously evasive or revelatory gestures of its narrative rendering, the rhetoric of dying must transpose life's terms into death, familiarize the ineffable by crowding death's infinite instant into the momentary and mundane syllables that phrase even as they fade over to it. The verbal and psychological space of this transition is discussed in Chapter 2 as the traversed interval of death in Dickens. With a main strand of Romanticism justly understood to be a systematic naturalizing of the supernatural, dying in the nineteenth-century novel follows suit by internalizing metaphysics as psychology, and so by naturalizing revelation as review rather than visionary access. The premise that death can be more lucid and communicative in the novel than in life does not contradict the fact that fictional dying is held to retrospect rather than loosed to prophecy; the fictional death scene, however richly pointed, must point back rather than forward.

This has little to do in major writing with the convenient formula

of characters routinely dying as they have lived; it is a formal consequence of the whole narrative enterprise. In our actual dying the
readiness may be all, an eagerness for appeasing surprise, even
epiphany, an eagerness however much chastened by a knowledge
that dying, even when free from agony or grief, may still be not only
uninstructive but dreary, negligible, perhaps unconscious. Fictional
dying, however, is bent on meaning, and so in novels the rightness
is all. Lives may bow to the random, the undreamed; story must be
ruled by congruity. The only thing fictional death has to connect with
is time rather than eternity. Whereas actual death may assuage or
beguile itself with conjecture, the death scene must fasten upon the
massed data of temporal existence up to that point, transposing life's
notations into the key of fatality. It is a practice that can be illuminated
even by the most naive instance, as when the coachman Tony Weller
in Dickens's first novel, *Pickwick Papers* (1836), attempting to narrate
the death of his wife in a letter to his son, imagines her atrophy as
a downhill race with "little luggage" past life's unavoidable "last
pike" (ch. 52).

Any dying character in a Victorian novel, struggling to utter last
words in the company of any auditor straining to catch them, may
dramatize the transaction between writer and reader when words of
this world are asked to edge themselves free of their ordinary field
of definition. Habitual manipulator of such last words and the pathos
of their dimming volume, Dickens would surely have sensed the
connection between his own narrative prose in the proximity of death
and the lapsing powers of voice on the part of his dying characters.
He does this with subtlest conjuring in the last set piece of sentimental
dying in his career, the death of Betty Higden in flight from the
poorhouse in *Our Mutual Friend*, a scene no less complex for being
unashamedly emotional. Standard articulation cedes to the mysterious
artistry of death's enunciation, where in Dickens more things are
communicated than are said or sayable. The badge of heroism for a
character is often the penchant for deathbed clairvoyance, as when
Lizzie Hexam witnesses Betty's death and is able to intuit meaning
where there seems only garbled silence, to translate conversation into
an exchange deeper than disabled speech. The communion between
Lizzie and Betty (their doubling hinted by alternative nicknames that
familiarize each half of Elizabeth) begins appropriately, with a paradox of predication justified by a faith in otherworldly sentience on

the part of the dying speaker: "Am I not dead?" We hear this arguably inapt grammar of being through the mediation of Dickensian narrative, but as if the speaker were indeed dead and ascended, its words do not easily reach their human auditor on the scene:

> "I cannot understand what you say. Your voice is so low and broken that I cannot hear you. Do you hear me?"
> "Yes."
> "Do you mean Yes?"
> "Yes."
> "I was coming from my work just now . . . and found you lying here."
> "What work, deary?"
> "Did you ask what work?" (III, ch. 8)

What is at issue here are ruptures of utterance, gaps of designation, that go far deeper than physically weakened enunciation. This oblique dialogue is part of a death scene whose local indirections combine for a parable of the very nature of language—always deflected, mediated, translated—when in confrontation with death's silence.

There is in this Dickensian encounter the "yes" that goes unheard as well as the assent that is somehow sensed along the lining of silence. Communion deep beneath the inadequacies of dialogue turns this exchange into a mysteriously meshed subliminal empathy that does in little what the scene as a whole sets out to do: inscribe the indecipherable. Betty now worries that she might be too disfigured for a last kiss. Again, direct speech is not necessary to mediate, only the language of feeling, lips uttering love without articulation after a comma where dialogue might otherwise have come: "The answer is, the ready pressure of her lips upon the cold but smiling mouth." Speech returns to Betty for a moment: "*Now* lift me, my love." And then the unsaid death: "Lizzie Hexam very softly raised the weather-stained grey head, and lifted her as high as Heaven." The balanced, momentarily stabilized chiastic assonance of "weather-stained grey head" passes through the aspirant iambic alliteration of "her as high as Heaven" in a suggested transcendence that needs no religious validation.

Subjective and objective rendering are thereby hinged about a slippery phrasing that seems half analogy, half hyperbole: so high it seemed like heaven; every bit as high as heaven. The euphemism or periphrasis we might expect at such a time—"she raised her beyond reach of any poorhouse"—is transformed into an indirect voucher of redemption that still avoids the mention of death while speeding to its visionary destination. A scene that begins with a curious break-down or discontinuity in the ordinary channels of dialogue thus ends with a greater indirection in narrative prose itself, raising an as-cending motion begun on this side of time to its eternal factor. In the calculus of such verbal style, the "as high as" transition is a differential that allows for the quantum leap of the last capitalized word. When Betty says "yes" earlier, we hear it at once, even as we overhear Lizzie strain to make it out. The authorial privileging of signification for reader rather than character is extended now into the very ambiguities of death as event, where the dying mind conveys itself directly to us through a pervasive subjectivity of report. Lizzie knows only that she lifts Betty's head a bit; it is granted us to recognize the completion of this alleviating, levitating gesture in a transposed key. The weariness of this world given over to the selfless arms of sympathy, the burden of being in time momentarily assumed by another and so indescribably lightened, all gravity removed by the grace of love—this is as close to any idea of heaven as Dickens feels most of us, still conscious, can come. Analogy, the gentle suasion of "as,"[11] guides the logic of this phrasing precisely because there is nothing in this world with which to compare such lightening of the mortal load.

Epitome. If the analogic ratio "as high as Heaven" in *Our Mutual Friend* had not only surrendered but managed to sum up Betty Hig-den's earthly existence ("lifted her," for instance, "as near to Heaven as she had always seemed"), it would thereby have inflected itself to an epitome.[12] In a brief, little-known, and never-reprinted essay from 1952, Kenneth Burke includes in his enumeration of the uses of death in poetry the "image of fulfilment (the 'entelechial' motif), in ac-cordance with the double meaning of the word 'end,' to name either the purpose of the cessation of an act."[13] It is a double meaning not unlike the joint sense of intent and destination in Freud's famous dictum that "the aim of all life is death."[14] Death by epitome is essence tested and found true (to itself), life raised to the power of its own (however negative) potential. It is what Fielding parodies as the scurrilous title figure's "Apotheosis" on the gallows in *Jonathan*

Wild—yet seen there entirely as a superficial "consummation," with no attempt to probe, as in a Romantic text, its psychological dimension.[15]

When the Christian afterlife cannot be taken as a spiritual certainty—as it no longer can for a transitional author such as Dickens or for most of the later masters of British fiction[16]—the agnostic writer's agility and imaginative guile strive to turn ambiguity no more than halfway to augury while, in the case of epitomizing death, striving also to point the language of death back at life in an encompassing sense. It is in the time-bound nature of narrative art, with its ambitions toward maximized significance, that the act of transposition will often amount to a definition of the temporal self it takes as subject, the resulting epitome computed as a spiritual sum at the departure of substance. The first on-stage death in the main body of *Pickwick Papers* befalls the Chancery prisoner in the Fleet, a dying that arrives as the end point of the self's entelechy, his lifelong dream of release from the prison of his quarters and of his life: "He got his discharge, by G——!" (ch. 44), where the speaker's last phrase seems one of agency as well as exclamation. Whether in the voice of narrator, bystander, or dying character, idioms and colloquialisms can at such turning points sharpen to a deadly edge, with some familiar phrase refashioned in an oracular flash, an identifying tag line aggrandized into a momentous last word, a euphemism ironically reconstrued, a dead metaphor suddenly exhumed, a cliché pitched back (not over) into revelation. At the moment of death in fiction, even when never before for a given character, life refuses to go without saying. Decease takes reflexive definition from pure antecedence. There is a well-worn vernacular formula for this that is still very much with us: the villain who "got his." Alluding to this summarizing power of death in poetry, as well as to its inevitable transposition into figurative language, Dylan Thomas wrote that "Death is all metaphors, shape in one history."[17] Living is in this sense both troped and summarily disposed by the literary death scene, a moment, as Alice James said in anticipation of her own death, when "living becomes life."[18]

Thus the death of Barkis in *David Copperfield* coincides with his last repetition of the identifying line, "Barkis is willin'," that paradoxically noncommittal idiom of will which, long before, he passed through David to Peggotty as a proposal of marriage and which now, as his three last words, balances poignantly between catch phrase of recognition and testament of happy resignation:

> I was on the point of asking him if he knew me, when he tried to stretch out his arm, and said to me distinctly, with a pleasant smile,—
> "Barkis is willin'!"
> And, it being low water, he went out with the tide. (ch. 30)

Years before, Barkis's second-hand marriage proposal, delivered by his go-between, David, took fate slyly into its own hands under the guise of mere passive acquiescence, while by these same words at the moment of death, this time unmediated, Barkis, either with full responsibility or with a smiling lassitude, opens his hands to fate. It is an epitome designed to accompany and deepen the closing transposition from life to death upon the ebb of a tidal metaphor.

Even if a character is not granted the self-conscious epitome of spoken last words, the narrative treatment may itself compact his or her identity into a single phrase. Beyond all the other uses of death in narrative, fatality is an event linked directly to the evolution of the fictional self for the obvious but often unstated reason that whatever that temporal self is to become, rather than might have become, it has become at the moment when death consigns it to nonentity. Death, whether the self knows it or not, turns living to the finality of life in a single instant. If that moment, as phrased by narrative, encapsulates as well as dispatches the self, organizes the finished life toward compressed biography, then such an epitomizing death may become art's invaluable model for one of the few agnostic graces of deathbed consciousness—the revelation (just) in time of the self in time, identity's fullest because final (and so complete) unfolding to itself.

This flexible effect is equally useful for the death of a major villain as for that of a minor eccentric such as Barkis or a full-scale hero or heroine. In *Little Dorrit* the loathsome Rigaud ends as befits him, found dead rather than seen dying, in an elliptical death scene not worth mentioning; it is elided instead into the neutering of his person not only by metaphor but by a periphrastic subordination that phases out identity altogether. Perjuring himself with a facile version of mortal epitome in a narcissistic second-person address, "You have lived a gentleman; you will die a gentleman" (II, ch. 31), he is shortly discovered as a shattered corpse under the collapsed Clennam house—obliterated to his essence, dirt to dirt—and mourned there by circumlocution as "the dirty heap of rubbish that had been the foreigner." To tighten this effect, one assumes, Dickens dropped the dubiously humanizing adjective "dishonoured" before "dirty" in the proof,[19] holding back the symbolic irony of "rubbish" from slipping over into a mere figure of speech.

Displacement. A different sort of dehumanizing transformation in *Dombey and Son*, this time from active to passive predication, seems to mark the staged but at the same time elided moment of death for another villain. It is a death by displacement—by which I am suggesting a death undergone by proxy so that it can be overseen by a surviving protagonist—that serves to defray the psychic expenditure of an equivalent fatality in the onlooking consciousness. Here is Carker's end under the wheels of a train and the eyes of Mr. Dombey, his past victim and present nemesis:

> He heard a shout—another—saw the face change from its vindictive passion to a faint sickness and terror—felt the earth tremble—knew in a moment that the rush was come—uttered a shriek—looked round—saw the red eyes, bleared and dim in the daylight, close upon him, was beaten down, caught up, and whirled away upon a jagged mill that spun him round and round, and struck him limb from limb, and licked his stream of life up with its fiery heat, and cast his mutilated fragments in the air. (ch. 55)

The paratactic accumulation races breathlessly from verbs of mere perception such as "heard" and "saw" through the certainty of "knew" to forms of almost involuntary reaction, as in "uttered a shriek," where that noun of inarticulate cry answers to the repeated "shrieks" of the train wheels earlier and the more immediate "shout" of Carker's horrified avenger facing him from this side of annihilation.

In the penultimate paragraph of his life, Carker, chased down by Dombey, "looked at his pursuer, breathing short and quick." That participial uncertainty begins a referential blending of these arch-enemies just as the railroad, symbol of the aggressive economic progress for which they both stand, brings Carker to his bloody end. His death is a mechanized violence portrayed as the disintegration of that very principle of self, headlong driven will, which has led to its own extinction. Identity virtually effaced by terror, Carker must read what should be his own reactions to the closing in of death on the face of his sexual rival and capitalist alter ego, who finally utters the shouts of horror that rightly belong to Carker. It seems directly to the point here that at the proof stage Dickens altered to "passion" his abstract noun in the manuscript's original "saw the face change from its vindictive hatred."[20] Raving subject and quailing object are more closely allied in the revised version, the rage generalized beyond "revenge" to include all self-vindictive excesses.

A further breakdown in the clear demarcation between Carker and the furious setting of his death occurs when even the personified locomotive drains off the victim's emotion and mirrors his bloodshot, long-sleepless stare. It is at exactly this verge of impending extinction that the metamorphic play in Dickensian syntax implies a subverbal transposition dislodging the villain from subject to object—just an instant before the transition to passive dismemberment at "was beaten down."[21] No sooner has Carker seen that the bleary eyes of the train were "close upon him" than he must see them, given their inexorable speed, thrust forward at and in the transitive sense "close upon him," ending his consciousness. The gap—or in temporal terms the in-terval—between adjective and verb in this wavering locution is the infinitesimal space to which life has contracted. This distance, tra-versed in the split second of recognition, is enough to close out recognition forever. As Dombey undergoes his symbolic mutilation in the delegated person of his manager, he thus begins a slow release from the displaced vision of his own death to the arduous term of his rebirth—climaxed by the humanizing reunion with his daughter, Flor-ence, after his later illness and debilitation.

Released in this way by the decease of a proxy or surrogate—a displaced fatality—Dombey points up a widespread tendency in the post-Romantic handling of fictional psychology. With its emphasis on childhood as phase of rather than preface to identity, on time's movement as a cumulative rite of passage, on self-fulfillment as a teleology of being—in all this and more, Romanticism establishes the language of death as a rhetoric of the self's transition. With life no longer religiously imagined as a probation for eternity, literary death turns in the first place retroactive, a comment back on life, and then rhetorical, a figure or analogue for some decisive change in other lives or other vital phases of the self's continuum. The child might be father of the man, but the man is also undertaker to the child—or mourner of himself in the remains of an outgrown or outlived double. Death in nineteenth-century fiction becomes an emphatic way to name by metaphor or embody by alter ego certain changes too violent and disjunctive for the alternative Romantic metaphors of organic growth. Tolstoy's greatest heroine asks just at the moment of her suicide, "Where am I? What am I doing? Why?" (*Anna Karenina*, ch. 31). Her questions, crucially transformed, survive her death— and that of the hero's brother before her—to be willed redemptively to the hero himself in a much later contemplation of that fraternal death. When Levin asks, "What then am I? Where am I? Why am I here?" (VIII, ch. 11), the interrogative stess applied by death has been shifted to the very essence of identity as well as to an ontological rather than local questioning of place, of mortal role more than lo- cation. From Anna's articulate but blinkered query, through the mute provocation of a remembered corpse, to the spiritual restitution of the hero at two removes, the pattern of displacement is itself dis- placed, doubled.

Avenues of maturation for fictional selves in the aftermath of Ro- manticism may often route the "I" toward figurative rebirth through the sacrificial death of a counterself, as Dombey is immobilized before the mutilation of his former second in command and then returned slowly toward feeling. The strategic use of psychic doubles, mortal alter egos, surrogates of the self's disintegration, delegates of its renewal may also serve to reflect self-consciously on the process of reading about death from the security of aesthetic distance. Through such encounters within the text turned to parables of textual under- standing—again, such displacements displaced—the death of others is often seen to encode our own, a fate to which we must, at one depth of consciousness or another, own up. When Emily Dickinson writes that "The Figures I have seen / Set orderly, for Burial, / Re- minded me, of mine,"[22] the ambiguous possessive pronoun (my fu- neral? my body?) merely suggests a thoroughness of identification that would be no less potent if the "figures" were only rhetorical representations of death "set" in a printed text. Characters in countless novels likewise survey indirectly their own corpses while we look on, read on. At two levels, then, a narrated death often becomes, borrowing from another Dickinson poem, a "funeral in the brain."[23] When literature confronts a hero with the death of a double, the eyes of the scapegoat glazing over into mirrors, such scenes, whatever their purpose within plot, are also plot's parable—where in figures laid out for burial we readers read our own. As we shall see later in this chapter, commentators as different as Sigmund Freud and Walter Benjamin have had much to say on this issue as the very sanction of fiction. In this context one may call to mind the other, older meaning of *demise* itself, referring not to death per se but to the postmortem conveyance of an estate or the transferral of sovereignty to a successor. (We have this same alternative in modern idiom with the overlap of decease and legacy in *pass on.*) When fictional death is demised to us, it is bequeathed by a given text through the operations of catharsis and artistic comprehension.

□   □   □

What we are beginning to explore are the theatrics of the secular death scene by which it maximizes its passing chance for meaning. Peter Brooks's comments on melodramatic form in nineteenth-century fiction as a "mode of excess" trace it back to the desacralizing tendencies of the Enlightenment and the subsequent efforts of Romanticism to recover the options of moral and spiritual revelation. The hyperbolic gestures of melodrama, for characters and in turn for authors, are seen as an attempt to wrest expressive power from the voided center of meaning which the creative suffering of tragedy used to fill. As we might expect, several of Brooks's examples come from melodramatic death scenes and mortuary perspectives. Indeed, Brooks's stress on "document" pressed to "vision," the extrapolation of figure from fact, and his support from I. A. Richards's "encompassing definition of metaphor as a 'transaction between contexts,' "[24] aligns his view of the melodramatic penchant with what we have already begun to investigate as the mortal necessities of "transposition," the death that is "all metaphors." Death becomes a figurative projection beyond the limits of the temporal—in and across the inflected "interval" of the death moment. Peter Brooks's sense that post-Enlightenment melodrama is premised in a "moral occult,"[25] requiring articulation to redeem it from torpor, may never be more apparent than in the whole lexicon of expressive gestures and phrases of the secularized death moment, where meaning is construed in the face of void.[26] The nineteenth-century death scene—with its often frustrated impulse toward a revelation not necessarily numinous, as in the high Romantic poem, but retrospectively illuminating—is thus the mode of excess in extremis, the ultimate occulting of vision at what Conrad would later call in *Heart of Darkness* the "threshold of the invisible."

It is a threshold flagrantly transgressed in an exemplary brief narrative from the American Romantic period that has been much discussed for its deconstructive overtones, Poe's "The Facts in the Case of M. Valdemar" (1845).[27] This story, as I read it, presses the case of death's representation beyond typical Romantic melodrama into the realm of the uncanny in order, among other things, to offer a parable of death's more ordinary operation in prose fiction. The death moment of the title figure is arrested by hypnotic trance, his agonized and paradoxical predication "*I am dead*" seeming to well up from the void over which he is artificially suspended, a locution distanced by italics as the most foreign of all utterances. Implicated even in this aberration is the general principle that any narrative, insofar as it must inevitably render death in discursive rather than mortal time, depends in a sense on mesmerizing the death moment into distension so as to give it voice. When Poe's narrating scientist explains at the start that "no person had as yet been mesmerized 'in articulo mortis,' " the Latin idiom for mortal "turning point" seems to anticipate the story's coming emphasis on deathbed utterance through a play on the English sense of *articulation* as "speech," a double suggestion which Conrad would later activate in *Lord Jim*. At the same time, Poe's intensive mortal instant seems in its both experimental and discursive extension to structure at reduced scale the larger machinations of plot itself. By delaying its narrative climax through and even beyond the voicing of "*I am dead*," a paradoxical condition prolonged until the release and instantaneous degeneration of the forestalled corpse, Poe's story of pure metageneric suspense has thus disclosed those operative strategies of postponement and deferral that compose any and all story, that keep narrative—and here is the closural implication of Poe's tale—not just from stasis but from something like decomposition.

Another way of couching the dichotomy between an intensive death moment and its extensive representation as text is to take up a further claim by Peter Brooks about the place of metaphor in narrative. Not just a "transaction" between realms of designation, metaphor as a master trope is stressed in Brooks's more recent work as a "totalizing" function tending to arrest plot, so that "the key figure of narrative must in some sense be not metaphor but metonymy: the figure of contiguity and combination, the figure of syntagmatic relations."[28] Opening rather than troping an episode, metonymy gets plot going, breaks with stasis, negotiates a reprieve from premature closure. In Poe's story the otherwise totalizing equivalence "*I am dead*" (framed indeed by what grammar calls an equative clause) must be dislodged, destabilized, made to generate not just the reiterated and varied "*I am dead . . . dead! dead!*" (p. 103), with attribute detached from clause of presence, but all the scientific ministrations that attend this phenomenon in the course of the story. These metonymic efforts must be made to dispell stasis long enough to propel plot.

Before moving on to further fictional instances, we need to stand back a bit farther yet. There should be little doubt that the phenomenon of the melodramatic death moment in fiction is increasingly to be found in the fiction that follows from Romanticism. Richards's "transaction" may offer a useful term for the dynamics of such moments, but toward what conceivable field of meaning is their metaphoric action to be transposed or negotiated? In setting off the novelists from Dickens on as characterized by a specifically post-Romantic attitude toward the relation of death to identity, I do not claim that the narrative rhetoric of death since the inception of the novel—a genre inevitably materialist in the bearings of its mimesis—ever had a choice but to be retrospective in its metaphoric format, nor that the novelistic handling of death knows no prototypes from earlier genres. Romanticism merely increased and diversified the metaphoric cast of fictional mortality, which as a result was encouraged to draw more widely on the figural daring of previous experimentation. Indeed, Elizabethan and Jacobean theater is often closer to the dramatized emphases of Victorian death scenes than are other, nearer precedents in prose. The link between a tragic Shakespeare, say, and a melodramatic Dickens in this regard has to do with the playwright's need, and the salience of invention answering to it, for a language in which to externalize by irony and ambiguity, whether in dialogue or soliloquies, that poetic justice in death that no narrator is on hand to arbitrate and articulate.

The inveterate rhetorician Othello, concerned even at the end with the way history will narrate his tragic blindness, slays himself in the very execution of his verbal death sentence, a suicidal soliloquy gone public:

> Set you down this.
> And say besides that in Aleppo once,
> Where a malignant and a turbaned Turk
> Beat a Venetian and traduced the state,
> I took by th' throat the circumcisèd dog
> And smote him—thus. (V.ii.347–352)

The analogy to past service done the state, hinged about the temporally doubled adverb "thus" and closing upon the suicidal instant of death's (re)presentation, instances the violent swerve from heroic nostalgia to mortal negation. The momentum of metonymy (I did thus and so, once upon a time) is abruptly canceled upon its collision with a silencing analogue or metaphor (It was thus with him, as now with me). The closural "thus" adverts and converts at once, shifting the syntagmatic axis of recounted heroism to the paradigmtic axis of equated and interchangeable retribution. Lodovico's immediately following exclamation, driving home an image of the wounding puncture, "O bloody period!" (V.ii.353), besides its choric sense of a grievous "end," further points up the syntactic and metanarrative irony of Othello's account for posterity. The phrase connotes at once the whole historical span defined by the interval between these two state murders, the end-stopped punctuation that closes the speech as syntax, and the suspended rhetorical "period" that has driven toward even while deferring this finish. This passage of course transpires without local figuration at all, whether by metaphor, simile, or other specific figures. Its primary stylistic transaction—in terms of the master tropes of metonymy versus metaphor—is that instantaneous adverbial transit from former to present enemy of the state in a "metaphoric" equivalence both total and eradicating. The tension and then collapsed gap between past action and present recounting, even as they converge in a form of ritual reenactment, puts the linguistic shifter "thus" to full work as an unstable marker between history and discourse. If we assume that Othello not only stabs himself but grabs his own throat in miming the earlier event, then the point is further dramatized that his fatal rhetorical flourish can only lead to the strangulation of the very language in which he has been glorying this one last time. Like the Romantic poem and post-Romantic novel, Shakespearean drama, here as well as in its more figural textures, recognizes the death sentence or period as preeminently a test of discourse in narrowing confrontation with language's own limits.

Unaccompanied by the omniscient description possible to the novel, Shakespearean characters are often precipitated into such self-conscious meditation as Sir John of Gaunt takes to extremes in his half-dozen deathbed quibbles on the teleology of his name. The first turns on a chiastic inversion from living identification to deathly premonition: "Old Gaunt indeed, and gaunt in being old!" This is immediately preceded by an establishing line which plays on the textual ironies of this created character, however historical, musing over the theatrical tag that designates him as player: "O, how that name befits my composition!" (*Richard II*, II.i.73–74). It was the greatest critic of the Romantic age who turned specifically to this speech for psychological commentary on its mortuary word play. The whole bequest of literary death as linguistic occasion seems summarized by example in Coleridge's defense of Shakespearean deathbed punning for its deep congruence with the essential "equivocation" of death.[29] What's in a name? It may well contain the premonitory denomination of a fate. When Nell, in Dickens, is knelled out of the world, Carker turned to dismembered carcase, Mrs. Skewton to skeleton in the same book, the self-styled Nemo in *Bleak House* emaciated to no one at all, Headstone in *Our Mutual Friend* surmounted and secured by his namesake, even Steerforth piloting his aimless way to a death by drowning in *David Copperfield*, we see that Dickens will stop at nothing to claim this verbal legacy. To enlarge the issue of fatal naming to its full width, when the application of language to mortality is not localized in the single referential act of designating the negated self as noun but is found rather to predicate in metaphors the action of the self's fate as a fatality, the same retrospective obligation is in place. Language always looks back at such points in fiction, there being nothing to figure at death, and no figures for it, but that which precedes the moment of dying, resting there both as human past and as temporal matrix for the metaphors of its surrender.

In a transitional Romantic writer such as Sir Walter Scott, still close to his eighteenth-century forebears, we find the trusted formulas of the early fictional death scene as if neatly alluded to by the title *Old Mortality*. Scott's figurative transpositions are explicit and free of metaphysical risk, his epitomizing moments predictable in psychology and more or less objective and externalized in phrasing. In *The Fair Maid of Perth* (1828) the severance of fatality is seen at one point to have "divorced the immortal spirit from its mangled tenement" (ch. 23). Life is an inhabitation of the world, death an eviction. Here from *Old Mortality* (1816) is a gesture toward the often accompanying formula of death by epitome, a rhetorical capstone so explicit as to leave metaphor behind entirely, the hero Macbriar dying "with the same enthusiastic firmness which his whole life had evinced" (ch. 36). Death tends to generalize life, or at least *from* life, in the older and dominant mortalities until Dickens, after which demise begins to reestimate temporal identity at a new depth—a difference in the rhetoric of retrospect of degree rather than kind.

Even when the pre-Dickensian treatment of death was far more self-conscious than in Scott, its eighteenth-century practitioners still tended to study it from the outside. Richardson's *Clarissa* (1747–1748) so lugubriously prefigures death as a rewriting of the world's terms that an actual death scene would be a redundancy. Richardson's novel details toward the end the heroine's attempt almost to enter upon her own metaphors as the mechanism of release, to make the rhetoric of transposition a warrantee of transcendence. Long besieged and at last violated by Lovelace, Clarissa Harlowe slowly embraces death, and through it the conceit of Christ as her better Bridegroom, rather than be wed to her treacherous earthly suitor. To escape him successfully long enough to do her dying in peace, she must quibble over the terms of a rendezvous at her "father's house." The earthly counterpart she has in mind, the only haven where Lovelace can expect to find her, is in the narrow last lodging of her "furnished" coffin. Turning inside out Scott's later metaphor of the body as evacuated tenement at death, Clarissa's is the transposition from domestic architecture to burial metaphor. Such a figure for a secular construction funereally reconstrued also appears the next year in the more comedic cast of Fielding's memento mori at the death of Captain Blifil, early on in the worldly progress of *Tom Jones* (1749), a passage derived from Horace about our vain tendency to "build houses of five hundred by a hundred feet, forgetting that of two by six" (II, ch. 8). In his letter of September 1, near the end of Richardson's novel, Belford alludes to Clarissa's pun on the "closing-day," when, after her painful secular escrow, she will take up residence in her coffin. Though Lovelace is hypocritically outraged by her "lies," nevertheless the double edge of Clarissa's punning, eluding his understanding and thus his pursuit, offers both retribution and deliverance, language fallen, debased, and evasive only when it falls on profane ears. For the heroine this self-conscious rhetoric of transposition is an italics of finer emphasis—and a secret code of freedom. Trademark of the later Victorian death scene, the pun's very liberation from semantic stasis has "transacted" her freedom from earthly imprisonment.

After Richardson, in the predominantly comic mode of the rest of the eighteenth-century novelists, there is Laurence Sterne's *Tristram Shandy* (1759–1767), a novel in part concerned explicitly with the linguistic demands made by death. At the demise of Tristram's brother, Bobby, his father is beset by an encyclopedic paroxysm of mortal sententiae, the aphorisms moral and portable: "Philosophy has a fine saying for every thing.—For *Death* it has an entire set; the misery was, they all at once rushed into my father's head" (V, ch. 3). This blast of maxims amounts to an exacerbated exercise in metaphoric transposition, reading death from life as "first statute in Magna Charta," central dictate in the "everlasting act of parliament," that "great debt and tribute due nature." Before this local parody of the figurative bromides of mortality, Sterne also lampoons the rhetoric of senti-mental consolation. After borrowing from Shakespeare to lament the death of Parson Yorick, two notorious pages in the twelfth chapter of the first volume are made to wear mute black in their grief, either so as to picture the muffling crepe of an unspeakable mourning or to inscribe a parodic density of expression of the sort that later gurgles from the lips of Mr. Shandy. In scriptive terms black is presence, a superflux of utterance. True to the metanarrative bravura of Sterne's text the seemingly blank pages of respectful silence, gone politely black, may well provide a plethora of scribbled lament rather than its temporary intermission. Meaning becomes replete but unreadable.

In a later story, attempted once by Corporal Trim and resumed by Tristram, we hear how Lieutenant Le Fever is stricken with an un-specified illness to the nature of which there is no clue but his portentous Gallic name, a new version of the ailing and emaciation of Gaunt as the etiology rather than etymology of a name. As with the nautical metaphors for Smollett's dying seamen,[30] the trooper Le Fever also takes his leave of life as a final factor of his vocation, for, in Trim's reported account, "the lieutenant's last day's march is over" (VI, ch. 8). It is a metaphor suited to the corporal who phrases it as well as to the lieutenant whose pathetic death it salutes. This figurative orientation is then inherited by Tristram's own description of the lieutenant's wavering pulse, characterized by a martial metaphor for life's beleaguered withdrawal to an armed fortress: "The blood and spirits of *Le Fever*, which . . . were retreating to their last citadel, the heart,—rallied back" (VI, ch. 8). But when his subject's pulse fails again, the narrator arrests his rendering just before the end: "Shall I go on?—No." The next chapter begins with Tristram anxious to return to "my own story" and dismissing Le Fever's last moments with a jump forward to his burial day. Metaphorical transposition and epitome, both dramatically justified by the argot of Trim's original account, have accompanied the sentimental displacement of the death scene onto the narrator's intermediary consciousness, where the ultimate suppression of the death moment is nevertheless explained away as impatience rather than sentimental euphemism. In all this we are still rather far from the Romantic deployment in depth of these structural features. The motive for this unconsummated interpolation embodies even as it mocks the general tendency of eighteenth-century fiction to veer away from the expanded moment if not the fact of death, as a privacy plot should not invade. Though prose must subsequently dwell on, even while the narrating hero flees, death, Tristram's itinerary of avoidance at the close may be seen, from a later perspective, to have narrativized the very aversion to death as renderable moment in the period as a whole. Textuality in this novel becomes increasingly a dialogue with mortality, so that "when DEATH himself knocked at my door" (VII, ch. 1), Tristram's vital spirits keep the closural threat at the threshold, a merely liminal specter, by invoking the very imperative of narrative continuance. "Now there is nothing in this world I abominate worse, than to be interrupted in a story——," writes Tristram, meaning both the salacious anecdote with which he is about to tease the reader and the whole fiction itself within which he is found relating it to another character. Enemy at once of plot and discourse, Thanatos as closure must be held off by precisely the erotic will of any and all story. If death is unavoidable, however, as in the inset narrative of Le Fever's end, then interruption is suddenly welcome.

Zest for life, and no little lust, spirited materialism, worldly wit and wisdom, social satire—these are among the common passwords of the eighteenth-century novel. However much such a sketch might seem to simplify a great age of invention and variety, it does fairly suggest the peripheral nature of death: a terminus acknowledged, but not too often; an ultimate limitation upon animal spirits, quick parts, fortune, fame, and affection, but not too soon; a dark cloud noted on the horizon, but swept continually to the side by other, breezier currents, lest all life's bustle, bravery, and passion lose their luster under its shadow; an invitation to narrative sentiment, but a precarious one, which should not too unguardedly be indulged lest it topple pathos into morbidity. Death for the novel in its early years was, of course, an ineluctable rite of passage after those other three mainstays of fiction—birth, baptism, and marriage—but it was not to be anticipated with so sharp an eye that its closural absolute be allowed to contaminate the marital stasis toward which plot is so often propelled, as for example in the exclusively domestic enclaves of Austen's books at the turn of the century. Intead, death in the novel's first century, even down through Scott, is a fortuity and an external fact, of concern largely insofar as it was at all costs to be avoided in encounters with plagues, enemy bullets, highway robbers, or contagious relatives.

Romanticism as a rule asks more of death, and this in the form of a stricter interrogation. Answers, as we would expect, are for the most part retrospective and secular rather than religious. Even a Romantic narrative poem in a comic vein such as Thomas Hood's "Death's Ramble,"[31] which personifies "King Death" in a medieval fashion and sends him abroad in the land on horseback, illustrates by association the increasingly complex novelistic logic of appropriate (which is to say retrospective and analogic) dying. The process of making a living evinces the makeup of one's dying, professions or vocations transposed to effacement even as the protean shape of death is figured by them. Thus a dustman is summoned by King Death exactly because the latter is "contractor for all our dust," a coffin maker epitomized in a death that will employ his own retained mutes to "mourn for the undertaker," and a snoring watchman passed over by Death because "his sleep / Can never be more eternal." Puns are rampant in this poem, just as they proliferate in any treatment of death as an ambiguous extrapolation from life. The best of such duplicitous diction is pivoted in its equivocation directly around the point of transposition from life into death. Having come upon two card players, Death "quickly laid them flat with a spade, / To wait for the final trump!" The gamester's pun on "trump" for the archangel's "trumpet" at Judgment Day plays off against the "spade" as both suit and burial tool, sign of temporal bad luck and instrument of admittance to the interregnum between all chance and apocalypse.

Even more characteristic of mythic aspirations in the nineteenth-century treatment of death is Shelley's need as authorial persona in *Adonais* actually to enter the vaults of death with his dead hero. Illustrated, as we shall see, by Keats's own *Fall of Hyperion*, Romanticism brings to the fore the relation of heroism to death as rendered and even embodied by the artist, that implicit need for mortal extremity as the credential of narrative that does not appear in most of the novelists before Dickens. A further stanza in Hood's "Death's Ramble" makes ironic capital of this hubris of authorial Orphism in the case of autobiography, where "The End" is always premature, never coterminous with final unconsciousness. Hood's personified Death finds "an author writing his life" but stops him in midsentence because he is "jealous of all self-murther!" A writer foolhardy enough to attempt the vanity of autobiography—this would seem the major satiric pressure behind the stanza—takes his life into his own hands in a double sense and deserves whatever assassination he gets from friends or press. Part of the joke seems also to involve the thought that if a life could really be written in full, it would have to include a self-scripted and thus, from King Death's point of view, preemptive scene of dying. In a verbally subversive sense, too, all autobiographical endeavor is perpetual "self-murther," life giving out by being given up to its reembodiment as history. It is a transaction that therefore further usurps King Death's ordinary prerogative in being the sole agent who can remove a self, whether to immortality or not, from presence in the living world. Hood's King Death is jealous of the whole idea of textuality.

Apart from such an autobiographical closed circle, any narrative that comes upon a death scene is, in a certain Romantic sense, a "self-murther" for the narrating voice, an empathetic projection into death and the heroic return from its shadows. It is in this sense that Shelley in *Adonais* must descend into the Roman sepulcher of the dead Keats, overseeing there the imaginatively prolonged struggle for life between the breath of the Muse and the silence of death. It is in this same sense that any engaged narrator must enter upon the dying he engraves, his poem an Orphic ordeal of descent and reassimilation. The Romantic art of the death scene, with its fictional derivatives, stands again and again as a double act of participation and epitaph, with numerous novels specifying this, as we shall see, in a symbolic drowning and its displaced fictional transcription.

The nineteenth-century locus classicus for this deathlike call to the narration of death images the Orphic descent as a kind of inverted *gradus ad Parnassum*, the depths of suffering as the price of Olympian eloquence. In Keats's most ambitious narrative poem, *The Fall of Hyperion*, we thus find a parable for all narrative's struggle with death as subject. Beyond the general encounter of language with the ineffable, there is a displacement of mortal consciousness not between speaking character and some dying double but rather between the narrating protagonist and an internal narrator of wider ken. It is a transference imaged in *The Fall* as a dark knowledge passed to the hero as hearer through the mediating goddess of articulate tragic memory, even before the listening and so initiated poet has begun to inscribe this knowledge in his own narrative verse. Just such an identification with death and suffering, as it happens, is the experience we have seen deflected by sentimental trepidation in Trim's narrative within *Tristram Shandy*, travesty of the facile bathos of death as fictional subject in an earlier era.

At the core of Keats's narrative is the story not just of personal death but of the death of an entire race, and a race of erstwhile gods at that, of Titans who had never before known death. As such it is a parable not of gods demoted to mortals so much as of creatures, any creatures, recognizing the truth that they must die. Saturn moans out the prophecy of this doom as an instantaneous transition across a caesura, "There is no death in all the Universe, / No smell of death—there shall be death" (I, ll. 423–424). It is almost the imperative language of fiat, yet deflated here to mere prediction and revenged upon a god powerless to gainsay it. What we find at the center of Keats's poem, then, seems the Ur-narrative of mortality in the classical tradition—the scene that, like Genesis in the Bible, first brought death into the world. It is a tragic plot enfolded by a visionary parable, a Classic action played out under a Romantic proscenium arch. Keats's narrative takes as its poetic subject precisely poetry's ability to encompass such a subject in the first place. The origin of this tale of the leveled Titans is the goddess Moneta, her countenance "deathwards progressing / To no death" (I, ll. 620–621) in its own immortal memory of lost immortality. If Moneta's story of Saturn, Hyperion, and the other Titans can be taken to represent the original death scene in one line of the Western narrrative tradition, in the shady sadness of the first mortal vale, then the goddess's eternal telling makes her the original narrator of death, dying always in order to disclose.

Moneta becomes the type of all tragic bards, and to her sacrificial altar Keats must lift himself, suffering not so much in his own person as in the body of his imagination a kind of death. There is a similar, if less explicit, version of this after Jane Eyre's first-person account to Rochester of the death of her aunt: "I have been with my aunt, sir, who is dead" (ch. 22). His ironic mistaking of her temporal grammar plays not only upon her supposed supernatural gifts but implicitly on her role as a narrator, harrowing death so as to strengthen her autobiographical record against recurrent instances of human closure: "A true Janian reply! . . . She comes from the other world— from the abode of people who are dead." In Keats's rescue from final silence into tragic utterance "One minute before death" (I, l. 132), we see the artist as hero all but die into godlike and so immortal knowledge of those gods who, becoming mortal, died into perennial story. The displacement of this tragic disclosure from the goddess of total—and so lethal—recall necessitates the transposition of her language from the primordial enormity of this mournful story to the terms of human—that is, historical—grief: "Mortal, that thou may'st understand aright, / I humanize my saying to thine ear" (II, l. 2). It could also be called a temporalizing of things lost to our perception before or beyond time, a lending to eternal themes the local habitation and the name of plot. It could certainly be called a Romantic preoccupation and a nineteenth-century fictional hallmark.

□   □   □

Part of the Romantic preoccupation with accessible death centers around a particular mode of dying in fiction. It is a terminal moment that in a double sense, both empirical and Romantic, naturalizes the structural operations of dying at large in fiction: by grounding death's literary utility in common experience and by returning the corpse into the element of nature itself. This moment is the scene of drowning. Of course, to speak of the empirical in connection with a drowning vision is to use the term only loosely, since nothing of this sort admits of verification. Yet popular superstition, unsupported by scientific evidence but abetted by countless fictional instances, maintains that the drowning mind, having nowhere to look but back, abridges its existence in a single instant of vision too swift for utterance, though not, of course, for narrative phrasing. According to this assumption, death becomes a sudden anthology of life's impressions in a last flash of self. It is an epitome detached from literary formula into reputed psychological phenomenon.

So too the hanged man is thought to have time for the rehearsal of life: hence, such a trick case of narrative duration discovered to be a mere death moment in disguise as we get in Ambrose Bierce's *Occurrence at Owl Creek Bridge* (1891). Drowning adds to this compacted temporal summary the unique Romantic possibilities of the self reentered at death upon an undifferentiated natural relation, swallowed up by the physical universe itself. Drowning thus lends itself to narrative symbol by being the only manner of death—as the Wordsworth of "Lucy Gray," for instance, elliptically implies—in which the self returns before burial, indeed in the very manner of burial, into the either stilled or churning element of nature. Drowning amounts in this way to a reincorporation of the temporal self into the mythic element of time when viewed from the perspective of eternity, an absorption of presence into a medium suggestive of both fluidity and immutability. Yet by being not only a death in and then from time but also a dying crisis suspended over time in the distended moment of review, drowning declares its parallels to the literary work of epiphany or synopsis at the instant of decease, duration subsumed to understood shape, living to life.

Drowning is thus a scene entitled within narrative—or, if only metaphoric, a figure privileged—to example the mechanism of narrative itself as a wording into shape of lives passed into completion, lapsed to report. Though its asphyxiation cancels in realistic terms all chance for spoken, let alone written, language as an articulate scanning of a character's own past, drowning still offers frequently in fiction an enactment of identity exchanged for story as the summation of a self. Authorized by a popular belief free of religious premises, style may thus play out at full extent in the literature of drowning what is otherwise and repeatedly its narrative intent: to word the evident on the cutting edge of the invisible, epitomizing the self at its obliteration. The drowning mind thus offers the perfect model for agnostic epiphany, its revelation held to what has already been seen if not known. As mapped by the epigraphs beginning here with Hart Crane, my discussion will often center on the archetype of drowning retrospect—not out of any particular interest this book ought to take in the literary treatment of death by water as a clinical fatality but out of a sense—raised to self-consciousness in the greatest of such scenes—that the narrative act is in its own right analogous to drowning, to its symbol of flux interrupted by absolute fixity and deepened by retrospect.

The metaphoric corollary of speech prevented by drowning is an absence of language figuratively represented for an otherwise dying character by association with such drowning. In *Our Mutual Friend*, Dickens renders the prolonged deathbed battle for life of a man retrieved from drowning after a waterside assault, a battle imaged in metaphors transferred from the original circumstances of his near death. Of the bedridden Eugene Wrayburn we hear, "This frequent rising of a drowning man from the deep, to sink again, was dreadful to the beholders" (IV, ch. 10). Through the revived dead metaphor of a "sinking" vitality, drowning becomes, as it would later for Virginia Woolf in *The Voyage Out*, for instance, a metaphor for the wordless withdrawal of a feverish mind into the vortex of its own annulment. This is a metaphoric descent in which the sinking mind strains, as Dickens's strained phrase from *Our Mutual Friend* has it, "in an unspeakable yearning to have speech."

Another way to put the case of fictional drowning is to suggest that psychological epitome—by being naturalized or justified by drowning—can become only the more reflexively textualized. Barkis's epitomizing end in *David Copperfield*, as we know, involves a revealing metaphoric turn in the actual death sentence, once his last brief speech is over: "And, it being low water, he went out with the tide." Literal drowning, though, tends to internalize even more completely than with Barkis's repeated tag line, "Barkis is willin'," the wholesale review of a life running past while running out. From *The Old Curiosity Shop* through to a contemporary story by Samuel Beckett called "La Fin," from Quilp, that is, to Beckett's drowning narrator in that late tale, or from a heroine such as Maggie Tulliver in *The Mill on the Floss* down through Hazel Shade in Nabokov's *Pale Fire*—even, as the autobiographical context will clarify, in the repeated metaphoric and literal drownings of *David Copperfield*—countless characters go to their death by water not only as a quintessence of their own lives in time but as a tacit inquiry into the narrative act that documents them. In this manner drowning effects a transposition and also a displacement, as it were, between story and discourse, event and narrative structure, again between plotted content and enclosing form.

Before considering more closely the fictive centrality of the scene of drowning, as encapsuled by its metanarrative implications in *Moby Dick*, we must take up its relation to another literary tradition, influencing and reinflected by Romanticism. In moving forward from Milton's *Lycidas*, for instance, to Shelley's *Adonais*, one can note those transformations in the symbolism of drowning that are crucial to the ongoing genre not only of prose fiction but of pastoral elegy. Archetypes of mortal revival and transfiguration are of course inherent in the latter. Still, the fact that the subject of Milton's elegy, Edward King, did actually drown at sea lends force to the imagery of "whelming tide" (l. 57) and "perilous flood" (l. 185) and to the hero's redemption by "him that walk'd the waves" (l. 164). Shelley later turns this catastophe to pure trope in lamenting Keats's disappearance into the "amourous Deep" (l. 25) of the "gulf of death" (l. 35), then extending this figuration with a transferred epithet in the evocation of a "deep and liquid rest" (l. 63). The metaphoric appropriation of drowning is further extended and reclaimed by the end of Shelley's poem. The faith in Keats's inspiration defying any effort to "quench" (l. 481) its posthumous fire makes it available for the secondary inspiration of the elegist himself—through a virtual displacement of the drowning imagery into a saving transport(ation)—when out upon the tides of visionary discovery "my spirit's bark is driven, / Far from the shore."

Though drowning predates the operations of mourning in Milton and figuratively reworks them in Shelley, this fatal event is not a narrated aspect of either elegy. It seems to emerge instead as a kind of implicit analogue for the very fact of elegy as retrospect. It is as if the notion of a mind replaying its life in drowning is itself displaced, or extruded, into the commemorative format of the entire elegy, whether it draws on archetypal or instead Christian models of invulnerability and continuance, on cyclic renewal or sheer miracle. The mythic pattern of the sunk and resuscitated, or the divinely impervious immortal triumphing over the sea of time, is refigured as the very act of memory, dredging up and bringing to light the lapsed genius in a surge of rehearsed achievement and inherited fervor. This is all the more clearly the case in Shelley's Romantic text, where the drowning itself is only in the first place an empathetic figure of poetic speech in the flow of the elegist's own transfiguring verse.

Much of the efficacy of the drowning pattern, in figuring the self's relation to the temporal world, is on view in a further contrast between a later Romantic elegy and a modern ironic subversion of the form, between Walt Whitman's "Out of the Cradle Endlessly Rocking" (1859) and T. S. Eliot's "Love Song of J. Alfred Prufrock" (1917). A decade after the mysterious articulating waves of Dickens's *Dombey and Son*, Whitman is, like Shelley, inspired by "some drown'd secret hissing, / To the out setting bard" (ll. 142–143) in words he expects to arise from the sibilant laps of "sea-waves" (l. 163). Indeed these cyclic waters "Lisp'd to me the low and delicious word death, / And again death, death, death, death" (ll. 168– 169), all five instances of the noun convened again to fill a single monosyllabic pentameter line at the close of this penultimate stanza: "Death, death, death, death, death" (l. 173). The final verses of the poem then introduce a remarkable elision between the grammar of uttered finality and the reflexive reaffirmation of self, when a long periodic suspension (very much as in the later prose manner of Virginia Woolf) separates the allusion to death in "That strong and delicious word which . . ." far enough from the final isolated line of the text to insure the hovering of its last word between direct and indirect object, "The sea whisper'd me."

The closural whisperings of the sea in Eliot's "Prufrock" are meant instead to decompose rather than reintegrate identity in the face of death. The submerged metaphor of tidal enormity in the persona's "overwhelming question" (l. 93) and then as well his frail travesty in the next line of "Lazarus, come from the dead" decline toward the imagery of drowning at the close as an elegiac condensation of temporality turned inside out. Elusively verbalized here is an abdication of normal grammar and chronology. "We *have* lingered" undersea, admits Prufrock, with his typically ambiguous plural (and my temporal emphasis), "Till human voices wake us, and we drown." Not so much Lazarus as the already drowned Phoenician sailor from "Death by Water" in *The Waste Land*, Prufrock by his very grammar despairs of that confident reclamation of self from the flux of effacement achieved by Whitman. Prufrock doesn't say that he *once* lingered until he drowned, nor that he has continuously lingered, and will continue to do so, until he *shall* drown. Malingering is instead glimpsed as an asphyxiating fatality in itself: "We have lingered . . . till we drown," here and now, in the very voicing of it—a Joycean waking and a wake at once. Preterite and present tense collapse upon each other in the suggestion that the whole text is, has been, the excruciating review, the succumbing retrospect of a life mired and sinking in its own timorous evasions. Grammatically and psychologically the monologue's very point of departure is its lethal fait accompli.

It is another Lazarian corpse whose rising to the sea's surface is awaited five years later in *Ulysses*, Joyce's "man that was drowned" (p. 21) threatening to become the first on-stage corpse in the novel after Stephen's dream of his mother's recent deathbed agonies (p. 5). The sea having been "hailed as a great sweet mother," what the "nine days" drowned corpse suggests, in its imminent emergence, is a telescoped parody of rebirth after nine months of gestation—the search party "waiting for a swollen bundle to bob up, roll over to the sun a puffy face, salt white. Here I am" (p. 21). As a declaration of presence upon the fluctuating face of eternity, that last three-syllable sentence echoes the archetypal answering of the Lord's call which has figured with increasing irony in such earlier deathbed scenes in British fiction as Thackeray's *The Newcomes* and Hardy's *Jude the Obscure* (see Chapter 3). Here now for Joyce, as if in an objectification of elegiac review in the returned corporeal body of the self, is the symbolic incarnation of drowning as an owning up of identity.

No prose text of either the nineteenth or the twentieth century could more fully exemplify what death by drowning is empowered to "bequeath" (in the epigraph's words from Hart Crane's "At Melville's Tomb"), both within and by fictional plot, than Melville's own *Moby Dick* (1851). Death by water is of course the chief fatality in the seafaring world of *Moby Dick*. In the curt summary of the narrator, Ishmael, "Death in this business of whaling" is "a speechless quick chaotic bundling of man into Eternity" (ch. 7), where Joyce's noun "bundle" is anticipated in the very verb of this description. The emphasis on speechlessness, which is to be cured at the end by another cryptic form of articulation, reminds us of the peculiar utility of the drowning scene in fiction as model for the novelizing act itself. As distinguished from extended deathbed scenes, for instance, there is no conceivable room for speech in the instant of drowning suffocation, and so the meaning projected from a dying mind into fictional narrative becomes a manifest exercise in pure style. So it will have become by the end of Melville's novel. It is a climax no more than dimly adumbrated by the retrospective narrator, through a metaphor transposed from temporal routine, in anticipating the moment when "poor Queequeg took his last long dive" (ch. 13). The manner in which the closural scene symbolizes an apotheosis of that drowning black seaman is worlds apart from the formulaic epitome elsewhere phrased for the crazed boy Pip as an ascension "to the great quarter deck on high" (ch. 27), a facile turn of phrase in the manner of Smollett's comic epitaphs for his nautical heroes.

The first scene of drowning in *Moby Dick*, ambiguously suicide or accident, befalls the mysterious sailor Bulkington and predicts the pattern of later symbolic deaths by water. Melville's own chapter on Bulkington's death is self-consciously identified as a fleeting, an unfixed, a coded but ultimately indecipherable trace of such drowning: "Wonderfullest things are ever the unmentionable; deep memories yield no epitaphs; this six-inch chapter is the stoneless grave of Bulkington" (ch. 13).[32] One would ordinarily expect prose to court the analogy to epitaph, the inscription by which memory and meaning are secured. As in any story the scene of death is a virtual grave, but Melville's narrative at this early turn refuses to meet such an expectation with a complacent epitaph about the cause of death. This chapter comprises a death scene without detail completing a life without biography, a definition of life only in terms of death. The instant of demise is "unmentionable" ("let me only say that it fared with him as with the storm tossed ship") not because Ishmael is euphemizing a probable suicide, but because adventure and self-slaughter offer a false dichotomy for a life that is nothing if not a pitting of self (without the rage of Ahab) against the forces of otherness, of identity against negation. Bulkington is known to us only as the risk taker, and in this single chapter he is buried without being sacrificed to a significance beyond the common denominator of existential presence. The chapter's stoneless grave, its paradoxical engraving in prose of an import beyond inscription, ends with one of the most explicit formulations of an epitomizing moment in literature: "Up from the spray of thy ocean-perishing—straight up, leaps thy apotheosis!" (ch. 13). Bulkington's death *is* his life at its furthest reach, the moment of impact between man and the sea recognized as the apotheosis of a being energized solely by this ever-present fatal contingency.

The negative image of this genuine death (in what Conrad would later call the "destructive element") does not so much yield to otherness as rail and flail against it. The perverse relation of self to world is symbolized in the novel's last rather than first enacted drowning, that of Tashtego on the masthead as the Pequod sinks out of sight. In this vanishing interval Ahab's right-hand man—*only* the savage's hand visible now above the water—is attempting to secure Ahab's flag, the true colors of the captain's monomania. In doing so he nails a hawk's wing to the masthead. In the very moment of his drowning, "feeling that etherial thrill, the submerged savage beneath, in his death-gasp, kept his hammer frozen there; and so the bird of heaven, with archangelic shrieks, . . . folded in the flag of Ahab, went down with his ship" (ch. 135). Community under the ensign of a single reductive purpose, Ahab's banner enfolds the object of its quest, the harbinger of nonhuman nature, as the very definition of death for his surrogate, Tashtego. An editorial oddity in the publishing history of the novel suggests the logic of this symbolic last hammer-stroke and its syllabic reverberations. The English edition has Tashtego freezing the bird in his "death-grasp," while the American wording spells this instant as fatal to the human agent, a "death-gasp."[33] The textual gap between editions—and, more important, the likely echo of either phrasing in the other—inscribes (as between the two grammars of "close upon him" at Carker's death) merely a slipknot's distance between cause and effect, here between the bludgeoning of the universe into supposed submission and the suffocation and effacement of human identity that results.

But there is another drowning that has transpired unsung amid the mass catastrophe of the sinking ship, a drowning alluded to only after the fact, when the coffin prepared for its victim has surfaced, empty, to save the narrator's life. Ishmael has earlier looked with "sympathetic awe" upon Bulkington in his vanishing self-revelation, and it is this human sympathy that is explored in the rest of the novel between men who would form a community with Bulkington, who would know life as the perpetual risking of death, but would know it together, strengthened by human felllowship. Such heroic bonding comes to a very different apotheosis from Bulkington's at the end of the novel. Up from the whirlpool of the sinking ship leaps the epitomizing emblem of Queequeg's offered salvation, his empty and thus buoyant coffin, etched over with the cryptic tattooing that has adorned his living form. Recovering earlier from a near-fatal fever only to carve these markings on the lid of his coffin, Queequeg leaves this chiseled text now to the salvation of another. For Ishmael it is his friend's body as the symbolic vessel of a sustaining human contact, and it outlives Queequeg to bequeath survival to his friend.

Among the other "hieroglyphic marks" once painted on Queequeg's savage skin by the "departed prophet and seer of his island" is "a mystical treatise on the art of attaining truth; so that Queequeg in his own proper person was a riddle to unfold; a wondrous work in one volume; but whose mysteries not even himself could read, through his own live heart beat against them" (ch. 110). In all this Queequeg is only Everyman, any of us, just more visibly illegible to others and himself, a text of unreadable secrets in a nonmetaphoric sense. It is almost as if Hart Crane's lines from the epigraph about the wreckstrewn flood have Queequeg in mind with their image of the "scattered chapter, livid hieroglyph." By such emblazoned secrets, abstracted from the living flesh that is their original medium, Queequeg first and then Ishamel in turn are brought back from the abyss. The same mystery of the body's opacity—which in its nonhuman manifestation, as the body of the natural world in the warring shape of the whale, tortures Ahab into suicidal fury—can also release identity into acceptance and self-determination.

In so demonstrating, the parable of the coffin takes one more turn—

back to its own cryptic textuality. Without being able to interpret it, Queequeg has transferred his body's text into a sacred tablet upon the coffin lid, an engraved inscription that becomes an epigraph not by distilling the self to significance but by replicating its hieroglyphic mystery. By turning immediately after recovery from fever to the decoration of the coffin in which he lay for so long, Queequeg seems to identify this scriptive work with another version of outlasted death. By transcribing, as it were, his own person so as to be able to read himself upon the surface of his coffin, he displaces and disinfects his threatened end. His body a transferable if indecipherable code, Queequeg is himself translated to mere inscription after his actual death, to mere (though still withheld) meaning. He goes to his undersea burial, unmourned, with the rest of the crew, and his replica in wood, not as human form but as human content externalized in a mystic style, bursts forth as his only remains. What keeps Ishmael afloat, then, is not only a symbol of his friend's body as sustaining presence but the representation of the man *as* representation, as if Ishmael too were saved by reading, by taking support from a man-made text and a man made over into text. Queequeg's mystery in essence, his tattooed epitome, remains his only epitaph, and by the volume of its saving truth, as well as by the volume of water it displaces, his friend is redeemed from what John T. Irwin calls the novel's "*vor*-textual" abyss.[34] More obviously even than in the textualized recollections of pastoral elegy and its motifs of rescue from watery oblivion, here the rehearsal of life in drowning is objectified—what Queequeg wishes remembered of his person and his past—in the wooden text of his intended resting place.

Like Ishmael received back into the living world, so at one remove are we as readers of the whole narrative—as well as of Queequeg's history, his fever, his later death—renewed by the chill waters of his unenacted drowning and its redemptive legacy. In the chapter "Queequeg in His Coffin," Ishmael, narrator of a book called *Moby Dick*, stops to comment on the ungraspable phantom of deathbed revelation which is always beyond reach of inscription: "For whatever is truly wondrous and fearful in man, never yet was put into words or books. And the drawing near of Death, which alike levels all, alike impresses all with a last revelation, which only an author from the dead could adequately tell" (ch. 110). Yet Ishmael as man rather than as narrator, or as man so as to signal his service to us as narrator, *is* in reach of such a wonder in words on the floating coffin of his friend, where the meaning of death and the mystery of identity are transcribed (or in Melville's indirect texual allusion, "impressed") apart from the body of life as a way of representing that body invulnerably.

Ishmael's philosophical balance and spiritual buoyancy are epitomized by a death he is allowed to live through. He surfaces as a narrator returned more literally than most from the dead, a speaking voice that has harrowed oblivion and come back bearing, and borne by, hieroglyphic signs of a surviving if untranslated truth (certainly by us doubly unreadable, for we never even see these signs on the page). By Queequeg's epitaph of so many wood-hewn inches is Ishmael saved, resurrected, immortalized as the narrator of this very salvation. It is the Orphic displacement of death upon the storyteller, elegy as the essential energy of narration. As Keats showed earlier, deathly revelation is the last responsibility of hero as narrator, who must be ready to undergo his own going and survive it, the reader with him. Doing so, such a hero is delegated in turn to allegorize the fact that every great novelist is in some comparable sense an "author from the dead," every reader a fellow traveler in regions outside the daily limits of this life.

□   □   □

With the archetypal overtones of the drowning motif alone—in such myths as that of the sea god Poseidon, brother of Hades himself; of the drowned and resurfaced head of the dismembered Orpheus; of the cyclic power of the Fisher King; and of Christ, fisher of men, who himself could walk the waves—it is clear at least in one way how readily the literary death scene can lend itself to mythopoetic interpretation. Part of the reason for beginning with William Empson, however, was to suggest more broadly the potential centrality of the death scene, in all its verbal, thematic, psychological, mythic, and structural bearing, for the various revolutions in critical theory that have redirected by turns the course of literary study in this century, from the textual breakthroughs of the New Critics to the scriptive breakdowns of deconstruction. At the risk of oversimplification, I want to suggest the utility of the death sentence as a focal moment for various practical and theoretical methodologies before turning to stylistic analysis. Archetypal or psychoanalytic approaches, for instance, will naturally claim some attention. More important, however, my approach to the language of mortality in fiction—starting from the hypothesis that death is a structural microcosm of both duration inflected toward closure and utterance differentiated from blankness—calls for the exploration of the death scene as a narrative phenomenon uniquely equipped to negotiate a rapport between what has come to be called narratology and the more linguistic orientation of deconstructive reading. Since it is congenial to the meticulous stylistic scrutiny that the death sentence as rhetorical vaunt so often invites, this approach should also help account for the longevity of the death scene, from Dickens through Conrad to Beckett, as a sounding board of fictional invention and authority, as well as a test case for critical theory.

The assumption of an entirely self-contained verbal structure in the ideal New Critical text, defined by the isolated differentials of ambiguous discourse rather than by recourse to external verifications beyond the play of phrase, is an assumption carried beyond preference or method in the radically closed system of a written death scene. At the outer limits of narratability, no extraverbal experience can possibly be appealed to. Sealed off from the normal channels of information and report, the text of death is the most purely wrought, rather than recorded, of artifacts: the closed text in extremis, so to speak. It is Cleanth Brooks's "well-wrought urn" as the very space of narrative memorial. For the psychoanalytic critic, the death scene toward which so many texts direct themselves is also a privileged moment. Mortal recognition constituting one of the primal traumas of mental life, any narrative pointed toward or focused around the scene of death can become so self-conscious about its condensations and displacements of the death moment, erotic and otherwise, that an entire novel, such as Beckett's *Malone Dies*, can emerge as one long working through, in Freud's terms, of the death anxiety. Not only the polar opposite of Eros but of everything else in the conscious or unconscious life, death thus lends itself as well to the binary distinctions of structuralism in any of its guises. The voiding fact of death can well be taken to organize such random dichotomies as that between time and eternity, declaration and negation, self and other,

presence and absence. When structuralism yields place to a deconstructive critique, the death scene still retains its binary cutting edge.
Yet what might previously have been assumed as death's ultimate
opposition, between being and nothingness, is now seen, certainly
in any text, to be subordinated to the grounding duality of speech
and silence, not after all a difference between presence and absence
but only a deferral of erasure by articulation.

The thoroughgoing revisionism that attends the stress on this last
opposition between utterance and silence throws the poststructuralist
program into sharp relief against another of its more recent forebears.
Whereas Jacques Derrida, for instance, with far more than Empsonian
rigor, would cordon off the arbitrary sign systems of discourse from
the phenomena or intercourse of any separately conceivable world,
as well as from all authorial intention, the work of a phenomenological
critic such as Georges Poulet is instead a kind of intentionalism turned
inside out. Poulet and the other critics of consciousness imagine the
gathering of a writer's words toward a discrete and codifiable world
of their own, the continuous manifestation of a writer's imaginative
presence in language, to which only sympathetic interpretation can
gain full access. Death could thus, in this phenomenological approach, well become that definitive point of limit where the necessary
suspension of verbal referent at the verge of void would also hold in
arrest the imagined phenomena of the writer's whole invoked world.
In another sense, the death scene—and especially for Poulet the
scene of drowning, with its premise of retrospect and compression—
becomes the model of all story at the far edge of phenomenality.
Deriving his claim for literature as textualized transience, as a major
cultural effort toward the spatialization of time, from Henri Bergson's
philosophy of human duration, Poulet takes special note of Bergson's
interest in the temporally condensed (as if spatially compacted) moment of drowning, with its "panoramic" projection of lapsed time as
legible tableau—or text.[35] Such metanarrative implications for the
scene of drowning in fiction, or of related modes of death, also connect
phenomenological theory with structuralist studies of the text, where
death not only offers a special address to questions of closure but
also acts to circumscribe that point where plot must pass through
whatever level of imagined mimesis to pure discourse, of reference
and evocation to the sheer epiphenomenon of the verbal trace.

Once recognized as a narratological checkpoint somewhere between the phenomenological and the deconstructive models—not trapped between as half-measure but moving between as flexible examplar— the death scene in fiction tends not only to be most fully illuminated by literary theory but to teach in turn what it has to teach about the nature of narrative and the mortal need for it. The great leveler, death is also a great reconciler, at least an instructive point of coincidence between post-Romantic philosophy's program of nonmetaphysical humanism and the pervasive skepticism of its latter-day deconstruction. In the postponements, relays, and elisions of the fictional death sentence, with its barest—its laid-bare—differentiation of narrative from its own erasure, utterance from absence, the stylistic procedures of a text articulate—as never so directly elsewhere—not only the latent void of their local subject, death, but what recent theory would call the actual project of textuality and its own paradoxes of void versus graphic trace. Death as fictional subject educes the very work of narrative from its particular stylistic workings.[36] A sense of death's (emptied) centrality in such textual matters can be seen to develop from Hegel through Nietzsche and Freud to Walter Benjamin, Georges Bataille, Maurice Blanchot, and on into Barthes and Derrida, with the represented moment of dying emphasized as revelatory touchstone not only for the textual image as admitted mirage stretched over negation but for the whole task of fiction as mortal intercession.

Walter Benjamin is only the most eloquent, humanistic, indeed almost sentimental of this company when, in a neo-Freudian vision of narratological transference, he writes that what "draws the reader to the novel is the hope of warming his shivering life with a death he reads about."[37] Freud meant as much when, in his wartime essay on the necessity of rescuing death for therapeutic meaning from the ravages of mass slaughter and medical sterility, he lamented the removal of death from the family hearth to the hospital or the battlefield. To counteract this we need the recuperative interventions of drama and stories, where we can "die with the hero with whom we have identified ourselves; yet we survive him, and are ready to die again just as safely with another hero."[38] Behind this would seem to lie Nietzsche's famous dictum, "We possess art lest we perish of the truth."[39] This proposition—recast as the thought that we have the death scene so that we do not die of, or to, the ultimate lucidity of retrospect and overview—returns us to the theoretical insight at the back of Benjamin's deceptive sentimentality. Death is a structural clarification as well as an empathetic or cathartic occasion. Benjamin, that is, would argue further that we die with Freud's "hero" (though Freud is not mentioned) because of the special kinship between any death scene and any revelatory narrative regardless of its subject, the cognate relation between death's intensification of meaning and the very process of narrativizing a duration into a discourse.

We go to novels in general, as in particular to their death scenes, looking for the kind of knowledge that is knowledge only insofar as it is pure retrospect, wrenched free from supposed experience into containment and clarity, displaced from inarticulate pain, for instance, to epiphany. Using the term "real life" where I have been using "identity," Benjamin argues that "not only a man's knowledge or wisdom, but above all his real life—and this is the stuff stories are made of—first assumes transmissible form at the moment of his death."[40] Benjamin seems to allude to the notion that dying men tend to replay their lives in their own minds, just as they may well do by physiological imperative at that moment of drowning far removed from any domestic deathbed. He suggests further the displaced impact of such definitive introspection on an adjacent consciousness at the scene: "Just as a sequence of images is set in motion inside a man as his life comes to an end—unfolding the views of himself under which he has encountered himself without being aware of it—suddenly in his expressions and looks the unforgettable emerges and imparts to everything that concerned him that authority which even the poorest wretch in dying possesses for the living around him." He adds, "This authority is at the very source of the story."[41] Benjamin has in mind a transferred bestowal of shape whereby the dying man, seeing his life turning into coherent record, is becoming to those near him not a man any longer, and not yet a corpse, but in the luminous transition a character.

Benjamin's premise about the power of a deathbed scene to transmit a memorable sense of identity to those other selves gathered round is certainly shared by most of the Victorian writers studied here. For them the deathbed is still usually on the domestic site, scrupulously attended, even luxuriated over. It is still felt by the community, familial or larger, as an access to precisely that form of knowing that comes of being over. To borrow a term from Benjamin's theory, elsewhere, of the power of the unreproduced artistic original, there seems to be a charged moment of mortal "aura" conveyed at a death-bed.[42] Along with the transmission and revaluation of its fictional devices from Victorian to modern practitioners, such dying deserves analysis partly because the death scene can be understood in this way as the circumscribed synecdoche of fictional form at large, the focal because final moment of interpretable event for an articulating consciousness.

The modes of displacement and symbolic doubling within a given plot that may deliberately point this up thereby stand as emblems for the ritual duplications at the root of the representational process itself. In *Hegel, Death, and Sacrifice*, Georges Bataille writes that "the sacrificer identifies with the animal struck by death," as does the larger communal audience, as would we as readers of such a scene. The voluntary violence of such an identification, like Freud's reader wishing to die with the hero and then return from that death into life, makes the sacrificial act a conjectural self-assassination. The "sacrificer" thus "dies while watching himself die, and even, after a fashion, dies of his own volition, at one with the sacrificial arm." The logic of surrogacy here "foreshadows the necessity of *spectacle*, or generally of *representation*, without the repetition of which we would remain foreign to and ignorant of death, as animals apparently remain."[43] Such an underlying definition of man as the mortality-conscious animal takes its place in a line of thought that includes Yeats among the post-Romantic poets, who in "Death" concludes that the "great man" or hero "knows death to the bone" of his own decomposition, for "Man has created death."[44] By conceiving death as an abstraction, man has also placed himself in dire need of its displaced experience and survival. "Many times he died, / Many times rose again," says Yeats of that man who is more than a "dying animal," who can anticipate the measure of his death in the mind. This is, of course, a deep motive of the whole tradition of pastoral elegy, as phrased by Shelley in his characterization of himself as one "Who in another's fate now wept his own" (*Adonais*, l. 300). Such mortal "repetitions," in Bataille's term, can be achieved only by some sort of representation or rehearsal, whether through a solitary struggle of the imagination, through the sacrifice of a nearby demise, or through the medium and mediation of art. Indeed, when Bataille continues his commentary on Hegel's view of sacrificial representation, he suggests that "nothing is less animal than the fiction, more or less removed from reality, of death."[45] By being the most human "fiction," death can be seen as the essential source of all fabulation.

Derrida, himself tacitly developing motifs from Blanchot's revisionary Orphism of the text,[46] has also taken up Bataille on these matters for his own purposes, extending the sacrificial model into the more absolute disparity between any text and any imagined original action, thus deritualizing the very nature of narrative to mere inscription. Yet death is by no means excluded as narrative emblem; it is merely bled of its humanist priority. For previous psychological or religious coordinates of the death moment Derrida substitutes the grammatological trope. Variously acknowledged in the past as the mother of beauty, the muse of philosophy, the father of tragedy, the nonidentical twin of closure, death is newly unveiled as the first-born bastard child of all discourse. Literary articulation is thus deconstructed into a double suicide, the belated and fading ghost of the designated world on the one hand and of the referring mind on the other. When Leopold Bloom in "Hades" reads the daily death column and thinks, with a pun on "characters" and an implicit half-rhyme with "extinct" in "inked," that once living men are now only "inked characters fast fading on the frayed breaking paper" (*Ulysses*, p. 91), Joyce, according to later linguistic thought, is only taking newsprint obituaries as an emblem for all textuality as a mourning of presence.

Long before Joyce's hints or any more recent novel's preoccupation with deconstructive conceits, and well before the theory risen to such fictional occasion, the novel as narrative genre had acknowledged that other pact, at least as binding, with death. It is one that Joyce also has his hero insinuate. While still within the precincts of "Hades," Bloom recovers his inveterate humanism by placing a reader's stress on the text in reception rather than a linguistic emphasis on the text as inscription: "Read your own obituary notice they say you live longer. Gives you second wind. New lease of life" (p. 109). Bloom's rumor about journalistic obituary is more closely in line with the literary tradition from which he and the "Hades" section derive than is, for instance, the monitory notion expressed by Alfred Jarry's

Antichrist: "See your double and die."[47] It would be truer to the twofold possibility of fictional displacement, for character and reader alike, to say, "See the death of your double, whether inside a plot or on the page, and survive."

This Hegelian doubling has to do, of course, with the nature of reading at least as much as of writing. Story explores its own deepest accord with death through narrative insight devolved upon the reader rather than, or as complement to, scriptive traces banished from the three-dimensional universe of their intended reference to mere rectangular page. The issue is one of narrative revelation more than referential evanescence, of visionary deflection upon an audience rather than some ontological decentering of story as sheer discourse, of aesthetic involvement more than textual involution. This is so, borrowing again from Melville's metatextual humanism at the close of *Moby Dick*, not primarily because every text, as Queequeg's coffin implies, comes to us severed from the already dead body of its origin, but mainly because every author, as phenomenological filter of consciousness, is in the long view an "author from the dead"—every text not just a sacrifice of presence for trace but every great text, at least, a cathartic sacrifice of facile mimesis for Orphic discovery.

All that narrative can ever promise in this regard is that fiction, though not necessarily any of its characters, will be able to make something of death, take from it a revelation vouchsafed only because it can be safely outlasted, lived through in reading. Recasting such a thought in the key terms of this chapter, the special case of verbal transpositon at death that I have been calling epitome is, like displacement, an issue of text as well as of plot. To find transpired import compressed into a single coherent disclosure, be it desperate or redemptive, is a literary as much as a deathbed impulse: every tome an epitome of sorts. Such is the compacted power of narrative rhetoric or symbolism as well as of mortal epiphany, a power in itself displaced from hero to reader. Lived sequence is transposed to finality from mere duration, wrung to quintessence, squeezed clean into meaning. This is the genius of mortal closure under order from art, a delegated disclosure for (because not yet in) ourselves. In everyday life a death scene may be terrible, pitiful, empty. Art alone may be counted on to take us out of ourselves long enough to entertain with vision the end of ourselves. In fiction, therefore, death is alive with meaning, for its heroes on saving occasions, for us forever.

The Frontispiece is a photograph of a sculpture by Daniel Chester French sometimes referred to as *Death Staying the Hand of the Sculptor*, a funerary monument for a fellow artist and for the funeral that is art. It portrays a serene, gently erotic angel of death arresting the male subject in the process of carving a relief of the Sphynx. The triangulated point of contact between a corporealized Death, the artist's body, and the body of his artifact makes a multiple emblematic point about creativity touched by death. In its aspect as immortality, we might say, Death appears almost to guide and steady the hand of the sculptor, to "stay" it in this sense, eternity always colluding in the works of time. (So too in the Arnold Böcklin self-portrait reproduced before the Conrad chapter, where the hand of Death at play in the world not only matches but seems to accompany in every way the brushwork of the recording artist.) In its complementary aspect of finality rather than eternity, however, Death in the Daniel French sculpture stops the artist's hand stone cold—as cold as the marble object upon which it works and into which, in like and inclusive working, it has itself been wrought. In this recessional arrangement from spectator or mourner past dying artist toward the Sphynx, the marble realization farthest removed from both completion and immediacy is an iconic portrayal of that metamorphic, riddling mediation between animal and human, desert and city, nature and culture, past and present, whose marmoreal marriage to silence and slow time provides a model for all art's mute and memorial truth. It is a truth—myth is implicitly enlisted to remind us—whose articulation in any medium must indeed be approached at peril of a kind of death. The world stilled into Sphynx-like, oracular art is always the world's mystery in an incomplete, if not an interrupted, decipherment, as well as that same world's inscription into the realm of permanence. No artifact could better recognize the artist's league with a Death he would at the same time tame and banish, brace himself against in both contradictory senses, at once wed and transcend. Moreover, we may borrow the terms of this funerary monument—but imagined simply as monument rather than as actual tombstone or mausoleum facade—to assess the connection between textuality per se and the death it often records, always in some sense corresponds to. We find that a text should not be thought to bury or entomb its characters in the process of their generation so much as to provide the virtual cenotaph of their conceived life, a memorial to the very idea of independent fictional existences constructed in the absence of any remains thereof at the site of writing.

If death in the Victorian novel can be taken to mark something like the intersection between (and at the same time final divergence of) sociology and psychology in their mutual plotting of identity within community, then the manifest removal of self from the populated world is also subjectively defined by an interval, either temporal or spatial, traversed within that self. If the arrival of modernism serves in part to specify this intersection between identity and otherness through the magnifying lens of a more and more acute self-consciousness, of both literary form and psychology, then death remains foregrounded as the field of *scientia* which the self can never connect with in time—whether in the realm of lived time or in fiction's temporal form. Conrad, for instance, goes as far to illustrate this special implication of enacted dying within the self-consciousness of modernist fiction—death becoming a structural crisis for point-of-view narration as well as for the problem of human subjectivity it is conceived to investigate—as Dickens did, for instance, in illustrating the implicit inwardness of dying even within the classic mode of omniscient fiction. As models of perception come and go, so goes death. When fictional history moves forward from the modernist epoch of formal and psychological self-consciousness to the self-constitutive linguistic agendas of postmodernism's reflexive textuality, death continues as the test of narrative's final transit—a transition not so much to insentience as to sheer sentence. Arresting characterization, death nevertheless steadies the scriptive hand of the text. The revision of phenomenological by deconstructive perspectives in much recent critical debate offers in this way a suggestive parallel to the shift from modernist to postmodernist narrative. The elegiac enterprise of Proust's fiction, for example, with its numerous enacted and recalled death scenes, finds one of its fullest responses in the criticism of consciousness practiced upon it by Georges Poulet. While Beckett's later trilogy often reads like the transcription of a single dying consciousness yielding its voice to void, his novels come to require a deconstructive commentary with an equal emphasis at least on the ceding of space to trace.

As sheer writing, then, but also as style and as plot, the death sentence persists across the history of post-Romantic fiction in providing the variously linguistic, descriptive, and structural fulcrum of fiction. Death stands as a pivotal moment for language on the edge of silence, for evocation on the verge of the invisible, for narratability on the brink of closure. Received by nineteenth-century novelists as virtually the mandate of their narrative mission and the highest calling of their prose, the inalienable bond between story and mortality— Romantically capitalized on by Dickens in numerous metanarrative parables, ironically tampered with by Thackeray, withered to the mere skeleton of its emotional efficacy in Hardy—turns out to be ratified anew, against greater and more subversive odds, by the modernists Conrad, Forster, Lawrence, and Woolf, the postmodernists Beckett and Nabokov. This literary history of continually reaffirmed confidence in death as signatory to the very charter of fiction is the main story this book about death in story sets out to tell.

2

Traversing the Interval

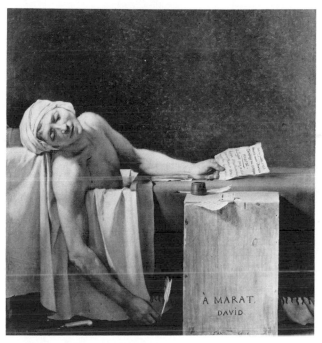

Marat Assassinated (detail), by Jacques Louis David
Courtesy Musées Royaux des Beaux-Arts, Brussels

Every beating heart in the hundreds of thousands of breasts
there, is, in some of its imaginings, a secret to the heart
nearest it! Something of the awfulness, even of Death itself, is
referable to this. No more can I turn the leaves of this dear
book that I loved, and vainly hope in time to read it all.

CHARLES DICKENS
A Tale of Two Cities

Man, how fast his firedint, his mark on mind, is gone!
Both are in an unfathomable, all is in an enormous dark
Drowned . . .
. . . death blots black out.

GERARD MANLEY HOPKINS
"That Nature Is a Heraclitean Fire"

that last
Wild pageant of the accumulated past
That clangs and flashes for a drowning man.

DANTE GABRIEL ROSSETTI
The House of Life

WHILE STROLLING through Paris early one morning late in his career and his life, Dickens noticed a motley procession turning round in front of Notre-Dame. Thinking it to be a christening or a marriage, those two transitional rites that figure with such prominence in his fiction, he soon discovered it related instead to the third. "Having never before chanced upon this initiation," he joined an eager crowd watching an anonymous corpse being delivered to the morgue. What he imagined others seeing in the person of this corpse affords a catalogue of the satirized vanities and selfish anxieties that so often attend death in his fiction. More to the point for the stylistic maneuvers by which death is necessarily rendered in narrative, Dickens notes in particular that all the stares of the crowd, his own included, "concurred in possessing the one underlying expression of *looking at something that could not return a look.*"[1]

To write of death is for the novelist to speak of something that cannot *talk* back, that must be worded from without, from this side of its arrival. Mimesis may itself seem inoperable, death being all presentiment, never direct presentation. This is the dilemma of death in narrative as well as its dispensation, a tolerance for all that it can never corroborate. Yet in one view all language is by nature grounded in definition, in things referable and finite, and so its expression in the face of death would hold on the verge, vibrate and break—not down so much as open. Set trembling before the imponderability of death, prose may shiver into ambivalent divisions where it can neither define nor with conviction divine, into puns rather than epiphanies. Hence Dickens's invoked first sense of "initiation," a metaphor deadened by the fact of death and hauled back through its etymology to a stiffening and literal sense of a corpse's "introduction" to the death house. At the same time, under the spell of curiosity and participation, the phrase seems dislodged from its true reference: the narrator's own "initiation" into the mystery of death as mortuary science.

Though this death, with its subsequent inquest, cannot be thought of as an initiation rite comparable to baptism or marriage, it does stand as another ceremony based on the receiving of a name, old rather than new. This Parisian corpse, awaiting identification by his people, waits for a wording of first and surname that will confer some kind of meaning, or at least verbal claim, on the mute identity of the anonymous body. This is just what prose style provides for dying within the body of a narrative death scene, a last wording that brings death to terms with denotation. Whether in the verbal apprehension of an onlooker or the last breath of a dying self, style in the fictional death scene must follow designation to the edge of negation. At that limit a name is only an emblem for the service of all language as a casting back to the life as lived—as given, expressed to itself, and then removed—even as such an identifying act of language may persist beyond the event of death as legal verification or epitaph.

It cannot too often be said that in his fictional practice, as well as in such a biographical anecdote, Dickens was doubly a man of his epoch: obsessed by death, fascinated by its demands upon articulation. To write of dying is often to stretch language's binding temporality—binding in the sense of both style's obligations and its ligatures—toward and across the point of threatened severance. This is frequently achieved in Dickens's fiction by a kind of calculus of decreasing intervals approaching the unknown at the pace and within the vanishing space of time-bound designation. In rhetorical particulars, such a stylistic task calls at various times upon a full array of assonance and alliteration, anaphora, ellipsis, the shifting interplay between subordinate, compound, and serial grammar, the subversions of paradox and ironic metaphor, all the ambiguities of diction and syntax at Dickens's command in order to convey the envisaged and traversed instant of death.

Even a pre-Romantic poem on the subject of death such as Gray's "Elegy Written in a Country Churchyard" (1751) is also likely to experiment with some of the transitional effects that both register and aestheticize the rupture of death—yet to do so without the interiorizing penchant of a Romantic text. The syntax of Gray's last two stanzas before "The Epitaph," for instance, moves forward from a grammatical structure begun with a temporal phrase, "one morn," then shifts from this adverbial modification to a new clause with the temporal des-ignation itself as subject, and then again, the moment of death already passed over, returns its temporal grammar to a subordinate place in the closing funereal action. "One morn I missed him," says the persona without yet the tone of lament. "Another morning" then "came," after which, while we still expect the subsequent phrase, "the next," as subject, it shifts to adverbial use; and so we get the retrospective allusion to death distended over both an enjambment and an internal rhyme: "The next with dirges due in sad array / Slow through the churchway path we saw him borne." Parallelism is itself discomfited within the disjuncture of fatality. What results is a sort of clausal chiasmus that, like an X marking the spot, inscribes the crossing, both over and so out, of death's chasm. Portraying nothing of the transitional moment within the dying mind, Gray's syntactic bracket nevertheless widens the gap of absence for the mourner in the muffled shock of confirmed finality.

Whereas Gray only indirectly suggests without enacting the dying interval between time and its cancellation, it is the peculiar genius of Dickensian rendering in a post-Romantic age to convey such an objective momentum as Gray gives us while also internalizing death's severance in a more immediately dramatic fashion. The purest form of the traversed interval between life and death in his work, pure because instantaneous and invisible, is the entirely subsumed death sentence for Stephen Blackpool in *Hard Times* (1854), the hero "borne" as in Gray's "Elegy" to his place of rest. Stephen's last reported thought, when he is brought up from the mine shaft, is his joy at finding "that they were about to take him in the direction whither the star seemed to him to lead" (III, ch. 6). Partly this implies, in astronomical rather than metaphysical terms, the optical illusion of receding movement in a typically Romantic projection of desire onto inanimate nature. As if already lying in state, Stephen has asked that his eyes be covered, presumably to follow his ideal trajectory in the mind's eye alone. His hope thus subjectively piloted by celestial rather than terrestrial coordinates, it is his hopeless bruised body alone that is carried homeward across the night terrain. Already internalized and redefined as spiritual promise, death has only the corporeal self left to assail. It does so in the very crevice of reference, death's removal of identity entirely removed from textual view. The absence of any violent spiritual disjuncture at Stephen's death is thus answered to in kind by the syncopation of prose report, a hole in time securing its own continuity. It is a death meant to be as illegible in the prose as it is negligible to the hero in his achieved peace of spirit. "They carried him very gently along the fields, and down the lanes"—still very much a creature of the earth—"and over the wide landscape . . . Very few whispers broke the mournful silence. It was soon a funeral procession." Suppressed rupture is turned to suture. At such moments the hoary rhetorical figure of *metastasis* (described in the *OED* as "a rapid transition from one point to another . . . Puttenham: 'the flitting figure, or the Remove' ") seems recast for dramatic agency. The downplayed metastasis (or *transitio*, elsewhere called *transmotio*) of Dickens's prose animates itself across the temporal stasis brought about in the wake of death's violent "remove" of self. The hero may be taken as far "out of the world" as in a novel by Defoe or Fielding, but it is the instantaneousness of the going, rather than the sheer distance, that now carries interest.

Stephen Blackpool's death moment, in dropping out of the text, sends shock waves through the adjacent syntax. No noun is assigned to the progress across the landscape in that initial serial grammar ("along . . . and down . . . and over"), yet some antecedence is assumed by the final subject, "it," as the plotted sequence moves from mournful anticipation to mortuary aftermath. The logged but temporarily unnamed motion of the homeward march overlaps with another, more striking suppression of reference when the unmentionable fact of death is left unspoken in the blank silence between sentences, a "period" by association. The inevitable split second between any death and its recognition by others is split open even further here by way of severing all reference whatsoever. Jacques Derrida, who takes death to be not only forbidding but "ineffable, unnarratable," the ultimate "interdiction,"[2] could, in the spirit of his own etymological word play, have gone on to note that the style of dying is often a rhetoric of inter-diction. Stephen's elided death moment, within its continuously presented scene, thus offers a kind of transposition in discourse (though with neither subjective rendering nor transcendental tendency in this terminal phase of the scene) which comes to pass with no transition enacted: the mere redefinition of trek as cortege. The unmarked juncture of style becomes the very locus of death. In this unusually concentrated instance from *Hard Times*, setting the vector of star-led transcendence aside, dying may be traversal, grief a going on, but death is all interval—preemptive, empty. Again and again in Dickens, death plays both sides against the excluded middle.

In the manner of her own revisionary Romanticism, Emily Dickinson, working virtually unknown in America at the height of Dickens's powers and renown, is the only comparable master of the compressed and polysemous death sentence—or its elision. In her most famous deathbed poem, "I heard a Fly buzz—when I died—," Dickinson's persona, after the signing of a last will, enters upon the interval of annihilation across an enjambment: ". . . and then it was / There interposed a Fly—." The grammatical format contracted here is "then it was *that*," the onset of mortality obliterating the very logic of subordination. At the same time the enjambment is invited to swell this fatal phrase briefly into the continuous thought "then it was / There," an adverbial emphasis on the then and where of death that immediately dissipates in the enveloping grammar of idiomatic inversion. Except for the metrical run-on at just the point of interposition and discontinuity, this is a death sentence whose poetry, of dislocation and elision, is available to prose as well. It is a poetry of that negotiable gap to which Dickinson gives the explicit name of "interval" in another of her lyrics. Exemplifying such syllabic and prosodic transpositions in a defiant warping of her own syntactic period, in a poem whose opening subject is "This Consciousness . . . aware of Death," she writes of

> the interval
> Experience between
> And most profound experiment
> Appointed unto Men–

The contrasting nouns of elapsed life and approached death, played off each other in partial echo ("experi——"), are wedged apart in a grammatical extremity that does violence to the logic of all articulation, and this across the enjambed intervention of death's ultimate "between."[3]

There is also something much like Dickinson's appointed "interval" suggested by a later and even more revisionary romantic, Wallace Stevens, in his poem on the death of George Santayana. There, on the "threshold of heaven," syllabic tampering evokes eternity from the alliterative intonations of this world, one gerund gentled over the line ending into its endless resonance: "The newsboys' muttering / Becomes another murmuring."[4] The hawking of dailiness is smoothed into near rhyme with the more completely iterative onomatopoeia of eternity. It is that transposition across an interval, made immediately visible in verse delineation, which operates also at the syntactic and metaphoric level in the prose of Dickens's death scenes, even when it is based on a teleology of closure rather than transcendence. Another way to put this is to say that the prose of death in narrative must arrange its own run-ons across grammatical intervals, must experiment with the prosody of syntax itself. In prose as in poetry, whole lifelines can be enjambed. And no fictional prose before that of Lawrence or Woolf has a comparable way with the play of expanding and contracting intervals—with the bridgings of alliteration, the manipulation of ellipsis and elision, the pacing and grading of syntax, the elusive folds of simile, the increments of parallelism—than does the prose of Dickens. Yet whether enjambed or elided, bridged or smudged, the interval of death looms eloquent in its delineation of absence, as much in Dickens as in writers far more nihilistic. Death may or may not erase human presence, but death's own essence remains ineradicable. The interruptions of prose offer not euphemism but proof of this, the invincibility of death getting coded by its very invisibility in so many passages. It cannot be got at or gone round, only given over to as void, absence reified as textual gap.

□   □   □

With Stephen Blackpool's unsaid death as unusually rigorous paradigm let us begin the chronological survey of this section with the first extended mortal set piece in Dickens, which happens to be the extravagant drowning of the villain, Quilp, in *The Old Curiosity Shop* (1840–1841). According to formula, Quilp goes down only to resurface before the final loss of consciousness. If there is any internalized rehearsal of his life, as superstition also has it, it is never brought to light by the prose—except by an elaborate symbolic displacement, quite outside of Quilp's consciousness, whereby the epitomizing manner of his death caps his sadistic misanthropy in life. A sustained and subdivided structure of grammatical parallelism organizes the cognitive impact of this fatality upon the mind of Quilp, without a trace of moral recognition. At the same time the inexorability of the structure's own formal momentum suggests the inevitability of this death as a spiritual consequence of the very life struggling bodily against it. The syntax is girded across two paragraphs by verbs of enabled sensation: "he could hear . . . could hear . . . could recognize . . . could understand that they . . . that they . . . that they . . . that he himself . . . could touch." (ch. 67). After stumbling into the river in flight from pursuers, Quilp hears their knocking at a gate which he himself has barred (a symbol of his self-willed exclusion from humanity), hears and recognizes a voice among them that might help, understands that they are close enough either to save him or to look on as he drowns, and further recognizes that he is the agent of their shutting out.

Quilp now answers with a yell, is swept on and down by the tide, rises to scream again when he is near enough to touch a passing boat, but is finally engulfed for the last time by the churning waters. "One loud cry now—but the resistless water bore him down before he could give it utterance, and, driving him under it, carried away a corpse." The parallelisms of internal consciousness, orderly and subordinated even in the turmoil of his terror, now give way to the conjunctive and progressive grammar of his inertia as mere body. Prose devolves from the "but" of frustrated disjunction to the "and" of fatal continuity in the flux of inanimate otherness. What is especially arresting about this passage is the ambiguity that slams up against that pivotal caesura. Dickens does not write, "A loud cry now would save him— but . . ." Rather, ambivalent phrasing makes available to interpretation the thought that the loud cry is indeed cried somewhere deep within the dying mind, actually willed, predicated, but cannot reach up to articulate scream. The ellipsis thus pries open the kind of interval we are investigating, here again (as with Betty Higden's barely managed last gasps in *Our Mutual Friend*) between inner speech and its utterance. In his gap, unbridgeable across the border of Quilp's now impotent because voiceless assertion of presence, the personal pronoun is then swallowed up in the doubly impersonal collocation of article and noun in "a corpse." It is just this frustrated rage for language in the approach to death, literalized by drowning in Quilp's case, that later shapes the metaphoric drowning of Eugene Wrayburn in *Our Mutual Friend*, where the "yearning to . . . make a communication" only hastens the sinking of his energy: "As the man rising from the deep would disappear the sooner for fighting with the water, so he in his desperate struggle went down again" (IV, ch. 10).

The frenetically animated Quilp, verbally energized and effusive, who has treated other people almost as the insentient objects of his vituperation, bitter wit, and actual physical assault, who at one point sets up a recovered ship's figurehead as a fetishlike surrogate for his nemesis, Kit, and sadistically hacks at and bludgeons it, is then, once become "a corpse," soon washed ashore as the beached figurehead of his own living person. The moment is marked by a transitional neutering from man to thing that secures the irony of his retribution. The paragraph following "carried away a corpse" describes the water as it "toyed and sported with its ghastly freight, now bruising it against the slimy piles, now hiding it in mud or long lank grass" (ch. 67) and so on through five more iterations of that neuter pronoun which Quilp's "him" has become. This transposition from "him" to "it" is one of the most frequent stylistic devices in the Dickensian death scene. This pronominal lapse to spiritual evisceration is in two senses a declension even within third person, whereby the very idea of person is shifted away from identity to misnomer at the instant of death, he or she declined to it. The most conspicuous example appears in Dickens's last completed novel. Says a police inspector in *Our Mutual Friend* (1864–1865) over the drowned corpse of Gaffer Hexam, " 'I'll find the nearest of our men to come and take charge of him;—I still call it *him*, you see,' said Mr. Inspector, looking back as he went, with a philosophical smile upon the force of habit" (I, ch. 14). This effect represents, in fact, a crucial emendation at the proof stage, for Dickens's manuscript reads, without the pronominal contrast to which he was elsewhere so committed, "I still call him *him*.[5]

Neutered not only from him to it, man to thing, Quilp has degenerated further to the "ugly plaything" of the elements, fit punitive
return for the misanthrope who mocked everyone and everything
around him when alive. At the same time this posthumous tableau
becomes a grotesque charade of continued existence on the corpse's
part, captured in a periodic sentence that in its own central, suspended interval reverts to the living *idée fixe* even in the act of
inscribing its emptied simulation by external circumstance: "The hair,
stirred by the damp breeze, played in a kind of mockery of death—
such a mockery as the dead man himself would have revelled in when
alive—about its head, and its dress fluttered idly in the night wind"
(ch. 67). After that inserted "such a" clause added in the manuscript
margin as a clarifying epitome[6]—its analogue to living consciousness
interrupting the terminal grammar—there is the abrupt neutering
return to the double "its," an idling of the villain's animate will once
and for all into a fortuitous counterfeit of life.

The relevant fatal intervals of the prose here, first within and then
across a phrase, conceptually ambiguous, then syntactic and successive—the uncertain predication of "One loud cry now" followed
by the grammatical slippage from "him under it" to "a corpse"—
combine to satirize the stifled fellow feeling and general inhumanity
of the corpse while alive. But the rhetoric of evasive intervals can
also be used in nonironic contexts, as shortly afterwards in this same
novel, to smooth religious doubt into spiritual celebration. In the
unscrambled chronology of the contrapuntal narrative at this climactic
point in *The Old Curiosity Shop*, the angelic heroine's death is virtually
simultaneous with that of her demonic counterpart.[7] Nell is found
dead by an entourage from the city, and in indirect discourse we hear
about what are nearly her last words with a dead metaphor of ab-
sconded godhead: those delirious wanderings about "beautiful music
which she said was in the air. God knows. It may have been" (ch.
72). That isolated pivotal sentence of two words bridges gingerly, in
its own play between baffled idiom and high surety, the transposition
between secular argot and the vocabulary of faith—with an expletive
like "God only knows" hovering uncertainly before its other understanding as the heavenly locus of confirmation. Prose opens an interval
its worldly referents have no way to negotiate, only to glimpse. Being
explicit and discursive where at Stephen's death in *Hard Times* a

similar elided dying is managed by the syncopated rhythm of style itself, Dickens writes, "They did not know that she was dead, at first."

In contrast to the neutering humiliation of a corpse in the drowning of Quilp, the language of death is largely deflected in Nell's case: "For the rest, she had never murmured or complained; but, with a quiet mind . . . faded like the light upon a summer's evening" (ch. 72). Opposite to the sullen glare of the actual evening sky reflected on Quilp's dead face, pure metaphor (not "died" plus the simile "like the light") muffles Nell's going in the figure of mere subsidence which follows that transitional phrase couched in the idiom of afterthought turned to peace: "For the rest." It is the shadow of a pun at least as old as the author Dickens knew best: "The rest is silence." When Nell is said figuratively to have faded like the sunset, we are to imagine the complementary arc of the sun's course that keeps the metaphoric vehicle in motion across death's horizon. To review those categories outlined in the first chapter, no transposition by simile from cycles of this life to the implicit hemisphere of another dawning could at the same time more succinctly epitomize the frail clouded life it ushers out; nor could the displacement of this absence upon a secondary character be more direct than with the malaise and death, within days, of the old man Trent. Her grandfather's whole reason for living dies with this vessel of innocence by whose ailing presence he could alone justify his own gambling and debasement, yet in another sense whose certain lingering doom finds ironic analogy in his own hopeless defiance of chance.

After Nell, the most famous death of a young child in Dickens is that of Paul Dombey the younger in *Dombey and Son* (1846–1848). It is a scene framed not in terms of that summarizing retrospect familiar from scenes of symbolic drowning but phrased rather as the peaceful drifting away on a deathless tide. Waiting for his old nurse to come and wean him from life, Paul anxiously asks, in a paradoxical transcendence of diurnal intervals, "Is it tomorrow? Is she come?" (ch. 16). The chapter is called "What the Waves Were Always Saying," drawing not only on Paul's lifelong curiosity about their distant murmur but on his own metaphor for the river that runs through and past his brief life toward eternity. What narrative style is here enabled to verbalize, as with the airy music in either Nell's hearing or her mind, complements a dramatized audition that goes in one ear of the prose and out the other without being worded into certainty—or, in Paul's case, even into specific articulation. All he knows is that life's river is "very near the sea. I hear the waves! They always said so!" In this scene of oceanic summons rather than drowning, the interval of revelation (what after all *do* they say?) is elided out entirely, referred away to the unavailable in the consoling monotone of mere recurrence. Retrospective, compact of all previous iterations of this lulling signifier without a signified—in the waves' murmuring utterance of time itself in motion—the transposition from life to death is thus inevitably elliptical. And this in itself provides a fit epitome for Paul's otherworldly imagination, whose fantasies could never be humanized into a normal vocabulary. Again we get no specified death moment. There is Paul's allusion to Christ's aureole in a print at school, whose "light" is "shining on me as I go," followed by a less than luminous white blank in the text and then the notorious oratorical paragraph about death as the "old, old fashion." It is here that the teleology of the universe looks forward to its own virtual textualization with the advent of apocalypse, "the wide firmament . . . rolled up like a scroll."

Death is again defined by the interface between private radiance and narrative peroration at the death in *Bleak House* (1852–1853) of Jo the crossing sweeper, who, unlike Paul, dies in the middle of a last spoken clause. When Jo, in his own idiomatic confusion, epitomizes the laborious burden of his life by imagining his breath "drawing" at the end "as heavy as a cart," Dickens interjects an allusion to the proverbial death rattle, "He might add, 'and rattles like it' " (ch. 47). Jo is asked by Woodcourt to summon his failing breath for a repetition of the "Our Father." Set in counterpoint to this prayer, itself set in caps at the proof stage to emphasize the disparity between sacred text and the boy's incomprehending recitation,[8] are Jo's feeble, lower-case responses. When Woodcourt's rendering of the Lord's Prayer arrives at "HALLOWED BE THY NAME," Dickens originally had Jo answer the line in full and then fade away as if by enjambment into the gaping margin. The denominated "name" in Jo's response, however, was crossed out at the proof stage, so that at the moment of death all reference, not least the name of eternity, falls not only from enunciation but even from allusion. (Not to mention that it is exactly the name of the father which this orphan has never known.)

As if the truncated blank space where the noun of the name should come is an interval flooded with revelation, omniscience intercedes for Jo with "The light is come upon the dark benighted way." The violence of death's severance seems suppressed by the onset of revelation. Yet the detached participial grammar of finality intrudes just after the death sentence with the exclamatory fragment, "Dead!" (The structure here might be taken as a grammatical decontraction of such a clause as "The light is finally come upon him, dead," anticipating Conrad's stripped syntax for the death of Lord Jim, "fell forward, dead.") The abrupt past participle next precipitates out, in turn, an entire paragraph of harangue in which the lamentory word "dead" seems to bleed into an accusation against the unheeding observers of Jo's degradation. Heard as spoken apostrophe, without clarifying punctuation, the culminating antithetical syntax of "Dead, men and women, born with heavenly compassion in your hearts. And dying thus around us every day" tends to snare the auditors in its grammatical bracketing of the moribund. The light come is thus instantaneously shed on the moral darkness of an accusatory death scene by social proxy.

It is again the imagery of light that organizes the end of Mrs. Gradgrind in *Hard Times* (1854), a deathbed passage balanced generously between satire and sympathetic salute—and balanced there across the swift elision (rather than mere ellipsis, as in the waves' confirmed saying in *Dombey and Son*) of a syntactic interval almost ineffable in its effect. The scene appears under a title which, like so many in Dickens, has in itself an ambiguous referential function partly dictated by the laws of suspense. (To let us guess a death from the table of contents gives the narrator's game away before the character's.) "Hearing the Last of It" (II, ch. 9) transposes to finality the woman's hyperbole for her husband's badgering whenever she tried to express herself ("I have never heard the last of it") while commenting on our own hearing of her story as it closes down in death, with a hinted decline there of her to "it" as well.

Everything else in the death scene of Mrs. Gradgrind follows from this hinging of the title as it swings over from perpetual grievance to negation, from living refrain to fatal circumlocution. She is early said to resemble "an indifferently executed transparency of a small female figure, without enough light behind it" (I, ch. 4). Not self so much as faint simulacrum, at one point she "departed this life for the time being" after delivering a "codicil" to "remarks already executed" (I, ch. 16). Actual death merely transposes this manner of speaking about Mrs. Gradgrind's exits into virtual nescience, shifts it from metaphor to literal truth, even as we see her trying to inscribe one final codicil to her last will and testament. Wanting to write to her husband about some missing ingredient in the Gradgrind system, she thinks mistakenly that she has been given a pen. "It matters little what figures of wonderful no-meaning she began to trace upon her wrappers. The hand soon stopped in the midst of them; the light that had always been feeble and dim behind the weak transparency, went out." The imagined pen is the very implement of imagination, the addled Mrs. Gradgrind joining Dickens as a scriptural fantasist of benign signs. In the act of struggling to pose some antidote to the mental constraint of her husband's "Never Wonder" ethic, her success is implicit in the cryptic jottings which enact, even though they cannot articulate, the alternative of which she dreams. They are not said to be pointless, only of "no-meaning," the opposite of discursive fact. Scribbling them in mid-air, Mrs. Gradgrind stops not in the middle of this act of desultory and delusory writing, as Dickens's wording could easily have suggested, but in the palpable "midst" of these figures—as credibly posited by his own imaginative diction. Her identity is gladly yielded up within a density of newly felt intent where her hand and her life have come to rest. Tennyson hits upon a comparable image of mortal self-containment for one of his earliest efforts in the vein of Romantic allegory. "Singing in her song she died," he writes in *The Lady of Shalott* (without a comma setting off the participle), so that the prepositional phrase "in her song" becomes an adverbial modifier not so much of suspended duration as of introverted creative space.

For Mrs. Gradgrind, too, lost in her own figural emanations, the light that repeatedly "died away" in the presence of inimical otherness fails forever as the dead metaphor becomes literal, thus epitomizing the waning life it ends. There remains one clause to this death sentence, one turn of wording well past the woman's last words, which follows from the imagery of faded light across the softening caesura of the semicolon: the light "went out; and even Mrs. Gradgrind, emerged from the shadow in which man walketh and disquieteth himself in vain, took upon her the dread solemnity of the sages and patriarchs." With prose's own transition solemnized by the shift into biblical diction, a dying life transposed toward the sanctity of the greatest of texts, the pivotal "and" institutes a continuity where there is only expected rupture. What ensues is an elusive subordination whose all but subliminal syntactic shift creates one final transposition in the passage, this time from grammatical action to spiritual passivity. Dickens changed the following compound clause in proof,[9] reducing it to a single complex (and syntactically unorthodox) one: "and *then* Mrs. Gradgrind, emerged from the shadow in which man walketh and disquieteth himself in vain, *and* took upon her the dead solemnity of the sages and patriarchs" (my emphasis on the words changed, the first to "even," the second deleted altogether). Since even in the revised version we cannot at first understand "emerged" as anything but an intransitive form, we think we are engaged upon the main action of the clause, the shadowy Mrs. Gradgrind's emergence from the Valley of the Shadow in a still finite verb phrase, only to realize that the sentence must in fact parse as turning about a faintly false passive with unstated agent—"having (been) emerged"— dependent upon the subsequent main verb phrase, "took upon." This strained passive aura is evocatively in phase with Mrs. Gradgrind's diminished force of character yet again (and quintessentially) in death. Somewhere, unsaid, between "went out"and the grammatical disembodiment of "emerged" lies the evasive interval of that death.

In *Little Dorrit* (1855–1857) Dickens gives us in metaphysical terms a phrase that neatly covers the syntactical elisions and metaphoric leaps of his death sentences, calling the interval between life and death an "untraversable distance" (II, ch. 19). It may be determined, that is, by bordering coordinates, but its transit resists mapping. As suggested earlier, it is a crossing over and, by avoidance, a crossing out, taking definition from the void it (in a double sense) bounds. The notion of a mortuary stasis as plastic image, in the backlit transparency at Mrs. Gradgrind's death, also returns in the form of sculptural allusions in *Little Dorrit*. They are deployed climactically to portray, after the fact, the off-stage fatality of the Dorrit brothers, who are figuratively "translated" to heaven (in both senses: linguistic and theological) without the intervention of a dramatized traverse, their bodies remaining behind as figural remnants in the sculptural sense. As much as for Esther Summerson in *Bleak House*, such death scenes of related characters may symbolically inscribe an ordeal of survival, even rebirth, for the heroine, Amy Dorrit, especially the coterminous removal of the blocking figures of father and uncle. Esther is herself an intermittent narrator in *Bleak House*, overcoming through empathy and projection those deaths she herself must transcribe, searching them more or less consciously for the revealing displacements—for her or for others—they may entail. Though Little Dorrit is not the general narrator or the novel named for her, nor in particular of the death scene of her father and uncle, it is this compounded, epitomizing, and then displaced fatality that releases her as well to a narrated act of transcription symbolic of new life: the closural enrolling of her own name in the book of marriage.

We feel the internal logic of the brothers' double death scene in large part through its preparation by those numerous allusions to the lifelessness of pictorial or plastic arts. They give the scene's funerary metaphors a context in the novel's whole satire of artifice and stiffening pretense. The nearest such glance at nonliterary art, with the most directly relevant leverage on the death shortly following, has William, Amy's indifferent father, returning to Rome to find her in a warm domestic "scene" (Dickens's pictorial term for it) with her beloved uncle. In a rare instant of understanding, William senses his own filial bond with Frederick, which he usually patronizes into nonexistence. "Allowing for the great difference in the still-life of the picture, the figures were much the same as of old: his brother being sufficiently like himself to represent himself, for a moment, in the composition" (II, ch. 19). Reflexive grammar repeats itself there, ambiguously, as if the distance of brother from brother is equivalent to that of self from self in this divisive world. Any congruence must be an act of sympathetic imagination, in William's case too long belated—indeed all but posthumous, as the rest of the chapter goes to show.

This "composition" is a "still-life" that anticipates the twinned displacement from life into death of both brothers together later in the chapter. There we ourselves look on at stilled "figures" rather than mortal forms creating a stately sarcophagus, the whole scene a *tableau mourant* which Dickens carefully modified in manuscript.[10] It is a scene that Dickens's illustrator captured perfectly in the accompanying plate by showing the dead brothers flanked by such representatives of the plastic arts as a portrait, an ornately bordered, desolate landscape, and a piece of sculpture. "Two figures were within the room; two figures, equally still and impassive, equally removed by an untraversable distance from the teeming earth and all that it contains, though soon to lie in it" (II, ch. 19). Catching the metaphysical paradox of presence and removal, of an existence that is also an irreversible distance from living, is just this surrender of breath to virtual plastic figuration: "One figure reposed upon the bed. The other . . . drooped over it . . . so that the lips touched the hand over which with its last breath it had bent. The two brothers were before their Father; far beyond the twilight judgment of this world; high above its mists and obscurities." Dickens's characteristic agnosticism, even when his prose tries rising above it, still lets his text sight no more than the far edge of fatality. The "distance" of death, even when testified to, cannot be "traversed" by language, and the very moment of death's "interval" is once more shunted entirely offstage.

As so often in fiction, however, death identifies, affixes the self in its role. In the ironic context of *Little Dorrit*, death alone reanimates the familial, returns us to a proper idea of the "Father" in this novel about its selfish perversions and reverse dependencies. The capitalizing mechanics of Christian metaphor may clank a bit in Dickens's portentous engineering, but the symbolic superstructure of the death scene is earned and sturdy. Frederick's now admittedly fatal relation to his unfeeling brother is that of a well-intentioned parasitic twin, living only for the other's life in an abnegatory suspension of all private motive. But Frederick's automatic, self-willed death is not only the final masochistic emblem of a defective, however generous, integrity of being. It is also, resurrection notwithstanding, the symbolic return to a fathering unity before that fall into primal division between otherness and identity, selflessness and egocentricity, which has infected at the center of plot the heroine's stunting deference to her father. What is for Fredrick a necessary end at the death of William is in the next generation Amy's only chance for initiated maturity as a future self. Hers is a belated release from that emotionally incestuous parental deadlock into autonomy and sexual possibility—a belated birthing out of death.

This is a recouped option for the passionate self which so often in Dickens, and long before the Lawrencian ethic of identity as "utterance," invites written declaration. Esther in *Bleak House* tells tentatively her own story until she can mature into a serious claim on it, rescued from the precincts of nonentity through her narrative encounters with death. Such is the case indirectly with Amy Dorrit, later with Pip and, in a complicated and implicit sense, with Sydney Carton—and also, of course, inaugurating this sequence of late heroes and heroines, with the autobiographical agent of *David Copperfield*, transcriber of his own life in order to make it his. In *Little Dorrit* the antithetical author figure, counterpart to the hero and heroine at the end, is the disappointed John Chivery, perpetually composing epitaphs for himself as a doomed young man cut off in his prime by unrequited passion. Amy's life having been lived until now as an epitaph of a human potential curtailed and defeated by circumstance, she can at last begin to live it anew as a self-styled autobiography of desire. Together with Arthur, she takes pen in hand to engrave her new hope for conjugal vitality in that public marriage book whose pages lie open at the novel's close, the new volume of the lovers' union and continuance. Amy had much earlier been offered a burial register as a pillow when she was forced to sleep overnight at the church near the Marshalsea. Fifty-five chapters after her ominous, potentially nightmarish repose on this "book of fate" (I, ch. 14), two paragraphs before the end of the novel, she takes up a pen to inscribe in another such register a new version of her private history.

Says her old friend at the church, "Her birth is what I call the first volume, she lay asleep, on this very floor, with her pretty head on what I call the second volume, and she's now a-writing her little name as a bride in what I call the third volume" (II, ch. 34). As the first "little" noun of this name (diminutive in length as is her living stature: typical Dickensian coincidence of signifier and signified) the three letters *A-M-Y* provide the open-ended marital closure that counters separation and death with convergence and renewed direction. They finish off Dickens's two-volume novel by having its heroine coauthor with its hero the third restorative installment. The mutual *A*'s of their names begin a new alphabet of affection and a new prose of hope. Those pictorial metaphors throughout *Little Dorrit* that reduce life to trace, entablature, graphic epitaph, sculptural simulacrum, along with the morbid verbal imagination of John Chivery that does the same for the texts rather than tableaux of existence—all are now reclaimed and reanimated by the identifying and inscribed Word. There is a perfect symmetry here with the novel's opening chapter, where Dickens discretely alludes in passing to the death scenes of the world's heartless governors, "the said great personages dying in bed, making exemplary ends and sounding speeches; and polite history, more servile than their instruments, embalming them!" There are no speeches sounded at the closural marriage ceremony, just a quiet dedication enrolled, each to each in the name of the other. The irony about prose as a mortician's art is thus answered at the close by the generic resurrection of the novel out of "polite history." What *Litte Dorrit* cedes to at its closure, we are to think, is Little Dorrit, girl grown woman and wife. Heroine has broken from title to write her name afresh, inscribing as a character the first characters of a "life" spread before her. The book that Dickens's book closes by entitling would thus become a new testament of vitality begun as the true baptismal register in a metropolis of the embalmed great and the nameless dead.

□   □   □

Little Dorrit ends where *David Copperfield* (1849–1850) had ended, with a marital union testified to in a first-person singular inscription, in that case David's hymn to Agnes. But that earlier novel had been just such an act of inscription from first to last, an autobiography written by its title character and narrator. More than in *Little Dorrit*, the work *David Copperfield* takes the shape of the life it names— style, as it were, the man. Having surveyed the variety of stylistic devices by which the interval of death is commonly traversed in a Dickens text, and before concluding with figurative death by flood and its narratological implications in *A Tale of Two Cities*, we must explore the earlier autobiographical use of drowning in its own curious links to the retrospective aspect of textuality itself. Given the received (if never more than conjectural) opinion on the actual phenomenon of drowning—its rumored flood of review in the vanishing space before effacement—such a scene, in fiction, is primed to figure symbolically or actually precipitate from within an epitomizing reprise of character and event. The prevalence of both narrated and analogized drowning

in *David Copperfield*, and its superstitious connection there with a
hero congenitally immune to such dying as a private fatality because
of an accident of his birth, his "caul," sends us not only to the book's
actual scenes of drowning, with their symbolic externalization of
inward review in last words or in the retrieved posture of a corpse,
but also to the whole story's sense of itself as explicitly written epitaph
for lives flashed past and gone under. At the center of the Dickensian
canon, *David Copperfield* vividly convenes the issues on which this
chapter is focused. As rhetoric, as subjective revelation, as narrative
raison d'être—in its coordinated linguistic, psychological, and narratological aspects, that is—death is clarified in *David Copperfield*
by the symbolic proliferation of the scene of drowning. With Mr.
Peggotty's conflated coinage "drowndead" (p. 3), *David Copperfield*
is indeed the only novel I know before *Malone Dies* that has invented
a new word for death, the portmanteau past participles compact of
cause and effect across their own invisible interval. The novel has,
beyond this, far more than a word to add to the idea of death as a
test of wording.

Apart from its incidental denomination, any central definition of
death in this fictive autobiography must fashion itself in contrast to
the pun on ontology and narrative on the opening page: "To begin
my life with the beginning of my life I record that I was born."
Interchangeably biological and biographical, the oscillating sense of
"life" vibrates throughout the novel, giving a special resonance to
any number of otherwise neutral metaphors. Hinged around the textual consciousness versus the existential, turning the narrator's whole
"life story" into a kind of discourse, such ambiguities manage to
riddle the text in two ways, both pervade it and interrogate its status
as a narrative document, so that periods in David's dim infancy are
not just obscurities but "blanks" in the collected leaves of time;
actions do not have consequences pure and simple, but "sequels,"
with discernible phases of a life called "chapters," stretches of time
"passages." When David is afraid after his first dissipation of following
in the misbegotten footsteps of the previous London lodger in his
rooms, who died of smoke and drink, he shudders at the thought that
he should "succeed to his dismal story" (ch. 24). And in a later
instance of life and death imaged as the extent and terminus of a
narrative, the death of his child-bride, Dora, evokes from David the

lament that her "tender story was closed forever." He then closes his own "Retrospect" on her death scene with the admission that "for a time, all things are blotted out of my remembrance" (ch. 53). It is a displaced extinction whose scriptive metaphor resembles Hopkins's "mark on mind" from this chapter's epigraph, the trace that "death blots black out."

With a metaphor like "tender story . . . closed forever," narrative becomes the very vessel of death as an understood event. Of the some dozen mentioned and lamented deaths that precede and impinge upon the plot of *David Copperfield* (first, in order of appearance, that of David's own father and namesake),[11] and of the six characters who die within the circuit of plot, whether on-stage or just off (including Mrs. Copperfield, Barkis, Mr. Spenlow, Dora, Ham, and Steerforth), it is the first of these narrated fatalities, David's mother's, that sets the pattern for the rest. It does so in part by being reported, unlike the other major deaths, by an intermediate narrator, and so by placing David where Pip will later find himself—not only orphaned but forced to recover images of his origin from the record left behind, in Pip's case on a tombstone, in David's case in one of the oral stories of greatest weight in all of Dickens. David is summoned home from school with the news that his mother has died, the death of his newborn brother following a day late, ironically coinciding with the "anniversary of my birthday." His grief at first makes him feel "distinguished" among the other boys, and throws him back on an acute self-consciousness. "I stood upon a chair when I was left alone, and looked into the glass to see how red my eyes were, and how sorrowful my face" (ch. 9). It is only later that the full emblematic mirroring occasioned by this grief—its deflection upon the lives it bereaves as a reflected death by proxy for the still-living son—is made clear by Peggotty's "narrative" of the actual dying, set in place where, in Q. D. Leavis's words, "Dickens forbore to give us an actual death-bed scene, witnessed by David."[12] This indirect telling spells out as well something crucial about both the symbolic and the therapeutic aptitudes of the novel as a whole in the handling of death.

David has ample time to assimilate the fact of death before its story, and so the scene of Peggotty's report is cleared for interpretation as well as for painful reception. Even though couched in the nurse's only rudimentary instinct for metaphoric language as a humanizing of the all but unsayable, still her story becomes a compound illustration, before its self-conscious displacement, of the other two main features of dying rhetoric in Dickens, the two ratios of death to life out of which language can generate meaning. In the first place, death must draw its terms from the vocabulary of life, here by means of a direct simile: "She died like a child that had gone to sleep" (ch. 9). By the logic of its analogy, this is also the special case not just of figurative transposition but of symbolic epitome. This childlike woman, innocent and withered before the Murdstone rigor, by going as if simply to sleep merely symbolizes her trusting and submissive lassitude in life. Yet though the scene feels, in typifying a life, typically Dickensian, we register the suggestiveness of its secondary rendering by a naive narrator in part through the rare appearance of the explicit verb "died." Unlike the figuring of Nell's death by the metaphoric verb "faded," here death is at first directly predicated and then interpreted by simile.[13]

Following the last mortal image of childlike "sleep" by which Peggotty tries to search out the emotional truth of death and muffle the blow for David, we hear from him, "Thus ended Peggotty's narration" (ch. 9). And then immediately, referring to the time of the first announcement of his mother's death back at school, "From the moment of my knowing of the death of my mother, the idea of her as she had been of late had vanished fom me." Peggotty's oral story "was so far from bringing me back to the later period, that it rooted the earlier image in my mind." It is a rooting that is also a double interment. Peggotty's story not only transfers life's terms into death but induces a displacement of those terms upon the present consciousness of the son, who, thanks to her story, oversees the death in his mind and, in so doing, undergoes it as a private rite of passage for his own identity. Here is yet another Dickensian effect secured at the proof stage: "The mother who lay in the grave, was the mother of my infancy; the little creature in her arms, was myself, as I had once been, hushed for ever on her bosom."[14] It is a memorable birthday indeed that memorializes its own fled bliss in the death of a brother as a surrogate self.

A death scene told rather than attended, or told so as to induce participation, opens itself to a peculiar scrutiny, to options of interpretation and so of conveyable power. David's parable of auditing and then transcribing for us the fateful story, as if she were his mentor in narrative, shows the hero apprenticing himself through her nurturing example to mature and purposeful storytelling. It leads directly to the report in his own voice on the death scene of Peggotty's husband, Barkis, and after that to those more melodramatic fatalities in the Yarmouth storm. The novel's first on-stage death overheard in review, the others worked through in the hero's unmediated voice, the first his own lost innocence displaced in the corpse of a younger brother and former self, the last, of Steerforth, serving much the same purpose, though not in David's own troubled words—these deaths in sequence not only allegorize the hero's transitions as mortal crises but also illustrate his verbal development as narrator of this very history as a retrospective "life."

Though it precedes the two major scenes of drowning in the novel, the death of the bedridden Barkis is, suggestively enough, imaged in terms of a watery end, a washing out with the tide. Other metaphors preparatory to the actual death scene begin to offer reasons for this in line with the logic of epitome. For all our sympathy with the gruff and scruffy coachman, his close-fisted miserliness as he nears death places him by verbal irony in the Vanitas tradition as a typical negative exemplum. Barkis claims early on that "nothing's truer than" taxes (ch. 30). What he has forgotten in this penurious skewing of the truism, the plot (as well as its rhetoric) will before long recall. As Barkis moves into his debilitating decline, his wife Peggotty explains to David that he is "a little nearer" yet, where the compound sense conveys his being both closer to the end and tighter with his funds. Just as death itself is about to levy life's final tax the callous wit Steerforth appears on the scene to enter a satirized because unfelt instance of epitomizing rhetoric for this old coachman on the Blunderstone line. When Steerforth says, in an occupational metaphor raised to metaphysical conceit for life's long pilgrimage, that "the carrier was making his last journey rather fast," the phrase stands as a facile co-option of Dickensian gesture.

David must assert himself as narrator at this point, developing metaphors feelingly from within. What follows is so compact an instance of death as life's rehearsal and quintessence that it has already been examined for its paradigmatic contours in the first chapter: a life summed up in the multiple import of the dying words, "Barkis is willin'.'" The tag line by which Dickens ordinarily tickets his characters for easy identification is here taken inward from narrative tactic to private psychology, as if a lifetime of receptive passivity is something Barkis has learned, on his deathbed, about his own identity. Another figure of speech by which the whole scene is framed associates this modest revelation with the mythology of drowning as a review of life. Mr. Peggotty has explained to David that people living along the coast tend to hold off their deaths until the tide turns, and David borrows this metaphor—from the colloquial poet of death who also coined the term "drowndead"—in his own rhetorical substitution of pure natural metaphor for the diction of mortality. No sooner has Barkis seemingly looked back upon and summed up his life, with a phrase that also negotiates the interval between worldly and otherworldly objects of his willingness, than the narrator submerges the expected but unsaid verb *died* within a swift figurative withdrawal, for an epitaphic last paragraph all its own: "And, it being low water, he went out with the tide" (ch. 30). Opening with a conjunction to rebuke the very idea of abrupt closure, Dickens's phrasing insists on continuity even as the apparent combinative logic of sequence gives way to metaphoric equivalence. Swelled and held in the gathering progressive grammar of the suspended absolute phrase, this death sentence then levels off in anapestic monosyllables for the smooth subsidence and removal of its own fluid rhetoric, crested, ebbed, empathetic—altogether a deep narrative participation in the rhythms of transition without arrest.

If Peggotty has in a sense helped teach David how to handle a death scene in narration, whose mastery is a central Dickensian touchstone of the storyteller's capacity to word the movements of the world, then the idea of apprenticeship is only enlarged upon by what follows. At this chronological point in the plot David does not know he is to become a writer; he thinks instead of the law as his eventual profession. The first trial of his legal skills, his indoctrination into the practical rather than creative terminology and rhetoric of the law, is the "proving" of Barkis's will for Peggotty. It is a display of expertise comparable to that which retrospectively, as novelist, has just proved his own powers—as well as Barkis's integrity as a character—by that terminal play on "will" and "willingness."

Two domestic deathbed scenes—one narrated second hand by

Peggotty and interpreted by David into displaced relevance for himself, one then narrated directly, complete with last words, by the very
self who has outlived the symbolic death of his own alter ego in the
first scene—are followed now by the description of two found corpses,
both "drowndead." Though the moment of extinction is not registered
by prose, still the myth of drowning as retrospect seems to dictate
the rehearsal of lost lives in an objectified tableau rather than an
internal review. Ham's corpse is found washed ashore in the state of
suspended heartbeat which sums up the destitution of his life since
his desertion by Little Emily. All we hear, with an unsettling dissociation of the verb *beat* from the "heart" of life, is that "he had
been beaten to death by the great wave, and his generous heart was
stilled forever" (ch. 55). David is shortly told of another body washed
ashore. His "do I know it?" seems deliberately to distance and de-
personalize the truth he suspects. In his coming description, the dead
"it" is never reiterated or even specified as an identifed corpse but
instead repersonified as an earlier and idealized image of Steerforth.
The old friend is not dead so much as dormant, trapped somewhere
in the unwakable past amid the symbolic devastation of the Peggotty
hearth. For "among the ruins of the home he had wronged—I saw
him lying with his head upon his arm, as I had often seen him lie at
school." As in the case of the police inspector in *Our Mutual Friend*,
David still calls it "him"—but from more than force of habit.

Quite apart from the "lie" Steerforth's counterfeit of sleep amounts
to in its meliorating transposition from the language of life, we find
here a death pose that not only epitomizes the character's ethical
posture in life—supine, oblivious—but by displacement also replays
the narrator's own earlier vision of a perfect self. For David, his false
friend Steerforth was a myth generated out of the long moral sleep,
that suspension of critical consciousness, into which David was betrayed by his adolescent identification with his idol as the incarnated
dream of invincible vitality and charm. It is a dream laid to rest here
as irreversibly as the earlier vision of an Edenic David upon the
breast of his dead mother.[15] The projective identification induced by
Peggotty's narrative can now be managed by the adult David for
himself in this depiction of a razed ideal. Steerforth's dying has
transferred the ordinary mechanism of retrospect and instantaneous,
fleeting recovery (associated in common thought with death by drown-

ing) from a corpse long dead morally, whose actual death throes are thus elliptically dismissed, to the secret emotional life of his double—and his narrator. Which is a way of saying that Steerforth drowns so that David can review again their time together, look back once and for all on his dream of an invulnerable identity. In speaking implicitly of this dream over the corpse of its incarnation, the narrator fixes his ideal there, as something outside of him and lost in time—a model for the self as completely outmoded as that cradled brother in the deathbed tableau conjured indirectly by Peggotty's words about his mother's death.

That something dies in the hero with the death of Steerforth is made clear by the further displacement of fatality in the identity crisis to follow. David compares his desolation to a "mortal hurt" in the chapter called "Absence," whose title describes not only his expatriation to the Continent but the sudden vacuum at the center of his emotional life. When "this despondency was at its worst," writes David, "I believed that I should die" (ch. 58). Like Clara Copperfield reclined on Clara Peggotty's arm at her death in the latter's narrative, like Steerforth on his own arm in the symbolic solipsism of his languourous and finally fatal contentment, David now assumes roughly the recumbent position associated repeatedly with death in the novel. Only this time, in the neo-Wordsworthian Alps, it becomes the posture of humility and restitution: "All at once, in this serenity, great nature spoke to me; and soothed me to lay down my weary head upon the grass, and weep as I had not wept, since Dora died!" Instead of drowning in the flood of morose self-pity that followed the death of Steerforth—temporary funeral of all life's dreams of self-realization—now David is cleansed by his own renovating tears, baptised anew to purpose. With a wavelike resurgence, "Absence" yields to the next chapter's "Return," the bearings again internal as well as geographical. David's homecoming is the return of as well as to, an emotional retrieval as well as a reversed itinerary. The past, retraced, is ready for transmission first to text and then to print as the novel *David Copperfield*, whose "life" is the inscription of being in the form of meaning.

This has everything to do with the motif of drowning in the novel as symbolic scene of retrospect. Barkis goes out metaphorically with the tide, summing up his terrestrial self; Ham and Steerforth, after a joint death at sea, are washed ashore with the tide to materialize extreme and contrary options for the narrator's identity, saintly and effacing goodness and destructive egotism; the aftermath of this mortuary trauma then induces a review of David's life at one remove, the void of their death opening upon the vacuum of his "Absence." From this hollowing out of desire David at last recovers, one might say, in the very form of recovery, not reverting to a time out of time, as Steerforth's corpse has done in the narrator's reading of its posture, but converting time into fictional chronology, life to "life," by living on long enough to write of it.

In this, as author of memory and its transmutation, David must be compared to the other memorialist in the novel, Mr. Dick, whose name is meant, as everyone sees, to truncate that of the fictional author of *David Copperfield* itself. This version of "Mr. Dickens" is severed between syllables because Mr. Dick's own work is always arrested in midstream. Would-be author of a memorial about we know not what or whom, perhaps an autobiography in its own right, Mr. Dick balks when the idea of King Charles's (his lordly author's?) decapitation repeatedly gets in the way of his creativity, another macabre symbol of truncation and brainless impasse. Comparably, the third author within this authored structure of words is Dr. Strong, whose dictionary by the end of *David Copperfield* gets only as·far as *D*, as if, reflexively, for "dictionary," as well as for "David," "Dickens," "Dick," and perhaps "death" itself. Yet David the memorialist can get farther, can word his life to completion in the work of its telling. He can get beyond death and its recurrent scene because, unlike Mr. Dick with his headless Charles, David can in a sense put his dead back together again, take their "trouble" into his own head by the agency of narration—displacing it upon himself as a sacrificial passage come out the other side into an articulate memorial or record.

This the opening two paragraphs of the novel demonstrate when taken together with the last two of its main chronology, before the future compendium of "A Last Retrospect." When David tells of that life-preserving "caul" born into the world with him by obstetric accident from the protective flesh of his mother, he also mentions another curiosity of his birth that connects with a local superstition less cheering to his excitable child's imagination: the belief of certain "sage women" in the neighborhood that he was "privileged to see ghosts and spirits" because he was born at the very stroke of midnight. Entering the world at a diurnal point of transition, David is somehow thought gifted with peculiar prescience as regards another border state, the no man's land between life and death. Says David ungratefully about this unwanted gift for seeing ghosts, "I will only remark, that unless I ran through that part of my inheritance while I was still a baby, I have not come into it yet." The legacy transmitted across death's limit from one generation to the next is precisely the gift for erasing that limit, for permitting the dead entrance into his present world. The point that no naturalistic denial of such talent can evade is that this is indeed his true natal gift, his native power as a novelist. Allegorized here is the privilege of seeing ghosts in the form of those "phantoms" (his own frequent, unguarded word for them) summoned from the past to people his retrospects, including that icon of his former self dead in the imaged security of his young mother's arms. His is a memoirist's access to absent lives that can be drawn upon therapeutically to lay old ghosts, exorcise demons, disinfect and embalm traumas, and of course to preserve love. David's congenital if surgically corrected invulnerability to the very drowning that forms a major motif in the novel thus meets halfway on that first page— balances with and complements—his power to rescue other corpses from the ebb and flow of time, to animate ghosts in the mind's eye of his own transpired but transcribed past. He is thus in an allied and final sense born with a call,[16] a vocation that destines him to traffic in phantoms.

It is against this opening suggestion of watery death and ghostly perpetuation that the last act of the main chronology can finally be silhouetted. There we see David, the internationally famous writer, in the act of copying out a piece of prose of his own device on a slip of paper for Mr. Peggotty. It is his long-ago drafted and later chiseled epitaph for his drowned friend, Ham. "While I was copying the plain inscription for him at his request, I saw him stoop and gather a tuft of grass from the grave, and a little earth." The last paragraph: " 'For Emily,' he said, as he put it in his breast. 'I Promised, Mas'r Davy' " (ch. 63). This is, of course, not the literal dust into which Ham has been returned but rather the earth he once trod as a living man and the natural growth renewed from it even in his absence, a metaphor for love's continuance within the drift of time. Yet, though Mr. Peggotty does not take back to Australia a burial urn full of ashes, dust of Ham's dust, in another sense, in that copied epitaph, he does. The symbolism is extraordinarily intersupportive. Copied epitaph and scooped sod, word and thing, text and transubstantiated body of the man it names and whose life or essence, however briefly, it narrates— together these emblems give us the full measure of David's achievement, not as long-time friend only but as chronicler, reproducing his work for a feeling readership.

But how is it that Dickens resists giving us the actual epitaph in a single poignant turn of David's wrist? Is this a missed chance or a final confirming emblem in its very absence? Surely the most eloquent epitaph for Ham when removed from the story is the story concerning him up to that point, complete with the epitomizing death of his "generous heart" in the attempt to save others from shipwreck. A memento from the grave plot becomes the memorial work of plot itself. In the novel's second chapter, the beginning of the hero's perceptual life called by title "I Observe," the child David, who loves even his book about ferocious crocodiles, is so terrified by the biblical story of Lazarus that he must be sped to the window and shown how the dead really do as a rule remain in their churchyard graves. But later David becomes an author of his own books, and has risen in one of them from his own near grave, from the displaced "mortal wounds" occasioned by the death of those he loved. In the main body of his autobiography he now takes leave of us in the very act of proving—through the agency of his verbal calling—that the dead need not stay in such a grave but can live on in the spectral shape of the unforgotten. They are incarnated in such shape not only by the earth they knew but by the prose that marks that knowing, that former presence, in its own effort to sum up and render transmissible.

Epitaphic artist immune from the first page forward to the drowning replay of his own history, but consigned in his autobiographic "life" to the perpetual resurrection of that history as a parade of phantoms otherwise lost in the backward wash of time: this is David as Mr. Dickens, memorialist for whom drowning is merely one of many symbolic fatalities or extended conceits for securing meaning as a function of finality, death as clarifying retrospect. With the least rhetorically elaborated and subjectively dramatized drownings in any Dickens novel containing such scenes, from Quilp's end in *The Old*

Curiosity Shop through to the joint death of the *Doppelgängers* Headstone and Riderhood in the weir of *Our Mutual Friend, David Copperfield* is nevertheless, or therefore, a crucial text for this motif. As in no other book by Dickens, this autobiographic chronicle makes the process of narration taken whole an enterprise profoundly comparable to the *topos* of drowning as a recovery of the past, as if minimizing the actual drama of the drowning scenes in order to accentuate their place in the larger analogue. The fluidity of prose narrative and its gift for distillation are under scrutiny in *David Copperfield* for the strategies of transposition a death scene of any kind may necessitate, the epitomizing views it permits, the psychological displacements it provides. Dickens's fictional autobiography also explores, as nowhere else so closely, not just the complexly plotted intervals of deathbed rhetoric, calibrated by ambiguity and braced by paradox, but also the psychology of narrating and receiving such scenes. In the person of its hero and the form of autobiographic heroism, it harrows and investigates the final breach (become reach) between experience and record. Dickens's eighth novel, like those before and after it to different degrees, thus shows prose traversing an interval in a manner possible to style only because of style's invulnerability to the very death that so often challenges its agency— challenges it both at and to the point of revelation.

□ □ □

With this sense of drowning in *David Copperfield* as a fatality correlative to the narrative activity of the retrospective text that reports it, we are ready for the gradually developed metaphors of death by water in *A Tale of Two Cities* (1859). These figures gather toward and help gloss the sacrificial death of the hero, dispatched of course by the blade and not by drowning, as that death is redeemed in and by narrative. One of the first full-scale renderings of the Parisian scene under the Reign of Terror comes to us filtered through its horrific revelation to the mind of Jarvis Lorry: "All this was seen in a moment, as the vision of a drowning man, or any human creature at any very great pass, could see a world if it were there" (III, ch. 3). Drowning is Dickens's definitive metaphor for this rite of perceptual passage, with the noun "vision" suspended in the periodic sentence long enough to stand for both effect and cause, vista and empowered eyesight.

Fortified by countless later analogies to the Terror as a bloody Flood come again, this simile foresees the visionary acuity that the hero himself achieves when he drowns symbolically in the tidal heave of revolutionary violence.

To place Sydney Carton's sacrifice within this larger historical context, we need to return to the first retributive scene of death in the novel, characterized by Dickens's usual verbal tension and ingenuity. The assassination of the vicious Marquis St. Evrémonde, portrayed as the initiating act of the revolution, leads at the public and private level directly to the execution of Carton, scapegoat of the Terror. The Marquis is only found dead by narration, not watched die. As in the case of Little Nell, though with an opposite moral implication, the very absence of dramatized transition from life into death is its epitomizing irony. With the Marquis's affectless sly ferocity and his heart of stone, it is only appropriate for prose to discover him unruffled by death, yet already stiffened in its aftermath. The word *death* is never mentioned, but the Gorgon of the ancestral mansion has found "the stone face for which it had waited through about two hundred years" (II, ch. 9). This face "lay back on the pillow of Monsieur the Marquis. It was like a fine mask, suddenly startled, made angry, and petrified." The marquis's face never more than a fine mask, the "it" to which it has degenerated is merely the epitomizing gist of its living nature, rigidified from within, until now, not by fear but by callousness. The final word in that serial syntax replaying the murder thus negotiates by ambiguity another familiar Dickensian interval (here only by retrospect and implication) between vanishing life and finality. The idiomatic reading of "petrified" in which an extremity of feeling would bring on a catalepsy of terror, a normative human reaction in the face of this sudden mortal violence, seems immediately absorbed into and ruled out by the more literal understanding of the term. The moral rigor mortis of the aristocracy is thus prolonged uninterruptedly into death from a life of chilling hauteur. The ultimate stylistic effect achieved by the reiterated severance of the "it"—stony face detached from stabbed torso—is to offer up the marquis, as inaugural victim of the Terror, to that epidemic of decapitation that will be rife in the land with the coming of la Guillotine.

Rage swollen to the breaking point, the floodgates of bloodshed

are now thrown open. This figurative sense of the nightmare to follow
is no dead metaphor in the novel. Murderous impulse is repeatedly
imaged as the impetus of inundation—as in those rivers of blood for
which that broken wine cask in the famous fifth chapter is a prototype.
The carnage grows intoxicating and inexorable. With the return of
the marquis to a stone-cold gargoyle in the dead edifice of his world,
Dickens begins the transformation from historical time into apocalyptic time, the fixating of the former with moribund stasis along with
the release of the latter into a set of images derived from the Flood
in Genesis. This is the ultimate manner, too, in which this first
dramatic death scene in the novel is channeled directly into, and
filtered clean by, the sacificial (and literal) decapitation of the hero,
Carton, where the apocalyptic images of flood that follow from the
marquis's murder are internalized as the private mind's "drowning"
vision. It is a vision compressed and, in the hero's access to narrative
grace, prophetic.

In a novel that drops in passing an apocalyptic hint about the Day
of Judgment when the "ocean is . . . to give up its dead" (II, 2), the
explicit imagery of flood and drowning begins innocuously enough as
a double turn of phrase in that very chapter, "The Wine-Shop," that
gives us in symbol the first overspill of revolutionary desperation.
The underprovided lamps of the Saint Antoine quarter are seen there
to provide merely "dim wicks" that "swung in a sickly manner over-
head, as if they were at sea" (I, ch. 5). The simile is then shifted
over to idiom and to omen: "Indeed they were at sea, and the ship
and crew were in peril of tempest." From that point on the metaphor
rarely lets up. Building toward the outbreak of violence, one chapter
closes in an eightfold paratactic spate of clauses begun with the rush
of literal water and sped quickly to metaphor: "The water of the
fountain ran, the swift river ran, the day ran into evening, so much
life in the city ran into death according to rule, time and tide waited
for no man," and so on as "all things ran their course" (II, ch. 7).
It is not long before the "living sea" of mob violence "rose, wave on
wave, depth on depth," a vast and "resistless . . . ocean" (II, ch.
21). The irreversible momentum of this flood runs straight into the
title of the subsequent chapter, "The Sea Still Rises," and from there
into the third book, where the "current" of death continues to "rend"
and "strew" (III, ch. 6) its victims.

By this third book, however, the figures are undergoing a certain internalization as well, so that Darnay in prison, hearing the distant "swell that rose" against him, also finds "scraps tossing and rolling upward from the depth of his mind" (III, ch. 1). His double, Carton, tending to see his own life as a merely troubled, restless, superficial swirl in the torrent of history, is more ironically self-conscious about the application of tidal analogies before an actual river: "The strong tide, so swift, so deep, and certain, was like a congenial friend" in which he sees glassed a replica of his own relation to it, "watching an eddy that turned and turned purposeless, until the stream absorbed it, and carried it on to the sea.—Like me!" (III, ch. 9). Just before that self-accusatory internal echo ("sea" / "me"), Carton's "chain" of reverie leads him back to thoughts of his father's funeral, retrieving its recited sacred text "like a rusty old ship's anchor from the deep." The tacit idiom "chain of association" is thus aptly literalized as the recovery of a previous being far submerged in the internal tides of mind. For this man who had once characterized himself to Lucie Manette as "like one who died young" (II, ch. 13), the memory of his father's funeral is a partial resurrection of his earlier self coincident with the now recalled words, "I am the Resurrection and the Life." A confession of Carton's previous psychic burial is cannily unlocked in this same paragraph within the most straightforward of idioms: "Long ago, when he had been famous among his earliest competitors as a youth of great promise, he had *followed his father to the grave*. His mother had died, years before" (my emphasis on Dickens's funereal duplicity). In a single phrase we find the justification for all that macabre comedy about grave robbing that centers around Jerry Cruncher as Resurrection Man. It is Carton, not only orphaned but interred, who must be "recalled to life" again in a lifting out of himself that raises him to the sacrificial scaffold, regardless of any further elevation by death itself.

Lazarus-like, making good on the first person of the Lord's annunciation, Carton ascends not through but to his death scene, from the stilled "deep" of his humanity into that public storm where "fifty-two were to roll that afternoon on the life-tide of the city to the boundless everlasting sea" (III, ch. 13). Even the figurative verb there is a threefold pun compounding the oceanic metaphor of death with its literal cause and effect in the remorseless roll of the condemned and the consequent roll of their heads under the guillotine. For the man whose mother had died in his infancy, his goal, shared with the seamstress whom he has befriended in his last hours, will be to rejoin the "Universal Mother" across the untraversable distance of death's "dark highway." It is a distance implicated in the interval of a nearby play on words, Carton and the girl hoping "to repair home together, and to rest in her bosom" (III, ch. 15), where the imagined journey to their long home overtakes and includes the sense of a "reparation" for all earthly losses.

There, as throughout the death scene, the violent revolutionary sea changes seem to set in motion a compensatory verbal rhythm of wavering and restitution. As Carton nears his and the book's end, the Dickensian rhetoric detaches crucial phrases from within, releases words to each other in new ways, submits the burden of the unsayable to the ebb and turn of surprising allusions, nuances, and ambiguities. Here is the death of the seamstress just before Carton: "She goes next before him—is gone; the knitting-women count Twenty-Two" (III, ch. 15). A semicolon keeps separate the ledger of vendetta— ticking off its corpses with mindless metronomic precision—from the empathetic prose of the dying, clocked to a more humane rhythm. Across the dash of the scaffold's inflexible continuity in numeration and its fatal hiatus, the verb of motion, "goes," becomes the past participle of absence in "is gone," a phrase inserted above the line in Dickens's manuscript as a masterly afterthought.[17] Similarly the adverb "next" and the preposition "before," each not only spatial but temporal, are evaporated with temporality itself into the paradoxical present tense of instantaneous removal, "is gone," predicating still what in the same interval it eradicates. Imagine the phrase otherwise and you hear what Dickensian tact has managed with the grammatical parataxis, "She goes next before him and is gone." With the refusal of ordinary conjunction in the world's terms, the suspended tense of "is" lingers across the split second of recorded absence as a softening consecration of the girl's impress, if not still her presence, for the man who came out of himself to care.

That phrase "next before him" is the last direct reference, even by pronoun, to the hero. After a paragraph reiterating the text of "I am the Resurrection and the Life," we pass to another elided interval: "The murmuring of many voices, the upturning of many faces, the pressing on of many footsteps in the outskirts of the crowd, so that it swells forward in a mass like one great heave of water, all flashes away. Twenty-Three." In that long periodic building toward recapitulated subject and burst verb for the death sentence, the final predication of the hostile mob at its falling away from the hero, his from it, compresses its gerundive forms, the named actions of the inimical world in all its otherness, weight, and forward thrust, lets its grammar heap forward even into a suspensive independent clause ("so that it swells"), and then, at the pivotal instant of similitude (the monosyllabic massing at "like one great heave of water") undercuts the whole cumulative grammar of the world's inertial resistance with a dismissive idiom. The phrase "flashes away" is not only a formulaic description of drowning quite common in literary treatments (see the Rossetti epigraph to this chapter, the Eliot for Chapter 3, the Nabokov for "Afterwords")—a description enforced by the explicit analogy to the heaving furrows of "water"—but it is also an echo of that earlier murder of Madame Defarge and the sacrificial impairment of Miss Pross: " 'I feel,' said Miss Pross, 'as if there had been a flash and a crash, and that crash was the last thing I should ever hear in this life' " (III, ch. 14). Locution there for an explosive burst of light, "flash" has gone from noun of ignition to a verb of extinguishment across a pattern of mortal displacement captured by Dickensian prose at the level of echoing monosyllables. For what Miss Pross, clinging to Madame Defarge "with more than the hold of a drowning woman," saw and heard, the murderousness of the world turned against itself, is what Carton will no longer be made to suffer, having taken the violence unto himself as his own liberating fate. The canceling "crash" that follows the earlier gunpowder "flash" has become the guillotine's twice-repeated "Crash!" by which the whole scene of terror, in a chiastic inversion of the earlier death scene and its rhetoric, is finally "flashed" away for Carton, at the moment when the ferocious ocean of hate both overtakes and cleanses him.

I invoke the notion of a purging inundation advisedly, for the executioner's "Number Twenty-Three"—in its mindless recoil from subjective to objective reality—is a terminal code for the name in which this death by symbolic drowning does in fact miraculously, if at one level deceptively, baptise Carton: the name of the man Darnay for whom he dies. This is, we may remember, the novel of so deft a liturgical wit that its comic denomination of Jerry Cruncher is referred back to baptism as "the youthful occasion of his renouncing by proxy the works of darkness" (II, ch. 1). So does Carton endure his more extreme renunciation as a proxy for his double and recent namesake. When the revolutionary violence, in its focal reception by Jarvis Lorry, is earlier compared to the "vision" of the drowning mind, that perception is described as empowering the synoptic access to an entire world "if it were there" (III, ch. 3). The "world" that Carton's later figurative incarnation of a "drowning man" might now envision "if it were there" is the world that, through his death, is brought into being—the world of the future that his doom ensures for the family whose safety he dies to make possible. At this "pass of a crisis," as that explicit earlier conceit of drowning had it—this mortal impasse and passing on—retrospect is replaced by prophecy for a man who has no past worth looking back on, only another's future worth dying for.

What follows is a typical Dickensian survey of the future fortunes of his cast internalized as if it were the "sublime and prophetic" insight of his dying hero. Yet his visionary coda retains also its aura of a textual prototype, as we will see, the moment of death discovered virtually to novelize its own succession in the vanishing interval of last consciousness. When Carton tells Lucy earlier in the novel, "I am like one who died young," he adds, "All my life might have been" (II, ch. 13). Indeed, Darnay is the living embodiment of what he might have been: alter ego of Carton's emotional desuetude in life, projected continuation of his identity across the defied severance of death. With any meaningful past only faintly conjectural, Carton has at least in death earned the right to have his legacy appear before him with the strange declarative certainty of the (the paradox seems inescapable) prophetically remembered. This unprecedented shift in perspective, in the distended interval of annulled consciousness, is the ultimate metastasis or "remove" of mortal transition in Dickens: the instantaneous break from time redirected into an unbroken futurity rhetorically set forth.

These last five paragraphs of the book, inscribed for us as if they had been transcribed by Carton, gain a portion of their force by falling in line with other deathbed narratives in the novel and their summarizing truth. Darnay, after all, is sentenced, Carton executed in his stead, because of the incriminating narrative document scribbled with his last strength by Dr. Manette in the Bastille during what he thought were his final days alive. This is a narrative of aristocratic cruelty for which the chief evidence, besides the doctor's incarceration itself, is his own transcription within it of another deathbed narrative, orally delivered, of the young man whose family was destroyed by the cruelty of the Evrémondes. Carton's hypothetical last words thus shift the emphasis of such nested tragic reports forward into a purgative futurity, delivered up into our narrative as if Carton had been handed quill and paper on the scaffold. Indeed we hear of the "remarkable" woman executed shortly before him who was "allowed to write down the thoughts that were inspiring her," thoughts authorized by finality, intensified by death. "If he had given an utterance to his, and they were prophetic, they would have been these" (III, ch. 15). Dickens drops out the second and expected "if" under cover of parallelism, so that these thoughts are in fact predicated and deemed prophetic apart from any mystery that might be thought to cloak them for want of transcription. Insinuated with the impunity of ellipsis, they *were* prophetic, written or not.

There is a further inside-out turn to this narrative involution at the close. That manuscript of accusation against the house of Evrémonde was not the only narrative composed by Doctor Manette in prison, nor the only one binding the far future to the present implications of a tale. Besides this political injunction to retributive murder, Manette was also a prophetic narrator of domestic eventualities, jotting down in his mind, not on paper, alternative scenarios for the future life of the child he never saw born. One of these unwritten mental fictions is a remarkable negative anticipation of the novel's own metanarrative close. On the eve of her marriage to Charles, Manette confesses to Lucie how in his worst prison fantasy he had imagined his own oblivion in his daughter's eyes. He uses the same parallel grammar as in Carton's multiple "I see's" at the end, pushing his reiterations forward to a just barely suppressed metaphor of textuality: "I have pictured my daughter, to myself, as perfectly forgetful of me," he recalls. "I have cast up the years of her age . . . I have seen her married . . . I have altogether perished from the remembrance of the living, and in the next generation my place was a blank" (II, ch. 17). It is this blank—not just emptiness but ellipsis, not just oblivion but textual hiatus in the imagined book of record—that death permits the redemptive hero to inscribe with better meaning, both for himself and for the descendants of Manette.

We are now ready to watch Carton watching—and tracing out for himself in a mental inscription—the very future precipitated by his present-tense sacrifice from the otherwise effacing flow of time. Early in the novel, anticipating the "I see" pattern at the close, Carton "saw for a moment . . . a mirage of honorable ambition, self-denial, and perseverance." The paradisal "fair city of this vision," with "airy galleries from which the loves and graces looked upon him" (II, ch. 5), is to be replaced by a fatal sacrifice of undreamed "self-denial" that sends forth identity not into some heavenly city of purpose but into the secular "perseverance" of history itself. The closural pattern of rhythmic repetition is one that Dickens visibly labored over at the manuscript stage, subdividing an already drafted clause at one point so as, by introducing more "I see's," to promote the momentum of this visionary anaphora. The metaphors of rising and resurrection are first contrasted—"I see Barsad, and Cly, Defarge, The Vengeance, the Jury-man, the Judge, long ranks of the new oppressors who *have risen* on the destruction of the old, perishing by this retributive instrument"—until the flood subsides and brotherhood reasserts itself: "I see a beautiful city and a brilliant people *rising* from this abyss" (my stress on the shift from preterite to prophetic participle). The next paragraph opens, "I see the lives for which I lay down my life, peaceful, useful, prosperous and happy, in that England which I shall see no more," where the ambiguous quartet of congratulatory adjectives could apply grammatically to Carton's own passing "life" as well in his moment of recaptured purpose. "I see Her with a child upon her bosom . . . I see the old man . . . passing tranquilly to his reward." Carton's vision then presses on from this future death scene into the next paragraph, where the conjugal embrace of Lucie and Charles is epitomized in their final closeness underground: "I see her and her husband, their course done, lying side by side in their last earthly bed . . . I see that child who lay upon her bosom and bore my name . . . foremost of just judges and honoured men, bringing a boy of my name . . . to this place—then fair to look upon" (like the "fair city" of his early "mirage"). In this way the present apocalyptic judgment extends, softened, into the inherited vocation that Carton as law clerk could never muster in his own person.

Enunciated in the unvoiced cadences of sublime confidence, style thus humanizes into visionary view the last interval of a death scene. The ordinary agnosticism of Dickensian dying, its end-stopped character, the opacity of its high finish—all is qualified by the flavor of augury, but not, in the other sense, of divination. Degenerated history, exploded toward revolution and apocalypse by the death of Marquis St. Evrémonde, is returned after the flood of bitter judgment into the flow of temporal history again, regenerate now, imaginable by narrative even in its merely eventual shapes. The frequent superimposition of narrated drowning and fictional self-consciousness, in their common penchant for retrospective order and summation, is layered yet further with this access to the future as a virtually narrative feat, almost as if the hero had "been allowed to write down" his consolatory thoughts after all. These thoughts are couched like all fiction in the self-confirming authority of pure invention. What rumor assures us— the rehearsal of life in drowning—here becomes in the other sense of preview or try-out the only real life there is for the hero to rehearse. Yet two things must be kept in mind so as to clarify the nature of this coda. First, Carton does not see into and through the grave of his own fate to some intimation of immortality, or at least not until the novel's last clause. From the edge of eternity he peers back into the world of time, and forward there, as if through eternity's sanction as an incomparable vantage on time, into confident earthly prefiguration. Second, it is the final decorum of the novel as record, however fictional, that the generations availed and so evoked by Carton's sacrifice do not outdistance the time elapsed between the Revolution and Dickens's writing of the novel in the middle of the next century. Even within the myth of clairvoyance the authority of fiction, like the authority of deathbed revelation, is held to the precincts of retrospect.

To assert further the connection between novel making and this visionary dispensation, all Carton's prophetic seeing closes down at the end upon an overheard story, the hero imagining Lucie's son narrating for her grandson, Sydney's namesake, the whole narrative of his life up to and including his death: "And I hear him tell the child my story, with a tender and faltering voice." It is as if the dying Hamlet were shown overhearing in his own mind's ear the explanatory oration he has ordered of Horatio. In the vanishing interval of final consciousness, Carton's metaphorically drowning mind does indeed look back on the story of his soul's dark night told over as conscious tragic narrative, a story of course transfigured by the death that offers it up as completed and transmissible tale. No novel could fasten more surely the always tacit bond between mortality and communicable narration. Carton's dramatized and consummating death scene is displaced into an articulate exemplum discovered at the very moment of his death to be recoverable in the telling, time out of mind. And so the tale recounted by Lucie's son becomes, in short—and of course in its shortened form—the title scene of *The Tale* that earns its closure by foreseeing it.

This metanarrative redoubling then gives way to the last sentence, comprising the last paragraph, of the novel, perhaps the most famous brief soliloquy in all of Dickens. It arrives as if to instance in abbreviated form the very "story" of Carton's life, summation in light of peripety and redemption, and to understand this story as precisely the province of last utterance, unvoiced or not: "It is a far, far better thing that I do, than I have ever done; it is a far, far better rest that I go to than I have ever known." Death emerges here as both heroic action and its reward, moral resolve and at the same time temporal resolution, the valiant doing and the having done with. It is at the core of their power that these lines do not vie with the novel's opening sentence as the most famous in Dickens but seem to eventuate from within that anarchic parataxis desperately struggling for containment by antithesis. In the initiating chapter called, with apocalyptic overtones of premature closure in a time out of joint, "The Period," we have heard, "It was the best of times, it was the worst of times, it was the age of wisdom, it was the age of foolishness," and so forth, back and forth toward chaos. What is so unforgettable about the novel's finishing pair of contrastive clauses is that they take up, work over, and reconstitute this paradoxical deadlock at the outset. There hyperbole is pitted against hyperbole in a specter of historical contradiction collapsed inward upon itself, imploded and immobilized. Any curative rhetoric must require a meliorating breadth between extremities sufficient to declare a direction. From the self-conscious barrage of the first weighted and heightened sentence, which boasts "the superlative degree of comparison only" (that phrasing itself almost a logical paradox), the novel must make its way toward the freed-up incremental style of the true comparative degree in "far, far better," twice repeated at the end in a triumph not over the previous worse or worst so much as over the historical ultimacy when acme and abjection are at one, where time itself as principle of movement and differentiation is fused shut in the insistent plural "times." The hero's communion with pure futurity at the end, when it returns him to the equal purity of completion and retrospect in the last sentence, is thus cadenced in 'a rectifying echo of the novel's opening. Deep within the rhetoric that attends the communal or fraternal sacrifice of a single life is found the attempted vindication of an epoch.

It happens that the last two pairs of antithetical statements strung on that pendulous syntax of the opening sentence—"we had everything before us, we had nothing before us, we were all going direct to Heaven, we were all going direct the other way"—describe nothing so much as a societal death scene under the aspect first of religion versus atheism, fronting on eternity or void, and then of the two alternatives within a Christian faith, heaven or hell. These simplistic, conflicting overstatements must all be moderated and remade by the rhythm of the novel's last sentence and the waiting ambivalence of its last word. However much the final sentence is designed in obliquely tunneled allusion to the book's opening, its chaos of contradiction now sorted to order, still it allows a final interval within a single verb that also makes it one last instance of immediacy phased forward into the advent of recognized rest and backward into retrospect. The novel's last word is the conduit of a kind of vocabular grace, acknowledging a peace perhaps blessed as well as merely absolute. The rest I take here and now, says (or thinks) Carton to himself, is better, because more complete, than any I have before *taken*; the rest I now set forth upon will not only be better than any I have ever had, but better than I have ever, in my spiritual doubts, known *it would or could be*. On the second understanding of "known" to mean conceptual rather than empirical knowledge, that fretless preknowing of belief, the phrase edges past fact into an elliptical expression of achieved faith, an expression elusively revealed in the very language that reiterates its lifelong absence.

The uncertain valence of "known" thus widens the final grammar only so as to draw it closed again across the semantic interval—a postponed model of death's own instantaneous shift of register—between a past prescience unfelt and an impending nescience momentarily reimagined as ecstatic stasis. Within the vigilant options of its own possibilities in this very last word of the novel, style has once more, and in more senses than one, seen a character through. From "all flashes away" in the actual subjective death sentence, across the period and textual break (suspension as well as severance) at "Number Twenty-Three," the phenomenal passes to the brutally numerical, while at the same time displacing the numenal forward into this whole last monologue. It is a mortal vision which, in its own verbal suspension, would seem to have reinhabited, or even to have broken from and outlasted, the very interval of evacuated consciousness at death.

Close study of Carton's death scene and its visionary coda should have made clear that the extended passage could scarcely have been conceived as the straightforward hallmark of Victorian moral fanfare and uplift, of pathos, threnody, and catharsis, in the guise of which it has passed into literary and popular history. It is not just an exercise in but an exploration of the style of dying as a narrative act, the clefts of its alert and crafted prose activated across narrative time to suggest the evanescent momentum of traversed intervals. It is also a study in the rhetorical power as well as the verbal implementation of death in narrative. Any such sense that the execution of Carton is not only enrolled on the rosters of vengeance but inscribed self-consciously in a novel, a rhetorically motivated sacrifice we as readers somehow demand, takes us back to the first chapter of real plot after the introductory vantage on the times, a plot that knows itself as plot, for Mr. Lorry is repeatedly described there, with a pun on mail-coach ticketing, as the "passenger booked by this history" (1, ch. 2). So is Carton "booked," first to be resurrected from his own past and then to be preserved by "this history" of Dickens. He dies so as to secure the shape of this history for others coming, which of course means only for us, even "generations hence."

In an accompanying turn of rhetorical bravura, Dickens indicates Carton's sacrificial role as suffering stand-in for the readers as well as for his private double and the Darnay circle. Immediately after Carton admits to the young seamstress that he is in fact "dying for him" (III, ch. 13), for the man she previously saw in his place—and shortly before the fatal blank at "all flashes away"—there is an earlier break in the text and an unsettling shift into first-person plural. We are suddenly catapulted into the scene of escape, deposited in the same carriage that rushes Darnay, Lucie, and the rest from Paris in a reversal of the coach journey toward France that began the plot. This time we too, in the double sense, are "booked by this history," so that it is we for whom the hero has acknowledged his sacrifice, we who benefit (through a melodramatic shift in pronouns) from the dispensation of displacement. As the chapter closes after paragraphs of frenetic first person, "the whole wild night is in pursuit of us; but, so far, we are pursued by nothing else." We are haunted only by the atmosphere of the novel we are reading, our imaginations alone taking "flight."

At this turn it is essential to recognize that such a narrative fore-grounding of sacrificial death, its redemption in and through reading, has nothing to do with aestheticized dying. Dickens is shortly to satirize just this with those "riders in the tumbrils" who choose to "cast upon the multitude such glances as they have seen in theatres, and in pictures" (III, ch. 15)—or, presumably, such as they have read about in novels. Avoiding this prettified good death, Carton's end, and the structural mechanics of chronology that lock it into place, provide a representational sacrifice for the engaged reader. Guided by that elaborate rhetoric of transposition that eases Carton toward and over the threshold of his dying, the hero's epitomizing end as Resurrection Man is then displaced into narrative prophecy, as we have seen, and made available there far into the future. The auspicious narrative the hero might have written down if he could have is the predictive story the narrator tells for him under the aus-pices of omniscience, closing (in on itself) as it does with a future hearing of the novel's own abridged *Tale* lived through to its point of meaning in selfless martyrdom. In this conversion of life line to story line, we realize that the imagery of drowning may well appear at the instant of Carton's death as a popular equivalent to the fictional self-involvement of Dickens's closure. Summoned here is the paradigm of mortal replay, which suggests that time is not abrogated by death so much as gathered up one time, life brought to shape as it is brought to a close, whether in a flash of memory or as a function of record.

Even before this, it is our own relation to the whole record of death that has been dramatized by that striking transition into first-person present tense. Rhetoric in recognition of its own service, the passage is designed to reorient us as fellow travelers with the Darnay party, "pursued" as "we are" from the scene of tragedy into the open-ended world of its true comprehension. Fictional death by proxy translates to a displacement of fatality for the reader as well as Darnay. *A Tale of Two Cities* thereby nears its close with not only a demonstration but also a parable of the fictional death sentence and its resonance, acknowledging those "booked" heroes who die for us at the arm's length of aesthetic distance. When history, made present to us on that road out of Paris by the shifting grammar of tense, further includes us by the encompassing grammar of number, Dickens has more self-consciously than in any other of his novels inscribed that narrative place, the safe and sometimes curative space, of fictional substitution and catharsis—the dying that is far, far better in art.

3

Transitions

The Death of Ophelia, by John Everett Millais
Courtesy of The Tate Gallery, London

She had suddenly passed away from that life which she had
been dreading: it was the transition of death, without its
agony.

GEORGE ELIOT
The Mill on the Floss

3

The drowning man, urged by the supreme agony, lives in an instant through all his happy and unhappy past . . . And even in those earlier crises, which are but types of death—when we are cut off abruptly from the life we have known . . . and find ourselves by some sudden shock on the confines of the unknown—there is often the same sort of lightning-flash through the dark and unfrequented chambers of memory.

GEORGE ELIOT, *Scenes of Clerical Life*

ITS ELEMENT THE TEMPORAL, any style of dying must trope what it cannot otherwise portray, replace representation by metaphor. It ordinarily does so in the space of retrospect pressed to essence. In the threefold operations of transposition, epitome, and displacement, the classic Dickensian death scene, as we have found, requires and therefore generates a rhetoric of intervals. They may also be termed transitions: between normal communicative vocabulary and the death which a strangely obligated language must attempt to humanize into a living medium; between life as lapsed and the last instant of condensation that may replay it in the mind or, objectifying it in symbol, convey something of life's essence to the reception of a secondary consciousness. The logic of transition in an unequivocally Christian death scene is more likely to be vertical than horizontal, the descent of judgment or the ascent of the soul. The axis shifts for the post-Romantic death scene, horizontal not only in the sense that linear time gets severed and private life lines tied up, but that lateral recognitions are more crucially impelled. These horizontal displacements of the Victorian psychology of dying generally verbalize a mode of transition communal, sexual, or textual, a transference from self to some familial or social other, from lover to lover in an erotic transfusion, or from presence over to page in the preservations of scripted record.

It is this last and ultimately self-reflexive issue which emerges so strongly in the intersecting metaphors of textuality and death at the close of Thackeray's novel *The Newcomes*, calling to mind similar terminal strategies in *David Copperfield* and *A Tale of Two Cities*. Before turning to *The Newcomes*, we must trace certain post-Dickensian variations on the style of mortal intervals in such other Victorian writers as the Brontës, Eliot, and Hardy. Whether style waxes sonorous and at times incantatory, as in Eliot's treatment of drowning in *The Mill on the Floss*, or pales to the lividly understated in Hardy, it is language itself that not only gauges but effects undertones of meaning otherwise inaudible. Tracking this gradual transition from Dickens through Hardy into modernism reveals that, though the rhetoric of death may grow less ornate, prosodic, or intricately figural, the narrative of dying since Dickens demands no less than ever from style. In the later Victorian death scenes after the breakthroughs of Dickensian verbal experiment, as well as in the modernist innovators who further refine and ironize the temporal intervals of mortal rhetoric, death requires a stylistics of transition within a narrative of human transience.

□   □   □

A rather prankish interlude in Victorian fictional history may in its allusive joke bury a clue to lines of influence in the nineteenth-century novel's treatment of mortality. When sketches by Elizabeth Gaskell collected from previous appearances in Dickens's periodical, *Household Words*, were published as the novel *Cranford* (1853), they included in an initiating episode the death of a man run down by a railroad train moments after reading *Pickwick Papers*. The split personality of Dickens's novel, in which grotesque interpolations of death and dementia provide macabre relief from the plot's episodic farce, becomes in Gaskell's book the occasion of a death that gets under way an Austenian comedy of manners. The novel within which the Victorian death scene enjoyed its first major try-out is now the novel around which, and in part because of whose distracting fascination, the legacy of fictional dying is maintained.

Elsewhere Gaskell's inheritance of the Dickensian management of death goes unmocked, uncontested, and deep. Nowhere is the influence more obvious, for her and such Victorian peers as Trollope and Eliot, working also under the inspiration and the shadow of Dickens, than in the deployment of ambiguous chapter titles both to prolong suspense and to entertain metaphysical alternatives.[1] Among the several deaths in Gaskell's *North and South* (1855), the heroine's mother, ironically named Mrs. Hale, dies in a chapter with the duplicitous title "Home at Last" (ch. 3), nominally describing the arrival of the long-absent son, Frederick, but metaphorically denoting the return to that eternity from which the mother's earthly trials have been a protracted exile. Her husband later follows to his "Journey's End" (ch. 4), where the figure is used, for one thing, without the picaresque overtones of its appearance in Defoe or Fielding; for another, the "journey" is, in the mode of post-Romantic secular entelechy, as much life's momentum toward death as death's beyond life. Mr. Hale travels not just back to Oxford for his first visit in seventeen years, however, nor even just to his death; anticipating the "untraversable distance" of *Little Dorrit*, he sets off as well toward the "immeasurably distant" spiritual destination to which his ecclesiastic life had always pointed. Repeatedly in Gaskell, as in other writers of this Dickensian cast, ambiguous titles hedge fatality until they can edge their way to its redefinition as a transference from living terminology. A stylist as overt and inventive as George Meredith may even show such mortal doubleness spun round on itself in a pivotal inversion, as when he says of his title figure in *Diana of the Crossways* (1885) that "the race she ran was with a shrouded figure no more, but with the figure of the shroud" (ch. 29). In a shift of the term "figure" from concrete to abstract noun, the shrouded mystery unveiled turns out to be the pending death of Arthur Warwick, and by displacement the figurative death of hope for the heroine. The style of chiasmus itself marks one of the novel's titular crossways. Here and in later scenes of fatality and its near escape, Meredith might have said of his heroine what Gaskell did of hers in *North and South*, that she was "afresh taught by death what life should be" (ch. 48).

This teaching is often an instruction in and by style. Jane Eyre's first spiritual crisis, occasioned by the pending death of her friend, Helen Burns, is in part a lesson in the Victorian language of euphemism and in the more honest grammar of the verb *to be* that figures so conspicuously in fiction as a counterpoint to the prose of dying. (It is such a syntax of being, as we will see, upon which Hardy capitalizes in the several ironic copulas of *Jude the Obscure*.) Brontë's scene begins with the familiar divergence between referential poles of the idiom for homecoming, here in the context of a conversation between two orphans. Knowing that Helen is expected to die, and yet disingenuously asking, "Are you going home?" when her friend tries to say good-bye, Jane forces Helen's knowledge from her lips in a commonplace biblical metaphor that is for Helen literal truth: "Yes; to my long home—my last home" (ch. 9). Jane crawls into bed with Helen as if to absorb her faith by osmosis, the two orphans in each other's arms awaiting the arms of "the same mighty, universal Parent." The closeness occasioned by the last kiss between the girls is then phrased elliptically so that it seems verging on a syntactic equation of their identities in this moment of clutched oneness: "She kissed me, and I her, and we both soon slumbered." There is no real syncope of the verb *was* in the second clause, nor could there be grammatically, yet the phantom language of being and identity seems to equate subject and object on the edge of death. Such an effect stands as prelude to the displacement of death onto the heroine in her role as surviving alter ego for the dying girl. It so happens that among Jane's first lessons at school with Helen were "the first two tenses of the verb Etre" (ch. 8), present and preterite, with the novel from Helen's death forward charting a renewed direction for the future tense of the heroine's becoming. Years later, achieved in her being in a way quite different from Helen's religious self-abnegation, the married Jane errects a tombstone to Helen inscribed in first-person Latin singular, "Resurgam" (ch. 9). It is as if the heroine herself, in a dead language recharged with feeling, has retrospectively engraved the tense of her own resurrection. Jane has, after all, been reborn from the embrace of martyrlike death to a sense of self as enfolded and defined by passionate love on earth.

Death in *Jane Eyre* requires, and provides, a further instruction in English verbal conjugation as well as the equivalent in French or Latin grammar. During her spiritual crisis over the death of Helen, Jane's ear for speech loses its innocence through a fall into acknowledged reality across the transitional touchstone of the English verb *to be*, which hovers somewhere between negated future tense and the tacit predication of a being elsewhere anticipated. Given the report of Helen's doctor that "she'll not be here long," Jane admits, "This phrase, uttered in my hearing yesterday, would have only conveyed the notion that she was about to be removed to Northumberland, to her own home. I should not have suspected that it meant she was dying" (ch. 9). Imminent death institutes a harsher tutelage, the euphemism seen through as if the true hearing of the phrase would require an accentual emphasis somewhere in the interval between locative adverb (not *here* long) and grammar of being (not *be* much longer).

Long before Hardy's nihilistic experiments with the circular syntax of copulative predication as virtual dead metaphor, Elizabeth Gaskell as well as Charlotte Brontë exploited the ambiguous possibilities of this verb of being in the vicinity of extinction. Gaskell does so notably in *North and South,* in a context similar to Brontë's, in which the heroine survives the symbolic death of a young double. Yet Gaskell's is an even more melodramatic structure meant to sublimate the very moment of death's rupture, lending it the stylistic impetus of continuity. When Gaskell writes to Dickens that she might have called her novel "Death and Variations,"[2] one assumes her to intend not only mortal episodes that serve as variations on a central theme (changes rung on the formulaic death scene) but also those systematic analogies drawn from dying that vary death into a symbol for some powerful transition in the proximate self, be it precipitous collapse, decay, or edification.

In a novel repeatedly interlaced, as in other of Gaskell's works, with epigraphs from the Victorian poetry of death, this ability for life to be tutored by finality in the premises and limits of being is most unmistakable in *North and South,* when the heroine's nineteen-year-old counterpart, Bessy Higgins, has her dying elusively redefined by a slippery demonstrative syntax. As Margaret looks upon her friend's inert body at rest in a deserved peace after so much pain, the vision objectifies a stasis toward which the heroine's adjacent turmoil gravitates, and within which it can be laid at least partly to rest. "The slow tears gathered into Margaret's eyes, but a deep calm entered into her soul. And that was death! It looked more peaceful than life" (ch. 28). The exclamatory "that was" clause, either dismissive, relieved, or elated, refers in its indirect discourse to the physical corpse laid out and made visible in its repose. But so too—especially by the logic of immediate grammatical reference and the persistence of the verb of being within a preterite frame—it must refer to that dead calm in the soul which introjects for Margaret the peace her ended friend embodies. She is a girl who will never be older than Margaret is now and who thus seems to symbolize the passing away of some previously unsettled phase of Margaret's own selfhood. An uncertainty of antecedence opens the space of this displacement. The linguistic ambiguities of copulative predication are made complicit in this effect by the fact that the verb *was* is set in the historical past tense of indirect discourse, "that was death" referring either to the death just done with, incarnate in the corpse, or to some reification of death as a power to suspend life's vexation, a power still present in the aftermath of the dying. By a manifold "variation" central to that rhetoric of death fashioned and sophisticated by Victorian fiction, death is thus demonstrated, thus denominated, as the very motive of mortal containment and instructed continuance. For the world-weary and spiritually receptive Bessy, joined with Margaret in an allegory of passage and maturation, what has quietly transpired is a composite process of transposition, epitome, and displacement—by which the surviving heroine is "afresh taught" the very mood of pushing on.

Death, we see, has a way of summoning stylistic ingenuity in authors far less disposed to rhetorical machinations than Dickens. A novelist of more or less transparent verbal texture such as Gaskell will nevertheless haze her prose with sufficient opacity to implement the innate ambiguities of death as thematic material. By contrast, Thackeray, inclined toward an opposite management of death as theme and scene, a stripped dismissal of its portentousness, works words round to his antirhetorical but no less stylistic ends. In *The Luck of Barry Lyndon* (1844) Thackeray conveys the death of Barry's son with the kind of throttled, curt death sentence so typical of his work—and which would not appear again with such regularity in any British writer, including Trollope or Hardy, before E. M. Forster. Yet Thackeray follows this characteristic sentence in the novel's last chapter with an ironic rendering of the reprobate father's mourning that utilizes a verbal ambiguity to execute a psychological displacement: "At last, after two days, he died. There he lay, the hope of my family, the pride of my manhood." The dead figure of speech that varies such a phrase as "issue of my proud manhood" into the more private and complete abstraction of "pride," in itself an entirely idiomatic turn, does nonetheless, because of its oblique logic of externalization and transference, ironically mark the death of a second, better self who might have sustained or channeled—not just embodied—the father's indulgent pride. Periphrasis can seldom rest easy in the face of death's concision.

It is no accident that the examples so far of death's ambiguous rhetoric, both figurative and grammatical—psychological transpositions blending into religious epitomes like "long home" or "universal Parent," dormant clichés momentarily recharged and subverted like "pride of my manhood," as well as such various euphemistic, vernacular, or quasiparadoxical derivations of the predicate of being as in "won't be here long" or "that was death"—all have to do with a foregrounding of the ordinary under duress from the inordinate, a reseeing of the given and its consequent resaying. This tendency often grows all the more obvious as the actual moment of death is approached, for there the necessity is most fully manifest for a rhetoric of transition from empirical evidence toward invisibility or mere void. There may be in the long run no words for death, but in the short run there are certainly none but what we have at hand. Death is a commonplace that remakes all others, its style based on a special penchant for the estrangement of linguistic expectations. The mundane or idiomatic expression, long habituated to the world's usage, may, alienated by mortal context, migrate toward surprise. Yet the rhetoric of death must rest somehow on the continuities of the referable world. It is a style of transition in need of a seamless medium, and must either resort to the grammar and figures of transposition as a primary mode of rendering or else refuse analogic connotations altogether.

The latter is Thackeray's tactic at his most terse and acerb. Alone among his Victorian peers, he tends to make no phrasal concessions to death as passage, to entertain as a rule no craving for its prose evocation as more than a negating event; for him dying is too empty or impervious to honor with sonorities, too enormous to worry with ambiguities. Death seals the lips of ordinary rhetoric, leaving room only for clinical report. And this is as much a style as any, more salient and self-declaring in its cryptic restraint than most. It also follows as much as any other stylistic strategy from the moral persuasion of the author's work. Thackeray wants death not as dramatic event but as leveling irony, the final rending fact of life, stripping bare the plumes of false pride. To intrude upon life without possibility of being converted to further self-flattery, death must be made to arrive not as a mirror of life but as a window on the void. As such, not only epitomizing ironies are minimized but the other complex modalities of the death scene as well, as if in Thackeray's prose there were a systematic dysfunction in the trusted rhetoric of dying; no longer a Victorian occasion for present meaning, death serves only for a chastening in prospect. This is what has been usefully called Thackeray's pervasive "argument *ad mortalitatem*,"[3] a rhetoric not of mortal symbolism but of digressive, if rigorous, admonition.

Quintessentially in *Vanity Fair* (1847–1848), Thackeray's broad satiric canvas—framed by deflated fatalities unlike anything else in the period, even in Hardy—reads like an extended Vanitas portrait of an entire society. Symbolic instruction by death has been edged out to an implicit caveat encircling the whole of plot. To settle on a single example of the kind of dying consonant with this view of the death scene's reduced spiritual efficacy in fiction, there is the offstage fate of Captain George Osborne in *Vanity Fair*. He leaves the plot very much alive in a martial procession: "He looked up, and smiled at Amelia, and passed on; and even the sound of the music died away" (ch. 30). The potential Victorian euphemism "passed on" seems proleptic, as does the metaphoric "died away"; language itself sustains at the level of dead metaphor the monitory perspective that lurks beneath the surface of all secular comings and goings. The actual description of Osborne's death, a subversion of all Scott's clangorous heroic fatalities on the battlefield, of anything weighted by rhetoric in Dickens and his followers, arrives without metaphoric adornment two chapters later: "Darkness came down on the field and city: and Amelia was praying for George, who was lying on his face, dead, with a bullet through his heart" (ch. 32). Death as foregone anticlimax in this omniscient aside is subordinated to a relative clause, and within that to the delayed past participle of mortal afterthought, pivotal cause to the prostrate effect of this glimpsed tableau. Inert and unnoticed, this isolated corpse is the narrative residue of an avoided rhetorical interval where the memorialized death might have been. George's death is denied transition or direction in the space between the auxiliary verb of being in "was lying" and the explanatory second participle, "dead," nailing down the death sentence with a monosyllabic slam.

☐   ☐   ☐

At any notch on the scale from understatement to melodrama, however, Victorian literature is full of death's passing between paired psyches in a lateral emphasis on that very meaning excluded from the death of George Osborne. The most famous paired deaths of the period in an unequivocally sexual context, each virtually suicidal and linked across plot by a tortuously sundered *Liebestod*, belong of course to the lovers in Emily Brontë's *Wuthering Heights*. Her heroine, Cathy, whose notorious "I am Heathcliff" (ch. 9) is a ceding of identity to erotic fusion—a madness of primal abdication—thus dies by epitome "of what was denominated a brain fever" (ch. 13) in childbirth, leaving behind the daughter of Edgar Linton. Death as quintessence, the familiar Victorian pattern, is reduced a chapter after Cathy's death to pure formula in the local doctor's words about the end of her brother, Hindley Earnshaw, who "died true to his character, drunk as a lord" (ch. 17). Similarly both essence and cessation of the self, the death of Cathy comes exactly midway in the novel's roster of fatalities—those of her parents, her brother's wife, and Mr. and Mrs. Linton before her, of Hindley first, then Isabella, Edgar, Linton, and finally Heathcliff after her—and so motivates the transition between the two generational phases of the novel. Cathy's death is at first described in Nelly Dean's running discourse to Lockwood with an unwitting hint, muffled by idiom, of reversion and epitome. The excess of Cathy's passion, we realize, has always been the prophecy of its own effacement. The language of being that would annex identity—I *am* the other—instead predicts its cancellation at the outset. Without momentous last words or any symbolic projection of dying psychology, still Nelly's style is surprisingly tapped in rendering the interval of Cathy's death, the idiom of temporality broken open into the grace of a negative revelation, of release and appeasement in an escape not only from but back to. Following upon Heathcliff's forced visit and the delivery of Cathy's child, two hours later "the mother died, having never recovered sufficient consciousness to miss Heathcliff or know Edgar." A circumscribed temporal sequence of a few hours' delirium seems under discussion, when in fact the prose hints at a recouping if never recuperative delusion that carries Cathy back to an unfettered passion before, by her own cowardice in part, she had been made to "miss" Heathcliff in her life, or to "know" Edgar's misbegotten place in it. Ordinary idiom has been opened by death's stylistic pressure to what we can only call a visionary amnesia, a lapse into reparation.

Having reported this once in her later narrative to Lockwood, Nelly goes on to recount the words in which she had originally narrated the death scene to Heathcliff at his insistence. Cathy's death needs shaping for Heathcliff as narrative, as that "true history" (ch. 16) he demands of Nelly: story for him now of all truth, closure of all history. The flight from time only implicit in the idiomatic phrasing of Nelly's passing report to Lockwood is literalized in the narrative to Heathcliff when Nelly says of the dying Cathy that "her latest ideas wandered back to pleasant early days," a direct account inflected by the simile "like a child." Mediated by representation as death must always be, if not always through such self-conscious delimiting within an inner narrative, mitigated in particular by the indirection of simile, and set off within a first-person report by a narrator who has served as nurse to both the dead woman and the male auditor, Nelly's "like a child reviving, and sinking again to sleep" would be echoed shortly afterward in *David Copperfield* by Peggotty's secondary "narration" to David of the death of his mother, "like a child that had gone to sleep" (ch. 9). Heathcliff, however, rejects this version of epitome in Cathy's case, since for him the very idea of her death and removal is a dissimulation; for the apotheosis of innocence he substitutes a reading of the "true history" as illustrating the principle of negative epitome: "Why, she's a liar to the end!" (ch. 16).

Nevertheless, if at some level Cathy *is* Heathcliff, returning in death to their time together, that death must have its commensurate trauma for the man who says of it, in a tautology that turns out, inside out, to be a reciprocal reification of Cathy as himself: "I cannot live without my life" (ch. 16). Her death is his own end not in turn so much as by definition: the logical outcome of their mutually annihilative definitions of each other. Like Cathy before him he starves himself, and like her at the open window of her bedroom exposes himself to cold and damp, all to feed a soul hungry for an elemental passion to which even the grave is no barrier. It is Nelly who finally comes upon his corpse: "Mr. Heathcliff was there—laid on his back. His eyes met mine so keen, and fierce, I started; and then, he seemed to smile" (ch. 34). The transitive sequence of the syntax in the second sentence, begun with "met," turns on a "then" that denotes the order of Nelly's perceptions, of course, but has the unavoidable effect, since we ourselves are not yet sure that Heathcliff is dead, of re-personifying the corpse in this truant interval. He seems a creature not fixed in but suddenly flashing a dark smile. It is an epitomizing grimace that posthumously defies us to guess whether his is a triumph over or merely in death. Style beguiles us with, even as it leaves in question, its own gothic conjectures.

Encasing in pallid words the most extravagant and violent double death in Victorian fiction is a wrong reading of this death by the very agent of its transmission, the outer narrator, Lockwood, a reading that is also a travesty of stylistic appreciation when confronted with the reported scene of death. Lockwood chooses to grant that Nelly "is, on the whole, a very fair narrator and I don't think I could improve her style" (ch. 15). He listens to this "style" at such a diffident distance from the recounted events that he might as well be reading a gothic novel. Even at his finicky remove from the tragic passion of the main plot, still Lockwood, ludicrously, fears infatuation with Cathy's daughter, yet speaks of her as if she were not only inside a romance but in herself a mere text rather than a fleshly creature: "I should be in a curious taking if I surrendered my heart to that young person, and the daughter turned out a second edition of the mother!" (ch. 14). The test of his involvement with Nelly's narrative, his negative touchstone for our own reading, comes with his coolness to the novel's most pathetic event, the central death of Cathy. He makes it over into a displacement of his own ailing crisis that stands as an emasculation of all fictional identification. Her death in early spring, as retold by Nelly, coincides with the remission of his own winter's illness in the present narrative, Lockwood liking to think that the former tragedy will be transvalued into his recovery: "I'll extract wholesome medicines from Mrs. Dean's bitter herbs" (ch. 14). Undercutting such powerful structures of displacement and identification as those that conjured the narrator's own death by proxy from Peggotty's inset narrative in *David Copperfield*, Lockwood makes us think again about the cathartic possibilities of narrative dying and of what one can too facilely expect to be "afresh taught by death" in fiction.

Before turning by contrast to perhaps the most extended such lesson in Victorian fiction, the joint death of the two siblings in *The Mill on the Floss*—where again, though less sarcastically, the reader's relation to cathartic revelation is dramatized from within the climactic plot—we must proceed briefly round that middle novel by Eliot to her later masterpiece, *Middlemarch*. We find there a fatal diptych meant to indict the moribund solipsism of the two victims, Featherstone and then Casaubon, in their petrifying distance from community and its voiced appeals to feeling. After the miser Featherstone's death as preparation, Eliot intrudes the fact of imminent death upon Casaubon in a Thackerayan passage of memento mori given the sting of the singular: "When the commonplace 'We must all die' transforms itself suddenly into the acute consciousness 'I must die—and soon,' then death grapples us, and his fingers are cruel" (ch. 42). The quotation of received opinion must first be thrust into first-person present tense, plural and then singular. The abstraction of death is also ominously personified by Eliot's style, at precisely this urgent turn in the conjugation of its grammar, so that the idea of dying is humanized to our corporeal ears. Note, however, that Eliot's editorial rhetoric still concludes with "grapples us," not "me." It is precisely because death is wrestled with never closer than at arm's length in narrative, displaced always to the clarity of aesthetic distance, that the story of Casaubon can have the power for us not of dull commonplace but of universal pertinence.

Not only does the etiology of Casaubon's ailment, a "degeneration of the heart," epitomize his spiritual debility, but a further perverse entelechy would preserve his "lifelong bias" even "to the other side of death" for its posthumous exercise of will, legal and otherwise, in the "dead hand" of the novel's next book. Eliot's dialogue is deliberately not inoculated against her character's deadness of heart; she has him insist on being "set to rest" on the promise of celibate dedication to his work that he is trying to wheedle from his wife. Casaubon is shortly denied a death scene for its undue momentousness, found instead only a little more rigid and impotent than usual. "Set" quite at "rest" at last, he is discovered leaning stiffly against a "stone table" that seems to symbolize what he has been unable to secure as the inflexible tablet of his law and perpetuity. Against the heroine's submissive approach to this corpse as poised authoritarian "figure" and would-be author of her future, the preceding death of Featherstone stands as complement. When Mary Garth slowly draws near the bed of the old misanthrope, after her refusal the night before to tamper with his will, she comes timidly with "inaudible steps" (ch. 33). No sooner do we discover him, as she does, a corpse, than the clinical precision of that adjective "inaudible" takes on a freezing irony, transferred from a presumed hyperbole for her gentle tread to the mortal fact of his condition. A parallel emphasis on the silence unto death at the discovered end of Casaubon gives over what might otherwise be a softening periphrasis to the grips of a bitter epitome. Dorothea calls to her husband to announce an acquiescence only his pending death could have wrung from her, but "the silence in her husband's ears was never more to be broken" (ch. 48). Emotionally deaf, fanatical, unflinching, Casaubon comes familiar to his end, a fitness already schematized in comparable terms for Featherstone's death. An internalized reification of absence as presence, the idiomatic "silence in" is a far cry from the euphemism it mordantly courts. The phrasing asserts a transition to absolute obliviousness that is only moral insentience intensified to finality.

□   □   □

The mortal doubling of Featherstone and Casaubon educes the force of analogy from the weight of sequence and association. In *The Mill on the Floss*, Eliot renders the deaths of Tom and Maggie Tulliver not only successive in the text but simultaneous in order to turn the one death into a metaphor for the other—displacement as overlay—and thus to explore the mutual recognition that at the same time both deals out and half heals this tragedy. More than portraying such a mortal convergence, style is also assigned to disclose the way in which the heroine's whole life has been a long delaying of the death moment, existence not only leading up to but led too much in the shape of a dark drowning, airless, desperately thrashing, obsessively retrospective, murky, expessionless, and blind. In this infamous Victorian death scene, unmatched in verbal flourish and nuance outside of Dickens, figurative drowning passes to fact in the symbolism of epitome. With more irony than is usually credited to Eliot's ending, her heroine seems liquidated in the quintessence of her own headlong being, pulled down by frustrated instincts to suffocation and effacement.

To charge this spectacle with cogency, to pursue it virtually to the ends of allegory, requires all of George Eliot's stylistic equipment. The exchange between death by water and its metaphoric equivalent in spiritual review is not new to Eliot. In her first novel, *Adam Bede* (1859), the discovered "watery death" of the hero's father is figuratively displaced onto the son in an inundation of empathy, fatality canalized into memory and amelioration as "Adam's mind rushed back over the past in a flood of relenting and pity" (ch. 4). Eliot also mastered the steely miniaturized precision of an ironically cadenced dying for the end of Mr. Tulliver earlier in *The Mill on the Floss*, but that would not suit her purposes at the climactic death of the daughter. His is the pointless attenuation of life into death, his last words trailing off into the leveling simulation of a phonic mutter smudged out in conjunction with dimming sight: "Soon they merged into mere mutterings; the eyes had ceased to discern; and then came the fatal silence" (V, ch. 7). Insentience carried in the alliterative drift of the narrator's own syllables traverses by blurring the very mortal interval that must be widened to ironic revelation at the death of Maggie. It is there that such a model of linked syllables expands to a concerted structure of syntactic and rhetorical parallelism bearing down upon the moment of death. The destined breaking of this continuity marks not just a baffled lapse to cessation but a violent if inevitable disjuncture between life and the very death prefigured in it as something torrential and ventless in the self's denied potential.

Like so many other Victorian writers, Eliot anticipates the event of death by its vocabulary, the moment by metaphor. Overseeing her father's bitter decline, severed from the affection of her callous brother, Tom, the heroine laments her lot in the language of denial as annihilation: "It is like death. I must part with everything I cared for when I was a child" (V, ch. 1). The Romantic simile of maturation as the funeral of one's former self seems taken up too literally by a mind given over to the equation of life with the dispersed myths of childhood. Death still serves as vehicle to the heroine's tenor of loss as we near the flood scene. When, in a final interview with Lucy, Maggie sacrifices her passion for Stephen by asking Lucy to forgive him, the words are "wrung forth from Maggie's soul, with an effort like the convulsed clutch of a drowning man" (VII, ch. 4). Eliot tries by such means to make the flood arrive as a psychic inevitability. In a preparation of the epitomizing moment all but unprecedented in Victorian fiction, the tidal imagery preceding the storm waters suggests that the heroine is both victim and fountainhead of her own defeat, swept forward by the impulsive rush of her deepest nature. Once she is seduced by Stephen into an irresponsible rowing excursion, the indifferent tide toys with her as an objective correlative for the listless but insistent drift of her own desire, her emotions "borne along by a wave too strong for her" (VI, ch. 7). She wishes that she "need no longer beat and struggle against this current, soft and yet strong as the summer stream!" (VI, ch. 11). Though Eliot explicitly introduces the threat of drowning as if it were a danger lurking within some destructive "submergence of our personality by another" (VI, ch. 13), it is clear that the true threat is a swamping of moral purpose by the heroine's inner turmoil.

We have learned earlier that Maggie's life presents itself to her "like the course of an unmapped river: we only know that the river is full and rapid, and that for all rivers there is the same final home" (VI, ch. 6). When the potentially instructive width of simile is clamped shut to equivalence, Maggie is ready for that long home whose earthly type has been closed to her by perversity and neglect. If the tide that overtakes her is meant to evoke the "awful Eagre" which, when she was a child, "used to come up like a hungry monster" and put her in mind of that symbolic mortal border in *Pilgrim's Progress*, "the river over which there is no bridge" (I, ch. 5), then this premonition would befit the awful eagerness of a life that could only surrender to the element of its own dammed hopes. We do not hear the name of the tide that rises for the final flood, but in the opening paragraph of the death chapter we are told how its first effect, upriver, is seen in the fact that the "harvest had been arrested." Downriver, too; for by the fruitless confusion of her life the heroine is halted, deluged, and engulfed. Style inscribes this in an interval over which there is no bridge, except for the projected gestures of rhetoric meant to traverse as well as render the gap of human negation within a world that endures.

When, driven out on the waters, Maggie cries, "Oh God, where am I? Which is the way home?" the question compacts both senses of the noun "home" from that previous simile of the unmapped river. Primarily Maggie hopes she can reach her earthly home soon enough, and just long enough, to rescue what is left of her family. It is clear that she has in mind not safety and salvation but "some undefined sense of reconcilement" with her brother, the dream of leniency come true in the face of death. She does not fear to die, only "to perish too soon." Once she has come upon Tom, his "lips found a word they could utter: the old childish—'Magsie!' " The phrase "the old childish" was added in proof,[4] not only as a reminder to the reader of the long dormant nickname but as an index to the emotional reversion with which the whole scene is concerned. The fond naming also suggests something more. The provincial Dodson creed, by which in part Maggie has long been victimized, holds as a central tenet in its system of belief that baptism is required solely in order to be properly buried (IV, ch. 1). At last in the reunion with Tom, despite this narrowness of familial belief and the other impediments to their love, and if only in watery death, Maggie is indeed baptized in the recovered name of affection.

No sooner are the siblings reunited than Tom sees "death rushing on them" in the shape of giant "fragments, clinging together in fatal fellowship" and racing toward them with the tide. By a massively objectified transference, the fragmented relationship of brother and sister is repaired only to meet its nemesis in a clinging fatality which mirrors their bond in the outer world. "It is coming, Maggie," says Tom with his last words. He uses his sister's adult nickname this time, not her "childish" one, but it is too late to rebuild a present relationship out of his "clasping her" to him, for "brother and sister had gone down in an embrace never to be parted: living through again in one supreme moment the days when they had clasped their little hands in love and roamed the daisied fields together" (VII, ch. 5). This is the critical sticking point, and U. C. Knoepflmacher puts well the widespread objections to this "antediluvian idyll." For him and many others, "George Eliot's reliance on the flood as a deus ex machina remains a mechanical device to bring about a harmony that brother and sister never experienced while alive . . . George Eliot's ending is at best pathetic, for it asks us to believe that the muddy waters of the Floss have briefly restored an Eden that never existed."[5] Yes, there is something about "little hands" and "daisied fields" that gives pause, but surely is meant to. The epitomizing impulse suggested by "supreme moment"—that phrase for death's clarity that

Conrad would use twice later, for instance, in *Heart of Darkness*—
has a dark underside in this context, for the narrator cannot expect
us to have forgotten how few were the days of idle pleasure and
fellowship, how easy it might be to relive them in an instant. And if
this instant is life's "supréme moment," what kind of a life has it
been? It is precisely the denial of sufficient affection to Maggie, both
as child and as adult, and especially by her brother Tom, that has
lamed her dreams and thrown her back on this virtually incestuous
fixation. The life unled rushes back in crisis to the point when its
vitalities were first blighted, as in the death scene of Cathy in *Wuthering Heights*, her mind wandering "back to pleasant early days" with
her lost "brother" Heathcliff.

It is not just that Maggie has returned in drowning to that one
coveted span of early happiness, but indeed that she has worked
back to her very first memory, canceling all that has intervened,
remaking the birth of consciousness into a single blissful swoon to
death. Recalling that she has said, "The first thing I ever remember
in my life is standing with Tom by the side of the Floss while he held
my hand; everything before that is dark to me" (V, 1), we understand
better the darkening ironic circularity of Maggie's life line. And it is
part of this irony that the adjective "supreme" in the seemingly
triumphant phrase "supreme moment" had a current usage for merely
"last" (see this chapter's epigraph from Eliot's own *Scenes*, "Janet's
Repentance," ch. 12), as if only by ending her travail could Maggie's
life achieve its sought peace. The "dark and unfrequented chambers
of memory" which are suddenly entered upon and illuminated by the
drowning mind, according to that passage from the *Scenes*, have
narrowed to the flooded chambers of the womb as tomb. For what
exactly is comprised by the title of the last book, "The Final Rescue"?
Transposed from the literal fact of Maggie's briefly successful gathering up of Tom into her frail boat, the title becomes a metaphor for
death as a lethal retreat into—and so retrieval of—the past, a brief
salvaging that is only in this sense a salvation, not divine relief but
only an emotional and momentary reclamation. An earlier dream of
drowning and rescue has presaged this irony. At the start of a chapter
with the jointly literal and ethical title "Waking," Maggie rouses
herself from moral torpor and refuses elopement with Stephen. Reaching out in the last stages of her sleep of judgment toward a dream

vision of Tom in a passing boat, she topples from her own vessel and begins to sink, "till with one spasm of dread she seemed to awake and find she was a child again in the parlour at evening twilight, and Tom was not really angry" (VI, ch. 14). Even as it prefigures the reversionary beatitude of the real drowning, this rescue of and by the past is merely a seeming, from which the subsequent "real waking" is "to the plash of water against the vessel." (VI, ch. 14). Here is the demystifying intrusion we are spared by the narrator at the actual death scene, when Maggie's consciousness is closed to us while still in the throes of mortal nostalgia.

Nevertheless, compacted syntactic details, in a rhetoric of ambivalent intervals, erode the resonance of death's "Final Rescue" as if from within the fluent medium of its own assertion. When we find brother and sister "living through again in one supreme moment" what is at least Maggie's private Edenic dream of their effortless affection, free, timeless, world excluding, we have more verbal encouragement even than "supreme" (in its less honorific sense as "last") for seeing the death scene as both a first and a last such moment of idyllic bonding. The preposition "through" is tied closely to the participle "living" as part of an idiom having less to do with direction than compression; it suggests an action more likely to be coterminous with the "moment" that permits and delimits it than to forge any surviving penetration beyond it. In a comparable way, when Tom and Maggie have "gone down in an embrace never to be parted," we may well wonder whether it is the physical clutch or the reestablished union, in a Christian understanding of its immortality, which is never to be severed. After the flood subsides, as with Lawrence's drowned pair in *Women in Love*, "two bodies were found in close embrace" and buried together, an insentient coupling which is all we have confirmed by narrative. This is the one and only sense in which the titular "Rescue" pertains for Maggie: release without rehabilitation, safety cut free from the claims of time. For all its providential convenience, Eliot's flood offers neither simple pathos nor facile uplift. More powerfully perhaps than in any other Victorian novel, though more riskily because the tragic irony circumscribes the sentiment with so fine a stylistic line that it can seem invisible, George Eliot has drawn for us the reversionary desires that *are* death.

But so far this is Maggie's flood, for her and finally of her, fulfillment of her turbid and curbless passion for a life beyond self-denial. So how is it that Tom can justly go down with her? He is not asked for his life by the plot solely to render punishment or to represent the recovery of something long sundered within Maggie's desire. In what flood then, what element true to his own mentality, is he swallowed up? It is only through a subtle blend of the prevalent water imagery, much of it scarcely surfaced above the implicit, that this double death scene can chart its linked purport. Stiff, pinched denizen of life's emotional shallows, Tom is launched at last upon those profundities he has never before tried to plumb, overcome by their tidal sway as they "rushed upon his mind." Moments later he is taken down by this thunderous burden, but for a split second of ecstatic illumination he endures "a new revelation to his spirit, of the depths in life"— the unfathomed reaches of his own filial identity and of that life which, knowing himself better, he could have helped make with Maggie, helped her to make for herself. Not unlike the remedial bliss of Maggie's epitomizing last moments of consciousness, Tom's drowning takes place in the depths of his own long stagnant nature. In the brief prelude to this submergence he comes upon what Maggie, in a more prolonged interval of revelation, has striven toward and at last achieved; swept out upon the flood, she "felt nothing, thought of nothing, but she had suddenly passed away from that life which she had been dreading: it was the transition of death, without its agony" (VII, ch. 5). The idiom "passed away" is sustained this side of the Victorian euphemism for death just long enough for a visionary broaching of the untraversable. Under pressure of repetition, that "nothing" she first conceives, then feels, inches its way toward voiding noun within the still transitive grammar of living subject and suspended object. The "transition"of such a nearly traversed interval is an encroachment upon the very abyss whose contemplation, by the staying power of "nothing" in its pronominal sense, is held briefly in abeyance, its terrors allayed.

In her reunion with Tom shortly following, Maggie lets this abyss be filled with the retrograde grace of her recovered nickname "Magsie." Style immediately spells out this ambivalent blessing in a homophonic pun heard with a clear ring on the underside of idiom. "Maggie could make no answer but a long deep sob of that mysterious wondrous happiness that is one with pain" (III, ch. 5). Instead of writing "at one with," Eliot phrases this spiritual equivalence so that the phonetic torsion from the second set of double epithets, especially the first syllable of "wondrous," turns the idiom of fusion ("one with") toward the achieved participle of a lethal victory, the triumph "won" only with the reavowed oneness of brother and sister. From the quiet glory of this pun is sprung the book's closing consolation, a vacillation of phrase stirring the whole denouement into seeing double. What begins as a paralleled rhetoric of emphatic and fateful repetition will soon extend across the abridged moment of death to become a litany of continuance in the epilogue, style itself enacting the traversed interval of renewal. Just before, an insistent repetition asserts itself against the strain of inversion: "The wide area of watery desolation was spread out in dreadful clearness around them—in dreadful clearness floated onwards the hurrying, threatening tide." That chiastic, focal pressure on the trapped protagonists, a syntactic cornering at the turn of the sentence, seems at the same time caught up in the clausal momentum of threat as well as its precarious locus. The prose runs now, in impelled repetition, with the inexorable swell of that tide by which the boat is soon engulfed. No sooner has the "keel of the boat reappeared" than sheer repetition gives way to the grammar of qualification: "The boat reappeared—but brother and sister had gone down." The recuperative impulse is here inanimate and mechanical only.

The blankly incantatory rhythm of this death scene, first diverted by chiastic inversion, then broken against the fatal disjunctive "but," now seems to score the iterative grooves along which the immediately following epilogue continues to move. It is a rhetorical displacement of this death upon the incremental grammar of endurance. "Nature repairs her ravages—repairs them with sunshine . . . Nature repairs her ravages, but not all." Across successive paragraphs, the restitutive beat of the world's perpetuity, measured and resolute, maintains an uneasy accord between reparation and lament that is not rhetorically indulgent so much as dramatically mutable, cumulative. Disconsolate monotony is taken up within the alliterative momentum of archetypal return as well as mechanical restoration—wooden vessel buoyed by the deluge, then drenched landscape refreshed by time in the eye of the world's warmth. The mysteries of recuperation, seasonal and even spiritual, dictate the rhythm of slow advance within flux that characterizes Eliot's closural refrain, pulled upon still by brutal truth of loss.

This whole orchestrated set piece collects, reexamines, and inter-
laces the threefold functions of the death scene we have been considering, with a clarity only the truer for Eliot's original adjustments
of the pattern. The logic of metaphoric transposition crystalized as
epitome which the flood as symbol annotates so strenuously (Maggie's
hopes sinking in her own turmoil) also requires for its emotional logic
a doubling or repetition that can be understood as a telescoping of
displacement for the reunited siblings, an overlapping of epiphanies.
Reclasping what only the other can complete in each, what is half
dead without conjunction, Tom and Maggie collapse the ordinarily
temporal distance between death and spiritual participation by another. Following upon this mutual simultaneity of death and illumination for brother and sister, the mode of displacement then makes
its more predictable division between victim and survivor, between
Maggie and the two men who have taken the definition of their desire
from her. The living intensities of her two suitors, Philip and Stephen,
are reified even as interred, capable of disembodiment only because
dead; the men's "keenest joy and keenest sorrow" were "forever
buried" in Maggie's grave. This familiar elegiac trope, dying as the
burial of another's dreams, throws into relief the more startling variant
on the pattern of mortal alter egos portrayed in the double death of
Maggie and Tom. Theirs has been the winning to reciprocal revelation
rather than the twinning into displacement of lament and identification.

For the culminating formal irony of drowning in *The Mill on the
Floss* it is not enough that Maggie succumbs to the retrospective
compulsion of an entire life, swallowed with Tom in the very stream
of time to which otherwise, and because of him, she resists submitting.
The drowning is followed by another burial of brother and sister, this
time in earth, and by a chiseled record on their tombstone which also
happens to be the book's initiating biblical quotation and inscribed
epigraph, "In their death they were not divided." Eliot elects this
return of text upon opening text to stress in part the singular noun
phrase "their death," one shared dying entered upon together, even
as it is the "divided" nature of each of them separately that death
rectifies. At the same time, that widespread ambiguity "in death" is
meant to chasten its own lurch toward eternity with the alternate
designation as a mere last moment, supreme only in the closural
sense. There is an interval traversed, but no eventuality.

We are now at the point of apprehending once again the deepest appeal of drowning, whether as scene or conceit, to the structural imagination of a novelist. Dickens introduced into *A Tale of Two Cities* the rhetoric of bloody inundation and apocalyptic flood, and kept pressing the metaphor toward the moment of death, in part so that he could open that moment to a visionary review, not only of past but of future, as if the fiction were itself submerged in the medium of its own translucency and temporal flow. Similarly, George Eliot gives us a retrospective death scene, undercut by a distrust of the very idyllic memory it would reanimate, so as to circle the heroine's identity round to its earlier desire and destitution. Scored on her tombstone along with the presumed dates of the two doomed life lines, the irony of epigraph turned epitaph—of inauguration as augury—enciphers the formal circularity answered to within plot by the familiar symbolism of drowning. Narrative destines its own ends as exempla, while life must somehow struggle to flee precisely that escape which is simply repetition and return, the consolatory promise of mere symmetry. Death marks, and names, this living effort come to grief, a grief, however, that only art can soften with the clarifying force of form itself. What Maggie Tulliver has offered herself to, and offered up to narrative history, is a definitive instance of the whole motive for the fictional death scene. She has made dying readable. Eliot's heroine, like her author for her, has negotiated that "transition of death, without its agony," that still interpretable ordeal, which is the very business of dying in a fictional text. Jude the Obscure, although with his own textual prototype in mind, must submit instead to death's agony without a genuine transition. Earlier, Thackeray's *The New-comes* closes on so exclusively metanarrative a plane that its last mortal transit takes place entirely across textual conventions or levels of authorial identification. Together these three texts divide up the styles of Victorian dying which modernist fiction will then have to investigate and revise.

□   □   □

More than a quarter of a century after *The Mill on the Floss*, yet with a comparable circularity of biblical prototype and tragic enactment, Thomas Hardy tortures the Victorian novel into the terms of a new century while summing up the ironic vision of his entire career. The hero of *Jude the Obscure* (1895) reverts self-consciously to the biblical precedent of Job, reading his own life against a textual archetype of creative suffering that both torments and outmodes him. The haunting thought that his own life is prejudged by a tragic parable not of his own dictation, a plot belated, derivative, and irrelevant, leads him more bleakly than even Maggie Tulliver to read his days and acts as a closed book even before the end—and so in the disheartened process to precipitate that end. This thought that death, one's own or another's, is or could be readable on the surfaces of things unwritten haunts more characters than Jude in Hardy's verse as well as his fiction. A bereaved persona in one of the poems, writing of the last encounter with a soon-to-be-dead woman, says of her characteristic, indeed epitomizing good-bye, that "I read no finis in it / As at the closing of a book."[6] The chance that anyone might have done so in Hardy gives a peculiar inflection to the scenes of immersion, drowning, or its threat in the novels; by contrast to its central use in *A Tale of Two Cities* or *The Mill on the Floss*, for instance, much of Hardy's interest in the imagery of death by water has more to do with the legibility of mirrored surfaces than with the compressed vision of the sinking mind, with illusory text rather than hallucinatory retrospect.

In *The Return of the Native* (1878) the death of Eustacia Vye, followed shortly by that of her lover, Wildeve, is at first recognized by him when the drowning pool is seen as a reflecting glass: "Across this gashed and puckered mirror a dark body was slowly borne by one of the backward currents" (V, ch. 9). The flow is retrograde in part because it returns the heroine named Vye, too long vying with the primitive elements of her narrowed prospect on the heath, to the insentient turmoil of her origination, as if death itself were that native thing which always returns. Moreover, the ghastly description of the water's reflecting surface suggests by predictive irony that what the splashes of its gashed, creased rippling do in effect mirror is the frantic, perhaps lacerated, certainly water-shriveled destiny that awaits the bewildered Wildeve. Eustacia herself has earlier sought a hieroglyph of her own virtually suicidal fate, studying her grandfather's pistols "as if they were the page of a book in which she read a new and strange matter" (V, ch. 4). Her existence is a text she would like not just closed in the long run but eradicated, phrasing her desire to flee the heath as a need to "efface herself from" (V, ch. 7), not just escape, the oppressive landscape. The narrator then sustains the idea of life's text (the life "history") with his final grammatical analogy for the double death scene in the mirroring weir, a lethal hyphenation giving way to the ellipsis of eternity by "cutting off their erratic histories with a catastrophic dash" (VI, ch. 1).

Just before Eustacia's drowning, a gruesome surrogate in wax— Susan Nonesuch's voodoo replica of her—is destroyed in another elemental cleansing by fire rather than water, the "effigy of Eustacia . . . melting to nothing" (V, ch. 9). This figuration of fate by effigy is taken up, in more direct connection yet with the motif of drowning, for the scene in *The Mayor of Casterbridge* (1886) in which the title figure finds a stuffed replica of himself floating upon "the pool he was intending to make his death-bed" (ch. 41). Before Henchard is checked by this visual duplication of his own intent, he perceives "with a sense of horror that it was *himself.* Not a man somewhat resembling him, but one in all respects his counterpart, his actual double . . . floating as if dead." The very sense of being is under siege by this vision of effigy, for the reflexive "himself," ordinarily an emphatic assertion of identity, represents here its mere detritus, inert and removed from the cognizant "I." When the self lapses either to mere text or mirror image, the gap between subject and object has become fatal. Hardy's drowning scenes, direct or by proxy, exclude the moment of internalized retrospect and offer instead as an object of gaze not the life history in review but its last sodden, shrunken page. The mayor now turns away from his would-be watery "death-bed" to a fate equally willed but less self-determined. Dying off-stage, wandering in absentia from the Casterbridge of his mayoral title and his former esteem, Henchard seals his fate with a last scrawled wish for an unmourned and unmarked burial. This last willing strikes his daughter as a further explicit epitome, "a piece of the same stuff that his whole life was made of" (ch. 45), where the very metaphor is transposed from the mayor's stuffed effigy in the pool. It is also a precise illustration of a hero at odds with an authorial project, Henchard's desired effacement running afoul of Hardy's literary tactics for, in J. Hillis Miller's phrase, the "safeguarding of the dead."[7]

In much the same funereal state of aimless self-exile does Jude Fawley live out his days a decade later. Yet the legible effigy of his fate is incarnate in his own male issue rather than an inorganic replica, even while the child is connected again to those metaphors of inscription which, throughout this novel and others by Hardy, foreground the scene of mortal recognition from the text of the narrative as a whole. Tricked into a remarriage with Arabella Donn late in *Jude the Obscure*, a woman whose ironic last name debases the donnish glories on which he had once set his clerical sights at the Christminster colleges, Jude admits with a loaded analogy that "how I came to be here with her I know no more than a dead man" (VI, ch. 8). Anticipating the reductive biblical allusion that constitutes his last words, he also reaches back into his reading of the classics to pronounce by another analogy his own wretched elegy: "As Antigone said, I am neither a dweller among men nor ghosts." Yet even this draws him closer to those "spirits of the dead," haunting such colleges as Sarcophagus, with whom since childhood he has longed to commune. There has always been something in a different way deadly, because doomed to defeat, in his yearning for the scholarly life, as hinted when his attempted mastery of the dead languages gets him only as far as the "funeral games in the twenty-third book of the Iliad" (I, ch. 6). It is also at this time that Jude is deciphering "the Latin inscriptions on fifteenth-century brasses and tombs" (I, ch. 5). Had he known what was coming, he might have read upon these mortuary surfaces the epitaph of his higher ambitions; instead, he wears himself out in frustrated attempts to achieve his dream. Even on his first visit to Christminster years before his death there, his isolation from the community of his aspiration is so withering that he feels like a "self-specter . . . almost his own ghost" (II, ch. 1). In the process his other, surer life as a skilled craftsman is progressively demoted until, after getting as close to the clerical sphere as he could by becoming a "cathedral mason," he ends up where Trollope's Sir Roger Scatcherd in *Doctor Thorne* (1858) begins: as a headstone engraver (V, ch. 1). While Trollope's irony, however, returns his character to the point of origin in an epitaphic monument whose "graphic diction" (ch. 30) pictures the man quite literally carving out his own doom, the "diction" of Jude's predicted fate (Hardy uses just this linguistic metaphor) comes chiseled in the gaunt features, the wrinkled and puckered mirror, of his living son.

With Jude already wishing by the close of the fourth chapter that he himself "had never been born," willing himself "out of the world" that holds no promise for him, his son's truncated and futile life line is staged as an allegory of his father's fate. When, long after Jude and Sue have had time to acquaint themselves with the child's bizarre fatalistic character, he is nevertheless renamed Little Jude, the point is clear. More than one critic has found his introduction into the novel an excrescence, a "redundancy,"[8] but this is Hardy's very point. By seeming an unwanted blight and burden, both as child and as a fictional invention, by doing nothing for the book but grafting on another version of the hero's own ennui and blasted hopes, the child takes it upon himself to rid the world of his own presence, just as his father later flees to his own self-determined nescience. The point is not that Jude's story is complete in itself, Little Jude's an unnecessary turn of the screw of futility; both the father and his namesake are equally redundant, excluded from any genuine development.

When Little Jude, removed from the hook upon which he has hung himself, is laid in state, his face expresses "the whole tale of their situation. On that little shape had converged all the inauspiciousness and shadow which had darkened the first union of Jude, and all the accidents, mistakes, fears, errors of the last" (VI, ch. 2). As probable issue of the first union, macabre charge and bond of the second, the dead child also stands by proxy for the common factor of the two marriages—Jude himself. This corpse is "their nodal point, their focus, their expression in a single term." Little Jude's whole existence, dead in his very origination, a repetition of a redundancy, has been less a life than a cryptic danger signal all along, a twice-told "tale" derivative and duplicatory of his father's sad story. His identity is a brief narrative whose veil of superficial event is peeled away to reveal meaning only at the moment of death, and then less as a character in the psychological than the textual sense, an expressive graphic "shape." Staring into the face of his living effigy, Jude could well have "read . . . finis in it" if he had been steeled to such an act of interpretation, for Jude the younger is a veritable reissue of his father in a "single term." True to the Victorian style of dying, once life is translated to text it is open to doubleness, even if that doubleness is only redundancy. The whole fatality of the defeated father is there in the choked-tight interval between the play on "terminus" and the word "term" for mere "word," as if every life history, closed in upon a single verbal rather than facial "expression," has thereby come to closure as a temporal event.

There is a further compressed expressiveness in Jude's story, erupting on his deathbed, that renders his own life as well as his son's even more openly, because again textually, derivative. This is the story of Job that seems to conflate both father and son in the nodal and annihilating shape of the single term "man child." Wasted by the symbolic debility of a consumption deliberately induced by exposure to the elements (shades of Cathy and Heathcliff, but without the Romantic sense of a surrender to nature), Hardy's hero gasps out his last painfully taken breaths with words not even his own. Jude thereby dies away into the first person of Job's displacing, scarcely consolatory prototype. In sarcastic counterpoint to his whispered tubercular collapse is the college graduation loudly celebrated just outside the chamber of his death, an irony borne in upon him by the roar of the crowd with a last spasm of recognition. "Ah—yes! The Remembrance games," he murmurs to himself, remembering all too well the world from which he has been excluded. "And I here" (VI, ch. 11). These three words are the last he says of himself; an elliptical positioning of identity without its predication, indeed without a name properly his own, they summon only a pronoun which is about to be absorbed into sheer biblical precedent. As if eerily inspired by the disjunction between the feeble wheezing of his own voice and the "hurrahs" of the crowd, Jude now goes out of this world—that last transition which is the only graduation he is ever to achieve—by fulfilling his preacherly vocation in a long quotation from his favorite biblical text, falling, of course, on deaf ears. With Job as Old Testament forerunner or type to his virtual crucifixion, Jude concludes by asking, "Why died I not from the womb?"

Before Jude has even met his putative issue, the son named Father Time, he has mused upon the agonies of Job: " 'Let the day perish wherein I was born, and the night in which it was said, There is a man child conceived.' That's what the boy—*my* boy, perhaps, will find himself saying before long!" (V, ch. 3). To clinch the peculiar fitness of the biblical idiom "man child" for this old-young creature, the guard on the coach journey immediately following Jude's prophetic lamentation calls the boy lightheartedly, as in a conversational irony out of Paul Dombey's story, "my man." Jude's exact lines from Job are then reprised much later at the beginning of his unattended dying sermon, followed repeatedly by the crowd's irrelevant parenthetical "Hurrah!" The postmortem interval between a private dying and the world's restorative continuance, as in *The Mill on the Floss*, for instance, is forced closed here to a contrapuntal dissonance. In the throes of these ghostly exhortations, Jude "delivers" himself at last in the combined form of reflexive funeral oration and valedictory address. For the never-matriculated hero, this Remembrance Day observance becomes both memorial ceremony and ironic commencement.

We get no actual moment of death for Jude, as if his "And I here" had summed up and surrendered his life in the very lapse from predicative status. There is only that whole appalling apotheosis of the hero as self-exorcising orator, and then a stark break in the text at the subsidence of voice. Arabella has seen that Jude is dying, leaves for the festivities, returns briefly to find his breathing inconveniently over—"the bumping of near thirty years had ceased"—but soon rejoins the celebration as if nothing has happened to the man, as in spiritual fact it hasn't. Only his animal functions, including the perpetual thumping in his chest as itself a humiliating masochistic assault called a "bumping"—only these have ceased; the rest had gone already, the hero so long disheartened as to leave no room for coronary diagnosis at the end. "By ten o'clock that night Jude was lying on the bedstead at his lodging covered with a sheet, and straight as an arrow" (V, ch. 3). The ghostly wanderer among men is now robed as one, and that ironically honed "arrow," which might have pointed straight through tragedy into spiritual hope in an earlier Victorian death scene, pierces only deeper into the unrelieved gloom of the scene. In Hardy death has no otherworldly direction. This swathed sarcophagal image of the rigidified hero may well be meant to recall an early inscription on a rock chiseled by Jude in his apprentice days as a stone carver, with its own arrowlike anatomical pointer toward the unreachable glories of Christminster (I, ch. 11):

THITHER

J. F.

It is carved on a milestone, but it might as well be Jude's epitaph on a tombstone, as with Trollope's Sir Roger, an encapsulating hieroglyph (without trace of heavenly destination) for a young man who knew early that his finest desires were always to be fatally caught up with a countering wish to be out of this world. Indeed, taken as Jude's mark, this insignia not only scores his doomed aspiration as student but etches his self-evacuation as hero, the man himself as if abbreviated by an anatomical index pointing elsewhere, displaced from identity by intent, inscribed by the very vector of his lack.

Following Jude's funereal peroration, his silence, and the stiffening aftermath, it is the choric mordancy of Arabella's voice, in alluding to Sue Bridehead, that sounds a verbal keynote of the whole narrative: "She's never found peace since she left his arms, and never will again till she's as he is now!" (VI, ch. 11). At least Arabella knew Jude well enough to understand that peace was just what he was seeking in death. Moreover, her last circumlocution for the extreme repose of his soul is a circular copula that ties off a pervasive motif of predication in the novel. Turns of this sort on the verb of being help elucidate the relation of identity to the many kinds of death in Hardy that deflect, stall, or cancel it. The grammar of being in such a case—since what Jude "is" is *not*—has an odd odor of the inappropriate, but Arabella is a past master of its libertine use, especially in self-serving tautologies. Pretending to a religious conversion at one point, she tells Jude, "I make no boast of my awakening, but I'm not what I was" (V, ch. 7), being willing to admit or specify neither what she had been nor what better thing she might have become. In any case, by the next chapter another colloquial tautology has led her back past hypocrisy to her primal instincts: "Feelings are feelings! . . . I must be as I was born!" Even a minor character such as Tinker Taylor is apt to preen himself with a formulaic "I shouldn't have been the man I am" (II, ch. 7). These recurrent copulas take on more thematic weight when Sue insists on her virginity in a related kind of grammar by saying, "I have never yielded myself to any lover, if that's what you mean! I have remained as I began" (III, ch. 4), where the sense of stale changelessness overlies the euphemistic periphrasis. Similarly questionable in its implied valuation of stasis is Jude's sexual jealousy when Sue marries Phillotson, for to him "Sue was not as she had been" (III, ch. 9).

The other side of the coin from this sexual reticence of indirect discourse is seen when Arabella tries to refer to her remarriage with

Jude and the phrase sticks in her throat: "Don't ask inconvenient questions, father. What we've to do is to keep him here till he and I are—as we were" (VI, ch. 7). Knowing what we know of her effect on Jude, this phrasing suggests a psychological as well as a sexual reversion that may recall one of the most pointed of these circular copulas, when Arabella meets Jude again after their long separation. She has thought him dead, "underground years ago," or "gone to glory" as she next euphemistically puts it, but their exchange shortly translates the notion of immortal ascendancy into secular terms: "Then you are not a Don yet? . . . Not even a Reverend?" No such glory for Jude, who might as well be dead and "gone," never having lived the life he strived for. And so he answers with a deterministic circularity, "I am as I was" (III, ch. 8). It is by such phrases that Hardy's novel anticipates the profoundly ranging ambiguities in the grammar of being that help define the consciousness of death in modern fiction.

What Hardy concentrates on as the end-stopped I-am-as-I-wasness of identity in derailed desire, D. H. Lawrence takes up, explicitly in his study of Hardy and implicitly in his own fiction, as a malfunction in the channels of proper becoming. Between Hardy and Lawrence, Conrad reinterprets the vital presence of identity to itself as an alternating current of ego and otherness brought into focus by the self's removal in death. His studies in the character of being and the being of character are followed by E. M. Forster's death-framed "I am I," where the mysteries of human presence are glimpsed by a vigilant epistemological intuition about the reality of the unseen in and beyond the individual mind. Further delving into the self, Woolf's modernist grammar of being is a subterranean tunneling into the fluidity not just of discrete identity but of an undulating consciousness streaming between characters in the medium of inner speech. Postmodernism then pursues such investigation to the very roots of identity with harder questions yet about the relation of language to presence. It is only to be expected that issues of selfhood elucidated through all these experiments in characterization should be addressed also, and crucially, by the termination of character in death—whether the impetus to becoming is blocked by the fatal paralysis of identity in characters as different as Eustacia, Henchard, and Jude; the ego grieved and frustrated to death by the world's refusal to meet its dream in Conrad; reality contaminated by inauthentic being in Forster until it dies away from the self, the self from it; identity slain by sexual imprisonment in Lawrence, or risen to an erotic transformation of state that makes way for the self's resurrection while still in the world; identity let lapse from synchronization with the flux of time in Woolf; self made to recognize in Beckett that whatever affirmation life can make available to it must be snatched from the nightmare of an existence coextensive with slow decay; or finally the expressive "I" in Nabokov whiling away its mortal hours in willed fantasies shored against effacement.

□   □   □

In our transition from Hardy into modernism we cannot leave behind the Victorian experiments in deathbed rhetoric—the post-Romantic novel's style of traversed intervals and ambiguous transitions—without considering an uncharacteristic and clairvoyant invention on Thackeray's part which anticipates much to come in the triangulation of textuality, death, and the grammar of presence. With the demise of the old colonel, the rhetoric of dramatized transit from life to death, of transposition and epitome, so often denied to Thackeray's characters by the leveling ironies of his secular ethic, makes an unexpected appearance at the end of *The Newcomes* (1854–1855). Just before the colonel's death, the narrator, Arthur Pendennis, in recording the death of Clive Newcome's wife and their newborn child, merely transcribes the previous record of these deaths from the daily press: "Among the announcements of Births was printed, 'On the 28th, in Howland Street, Mrs. Clive Newcome of a son still-born.' And a little lower, in the third division of the same column, appeared the words, 'On the 29th, in Howland Street, aged 26, Rosalind, wife of Clive Newcome, Esq.' " The euphemistic suppression of the rubric "Death" for this third section of what is sometimes called the "Transitions" column helps prepare for the reimaging of fatality as youthful reversion in the on-stage death of Colonel Newcome, which Rosey's fate in some measure precipitates. At the same time the narrator's second-hand consignment of life to text, even within his own text— "So, one day, shall the names of all of us be written there"—sets up expectations for the conversion of experience to record which will shape the novel's own elaborately nested closural strategy.

Following the reported death of Rosey framed by the transience and superficiality of newsprint commiseration, we turn to the authentic grief of the ailing colonel, whose sorrow is compounded by the sense that he is being punished by this added familial tragedy for his own sins of materialism and revenge. Willingly, almost eagerly, certainly with a flourish far beyond resignation, he takes upon himself this mortal scourge, seeming to stage his own deathbed scene both to complete his contrition and to permit a return to better times, as if reliving his life in its protracted moment of penance and departure. The colonel appears to sense the profoundly literary or aesthetic possibilities of dying as an exchange of duration for shape. To salvage meaning, even beauty, from the end of his days he must bring them to a resonant halt, must substitute certainty for flux, past for present, death for life. His death scene, an artfully contrived network of reverie, irony, and symbol, is so unlike the usual Thackerayan demise because it is the self-conscious performance of a more or less Dickensian mentality, sentimental, romantic, doting on the forms of portentous pathos.

In the company of Madame de Florac, Colonel Newcome displays his erstwhile chivalry one last time as he addresses "courtly old words of regard and kindness to the aged lady; anon he wandered in his talk, and spoke to her as if they still were young." The dead metaphor "wandered" revives some of its topographic force in this retracing of time's steps. The colonel's verbal grasp at recovery is also couched in an archaism, "anon," as a sign of narrator Pendennis's own at least unconscious empathy with the dying man. This feverish reversion is complete when the colonel wanders back through early manhood to the innocence of the schoolroom, for a recapitulating death that ranks with "Barkis is willin' " in its Dickensian twist, like a double helix returned upon itself after the unwinding of an entire life history: "And just as the last bell struck, a peculiar sweet smile shone over his face, and he lifted up his head a little, and quickly said, 'Adsum!' and fell back. It was the word we used at school, when names were called; and lo, he, whose heart was as that of a little child, had answered to his name, and stood in the presence of The Master." Like the familiar symbolism of demise in Dickens, this raising to exponential power and a capital letter of one of life's rites of passage, God becoming the Great Tutor, also epitomizes, in conjunction with the biblical overtones of "as . . . a child," the innocent heart of this man more sinned against than sinning.

Thackeray's death sentence itself is paced through a fourfold conjunctive pattern ("and just . . . and he . . . and quickly . . . and fell") moving gradedly to collapse at the ironic grammatical comedown of straightforward report, "fell back" (rather than such a schoolroom idiom and metaphysical antonym as "came forward"). The difference (or traversed interval) between childhood and age on the one hand, time and eternity on the other, in the double valence of the Latin form *"Adsum!"*—whose nostalgic import needs explanation in the subsequent editorial gloss—sets up a curious resonance. Its assumed meaning, "I am present," doubles disconcertingly for the instant of vanishing into mortal absence. The colonel's declaration in the foreign idiom of a dead language draws its meaning quite unabashedly from a separate sphere of reference; if he is present where he thinks he finds himself, the colonel is certainly gone from anyone on the scene. And it is important to add that all this is delivered uncritically in the voice of an invented and named narrator to whose Christian hope alone (and not Thackeray's) the description could be presumed to attest. The colonel's last word is a sentimental rendition of Abraham's "Here am I!" before the call of God, or Moses' later (both *"Adsum!"* in the Vulgate).[9] It therefore sheds new light on Hardy's Jobian ironies and the bitter twist of Jude's deleted because depleted verb of being in "And I here." From there it is only one more step into mortal irony until fictional history arrives at Joyce's parodistic vision of the articulate risen corpse with that drowned and resurfaced body anonymously announcing, "Here I am" (*Ulysses*, p. 21), examined as elegiac travesty in Chapter 1.

Following the colonel's death in *The Newcomes*, its narrator is swiftly dismissed after a white blank and a dividing line setting off the supposedly edited narrative from the confession of pure fabulation by the author. "As I write the last line with a rather sad heart, Pendennis and Laura, and Ethel and Clive, fade away into Fableland . . . And have we parted with them here on a sudden, and without so much as a shake of the hand?" So the author at last comes forward to ask, but which "last line" does he mean? Of the main plot? Of the coda, as each new sentence fades away to become the last one? Or does he mean "line" in the geometric rather than scriptive sense, as in what follows: "Is yonder line (_____) which I drew with my own pen, a barrier between me and Hades as it were, across which I can see those figures retreating and only dimly glimmering?" A typographical commonplace raised to ontological crux, the line he points to "yonder" by reduplicating interposes itself as follows the first time around, between the objective report and the editorial voice of Arthur Pendennis:

> had answered to his name, and stood in the presence of The
> Master.
> _____

> Two years ago, walking with my children in some pleasant
> fields . . .

As at the end of *Pickwick Papers*, after its wedding breakfast, to pass from the inner action of text to its externalization and dismissal as fiction is a crossing of the bar fully as extreme as that which follows upon "*Adsum*." It is only workably anachronistic, not inappropriate, I trust, to think here of the Saussurean bar (S/s) between signifier (in this case the narrative act) and signified (the narrated scene) in this fictional (re)signation of the author's "Fable-land" to its admitted status as verbal construct. Even the putative editor, Arthur Pendennis, is retired "to the shades" without answering the "sentimental question" upon which novels so often choose to end: whom did Clive marry after Rosey's death? The answer will have to be invented, and Ethel is the logical and sentimentally satisfying choice. The requirements of comic form and closure seem to be struggling with the preemptive threat of death. But nothing in this belated applique of a marital finish can erase the triple death at the end of the narrative proper, first of a stillborn child and its mother, eradicating a third generation and a marriage in the second, and then of the family progenitor himself, the old colonel. Any marriage that will then be confected must materialize *sub specie mortalitatis*, and doubly so since the whole tale is fading into the realm of shadows. Here, beyond the closural strategies of comic plotting, is that familiar textual displacement of the personal by the formal, of psychology by fictional phenomenology.

Pendennis "has disappeared," says the valedictory authorial voice, "as irrevocably as Eurydice," who dies in the very instant of being looked back upon—dies when a perceiving other tries to recapture, to reread, her image. Not to have stepped in with his fabrication of admittedly arbitrary futures for his cast would have left an aura of fictional permanence hovering about Thackeray's invented creatures. Instead a voice comes forward to admit that all writing, all narrative, is merely a ghostly trace that vanishes before our gaze line by line, whether the line be yet more text or the final linear bar between artifice and reality. "Ah, happy, harmless Fable-land, where these things are!" the author declares near the close, with the verb of being providing both placement and predication: they are there, not here; there only, not here, they *are*. It is the fiction's own "*Adsum*."

The question of receding presence is, as the authorial voice knows, a matter of infinite and concentric regression. If Pendennis's narrative, and he its speaking voice, are now passed over and away beyond the bar of signifying presence into trace, so too will the encompassing narrator be distanced by form itself. By way of suggesting this, there is a shift in pronoun toward the close from first to third person that is the metanarrative equivalent of that neutering within less metaphoric death scenes of "he" and "she" to "it." "Friendly reader! may you and the author meet there [in Fable-land] on some future day! He hopes so; as he yet keeps a lingering hold of your hand, and bids you fare well with a kind heart." So did the dying colonel hold out his hand to those near him. This is in an important sense, then, the deathbed valediction of a narrative voice that has already regretted the lack of a chance for handshakes with his fading creations, yet whose touch with his readers is maintained after all by that printed embodiment of his words which their hands must still have "hold of" even as they come upon the close. The *de te fabula* of incorporated reader consciousness has narrowed to a vanishing point at which our own imagination is the last presence on the scriptive scene, the narrative "I" receding past "he" into the Hades of completion. To activate the satire, we have always had to see ourselves in the anatomized follies of the characters; now just that consciousness of ourselves addressed by the text is all the text has left—or almost all.

As long as a novel named *The Newcomes* is still in the hands of the reader, it is the motive of Thackeray's closural device to suggest

that, even as his own articulating self is shunted to "he," such main-
tenance of the third person amounts all the same to a reclamation of
transience by text. It may be the death of the authorial "I," but it
also affords his preservation as a self-generated character, a still
narrated "he" within the remaining momentum of the discourse. Giving up no more than it gets in return, this is a saving of the text to
which we are alerted not as *a* strategy so much as *the* strategy of
fictional denomination, allegorized here by the precipitating figuration
of death as first the declaration, then the textual declension of presence: from *"Adsum!"* to the closural "he."[10] To enact the absenting
of presence which is any textual act, Thackeray alerts us to a sequence
of assertions which are at the same time withdrawals: narrative regress
as egress, all telling as sheer leave taking.

An old-fashioned epitomizing death scene, dramatized, credible,
summative, spiritually ambiguous while still soothing, turning duti-
fully upon the mysteries of presence in a world of mortally delimited
identity, is here preceded by ironies of textual memorial in the evanescence of newsprint and followed by a virtual (if not quite final)
deconstruction of its first plotted, then editorial, then authorial place
in the enshrinement of fictional narrative. The passage taps more
amply than perhaps any other of its century the narratological leverage
of a single death scene, as authored closure, on the authority of fiction
itself as a verbal articulation of human intentionality across time to
termination. The modernist crisis encroaches. All it takes is for a
character within the fiction, rather than its editor or narrative persona,
to raise such framing doubts about his or her own status as an act
(or accident) of verbally determined presence, doubts about the assumption of the *"Adsum"* in its very and every articulation,
and the classic novel has broken forward into the arduous self-
interrogation of this century. Conrad's Decoud, Woolf's Bernard, and
Beckett's Malone, among others, are characters agonized to an increasing degree over their own life, and its limit in death, as none
other than such a work of words.

Jude's articulated death scene makes him the transitional fore-
father, the embittered missing link. Surrendering his predicated hold
on presence with the elided grammar of "And I here"—the end of a
shapeless, merely consecutive, always intransigent life line with no
direction left—Jude then cedes his own "I" to quotations in first-

person singular from the text of Job, as if self is receding to sheer deadly precedent, withered to its own quotation by rote. The hero epitomized in this and in the other desertions of his last days, the interval of Jude's death becomes pure displacement. Essence converts to text in the way that the reconsecrated presence of the colonel in the eye of his origination is transferred away from spiritual drama to an Orphic parable of sacrificed presence in the retrospective making of any text. Yet unlike the colonel, Jude knows all too well that this is happening, that he is in fact doing himself in with his own self-evacuating last words. Nearing the turn of the century, Hardy's novel shows Jude's distance from self in death verging on a continuous dislocation of the "I" from any verb of being that would vest it with presence, verging on that lifelong alienation from an originating sense of self which so often in modern fiction goes under the name of death in the absence of its scene. If *Jude the Obscure* resembles Dickensian black comedy turned absurdist, the epitaphic aspirations of a John Chivery in *Little Dorrit* chilled to the bone, then the receding acknowledgment of Hades-bound presences in the narrative coda of *The Newcomes* provides the textual obverse of Amy Dorrit's confidence in closural inscription, which seems for her the open-ended predication of a new "life story."

In *Jude the Obscure* the formulas of fictional dying in the Victorian novel are turned inside out by Hardy and scraped dry. Jude's displacement from original selfhood is his epitome. There is for Hardy's last hero only reversion, belatedness, his prophetic biblical text merely an extirpation of all presence and potential. What is asserted by Jude in his consumptive, his self-devouring fatality is only the kind of eviscerated epitaphic lament that the novel *David Copperfield* would have become if the hero had conceived his own life, rather than the past of his drowned friend, Ham, to be only so many memorializing incisions on a sheet of stone. Moaning, mournful, and already extinct, excluded from the outer community he exhorts by self-example, a mere voice frittering itself away in a vacuum, Jude as sermonizer becomes not a preacher so much as a narrator, but one shackled to a received, involuntary, and repetitive plot, in the long run more a reader of his own life, out loud at the end, than a creator or motive force. Jude intones his fate by prototype in the absence of any immediate listeners, and thus turns experience back to the no better than scripted narrative which is always at two removes—being neither heard nor original—from the intended reality of and to which it would speak. His is the ultimate displacement from the priority of presence, reciting as he does his own finis by heart "as at the closing of a book." Supine and soliloquizing, his bed a bier, Jude's Jobian curses in solitude anticipate the cryptic ennui and inanition of *Malone Dies* half a century later. Jude Fawley, thither indeed.

4

Thresholds

Self-Portrait with Fiddling Death, by Arnold Böcklin
Courtesy of Nationalgalerie, Berlin

My task . . . is, before all, to make you *see* . . . And when it is accomplished—behold!—all the truth of life is there: a moment of vision, a sigh, a smile—and the return to an eternal rest.

JOSEPH CONRAD, preface to
The Nigger of the "Narcissus"

4

"A man that is born falls into a dream like a man who falls
into the sea. If he tries to climb out into the air as inexperi-
enced people endeavor to do, he drowns . . . The way is to
the destructive element submit yourself, and with the exer-
tions of your hands and feet in the water make the deep, deep
sea keep you up. So if you ask me—how to be? . . . In the
destructive element immerse."

JOSEPH CONRAD, *Lord Jim*

IN JUDE'S LAST ROOM, the lifelong desire of Hardy's hero to
find a plot for his life has come ultimately to grief. This spiritual
dead end also reads as a comment on the plot-making ambitions of
the British novel down through this final fiction of Thomas Hardy. In
Jude's textual transfer of dying presence to uttered biblical precedent,
narratology and fictional thanatology are collapsed upon each other
more apparently than ever before. Joseph Conrad was waiting at the
turn of the century to explore this often unholy alliance through the
complexities of his own experiments both in narrative point of view
and in the textual conversion of living to life. As with so many of his
paired characters, in Conrad's novels death and narration are repeatedly exposed as each other's doubles at the threshold of final
silence.

We have seen how the British death scene has evolved its verbal
features within the developing rhetoric of fiction. With this stylistic
lineage of its own, the death scene begins to seem not merely subordinate to the novel that surrounds it but correlative to it, not a
separable episode only but a model for the entire fictional enterprise.
Absolute mediation of the unseen by language, character crystallized
in words against the ground of silence, the very idea of narrative built
upon and pitched against effacement, temporal duration under duress
of inevitable containment, continuity ruled by closure, meaning no
sooner come to utterance than passed from the imagined presence of

its source or subject to sheer verbal trace, all phrasing at least vaguely epitaphic—to abstract the nature of prose fiction in this way is at one and the same time to anatomize the scene of death. Like characters within Conrad's stories, the fiction itself may well discover only in extremis its constitutional affinity with death. The rhetorical interval of a death scene may thus come to miniaturize the entire stylistic span of a narrative, a compressed articulation of life at the threshold of incommunicability.

It might be said that Dickens and Thackeray (the latter less in that uncharacteristically sentimental death of Colonel Newcome than generally) offer complementary models for Victorian fictional dying by coming at the moment of death from opposite directions: inside versus out. A similar watershed distinction for the modernist death scene can be found in its divergent investigation by Joseph Conrad and E. M. Forster. For Conrad dying strives to become an occasion of truth, however slaying; death yearns to be all revelation. For Forster it is the occlusion of any further truth; death is simply all. Between them Conrad and Forster submit mortality to an epistemological inquisition more rigorous and insistent than anything we have encountered so far in the British novel.

The first of these two writers to move the novel into the problematics of modern psychology, Conrad is perhaps most explicit on the issue of identity in his hero's post-Hardyesque obsession throughout *Lord Jim* (1904) with "how to be." In many of Conrad's other works too, earlier and later, such interrogation of being and becoming receives its final hearing (to borrow two phrases from *Heart of Darkness*) in that "supreme moment" when the struggling self is able to illuminate its life by transgressing the "threshold of the invisible." In context, however, Marlow's phrases refer to the bedeviled and hideous death of Kurtz, a victory of revelatory consciousness only in its unflinching nihilism. Unlike many later modernist characters, Conrad's protagonists look repeatedly to the scene of death with an avid hope of disclosures otherwise unavailable, even though their author more often than not (Kurtz's death being an exception) portrays the moment of death as blind or mute. Yet though they refuse any perfunctory displays of insight or solace at the "supreme moment," Conrad's plots are still nerved for revelation in death. A hero's disappointment comes through to us when the interval of traverse, promising a revelatory threshold, is blocked by a style of truncation or understatement, the narratable itself under arrest.

In the four tales on which I have chosen to concentrate we can see the analogy of mortality and story become increasingly energized within the actual workings of Conrad's plots. In *The Nigger of the "Narcissus"* (1897) the story (one long-delayed death scene in its own right as plot) is introduced by commentary on portentous storytelling of whatever sort in its relation to the inevitably fading flash of mortal insight. In the next year's *Heart of Darkness* the narrative persona has become a dramatized character encountering the powerful last words of the eventual subject of his tale, thus engaging more directly with the deathlike contract of all retrospective narrative. The Marlow narrator returns in *Lord Jim* (1900) to deflect this interest in the revelatory death scene, a scene in Jim's case deliberately ambiguous, toward a compensatory sense of death as the closural freedom of finis, epiphanic or not. And finally the travestied impulses toward revelatory death in *Nostromo* (1904) are subsumed by the ironic hero, Decoud, within the merely retrospective and memorializing function of written record. In a long and central epistolary episode, which happens to include within it another pivotal death scene, Decoud becomes in effect the autobiographical narrator of his own presently vanishing life. He thus brings forward to first-person crisis the definitive kinship between inscription itself and the ceded presence necessitated by any death. Only later in *Nostromo*, when the emphasis on the transcribed report of dying has given way at Decoud's death to Conrad's first sustained omniscient rendering of the mortal moment, only then do we see to what extent Conrad's modernism is able to co-opt, by way of revisionary strictures, the Victorian rhetoric of death as a stylistics of truncation, rupture, and continuance.

□   □   □

Probably Conrad's most often quoted summary of his fictional aesthetic comes from the preface to *The Nigger of the "Narcissus,"* where he announces that he wants to "make you *see*." It is no modest project, for "when it is accomplished—behold! all the truth of life is there: a moment of vision, a sigh, a smile—and the return to an eternal rest." Walter Benjamin's claim for the deathbed analogy of all storytelling finds here its most eloquent and succinct precedent. Conrad's sense of the epiphany of aesthetic perception is so much like a death scene that the satisfied sigh of recognition and acceptance is comparable to a last quiet gasp. The debated phrase "eternal rest" then seems to suggest the contemplative reward of such a genuine revelation.[1] This insinuated link between insight and a virtually fatal intensity of apprehension is in keeping with everything that follows in Conrad's fiction about the relation, increasingly ironic, between death's exit and he rumored access to extraordinary knowledge just across its threshold.

The Nigger of the "Narcissus" is the story of an inscrutable black seaman named Jimmy Wait dying of tuberculosis during the course of a dangerous sea voyage, a man around whom the crewmen of the *Narcissus* gather in periods of calm as if he could provide them with the kind of mortally tested insight which the novel offers the reader. The protagonist is introduced to us in a scene of almost farcical crossed purposes by a name that is mistaken for a verb. The mate is enrolling seamen for the voyage, and cannot make out the meaning of Jimmy's mark. " 'Wait!' cried a deep, ringing voice" (ch. 1), the monosyllable heard as a brazen injunction when in fact it is an explanation of the illegible surname. But this deep, sonorous voice, whose coughs grow steadily more explosive, metallic, and tubercular as events unfold, does in fact enjoin his fellow mortals to the long existential wait—for the very death he himself holds off as energetically as he can. It is an end inbred and irrevocable, whose death watch is interrupted by the redundant battle against drowning in a storm at sea. Jimmy's function is to intrude death into a sequence of adventures as a reminder, beyond the whims of contingency, of the death that cannot be deterred by effort or fortune—that is there waiting, like Jimmy, in the midst of all endeavor. The narrator's own idiomatic language suggests that Jimmy's knowledge of death becomes in itself contagious and irreversible, for (my emphasis on the metaphor of pathology) "we were always *incurably* anxious to hear what he had to say" (ch. 2).

After a violent storm at sea in which Jimmy and the rest nearly drown in the literalized "destructive element" upon which Conrad's seafaring plots are built, Wait suddenly feels released from the need to acknowledge his other, inner death, the fate beyond fortuity. Jimmy's false freedom maddens the crew. "His obstinate nonrecognition of the only certitude whose approach we could watch from day to day was as disquieting as the failure of some law of nature" (ch. 5). Jimmy's obstinacy fails "nature" so completely that he appears removed from the cycle of time: "He seemed to shout his denials already from beyond the awful border." He is in fact pushed over this threshold when he is forced by his scurrilous shipmate Donkin to own up to his dying. "I see you dying this minyt . . . before my eyes . . . . as good as dead already." Jimmy, stunned, musters enough strength to howl, "Go away! Murder!" (ch. 5). Death and its acknowledgment are coterminous in this tale—and again communicable, contagious; for when Donkin, having driven Jimmy wild by calling him "dead already," a "corpse," a "thing," a "nobody," watches him die at last, he sees no less than his own doom in the corpse. This man, so contemptuous of Jimmy's previous role as the living memento mori for the crew, now has the recognition driven home with "the anguishing grasp of a great sorrow in his heart at the thought that he himself, someday, would have to go through it all—just like this— perhaps!"

It is this recognition scene, toward which the whole plot has been aimed, that brings both halves of the title to new light. The dying Jimmy may well be cast as a black man to provide a kind of negative image of the white crew's vitality, and this may in turn help explain the name *Narcissus*. Every ship is of course one, poised as it is over its own reflection on the surface of the sea. But in the sense that this ship becomes a metonymy for its crew, what is it that they see, as a collective Narcissus, when they gather riveted around Jimmy's death bunk? What is it but an incarnate alternative—death from internal causes—to that prospective Narcissus-like drowning which is every sailor's threatened fate? Their inevitable deaths, beyond contingency, are seen through the glass, darkly, of Wait's black doom. By the end of the tale, the ship's docked, immobile bulk is described in a phrase that directly echoes the "ceased to breathe" (ch. 5) that marks the translation of Wait from man to dead hulk in the earlier death sentence: "The *Narcissus* came gently into her berth; the shadows of soulless walls fell upon her . . . She had ceased to live." The whole sea journey, itself a narrated voyage of discovery, has passed away from that "seeing" which is art to that quiescence already likened to the "eternal rest" of death.

□   □   □

Heart of Darkness is similarly concerned not only with the truths delivered by a mortal intensity of perception but with the lies and delusions that are the death of such truths. The anonymous narrative frame is retained, but between its dramatized yet impersonal voice on the Thames (rather like the "we" of the narrator on behalf of the crew in *The Nigger*) and the unfolding events—which in this case the outer narrator can only relay, not relate from first-hand knowledge—another narrator is inserted. This is one Charlie Marlow, who will enact the deathlike strenuousness of the encounter with truth as well as the deathly failure to sustain that knowledge in a heart made timid by its own darkness.[2]

On Marlow's way upriver to his displaced participation in the death of Kurtz, the structure of narcissistic confrontation and mortal doubling is tirelessly prepared for. Knowing intuitively the brotherhood of death to which he is made party when arriving at the Congo outpost, Marlow first seeks out the corpse of his predecessor in the jungle. It has become by now a skeletal memento mori with grass growing through its ribs, one of several other corpses en route that serve as surrogates for the narrator's own doom. Most crucial of these doublings on the journey toward Kurtz is the death of the black helmsman who was to get Marlow there. This is the "fool nigger" with whom Marlow had entered into a kind of functional "partnership" recognized only at the point of death, a filial link visible under the shadow of the universal fate. Stabbed to death by a spear, the helmsman "looked at me over his shoulder in an extraordinary, profound, familiar manner, and fell at my feet" (p. 46). This is for Marlow the brotherhood of a soul that knows its own death in the common body.[3] There are no last words, as there will be with Kurtz, no voice from beyond what is later called the "threshold of the invisible" (p. 72). Yet such a mortal demarcation is anticipated when the dying helmsman "frowned heavily" as though "in response to some sign we could not see," something waiting beyond the border or portal of death.

Even this power of undisclosed sighting is shortly drained away in a meticulously turned phrase that evokes the familiar sliding style of the mortal interval, the trusted Victorian rhetoric of transposition, but holds it to a mere transformation of syllables, with no transit beyond the immediate scene. In this jungle world, where death is so treacherously slurred with life in the very landscape, Conrad's mordant euphony blurs one noun into its stretched, sibilant negation, the gaze of life into the blank of death: "The lustre of inquiring glance faded swiftly into vacant glassiness" (p. 47). Marlow's stare into this dying eye does in one sense complete the role of the helmsman, who was to pilot Marlow not across the Congo as Stygian stream but along the length of this dark river to Kurtz's side. The helmsman's job is thus done when he brings Marlow eye to eye with death's threshold of invisibility, for this is just what Marlow is destined to come upon again in Kurtz. When we note later that the appeal of the dying helmsman, "like a claim of distant kinship affirmed in a supreme moment" (p. 52), finds its last phrase (already familiar to us from the closing deaths of Maggie and Tom in *The Mill on the Floss*) echoed in the "supreme moment" of Kurtz's death, we realize that it is not just a convenient Victorian idiom but a marker of convergence between Marlow's two direct encounters with death.

The symptoms of Kurtz's jungle fever, like the famous words that punctuate its final stage, may also be seen to derive from the Victorian rule of epitomizing death: as he has slain, so is he laid low; as he lusted, so death covets him. When we first encounter Kurtz, he is wasted to the inanimate matter of his greed and obsession, his face an ivory death mask; the maker of skeletons and corpses, he is collapsed now to a heap of bone. His terminal sickness is merely the pathological insignia of his soul's disease, for Kurtz dies lingeringly of a fever contracted at the heart of the primordial. Something he encounters there meets no resistance, immunological or spiritual; it first inflames then gradually emaciates him, gnawing at identity from within.

The manner in which Kurtz's end not only sums up the masking of Western imperialism by idealistic hubris and delusion but also reviews those narrative formulas by which sentimental idealism often assuages the specter of death is further exposed by the familiar codes of mortal rhetoric. Marlow himself comes to the death of Kurtz with expectations fashioned by popular myth or literature or both. "Did he live his life again," Marlow asks, in the recurrent formula for drowning retrospect which Peter Brooks has recently noted in this phrase,[4] "in every detail of desire, temptation, and surrender during that supreme moment of complete knowledge?" (p. 71). If so, then "surrender" at the end of this phrased sequence cannot be taken simply as implying his abject capitulation to physical death but rather as a reference to his earlier moral atrophy, in itself a metaphoric death to be replayed literally in the agony and shame of the deathbed.

Kurtz himself also harbors such an urge to formulate his death into expressible shape. The dying man has a further truism of terminus haltingly in mind in addition to Marlow's borrowing from the myth of drowning retrospect, as if Kurtz were consciously trying to wrest from his own bleak death the poetic justice of epitome. "I withdrew quietly," says Marlow, "but I heard him mutter, 'Live rightly, die, die . . .' I listened. There was nothing more." To such swallowed clichés has Kurtz's superb rhetorical gift dwindled. We strain to recognize a stuttered version, caught in Kurtz's throat, of some balked orthodox formula, like "Live rightly, die rightly," or "Live rightly, die, die nobly," as the manuscript originally had it.[5] Yet despite Marlow's later admiration for the dark insight of Kurtz's end, the dying man in his own voice cannot get beyond the sheer predication of closure—"die, die," the syllables battering at a threshold that will not yield to speech. It is partly this rage for relevant and articulate fatality that makes Marlow so sure about the enormity of Kurtz's "The horror! The horror!" (p. 71). Though it certainly may be no more than a last groan of agony or fear over the immediate misery of painful death, Marlow is confident that this "remarkable man" had therewith "summed up—he had judged" (p. 72). The doubled "horror" seems to Marlow both a retrospective assessment of Kurtz's life and a punitive verdict, the wretchedness behind him exposed as continuous with what may yawn beyond. This is what Marlow wants to think, would have us think; but that insistent "horror" may only be still more of those desperate, those all but inarticulate syllables massed at the impasse of death's threshold.

Marlow at this point insists on pressuring mortal closure to the point of import, yet when similar formulas from the literary history of death are enlisted by him later, they betray not simply a delusion but, worse, a deliberate ruse. If, beyond private retrospect and retribution, there is a strong suspicion at the time of Kurtz's death that his twinned phrasing of "The horror!" is meant to be divided up not only between past and future but between himself and his alter ego,

Marlow, this doubling is all the more true when Marlow colludes in
the perpetuation of a factitious idealism by lying to the Intended that
"the last word he pronounced was—your name" (p. 79). As Eloise
Knapp Hay has noted, this lie is fetched from the sentimental tradition
of the Dickensian deathbed, exact echo (allowing for the grammatical
shift of indirect discourse) of the letter reporting the death of Tom to
Louisa in the coda of *Hard Times,* "His last word being your name."
That we never know the fiancée's name in *Heart of Darkness,* so
awkwardly withheld from the reader, that indeed her title, "Intended,"
seems to incarnate in her all the original Kurtz's best intentions,
admits her even more readily into the sphere of his universal revelation
about the deadliness at the heart of such blinding idealism.

Marlow does not stop with that lone lie. Even as he tries to hedge
his further prevarications with ambivalence, his conversation with
the Intended continues traitorous to that horrible integrity of Kurtz's
death he had charged himself to transmit. Arguably conscious again
of his allusions to literary formula, he seems in league with Conrad
in a full-scale, multitargeted burlesque of the resonant death scene,
its temper consonant with life, a sounding board of moral sonorities.
Since Marlow's entire narrative is told from the advantage of retrospect, it is possible to detect his confused or hoodwinking rhetoric
even before the coda with the Intended. When Marlow realizes that
the name Kurtz, meaning "short" in German, is belied by the man's
considerable height, he says—as if forgetting the cauterizing truth
telling of Kurtz's last utterance—that "the name was as true as everything else in his life—and death" (p. 60). Marlow's own retrospective account seems colored, obscured, by the late meliorating
lie eventually summoned to smother Kurtz's black epiphany. There
is further evidence in the coda that Conrad, if not Marlow, has the
mortuary tradition in literature specifically in mind, with its often
rigorous equations between death and identity. When, hoping for
solace, the Intended clutches at the time-tested heroic prescription
"He died as he lived," Marlow's mock iteration, "His end was in
every way worthy of his life" (p. 78), not only secretly reverses the
moral judgment implicit in her faith, even as he preserves some of
that faith for her and for himself, but helps us see an additional irony.
The epitomizing apothegm of death is commonly phrased with a change
in tense—"He died as he *had* lived"—with pluperfect brought to

perfection (in the existential sense) in the preterite. The Intended, however, has unwittingly summarized the nature of a corrupt life coextensive with death and equivalent to it.

What must not be forgotten in all this, and what Conrad suggests should not have been so readily lost sight of by Marlow in his euphemizing white lies about it, is the "moral victory" of recognition thought to be achieved by the dying Kurtz. When Marlow subsequently falls ill and nearly dies, even though he "was within a hair's breadth of the last opportunity for pronouncement," he "found with humiliation that probably I would have nothing to say" (p. 72, my emphasis). The discovery is both humbling and in the etymological sense humanizing, defining the self, for all its timidities, as existing still on this side of mortality's terrible threshold. "And perhaps in this is the whole difference; perhaps all the wisdom, and all truth, and all sincerity, are just compressed into that inappreciable moment of time in which we step over the threshold of the invisible." Marlow here stands in awe of just the sort of distilled and transferable "wisdom" that Walter Benjamin sees as the authority of storytelling at the root of all prose fiction.[6] The imitative frontal "compression" of Marlow's syntax compacts the burden of discovery into a triad of appositional phrases gathered at the threshold of that "inappreciable moment" which may recall the "untraversable distance" of the death-bed interval in *Little Dorrit*, yet with a subversive difference. The adjective *inappreciable* does not speak so much of temporal rapidity as of the inapprehendable power of the moment and the later ingratitude of its denial by Marlow. For a recording consciousness still in this world, whether at the brink of his own death or, by displacement, at that of a double, Moneta's promise in Keats—to humanize the tragic profundity of death to the mortal ear—is a vain one. It becomes in Conrad only the mortal humiliation of revelations forever removed, mute, or unusable.

Held back at the threshold, all Marlow has heard from Kurtz are those famous words with which the dying man "had summed up . . . had judged." Not unlike Keats's doubled and redoubled syllable "-or-" in the repeated "forlorn" of the "Nightingale" ode, the echo of and within that twice-tolled "horror" (the very word is like a death bell) goes on reverberating all the way through Marlow's coda. It does so not because the dark truth lives on—cruel, invulnerable—but because even the narrator who believes that there is "a taint of death, a flavour of mortality in lies" (p. 27) has found himself induced to lie about this particular summation and judgment, to soften and baffle its impact. Mendacity is assassination, both of the true memory of Kurtz and even, by his own words, of its present deceiving mediator. Marlow, that is, has not only "laid the ghost of Kurtz's gifts," themselves deadly, with a deadly "lie" (p. 49), but he has also offered himself up as sacrificial victim on the altar of his own untruth in order to protect in the Intended, and preserve through her, the comforting idealism he takes her to incarnate.

Marlow's evasions at this point complicate enormously the moral and formal allegory of the tale. What is made abundantly obvious in the funereal gloom that haunts the coda of *Heart of Darkness*, where Marlow submits to the "taint of death" in his calculated deception before the Intended, is that Conrad has broadened the circle of his scrutiny well beyond the relation of narrative closure to "eternal rest" in *The Nigger*. The affinity between formal shape and mortal finality was given dramatic play in the actual plot of the dying seaman in the earlier story, as indeed it is again with the dying Kurtz. Yet the later tale, beyond the relation of narrative trace to human effacement, enlarges the issue by further shifting the ground of moral dilemma from the story of death to its discourse, from event to its subsequent enunciation, involving more deeply the mechanics of the narrative act. Having made the unsubstantiated, perhaps naive, certainly moralistic claim that Kurtz's summing-up was not only a neutral "victory" over transience but a "moral victory" of "wisdom" over evil, Marlow must seem doubly evil in his own eyes during his temporizing cover-up, with its knowing collusion in an idealistic lie.

Heart of Darkness thus compounds the parable of death as analogy for narrative closure with the moral parable of deceptive narration as a violence unto death. Whereas the "truth of life" in *The Nigger*, even when it turns out to be only an account of the universal fact of death, is followed by "eternal rest," a comparable truth at Kurtz's death is followed by the lethal act of false witness. The earlier tale settles for the allegory of text as epitaph. The later tale extends the question by an inquiry into the maneuvers of narration itself in its bond to the final and irreversible nature of narrative "truth"—or at least of accuracy and closure. The slaying lie not only lays the ghost of its subject, Kurtz, whose communicable horror Marlow might otherwise have survived at one remove from its original disclosure on the deathbed, but it also taints to death the narrator who tampers with and puts to premature "rest" the "truth of life" which Kurtz died divulging. The textual allegory of the coda is widened to the ethical. The heart of darkness is hereby exposed as deliberate narrative obscuration in and of itself, a sin against the Intended's specifically verbal faith that Kurtz's "words, at least, have not died" (p. 78).

☐ ☐ ☐

If *The Nigger of the "Narcissus"* constrasts its empty, wordless, externalized death scene with the illumination that the story as a whole, driving toward it, serves to provide before its own expiration as articulate narrative, and if *Heart to Darkness* reverses the process by letting an articulate "victory" in death, however horrible, get buried within the evasions of its dramatized retelling, *Lord Jim* steers an ambivalent middle course. Inheriting the Marlow narrator from the preceding tale, the novel champions through his voice the bitter Kurtz-like candor of Gentleman Brown's dying words, his power of expression "*in articulo mortis*" (ch. 41). The deceits of this very deathbed rhetoric send the hero, Jim, to his decidedly voiceless death and its undetermined revelation, a death whose barred threshold discloses for certain only its analogy to the nonepiphanic finis of narrative in general, not necessarily the resonant closure of moral fiction.

Jim's initial cowardice on board what he thought to be the sinking *Patna*, his version of the Romantic Narcissus voyage turned to despair, is a jump that is meant to save him from going down with the ship. Twice more the actual fate of drowning is portrayed in this novel so as gloss or allegorize Stein's figure of the "destructive element." Sitting in judgment on Jim in the trial over the *Patna* desertion, the egocentric Captain Brierly gradually degenerates under the strain of having another soul exposed before him, an extension of his own. So this alter ego for Jim as a hero of willed introspection jumps to his death through the mirroring threshold of the sea, after the "gates of the other world" have momentarily "swung open" to "receive him" (ch. 6). By the time Captain Chester and his crew, with whom Jim had nearly signed on next, have gone down in the Pacific, we are ready to find illustrated a figurative immersion in the "destructive element" which would have to do not with the risks of physical fatality but with the universal question of "how to be." This would have to do in turn with the internal rhyming—both a verbal and a spiritual reciprocation—implied by Stein's assonant phrasing in the epigraph to this chapter, the mutuality and balance needed to let "the deep, deep sea keep you up" (ch. 20).

The definitive limit for "how to be" is suggested in Marlow's comments on the off-stage drowning of Chester and his crew, when "not a sound came out of the waste. Finis!" (ch. 16). More literally than the *Narcissus*, this ship has "ceased to live," dying indeed a silent, unreadable death. Marlow repeats his at least implicitly textual analogy in the next sentence, in English as well as printer's Latin this time: "End! Finis!" He wants to claim this unvoiced epitaph as the only perspective "that makes the idea of death supportable," the one "potent word that exorcises from the house of life the haunting shadow of fate." Conrad seems here to be anticipating what he later reports Stein as having said about that immersion in the element of creative destruction: what is required is that the heroic self "follow the dream . . . *usque ad finem*" (ch. 20), pursuing desire through to its end.[7]

There is certainly a sense in which Jim has done this by the close, even while he has been duped by the dying Brown into a fatal course of action. Marlow is as impressed by Brown's volleys of speech "at the gate of the other world" (ch. 41) as he was with the curt utterance of Kurtz at that earlier threshold. Such summoned speech arrives as a "triumph" of expression at the mortal turning point, with "*in articulo mortis*," Marlow's own words, seeming to play on the English rather than Latin sense of terminal "articulation." Yet it is Jim this time, not the narrating Marlow, who identifies with Brown as a penumbral double, a point Marlow appears to hint at by describing Jim acceding to Brown's schemes in a dubious mutter "as if speaking to himself" (ch. 42). Jim has swallowed his own words even more completely when, at his own *articulo mortis*, he dies in a voiceless apotheosis of his private vision. When executed by Doramin for Brown's murder of Dain Waris, Jim reclaims from this sacrificial doubling a gesture of personal epitome: "They say that the white man sent right and left at all those faces a proud and unfliching glance. Then with his hand over his lips he fell forward, dead" (ch. 45). The distance between isolated self and the world of otherness, at this terminal disjuncture, is distinct enough to require the verb "sent" for such an instantaneous transmission across the space of that last look. With his hand stopping any possible burst of utterance in a mock-heraldic emblem of reticence, the hero, thwarted by a muteness of his own doing, topples to his destined finis as mere end. His is a death sentence delivered by Conrad so as at once to invite and to forbid the traditional interval of transposition or transit. No prose could more minutely, more mutedly tune itself to the vanishing interval of presence. As contrasted with Dickens's apostrophizing participial exclamation—"Dead!"—at the death of Jo in *Bleak House*, the very smallness of Conrad's effect is its ironic rhetoric. "Forward" only in the end-stopped sense of "forward, dead" is the sole direction Jim's dying can be sure to have.

Marlow allows that "it may very well be that in the short moment of his last proud and unflinching glance, he had beheld the face of that opportunity which, like an Eastern bride, had come veiled to his side" (ch. 45). But all we have had objectively confirmed is the death glance "sent," not any vision received. Then, too, Marlow says "*in* the *short* moment," rather than "*at* the moment" (and so potentially from then on). If there is a threshold crossed by this faintly eroticized romantic opportunity, it is merely instantaneous and spectral, not one over which Jim might move "forward" to glory. The monosyllabic clause beginning the brief coda after the death sentence says it all, all we can know: "And that's the end." Immersed in the destructive current of his idealism, on land as at sea, Jim has followed his often phantasmal dream *usque ad finem*. He has arrived, as far as narrative can verify, only at the finis which an exorcizing death shares with the fiction that recounts it, with the momentum toward closure of any story.

□   □   □

The aimless life history of the antihero Martin Decoud in *Nostromo* traces the *usque ad finem* of a life entirely without "the dream," without visions or illusions. Decoud too falls forward from a gunshot wound after a last prolonged stare, but he does so in an unceremonial scene of solitary execution administered out of his suicidal despair. Decoud is self as scapegoat to neither tribe nor ideal, ego glancing at vacancy. Unlike Jim, Decoud does not block the passage of his last articulate breath, yet his dying words are more explicitly final than Marlow's about Jim. Uttering for himself the equivalent of an uninflected and irrelevant finis just before a redundant drowning in the "destructive element," Decoud goes under in a dark gulf whose density cannot suspend him because he has weighted himself down with the symbolic burden of materialism in the shape of four silver ingots. Everything this present chapter needs to sketch out about the revelatory expectations of the death scene in Conrad—its invoked portals, gates, or thresholds, its victories of articulation *in articulo mortis*, its epitomizing reliance on finality as touchstone—all is reprised, queried, and turned grotesque by the suicide of Decoud and by the elaborately meshed network of allusions to other deaths in the novel which his last scene is there to draw taut. Despite the shift from Marlow's voice to third-person omniscience, everything Conrad has been at pains to suggest in his earlier tales about the narratively privileged moment of mortal summation and judgment, however ambiguous, everything about death as the patron genius of storytelling, is there too in *Nostromo*. It has been transferred from oral account to written text in the virtual deathbed memoir which Decoud pens before his fatal adventure on the gulf.

The move to omniscience also serves to call into more rigorous question the long-standing purpose of the Conradian narrator, Marlow in particular, in testing his stories against the revelatory vantage of death. Such a motive may still characterize Conrad's project as a writer, but it has been reabsorbed within the framing narrative mediation that puts plot before us. Instead of the death scene becoming more mysteriously lucid and probing once removed from the partial view of a Marlow-like narrator, omniscience would seem to surrender its perspective largely to the insufficient vision of the dying mind. The nostalgia for luminous dying in *Nostromo*, for thresholds broached, epiphanic transits guaranteed, is given over entirely to the troubled characters, and given short shrift there by the story's pervasive pessimism. Entering with almost clinical objectivity into the lesions and lapses of consciousness within the dying mind, as no dramatized narrator could be empowered to do, *Nostromo*'s omniscient prose, though impressed into manifold stylistic service, thus prescinds from any vestigial rhetoric of revelation in extremis.

In the first speech by any major character of *Nostromo*, Captain

Mitchell haltingly declares that "certain forms of death are—er—distasteful to a—a—er—respectable man" (I, ch. 2). Lifted out of its immediate context of mob violence, the remark seems to predict the logic of spiritual corruption—what Shelley had called "moral death,"[8] what Conrad later in this novel calls "intellectual death"—as it lies in wait for its literalizing occasion in the book's counterplay of epitomizing fatalities. The psychological exchange of terminal insight becomes dramatized within plot as a mode of interaction between heretofore isolated characters, as if by death alone they might break free enough from enveloping selfhood to become spiritually available to each other as objects of true curiosity. Then too, as with Kurtz, dying words uttered in the full consciousness of finality come into line with the whole motivation for retrospective narrative when seen as compounded of epitaph and legacy. *Nostromo* thus manifests again in Conrad that aspect of narrative which makes it, in and of itself, the scene of an irreversible absence akin to death, every page an opaque threshold beyond which the world apart from words is withheld from view.

None of this is, of course, the overt topic of *Nostromo*, whether as invented political history, ironic fiction, or moral fable. Yet the book's theme does make deep, repeated, and familiar demands on the scene of death both on- and off-stage. Amid the corruptions of power and the hypocrisies of its justification, the theme of *Nostromo* emerges as identity under the aspect of vanity, ego engorging all that resists it, even from within, in its hunger for self-assurance. Vanity is a denial of limits, of personal thresholds, a refusal to acknowledge the border where self might meet others or must cede to the not-I in death. The ego's inevitable circumscription by limits must therefore come to enactment in Conrad, whether by the premature demise of the spirit within a still-living body, by an actual death scene, or by the adjacent dying away of another self as moribund exemplum for an onlooking consciousness forced to respond—or of course by all three in sequence, as *Nostromo*'s plot goes out of its chronological way more than once to provide.

Into the revolution-torn South American republic of Costaguana the plot introduces three European-reared main characters. They are Charles Gould, the new English manager of the country's largest silver mine, the just repatriated national Martin Decoud, nihilistic man of letters, and the Italian-born Nostromo, adopted man of the people. What Conrad achieves, among other things, by their placement on this divisive political stage is a dramatization of a civil strife in the self, three sovereign souls divided not against each other but against themselves. Needing a faith, however soulless, whose mystery rests with a palpable incarnation, Charles Gould sells his soul to the "material interests" of the inherited mine, thinking in his hubris that he is immune to taint. Such pride leads paradoxically but inevitably to his self-effacement as man and moral agent. But then so does the privately absorbed selfhood of the other two major characters, an egotism widely divergent yet equally virulent. In his relentless cynicism and hauteur, Martin Decoud believes in nothing, not creed nor people nor material objects, and in the end extends this contempt even to himself. By contrast, Nostromo, self-styled hero of the people, is so obsessed with the world's view of him that he sacrifices his integrity to a mania for public recognition; his is a self hollowed at the center by its own notoriety.

It is Gould's story that first unfolds in the novel's account. Coming early, it gives initial definition to a prominent and dovetailed pair of motifs in this novel: the mortuary nature of a doomed man's text or missive, whether posted in extremis or not, and the testing of second-generation integrity against the wishes, written or otherwise, of the dying or the dead. In Charles Gould's case, the wisdom that seeks transference from the preceding generation to his own life is the entirely negative wisdom of caveat. Worn down by years of bitter frustration over the San Tomé silver mine, Charles's father has been in contact with his son, absent while being educated in Europe, only as a transcribed voice in letters. The father is a narrator obsessed by a source of wealth whose fascination but not ferocity communicates itself to the ambitious youth. The defeatism and decline of the father, a degeneration embodied, like the man himself, only in the prose of his dispatches, is both closed off and summed up by the "news" (I, ch. 6), either in a telegram or letter, of his actual demise. No more than text all along to the absent son, the father as subject and source of those letters has been replaced with a mortuary notification of the man turned object, constituting in itself his death as authorial origin.

A related sense of dying by indirection, also associated with a death-haunted last missive, frames the next mortal injunction and second-generation betrayal in the novel. When the patriot Don José whispers feebly to his godson, Decoud, that the latter should, in his plan for political separatism, go humbly in God's service, his is a wasted last breath, reported by the atheist Decoud in a final extended letter. This is the professional writer's last act of writing in the novel, an account dashed off to his sister in Europe just before setting out on the fatal mission with Nostromo to sequester a lode of silver. It is not the least of the reasons for taking this inscribed report as a model of the novel's narration as a whole—poised as it too is on the brink of the "eternal rest" which is silence—that in the letter we read of events in the plot nowhere else presented. Decoud takes over from Conrad to narrate that part of the novel which touches him most closely, trying to make continuous sense of the fatalities in which he is caught up. Just as in other Conrad stories a death scene may often miniaturize the maneuvers of narrative as a whole, so too in Decoud's last letter (itself compared to a scriptive extinction) there is a crucial death scene included at its center.

The deathbed enunciation of Don José's at the heart of the last document of Decoud's barely aspires to the threshold of the audible, be it benediction or warning; all the grand "oratorical efforts" (II, ch. 4) of the aged political reformer have shrunk to this. As if he were Marlow leaning over Kurtz, "I bent my ear to his withered lips," writes Decoud, and made out his whisper, something like, " 'In God's name, then, Martin, my son!' I don't know exactly. There was the name of God in it, I am certain" (II, ch. 7). "It seems to me," adds Decoud, "that I have caught his last breath—the breath of his departing soul on his lips." The familiar ambiguity of last words in fiction is reduced here to the unresonant confusion of mere imperceptibility. Yet whether a mixed blessing or a dubious imperative in seeming support of a separatist plan which is the antithesis of the old man's republican dream, Don José's death gasp at the Casa Gould includes for certain a sacred name that Decoud in his godless egotism cannot help but defile. And so a deathbed urging as spiritual legacy must again, inevitably, be betrayed and violated. Hearing that her father seems to have meant to give Decoud encouragement in his plan for a separate city-state, Antonia knows that this sentiment alone constitutes the extinction of the nationalist patriarch as dreamer: "Then, indeed, I fear he will never speak again" (II, ch. 7). Silence, for the writer, the rhetorician, the republican polemicist is in its own terms a definition of death. Decoud himself has, after all, admitted earlier that to write his impassioned political journalism without real feeling for the cause amounts to an "intellectual death" (II, ch. 5). Allegorized now in a father figure's suddenly mute decrepitude, the import of whose decline is reiterated within one last piece of Decoud's own prose—for once, but too late, in the form of a private letter felt and urgently addressed—this metaphor of "intellectual death" is soon literalized in the physical death waiting for Decoud.

Precisely that Victorian legacy which E. M. Forster attempts to resist in the minimalism of his death scenes Conrad ironically cashes in. The widely proliferated habit in Dickens of figurative deadness impelled toward a literalizing scene, especially in the punitive ironies associated with Dickensian villains, is a practice assimilated and modified by Conrad. Heroes and villains alike in his fiction, or those hybrid protagonists who are neither one nor the other, find their ends predicted by the passing metaphors in which they speak or are spoken of. Kurtz's physical death is merely a noxious concentration of the funereal figures of speech that precede it. In characteristic Victorian fashion, the consequent hint of foregone conclusion and so dramatic redundancy in his death shunts it a few steps off-stage ("Mistah Kurtz—he dead"). This is no less true of the just barely deflected, because already metaphorically predetermined, death scenes in *Nostromo*: those of Charles's father, Don José, Teresa Viola, the merchant Hirsch later, and even, until the plot doubles back upon it and style pries it open, that of Decoud himself.

It is immediately after Decoud finishes the letter to his sister, recounting as its central episode a death associated by symbolic contagion with his own moral collapse, that Nostromo arrives on the scene with a doctor for the dying Teresa. She pleads with the man who is virtually her adopted son to bring a priest instead, to see her through to her destiny. Yet Nostromo's egotism insists on the greater importance of his own mission and his role as hero at its center. Over and above her end he places his own continuity: "It concerns me to keep on being what I am." In her despair Teresa realizes that Nostromo has failed the "supreme test." That adjective familiar by now in Conrad (used as a parallel between the deaths of the helmsman and Kurtz) suggests this supplication as his mortal trial rather than hers. First Gould Senior by a letter to his son, then old José to his pending son-in-law as reported in the latter's own letter had each at death enjoined upon the second generation, in effect, the saving of the younger's soul. Now, at the actual scene of that letter writing by Decoud, Teresa pleads directly for the salvation of her own soul, knowing that compliance will also redeem her intended son-in-law. Soon giving up hope for herself and for Nostromo, she too dies away from the will to live, fading without benefit or necessity of an actual death scene.

The dying moment we think we have been spared (or deprived of) has in fact transpired by yet another displacement. From this point on it grows clear that Nostromo, by refusing to save a supplicating soul, has in the process lost his own. The deathbed confrontation of vanity and fatality has failed to chasten and reroute its hero, standing instead as a symbolic mirror of his spiritual decay, to be played out in detail later, and again by a kind of reverse mirror image, in the death of his alter ego, Decoud. If, in his love for Antonia, Decoud can identify himself in that letter to his sister as a man with "a passion, but without a mission" (II, ch. 7), his counterpart Nostromo collapses this very dichotomy to distort self-love into a public duty, identity become the puppet of its own repute. As Nostromo leaves the deathbed of Teresa, her eyes have fallen from him in defeat. In the passing local mention of his "disregarded figure" is inscribed the verbal assassination of this cynosure of all gaze—the man who lived in every sense for the world's external "regard."

This returns us to the motivation of Decoud's letter and the need for another's regard, or at least attention, that it bespeaks. Precisely because he knows he cannot, in all probability, keep on being, Decoud needs at last to set down what he has been. Decoud's is a prolonged inscription that becomes a death by displacement in a peculiarly causal sense: the preemption of temporal identity by text. Here we enter that concentrically structured space in the Conradian novel where the power of retrospect, so often associated with the scene of drowning in fiction, comes into focus as the force of textuality itself. Even in that version of ingrown vanity which contemns and dismisses the outer world, a character like Decoud aches to leave his identity etched upon that world, if not in fame then in a more familiar, or familial, knowing. So that even in this tendency of his ego, Decoud is an inward contrary or inverted double of Nostromo in the latter's tyrannical lust for publicity. "In the most sceptical heart there lurks at such moments, when the chances of existence are involved, a desire to leave a correct impression of the feelings, like a light by which the action may be seen when personality is gone, gone where no light of investigation can ever reach the truth which every death takes out of the world" (II, ch. 7). The prolonged dying cadences of his dual subordination, the repeated verb of departure or dissipation, *gone,* and the appositive trail stretched out from it at the end hold open in their own distended syntactic "impression" on the page that hovering verbal afterimage they are meant to figure. The chapter's carefully engineered succession of fatalities turned inside out to narrative encasement—one set of dying words (Don José's) inscribed in a sense by another (Decoud's last letter) and succeeding to another (Teresa's)—thus lends schematic emphasis to the relation between life itself and its last enunciation. Long before we watch Decoud's corpse drop into the gulf, the internalized pattern of drowning retrospect can be seen extruded as the textual endeavor of reminiscence and memorial.

In writing to his sister, Decoud is said to enjoy "almost an illusion of her presence" (II, ch. 7), as Gould had in reverse with his father until the letters stopped at his death. This reciprocity of scriptive illusions, vesting with presence an author and audience alike, bears from both directions on Decoud's final act of scriptive record. His illusion about the immanence of his sister is one he expects to have requited by her own faith in his posthumous presence, after his removal not only from the site of inscription but from the world of existence itself. The scriptive pun from which all this allegory of textual respite and presence seems spun is already there in Decoud's natural enough desire to leave an "accurate impression" of his last hours. His own "breathing image" thus moves toward closure as at one with the pen's mechanical "impress." Indeed, in a description of the begrimed Decoud that interrupts his letter early in its course, we hear that his once "rosy lips" are "blackened" with heat and smoke, as if the black ink of his letter were his own speech not transcribed so much as transferred directly from its speaking source in the "delay" that "gives me time to talk to you."

Decoud admits to his sister his besetting doubts about "whether to count myself with the living or the dead" (II, ch. 7). His hallucinatory presence to her as transcribed voice, Conrad means us to see, can only bear out this dubiety. And this implied relation between inscribing source and its reception is, again, recriprocal. If Decoud's vanishing thoughts are embalmed before her eyes as those more or less of a corpse, she thus inhabits even more obviously than otherwise the space of whatever immortality he can expect. So it is entirely appropriate that he feels his letter to be addressed to a recipient beyond the grave, to a "resolute angel," fixed and unflinching, beyond the threshold of his text and his extinction. As a matter of fact, her receiving presence is sketched as if it were in its own right a kind of otherworld. Decoud's words are dispatched beyond imminent death to "another existence." Her very being as other, abstracted by that phrase, is also, as suggested, the only afterlife to which he can aspire. When he shortly drowns in the gulf, because water takes no "impression" except for a transient narcissistic gaze, Decoud goes down "without a trace" (III, ch. 10)—or with none but that of the omniscient narrative which refuses to follow him through the "gates" (as *Lord Jim* had it) of his descent across the "threshold of the invisible."

"With the writing of the last line," closing off a letter running to well over twenty pages, "there came upon Decoud a moment of sudden and complete oblivion" (II, ch. 7). No sooner has the writer seemed to intuit the relation between personality and its articulated gestures toward others than he is convulsed by a premonition of his actual death in a merely scriptive finis: "He swayed over the table as if struck by a bullet." Alternating between ballistic fact and mere metaphor, this is symbolically the same bullet which—after it actually enters Decoud's heart from a gun aimed by the hand that earlier held the pen—will also pierce the breast of the cowardly Hirsch, the unrecognized Nostromo, and, coming full circle again to the merely figurative, the grieving heart of Linda Viola in the presence of Nostromo's slaying. In an even more indirect sense, it is also this same bullet that is the first sign of the fighting to invade the house of the Violas, as remarked later by old Viola to Nostromo in connection with Teresa's long-delayed death scene following the "shot . . . fired down here, which killed her as surely as if the bullet had struck her oppressed heart" (III, ch. 9). All five lethal bullets do mark in their way the penetrating pang of final isolation. Once introduced to mourn

the silenced filial bond between Decoud and his sister in the suspended impress of his last letter, the bullet then passes through the
subsequent fatalities of the plot, each death a denial of or violent
withdrawal from that sustaining communion, verbal or otherwise,
which, transcending ego into feeling, becomes the very definition of
life.

We can now move forward to the brutal gratuitousness of Nostromo's
murder and from there back to the extended death scene of Decoud,
against which Nostromo's end must be read as an elaborate parallel
and displacement. Foretold in his testamentary letter, Decoud's death
is the enacted vacuum into which all the other dyings funnel, and
which only prose not his own, the ironic style of omniscience, can
search to its empty center. The immediate connection forward from
Decoud's letter to the moral death of Nostromo in the room above,
and then forward from that "supreme test" with Teresa Viola to the
actual assassination of the fallen hero on the Viola property at the
end of the novel, retains its association with the motif of a dying
confession or injunction ignored—become at the end, by ironic reversal, Nostromo's own. For it is by disclosing the whereabouts of
the silver that Nostromo would vainly have hoped to author his way
back from thief to hero on his deathbed.

Says old Viola, after having mistakenly shot Nostromo with that
symbolically recurrent bullet through the chest, thinking he was Ra-
mirez come to rob his daughter's virtue, "Like a thief he came, and
like a thief he fell" (III, ch. 13). It is the formula equivocated in
Heart of Darkness—"He died as he lived"—given a new ironic twist
by the structure of double simile. Resting his actions on a justice
circumstantial and poetic, Viola requires only the fatal symmetries
of appearance, whatever the facts ("like . . . like"). The conceivably
saving distinction between the hero only pitifully mistaken for a thief
and some real degeneration of his stature is erased as soon as it is
articulated by what we know of Nostromo's recent debasement. Then,
too, the emphasis on simile, on the metaphoric determination of
death—the mortal moment an analogy come to literal and lethal
pass—aligns this murder with the logic of dying elsewhere in Conrad
and in the fictional tradition on which he so often ironically draws.

With Nostromo's heroic dream dead of its own original sin of pride,
into this symbolically despoiled Eden crashes the sound of original

death, "the first shot ever fired on the Great Isabel" (III, ch. 13). Completing the trajectory of that once metaphoric, four-times literal discharge, the lethal shot now pierces the heart of innocence itself: it is heard by Linda Viola, who has loved Nostromo selflessly and without return, "as though the bullet had struck her breast." The literal and lingering death scene from this wounding bullet is still to follow. Ever since his fixation on the silver, Nostromo's usual ennobling epithets have been replaced now and then with a blatant identifying phrase such as "the man whose soul was dead within him." The shriving of such a soul in confession, recalling the last wish he had in fact denied to Teresa Viola, is thus ruled out as redundant in advance, despite his frenzied efforts to confess to Mrs. Gould the whereabouts of the silver. He wants her to believe his excuse when he wails, "I die betrayed—betrayed by—" (III, ch. 13), where the truncated last words recall Kurtz's stumbling, half-hearted formulas from the tradition of the meaningful death scene. Yet the only grammar of completed action for Nostromo would be reflexive, sign of a closed and vicious circle of defeat and self-betrayal.

Refusing to hear more about the loathed silver, Mrs. Gould "averted her glance from the miserable subjection of the dying man" (III, ch. 13). As before, when Nostromo failed the "supreme test" with Teresa Viola, here in Mrs. Gould's "averted" glance the hero is once more and finally "disregarded." The retributive pattern is complete in Nostromo's frustrated attempt at confession, since once more last rites are disallowed. For the actual death sentence Conrad's style again adjusts its register between the poles of literal and figurative diction (my emphasis): "Then his head rolled back, his eyelids fell, and the capataz de cargadores died without a word or moan after an hour of immobility, broken by short shudders *testifying* to the most atrocious sufferings." With the hero of action now immobilized, except for this mute, spasmodic body language, the last verb of his existence emerges as the dead metaphor "testifying" submitted to a macabre reanimation. The hero's soul prematurely effaced, his dying will to confess foiled, all last rites, including those of revelatory passage, suspended—here on the bitter underside of diction is Nostromo's last and only testament.

The novel's major chronology can thus be taken to begin and end with, and include twice at its turning point, a shunned last utterance. All this mortal articulation falling on deaf ears throws into relief the climactic death of Decoud, solitary, unknown to any imagination save the narrator's, briefly articulate but entirely unheard. Yet Decoud's is a death which Nostromo, long before his own death, wishes to reinhabit so as to outlast with understanding, as he has been able in body to survive his own ignominious return to life from his earlier plunge into Golfo Placido at the moment when the two men separated. Instituting the structures of displacement that bind hero to antihero, and even confuse the distinction, throughout the later retrospective scene of Decoud's death, the narrative would appear to suggest that the suicide which sends Decoud headfirst into the gulf is also part of a pattern that completes the earlier spiritual death of Nostromo with a second mock resurrection. As if moving again through his desperate plunge and resurfacing only to find himself this time in the suicidal space of his alter ego, Nostromo, climbing aboard the deserted dinghy, "resembled a drowned corpse come up from the bottom" (III, ch. 10). As Nostromo wonders about the dried blood he finds on the gunwale, his morbid curiosity triggers the very narrative that explains it. The immersed and returned presence of the wondering hero is thus displaced in flashback by the disappearing presence of the antithetical spirit who preceded him there and who dropped out of sight in the gulf, never (in his own person) to reemerge again.

Conrad summons for the rehearsal of Decoud's death the most sophisticated structures of rhetorical prose—anaphora, chiasmus, synesthesia—so as to penetrate the dying psyche to the very threshold of narratability. Then, in an echoing paragraph immediately following, many of the same figurative and grammatical devices are reprised to describe Nostromo in the throes of his effort to imagine exactly this elapsed death scene. There is no other passage quite like it in Conrad: the death of a solitary self corresponding to the spiritual failing of another in the very rhythms of report. Indeed, we discover by the novel's end that the internalized and distended death of Decoud amounts to the only subjectively rendered dying that Conrad is to provide even for the hero Nostromo. The narrative is largely withdrawn, as we have seen, from his later deathbed sufferings to the objectivity of mere mention, as if his death too were virtually offstage. Postponed for one hundred fifty pages or so in order to be more strategically placed, Decoud's end is thus foregrounded, even in flashback, not only as the pivot for the novel's themes of mortality, egotism, and memento mori but also as the lone scrutinized repository of its otherwise deflected death scenes, with all their differing and desperate gestures at last words.

Nearing his later and actual death, Nostromo begins to speak in metaphors of spiritual onus, which we have already seen made literal in the death of Decoud. Nostromo comes to realize that his own story replicates the local myth of the thieving gringos, "neither dead nor alive, bound down to their conquest of unlawful wealth" (III, ch. 12). Decoud's is a parallel fate, for he too has been in a starkly factual sense "bound down" by (in the narrator's phrase "weighted by") the four silver ingots which guarantee his sinking out of sight. Nostromo's self-betrayal is thus offered up in this detail as metaphoric tenor to the literal vehicle of Decoud's earlier suicide. Almost every phrase in this retrospective death scene is loaded with the same earned weight. The passage is begun with the disclosure that Decoud died "from solitude" (III, ch. 10), an ironic overlay of cause and effect within a single prepositional phrase: the man slain in an epitomizing moment *by* his own emotional isolation and so fled *from* the excruciating consciousness of it through suicide. This emptiness he must die away from is that same "great solitude" mentioned in his letter and closed in upon him now. "Solitude from mere outward condition of existence becomes very swiftly a state of soul in which the affectations of irony and scepticism have no place," explains the narrator now, and in the quick, unpunctuated grammar of the clause we meet again a fatal transposition from objective to subjective register.

The satirical journalist is thrown back upon himself, with no external provocation for striking a pose against the world; Decoud's very "individuality," usually differentiated by ironic distance, "merged into the world of cloud and water, of natural forces and forms of nature" (III, ch. 10). What might describe the aftermath of drowning and natural reabsorption in a Romantic text is here more neutralizing and lugubrious. With that last alliterative and chiastic dichotomy between force and form—the indifferent order (and orderliness) of nature, of nonhuman impulse and nonhuman shapes—the dying moment is readied. Death arrives in a delirious synesthesia by which the aural void of silence is hallucinated by Decoud as an attenuated specter,[9] an incarnate "stretched" absence at the threshold of death.

The silence appeared again before him, stretched taut like a dark, thin string.

His eyes looked at it while, without haste, he shifted his seat from the thwart to the gunwale. *They looked* at it fixedly, while his hand, feeling about his waist, unbuttoned the flap of the leather case, drew the revolver, cocked it, brought it forward pointing at his breast, pulled the trigger, and, with convulsive force, sent the still-smoking weapon hurtling through the air. *His eyes looked* at it while he fell forward and hung with his breast on the gunwale and the fingers of his right hand hooked under the thwart. *They looked*——(III, ch. 10, my emphasis)

Prose itself drives toward and holds at the threshold, style asked to evince the invisible as invisible.

In the preceding tales we have considered, and so far in *Nostromo*, all important deaths have been transmitted second-hand by a mediating narrative voice. It may be safe to say that this is what has until now interested Conrad most about the traditional power of the death scene: its possibilities for wording. The anonymous voiced "we" of the narrating crewman in *The Nigger* recounts the death of Wait, Marlow the deaths of the helmsman and Kurtz in one novel, of Brierly, Chester, and Jim in another. A note or telegram we never read in *Nostromo* announces the death of Charles's father, and after that Decoud's letter mediates for us the death of Don José. The significance of dying in Conrad has thus far tended to surface when localized and locked into a foregrounded narrative frame. Yet in their handling of the actual death moment, neither the speaking voice of *The Nigger* nor Marlow is a self-conscious stylist of the kind to test his mettle on the rhetorical treatment of death. In his later written text to his sister, Decoud the gifted writer may be alert to the ambiguities and ellipses of a dying man's last words, but he too makes no attempt to inflect them with his own verbal interventions and imaged transitions. His is the journalistic and objective eye—and pen—at their most reserved and terse, testifying not to the possible flourishes of textualized death so much as to the conveyable force of its very fact. Conrad seems to insist on this—unembellished death as a reported phenomenon—before experimenting with the modes and limits of death's representation. In *Nostromo* we must still wait out the off-stage deaths of Donna Emilia and of the cowardly merchant Hirsch before Decoud's circumscribed and restrained writing about death is reciprocated by the death of the writer himself under the incisive eye of omniscence. Only then does the novelist let his prose requisition, however sarcastically, the full arsenal of Victorian style—not only the immediate verbal interval of transposition, the rhetorical strategies of epitome, and the structural mechanics of displacement but the whole exploratory figuration and syntax of the approached threshold, here ironically closed tight.

As the act of reading follows with its own eyes along the grooves of that remorseless parallelism of sighted silence at Decoud's death, grammar barrels through half a dozen serial clauses to the prose enjambment of "They looked——" trailing off there into the uninscribed absence to the right of that truncated syntax. Far removed from the prophetic parallelism of Sydney Carton's reiterated "I see," Decoud's looking is neutered to a mechanical implementation of "they" without even a visual, let alone visionary result. The passage thus installs the form of looking without seeing, act without function, exactly as a synecdoche for the dying mind. The dissociation of senses that reifies silence as a visible tense "string" in that synesthetic figure of speech is part of the same sensory disintegration that detaches the eyes and their predicated sight from any other conscious bodily function. We are a long way from the "profound" fading glance of the helmsman or even the "sent" stare of Jim; this is the gaze of and upon absence itself. Decoud the ironic journalist, the bitter and distanced satiric writer, is now, as we are, reading his fate at the threshold of the invisible, as if even the void of final silence were legible to him. So of course is silence visible to the textual reader of this climactic scene; it is inscribed in each spare, taut line stretched out before us in those silent—scripted, unspoken—words of narrative. Conrad's is a passage which, rather like Decoud's letter to his sister, and more self-consciously than most fictions, invokes as we read the "illusion of . . . presence," this time of third rather than second person, even as such an illusion is dispelled in that white blank of cancellation after the dash.

In this elided transposition from the paradox of seen invisibility to pure effacement, we also encounter a more overt typographic version of the mortal interval than in any of the preceding Victorian novels we have studied, a death sentence contracted to a vanishing intransitive clause: "They looked——." Death opens the hiatus between subject, already the merely synecdochic eyes, and unstated object across a suspended accusative grammar that is the end of all transaction with otherness, all transitivity. The passage thus provides a perfect epitome of this sneering man who so disregarded the world around him that his dying predication takes as little note as possible, except in its abrupt abrogation at the end, of the world's removal from him, his from it. Whereas the innate continuities of standard grammar served any number of Victorian writers in their efforts to suppress the inevitable rupture of death, Conrad's "They looked——" resists the securities of syntax to insist on death as severance, even in the middle of a clause.

The interlocked quartet of predications in that gripping, that tenacious paragraph ("His eyes looked . . . They looked . . . His eyes looked . . . They looked——") evoke only to break off the rhetorical momentum which a Victorian writer, in a less ironic and leveling way, might have used to finesse an ineffable transit. As much as any probable debt to *Hard Times* in Marlow's phrasing of Kurtz's death, there is a likely Dickensian precedent for Decoud's death as well, revealingly modified by Conrad. It is the death scene from *Dombey and Son* (ch. 58) of Alice Brown, Harriet Carker attending, with its own threefold parallelism (italicized here):

> *The lustrous eyes*, yet fixed upon her face, closed for a moment, then opened; and Alice kissed and blest her.
>
> *The same eyes* followed her to the door; and in their light, and on the tranquil face, there was a smile when it was closed.
>
> *They never turned away*. She laid her hand upon her breast, murmuring the sacred name that had been read to her; and life passed from her face, like light removed.

Conrad's is a thresholding without transcendental access compared to Dickens's delirious elision of tense at "never turned away." Dickens even coordinates that closing of the door with the departure of consciousness, so that Alice's inward release seems projected onto the symbolic detail of her friend's exit. Dickens's typically ambiguous redemptive adverb in "never turned away" then provides a hidden transposition from the secular to the atemporal register, as if to suggest a beatific last vision of affectionate fellowship on earth passing unbroken into eternity under impetus from the rhetorical repetition itself. Dickens's style relaxes into the forward drift of such syntax; Conrad's prose stiffens against it. Decoud's continuous fixed look suggests the glazed stare of rigor mortis before the fact rather than the dazed peace of the dying Alice, where even the varied returns of the controlling grammatical anaphora leave their stamp of elegant variation on the sliding last alliteration and assonance of "life . . . like . . . light." Instead, the blunt truncation of Conrad's passage is dedicated at least as much to the metaphysically as to the aesthetically arresting.

These conjoined passages illustrate a quintessential line of descent and mutation for the argument of this book. We have been studying the multiple, and manipulable, perspectives by which death in fiction is seen and set down in the transition from the nineteenth-century novel to the twentieth. With contrary results in this single pair of examples, Dickens and Conrad enact such seeing from within the very scene of death, localizing omniscience in the either transfigured or canceled "vision" of the character, the implied rise to sublime insight or the lapse to mechanical looking. As always, such seeing must in narrative also be said; visionary options, whether chosen or not, make their claim on the verbal. Rarely could the actions of prose style itself, the almost subliminal hum of its syntactic expectations, more markedly than in these passages humanize to our ears the temporal discontinuity of death, whether ironically succumbed to or wondrously overcome.

Just before death, when Decoud stops rowing on the placid gulf and gives up all direction and movement, he pulls in the oars with a meaningless noise that is a satire on all moments of annunciation, certainly terminal ones: "The hollow clatter they made in falling was the loudest noise he had ever heard in his life. It was a revelation" (III, ch. 10). In some sense Kurtz can be said to have achieved a revelation in death, and Lord Jim may well have been rewarded with a less awful one. But here the visionary influx is merely "hollow," just empty noise. Coming entirely from this side of Marlow's "threshold of the invisible," and slamming shut any further access, it is epiphany by parody. The character is left to a wholesale displacement of personal interiority at the moment of annihilation: "His last thought was 'I wonder how that capataz died.' " This death sentence, arguably simultaneous with Decoud's last looking and last saying, is immediately followed by a further parody of immersion in the destructive element more chilling than the reported scenes of drowning in *Lord Jim* because already posthumous, a mere burial at sea.

A man whose burden in life has been cast in the reflexive grammar less of egotism than of rebounding irony, a man victimized by that "fatal touch of contempt for himself to which his complex nature was subject" (II, ch. 8), encounters his ultimate subjection at the moment of his death, in a mode of verbal degeneration that anticipates the coming end of his double. Nostromo has been plagued, in his own solitude on the gulf, by a "revulsion of subjectiveness" (III, ch. 8); said nearer the close to be "subjective almost to insanity" (III, ch. 10), the would-be mythic figure declines from heroic subject to mere object when Mrs. Gould finally averts "her glance from the miserable *subjection* of the dying man" (III, ch. 13, my emphasis). A parallel declension within the language associated with Decoud marks his end. His "barren indifferentism" (II, ch. 3) sinks to its reduced echo when the cynical Decoud falls into the placid and implacable gulf, the ironist finally "swallowed up in the immense indifference of things" (III, ch. 10), immersed and interred. Like Nostromo in that final "subjection," his double, Decoud, seems to disappear somewhere in the degrading of subjectivity to objectivity, here in the midst of a verbal shift from personal indifferentism to external indifference. The least Romantic of drownings in our fictional examples so far, it marks merely the descent from a coldly removed stance to its blank objective correlative in the outer, the insentient universe.

The operations of vision by now only vestigial in the repeated "looked," and so the world excluded from view, still the man Nostromo knew as "the talker" requires some last word, whether of summation and judgment or merely of finis. Decoud had once said that the life of his native land was like a ludicrous opera in which "the blood flows all the time" (II, ch. 3), and this conceit (in both senses) is rendered corporeal, again literalized, when he comes to his own articulate end in a mockery of heroic sacrifice, speaking his version of Christ's last words: " 'It is done,' he stammered out, in a sudden flow of blood" (III, ch. 10). Into that fatal gap yawning wide in the catastrophic ellipsis of "They looked—" the uttermost word has been inserted. The man without a mission has been driven inexorably by plot toward this parodic Passion, but his *"Consummatum est"* is only another negative epitome. Conrad's narrative, repeatedly haunted by the attempt to check life against, or ratify it by, an expressive death scene, has now referred this urge back to the primal scene in Western culture for the authorizing of heroic myth by the moment of articulate dying. In Conrad's sacrificial revisionism, he who died so that others might live is the type of all those fictional characters who die so that articulate narrative can affirm a validity comparable to the testings of death.

While Decoud is wondering in the narratively reconstructed scene of his death about the death of his immediate double, as well as of his distant precursor in Christ, so is Nostromo, in the present tense that frames this retrospect, speculating about Decoud's end. The very fact, let alone the content, of Decoud's allusion to an earlier legendary death is a further function of the textual and psychological displacement at work in his summoning of Christ's dying utterance. Part of this circuitous irony is discovered by comparing Decoud's last words, "It is done," with the owl's scream that has earlier answered to Nostromo's troubled thoughts in his own isolation unto death on the island. At that point Nostromo's mind has also just reverted to another death scene from which he had absented himself, wondering if Teresa would have died by this time. Just then the owl's "appalling cry" comes in immediate, as well as sinister and accusatory response, that "Ya-acabo! Ya-acabo! (It is finished; it is finished) that announces calamity and death in the popular belief" (III, ch. 8). Since Nostromo is himself the incarnation of popular belief, a heroic principle embodied from within the people, this superstitious reading of the inhuman cry is located exactly in the realm of the hero's deification and so of his moral finish and effacement. To die in the people's belief is to lose the only life he has.

Decoud's biblical allusion naturally recalls the heroic *usque ad finem* and more neutral finis of *Lord Jim*, yet for Conrad's bitter cynic, the "done" of Decoud is an exorcism of fate without the grace of revealed form or significance. It is a finality that infects as well the would-be hero trapped in its orbit. The poetic justice to which death sentences Decoud is stylistically displaced almost at once upon his alter ego. Here is the whole complex last grammar: "A victim of the disillusioned weariness which is the retribution meted out to intellectual audacity, the brilliant Don Martin Decoud, weighted by the

bars of San Tomé silver, disappeared without a trace, swallowed up
in the immense indifference of things" (III, ch. 10). At the head of
the next paragraph: "The magnificent capataz de cargadores, victim
of the enchanted vanity which is the reward of audacious action, sat
in the weary pose of a hunted outcast through a night of sleeplessness
as tormenting as any known to Decoud, his companion in the most
desperate affair of his life. And he wondered how Decoud had died."
The status as victim is itself posited by a frontal appositive in Decoud's
case, only for his name to emerge slowly from it with the specification
of his death. By typifying contrast, the opening assertion of Nostromo's
identity, mediated by honorific title, is then undercut by the fact that
his real name is nowhere present, absorbed by the very myth of repute
that is mocked here by absolute solitude. Across the stylistic grid of
the paired passages, in the deviously reshuffled emphasis of phrasing,
the epithets in general shift from inner worth ironically extolled in
Decoud's case to outward show in Nostromo's, "brilliant" to the more
literal shimmer of "magnificent"; the ethically explicit "retribution"
becomes, in the vicinity of Nostromo's silver, the sarcastic "reward,"
all remuneration turning ultimately punitive if the soul is not in its
own hire; "intellectual" as a modifier of "audacity" is replaced by
"action" as the definitive noun modified by "audacious"; "disillusioned weariness" is not only revised to but explicated by the mock-
magical overtones of "disenchanted vanity" for the folk hero who
seemed to boast a charmed life. The pride that braces ego against
world, and would in Nostromo's case fire the mind into heroic action,
shrinks to self-exhaustion for both characters in the face of an unmalleable reality. Intellectual audacity and audacious action, halves
of a single heroic self incomplete without the coexistence of these
qualities, tend, when they remain sundered, to do themselves in.

   The desire of the mind to know death by entering upon but also
outlasting it, to compass it by proxy, as in the devolution of Kurtz's
deathly revelation upon Marlow, reaches its ironic nadir in *Nostromo*.
Only half a dozen sentences separate "His last thought was: 'I wonder
how that capataz died' " from "And he wondered how Decoud had
died." Six sentences and a vast psychological breach. Without the
interpretive vantage of an intermediary narrator, death in Conrad is,
for all its ironic point, loosening its hold on spiritual portent. Kurtz
is delivered over to horrible knowledge in death and retrieves it into

speech. Lord Jim may or may not come upon his grand vision at the brink, and in any case dies without uttering it. Decoud and Nostromo, their deaths interpenetrating, look into each other's abyss as well as their own and end without any revelation worth giving voice, deputized to no traded epiphanies but the hollowness of the void. The finish of Decoud recalls both Hardy's blistering pessimism and Thackeray's textual self-consciousness. Unlike the receding editorial voice of the narrator at the end of *The Newcomes*, however, Decoud in his last textual "impression" with that proleptic letter cannot continue to narrate his own presence even in third person. His energy and his pen give out, he feels slain, and not too long after he pulls a trigger to finish the job, speaking there no longer of the "I" or even the "he" of identity. At the moment of the bullet's impact, voicing the act ("It is done") to no one in particular, not even to his psychologically dissipated self, having even less grip than Jude's "And I here" on the vocabulary of being, he blurts out in third person, in a spurt of blood, the impersonal "it" of his finis as nothing more than an objective deed done.

Decoud's mythic last clause has a literary as well as religious lineage, it should also be said, with a notable appearance in the Russian master for whom Conrad had little use. Rejecting Tolstoy's transcendental streak, the mystical loopholes of his tragic plotting, Conrad is not likely to have taken an interest in his late work, *The Death of Ivan Illych* (1886). Yet what Conrad produced two decades later with the death of Decoud could not be a more effective parody if it had been planned as such. "It is finished" says "someone" over the presumed corpse of Tolstoy's title character, yet for the still-living Ivan the words echo "in his soul" until they resonate into redefinition. The idea of finality is transposed across a Christian interval from life's temporal end, through the advent and end of dying, on into the destination of eternal life. " 'Death is finished,' he said to himself. 'It is no more!' " Since this mystic shift of perspective is effected only by Ivan's sudden suffering on behalf of those faced with his grievous end, rather than just generated out of his own self-pity— since it is selflessness alone that has released the protagonist to revelation—Christ's last words on the Cross are fittingly evoked. Long after Tolstoy, there is a secularized reprise of this consummating utterance with Woolf's closural "It was finished" in *To the Lighthouse*

(1928). This occurs when Lily Briscoe (whose own quoted remark in present tense it seconds) has discovered the last stroke she needs to complete what amounts to a commemorative painting for her dead friend, Mrs. Ramsay, a displacement of death into the less ferocious sacrifice and finality of art.[10] In between Tolstoy's religious transfiguration and Woolf's reflexive modernist closure falls Conrad's *Nostromo*, rejecting the one by debased echo and anticipating the other with the implicitly metatextual link between the figurative bullet wound of Decoud's last letter and the long-withheld having "done" of his actual death by gunshot.

Without the previous mediating storytellers of Conrad's Marlow narratives, *Nostromo* gives a special stress to the decentering of record from reality. Deferring his fatal mission for as long as he keeps writing to his sister, Decoud is in another sense exiling all immediate life from the impressions he sets down. If *Heart of Darkness* turns the potential textual allegory of representation, the slaying replay of Kurtz's terror in Marlow's yarn, into a moral fable, making Marlow's tampering brand of retelling to Kurtz's fiancée not only a constituent of discourse but a sin, then *Nostromo* serves to reverse this pattern from the ethical back to the textual. By first spelling out bad writing, in the case of Decoud's hypocritical journalism, as an "intellectual death," Conrad's novel then goes on to enact the dilemma of any textuality as a different but inevitable dying away from the real. To this end, too, Decoud's last words, "It is done," do their work. Beyond its parodistic Christology, Decoud's last clause is underwritten, which is only to say undermined, by an ironic grammatology. Completing his letter's fading evocation of life with its literal revocation in the tabula rasa of the gulf, Decoud's last three monosyllables recall Derrida's notion that the purest speech act is the enunciation "I am dead,"[11] calling up in turn Hamlet's instance of this remark to Horatio. In a deconstructive reading, such a clause exposes that evacuation of referent which characterizes all discourse. Decoud's exit line, no "I" in sight,[12] further exposes this by the ambiguous neuter pronoun ending at once the "it" of his life and the deed of suicide that concludes it, compressing all duration to a single fugitive interval vanishing to absence, to past tense, as we read.

But here we come round again to the mythopoetic pitch of this last utterance, the deepest ironic point of its biblical allusion. Only one man could say "I am dead," or more to the point "It is finished," and not betray language into the vertigo of the abyss. And that man was no man only, not just any speaker, but the Logos itself made flesh, under a paradoxical dispensation resembling the premises of omniscient fiction. Dying not only under the sign of the Cross but with the grace of the Transcendental Sign itself, Christ as the Incarnate Word speaks as perfected signified to his own signifier. Nostromo, who feels himself mysteriously and even blasphemously betrayed, but who has in fact sold his own soul for silver, is the parody Christ, who dies without a word. Decoud, by contrast, is the suicidal scriptor as ironic modernist. He knows just how far his self-conscious last allusion falls short of any validating metaphysical illusion. For Decoud, in whose sarcastic "It is done" the self as embodied word suffers excision rather than ascension, nothing is finished, only over, nothing is in the root sense perfected, *per facere*; for nothing and no one is carried through. Not sacramental invocation but sacrilege, not creative utterance but mere literary allusion, Decoud's last words, along with that displaced wonder about his double's end, inscribe the irony of secondariness itself, the cannibalizing of another death at the empty center of his own.

This pitting of mere words against the abyss, however efficient as a synecdoche for cathartic fiction, is not in Conrad enough for a life— or a death. The cynical journalist and "talker," the self costumed and cocooned in words, would have to have passed more willingly across language's "threshold of the invisible," from the opacity of ironic phrase to the clear perception of otherness, in order to retrieve any dying "I" from the mock-scriptural abdication of "It is done"— to reclaim an existential cast of mind from a purely textual one. Yet the novel's double bind—this novel's, any novel's—results from the fact that genuine access to reality even for its characters is in some literal sense more readily said than done, the world's authenticity sooner enunciated than otherwise confronted, uttered than engaged. This is the most unsettling implication of Decoud's mentality when sent to its limit in death, and Conrad's text resists even while considering it. Dying is retired from the arena of verbal meanings in *Nostromo* in the name (far from Decoud's lips near his end) of that reality beyond speech which death not only obstructs but nullifies. Refusing language its classic privileges in educing truth from death can generate further questions about the availability, elsewhere and anywhere, of the world through words. Thematizing the very limits of his own medium, Conrad takes up as subject what he is up against as writer. He renders the death of an insistently verbal imagination so that the scene comes to be about the very precariousness of language that brings it about to begin with. The half-hundred pages that remain between Decoud's last words and Conrad's closure serve to measure, by being possible at all, the extent of Conrad's recoil from the full deconstructive implications of his own anxious insight. There is something left to present, to imagine representable, which Decoud's death, despite the questions of reference it vexes, has in one sense left behind: the renderable world apart from him, which survives his finis on the way to plot's own "End." Nearer closure, another character dies in the middle of a look as a further parable of reading itself in arrest. Recalling both the textual death of Decoud, when "he swayed over the table" at which he was finishing his last letter, and the objectless staring of his eyes during his subsequent suicide, there is the fatal collapse of Old Viola immediately after Nostromo's death. Wearily reading for the last time his cherished Bible, Viola "never detached his eyes from the book while he swayed forward, gently, gradually, till his snow-white head rested upon the open pages." With his body left "growing slowly cold," Conrad closes his most explicit scene of mortally interrupted reading, and this merely a page from the finis of his own fiction.

Before coming to Woolf's "It was finished" at the end of *To the Lighthouse*, we will also encounter the ironic Christ-like sacrifice of Gerald Crich in the ice world of Lawrence's *Women in Love* (1922), death a futile solution to the need for traversing the interval between, as the character himself puts it, the functionally "over" and the authentically "finished." On the way toward Lawrence, Woolf, and her postmodern heirs, we move forward now from the thresholding experiments of Conrad's fiction, narrative poised with its heroes on the articulated brink of extinction, to the connective parables of E. M. Forster. Even more than Conrad's, Forster's death scenes strive to reject the celebratory potential, theistic or aesthetic, of the more stabilizing "It is finished" for the flat, nonmetaphysical fact of "It is ended." They thus return the quest for order and cohesion entirely to the world of time.

5

Connective

Time, Death, and Judgment, by George Frederic Watts
Courtesy The Art Institute of Chicago

He had entered the cathedral partly to avoid the rain and partly to see a picture that had educated him in former years. But the light was bad, the picture ill placed, and Time and Judgment were inside him now. Death alone still charmed him, with her lap of poppies, on which all men shall sleep.

E. M. FORSTER, *Howards End*

5

We too take ship O soul,
Joyous we too launch out on trackless seas,
Fearless for unknown shores on waves of ecstasy to sail . . .

Thoughts, silent thoughts, of Time and Space and Death,
                              like waters flowing,
Whose air I breathe, whose ripples hear, lave me all over . . .

                    WHITMAN, "Passage to India"

Dead she was—committed to the deep while still on the
southward track . . . she was further in the tropics than she
ever achieved while on shore, when the sun touched her for
the last time and her body was lowered into yet another
India—the Indian Ocean.

                    FORSTER, *A Passage to India*

SEVENTY SOME YEARS after the publication of E. M. Forster's
The Longest Journey (1907), *The New Yorker* magazine ran the
following disgruntled query: "I have always been worried by the
abruptness of Gerald's death in Chapter 5 of E. M. Forster's 'The
Longest Journey.' What happened? Why did Forster do that?"[1] Despite the editor's flippant dismissal, these were questions all but
universal in the early reviews too, where worry took the form of
reproval. Abruptness is one thing, but the troublesome narrative then
doubles back to study Gerald's death with all the brutal understatement that characterizes Forster's shorn rhetoric in the handling of the
death scene.

"Gerald died that afternoon," the fifth chapter begins. "He was
broken up in a football match" (p. 55). The idiomatic metaphor for
psychological collapse seems pinched at first to a deadly literal irony.
Yet when we return to the dramatized scene of death, the phrase
"broken up" does also account, after all, for the emotionally crippled
temper of the dying. To the athlete's fiancée, Agnes, the whole grotesque, undignified, and meaningless death by accident presents itself

as a "curious joke." Forster's prose seems to take its parodistic tone in recoil from her emotional fatuity. The slow eviction from consciousness in the presence of a loved one calls up the form of a traditional dying without the ordinary content, the stage of pathos at once set and emptied. In the narrative's combined burden of pitiless irony and spiritually bereft pathos, this is one of the truly shocking moments in modern fiction. The novelistic options of the revelatory death scene are meant to wither before our eyes, travestied and vetoed. Forster is out to censure the assumed epiphanic ripeness of such occasions by choking off every sardonically evoked opportunity for emotional clarity, let alone consolation, dragging out a death as wooden and hollow as the coffin to which dying delivers the corpse. Nearly the athlete's last utterance is only a plea for the release from all speech: "I want—I don't want to talk" (p. 56). Muttering, "I can't see you," he "passed from her trembling with open eyes." Before the close of the twentieth century's first decade, the time-honored rhetoric of the death scene seems in danger of losing its voice entirely.

In his satire of mortuary expectation Forster draws subversively upon the traditional textured phrasing of the death moment, its lexical shifts, the swift ambivalence of its syntax, in precisely those phrases meant to deflate the ordinary force of this rhetoric. In "passed from her trembling with open eyes" there is the aura of an ambiguous interval or breach, both in vanishing time and between the lovers in space, which allows Forster's narrative its mordantly poignant dodge of cathartic rhetoric. There is, in other words, a potential grammatical slippage from the gerund phrase "her trembling," describing Agnes's condition at this crisis, to a lone participle modifying Gerald's shivering passage as he slides blinded from her grasp. But the former is rendered improbable by Agnes's bland, blank disbelief in death throughout the scene. When "he passed from her trembling," it is unlikely that she was convulsed with him at the violence of their rupture. With Agnes sharing neither the pain nor the terror, there is nothing between them in this scene but their separation, his eventual nothingness. Forster opens up the alternative reading only to have us reject it. The equivocal "trembling" which would index the lovers' convergence of response, however pitifully at this point, the ambiguity that would through its own tremulousness of designation fuse the two lovers in death, almost with the mutual spasms of a *Liebestod*—this passing equivocation is instead fixed by context, the softening doubleness harshly disallowed by what we know of Agnes. This is Forster's antirhetoric of the death scene, the plangency of absented eloquence. To use that word which becomes the most crucial touchstone of Forster's aesthetic and ethical theory, there is neither connection between the lovers nor connection forward on Gerald's part to anything beyond death. Gerald's protracted end capitulates to no inherited modes of fictional death scenes but rather parades an ironic squandering of their methods on a dying emptied of resonance. The stark pallor of this scene haunts the early part of the novel like the ghost of its own spiritual efficacy.

It must be stressed, however, that in any fiction the rhetoric of dying remains the only recourse even of its own outmoding. The sense of stylistic options must linger long enough to be sabotaged. Forster illustrates this everywhere. *The Longest Journey* is a novel one of whose early reviewers "pleasantly calculated," as Forster put it, that "the percentage of sudden deaths (infants excluded) amounted to over 44% of the adult population."[2] The first two of these deaths, striking in rapid succession the hero's hated father and his beloved mother, however shriveled the scenes' visionary rhetoric, have no place to go for their irony but to style. This is true even when prose is not called upon either to evidence or to defer the actual interval of the death moment. "At last he died," we hear of the father, with the temporal gauge of the adverb fading into its other sense as a tacit sigh of relief in indirect discourse. There is a more complex doubleness of style at the death—indeed precipitating the death—of the hero's revered mother. Mrs. Elliot and son have had words after her husband's death, and Rickie leaves the house refusing to put on his greatcoat. "I do wish you wouldn't keep on bothering" (p. 30), he whines. The transitive verb, taking himself peevishly as implied direct object, shades off to a generalized intransitive; "bothering" becomes a term for caring, for trying, and thus looms as the central predication of the mother's fretful being. Once she is invited to stop, her heart just seems to cease beating; no other explanation is given for her demise. Forster is at his most typical when he follows Rickie's testy departure with this stretch of decimated sentimentality, not irony so much as pathos inside out: "He did not catch cold, but while he was out his mother died. She only survived her husband eleven days, a coincidence which was recorded on their tombstone" (p. 30).

Whatever transposition from petulant idiom to inclusive understanding of life is asked of that participle "bothering," whatever pressure will be put on a possible doubleness within "trembling" later, neither verbal device is expected to connect across time to anything beyond it, to negotiate an interval except on this side of death. Gerald's "passed from her" is, for instance, decidedly not passed *on*; it is a euphemistic idiom held in wretched check. Similarly, to move to our second recurrent category of the fictional death scene, whatever epitome may be dimly implied in these dyings—of the father too emotionally dead to warrant an actual death, of the mother whose life of mere trial is over when the troubling is stopped, of the inexpressive, loutish athlete who has nothing to say for himself at the end—they are quintessential death moments unprovided with drama, voice, revelation, even emphasis. While still transacting the down-played functions of death in fiction, Forsterian irony sloughs off not only the grandeur but the adequacy of death as an opening to disclosure.

This revisionary program for fictional dying does not intend, of course, to incapacitate itself entirely for the treatment of heroic deaths. There are such occasions, yet nothing about their fictional disposition should imply their claim on any valuation beyond the secular. Death has no visionary largesse, nor even any special psychology for Forster. It is rarely given over to the subjective register, remaining a featureless intrusion upon the narrated life in time, aloof, laconic, and incorrigible. Typically, the one scene of drowning in Forster's major fiction involves only objective report pitched to symbolism, no inner rendering of the mind in rehearsal of its own history. In narrative terms the whole scene is a flashback, yet it enacts none within the private drama of its victim. It epitomizes the lapsing life in external gesture without making us privy to the mind's own awareness of this pitiable fitness. I am speaking of the death by water of Mrs. Elliot's lover, Robert, a cultured rustic who has a habit of hiding his worker's hands behind his back in society. In announcing his love to Mrs. Elliot, he hints at what would happen "if I once unhooked my hands" (p. 253). According to her later report of his "heroic" drowning, having already released his arms to the love he bore her but not willing now to have them bear her down to death, "he put his hands behind his back and sank. For he would only have drowned me with him" (pp. 256–257). None of the emblematic meaning of this last posture is given to us as it passes consciously through Robert's mind, or even through his lover's intermediary and suffering account. Behind her recapitulating dialogue of the bare facts, the epitomizing sense is there for us if we seek it: the gesture of humility sustained to the point of heroic self-control. It is, though, decidedly withheld from the narrative voice—by a touching reticence perhaps in this case, but also by programmatic abstention.

The same obliquity and stinted rhetoric usually accompany all three major structural functions of the death scene when they appear in Forster's novels. Transposition is a minimal play with idiom that bridges no metaphysical rift, epitome a faint shadow of its traditional role, and in this way too displacement is no direct doubling but a sly migration of referents. After the athlete Gerald's death, urging Agnes to feel his loss unguardedly, Rickie sets about to impress upon her that "it's your death as well as his" (p. 57). Yet to this convinced emotional corpse Rickie soon attaches himself in the lifelessness of his own desire. When Agnes is alone with Rickie at one point, the narrative sidles into indirect discourse without signaling the transition, precisely so as to displace its subject from suitor to corpse: "She was sitting down with his head on her lap. He had laid it there for a moment before he went out to die, and she had not let him take it away" (p. 80). There is only one possible way to read this all but impossible sequence, given that the hero now "sitting down with his head on her lap" is Rickie, who has many chapters to go yet before his own death by accident. No verbal displacement of the living by the dead could more completely discompose a transition. We must hear Agnes's inner voice (by the narrative deflection of implied internal monologue) to catch the drift of this, and the effect is almost hallucinatory.[3] We realize suddenly that the "he" in the second sentence has sheared off from the present-tense reference to Rickie in an involuntary invocation of the dead lover—but only through the subjective inflection in Agnes's own mind. *He*, that supposedly greater man, lay like this once; Rickie's poor head in her lap now is proof that "she had not let him take it away" even in death, but has replaced him with a second pale lover who dissolves into the original during such rare moments of grace, of present forgetfulness. In a displaced authenticity drawn in part from the novelist's own self-doubts and summing up the plot of the novel as a whole,[4] hero is here superimposed upon broken corpse in this spiritual palimpsest of a second-hand life. This is an omen confirmed by dialogue later when Rickie's robust half-brother, Stephen, is passionately mistaken by Agnes for the dead Gerald. When asked by Stephen where this man Gerald is now, Rickie answers, "Dead." Stephen follows with, "And then you——?" And "Rickie nodded" (p. 275). Ellipsis, with its lack of new predication, opens the gap of displacement. One lover dead, and then Rickie indeed—though Stephen intends only the sexual axis of comparison—dead by default and proxy.

At the time he was writing *The Longest Journey*, Forster delivered a lecture on "Pessimism in Literature" in which he remarked, "We do not judge a man by the words that he gasps on his deathbed. But we do judge a book by the words that are written on the last page."[5] It is a suggestive conjunction of ideas for any thinking about the relation of fictional closure to mortality, and we will return to it. For now, it implies one source of Forster's contempt for the inflated classic death scene, complete with reverberant last words. Untrue to life, such treatment is also untrue to the fiction pledged to that life. This notion is elaborated in proclamations drawn from Forster's biographical prose on the one hand and on the other from his theoretical pronouncements about the novel. Precisely the kind of writing about death which Forster eschews in a characteristic early novel such as *The Longest Journey* is its aestheticizing catharsis in such Victorian letters of bereavement as he describes in "The Deathbeds" chapter from his biography *Marianne Thornton* (1956). There he portrays a working out of grief that amounts more to obsessive narrative strategies than to mere elegiac expression. It is a morbid storytelling in its own right in which "symptoms are dwelt on, dying speeches and death moments repeated and extended," and where "sorrow is so persistently exhibited as joy that both become meaningless" (p. 69). It is both too much and too little like death in fiction. In *Aspects of the Novel* (1927) Forster does admit that though the fictional hero "is generally born off," he is certainly "capable of dying on" (p. 56). Despite his own novels' ironic austerity about death, Forster realizes that in general there is "scarcely anything" about dying that a novelist "may not profitably invent. The doors of that darkness lie open to him and he can even follow his characters through it, provided he is shod with imagination and does not try to bring us back scraps of seance information about the 'life beyond' " (p. 53).

As bearing on a further aspect of the novel, Forster mentions wryly that the corpse has an "apparatus for communicating" that is sadly "not attuned to our apparatus for reception" (p. 48). Any elaborate transposition across the epistemological limit of death, whether by visionary conjecture or mere figure of speech, is thus out of tune with those truths to which mimetic prose can be sure of its real "connection." Forster would instead honor the ineffable with the honestly uninflected. And he would go so far as to bury the retrospective along with the visionary portentousness of death, the articulate and perhaps epitomizing review of a life as well as the invented lurch beyond— rehearsal as well as searching reach. When he is at his most strict and contracted in the arrested rhetoric of dying, the quest for causality in all fictional casualty seems for the most part suspended. Arriving instead with the terse effrontery of the casual, death as event invites little meaning and less moral improvement, validates nothing. " 'The king died and then the queen died' is a story," Forster writes, while " 'The king died and then the queen died of grief' is a plot" (*Aspects*, p. 86). More than any novelist before him in English, Forster reduces death to the stuff of story rather than of plot, a bare fact in the drift of a fiction, inhospitable to explanation or import, neither vindictive nor vindicating.

We have followed the English novel to what in Conrad might well be thought of as the ironic cul-de-sac of a certain grand tradition in the handling of death in fiction, grand even in its squalor and enigma. Conrad's image of the threshold models our expectations, or at least those of his characters, in the arriving death scene, structures the hope of access and disclosure, inscribes the futilities of its portal's own occlusion. His fiction tends to deliver the architecture of revelation while defrauding it of its false content, an ironist of the irradiated moment. Though Forster works occasionally in this way, his more often parodistic approach, demoting to mockery the formulas Conrad meticulously undoes from within, is to undermine the very ground of vision in death. Every locus of terminal epiphany is hollowed to its instantaneous grave. *Mors* has no *articulum* in the major fiction of E. M. Forster; is nothing if not conclusive and mute; is nothing at all. His character Adela Quested in *A Passage to India*, forced to remember at one point that "we must all die," shows that she has not been reading her own author's fiction when she says, "I used to feel death selected people, it is a notion one gets from novels, because some of the characters are usually left talking at the end. Now 'death spares no one' begins to be real" (p. 264). Here is one of Forster's rare narratological openings—indeed ruptures, where we drop straight through plot to a theory of its operation—and it is quickly passed over. Despite the inevitable consignment to still-living fixity of certain characters at the end of a book, or perhaps because of this and its deceptive implications, Forster makes sure that his own narrative deployment of death, extraordinarily frequent and evenhanded, insists on contingency, its scene for the most part precipitous, unprophesied, and absurd, its instant void of traditional sense or solace. Each time a character drops dead on Forster's remorseless pages, the thud reverberates against English and Continental fiction's formulaic death scenes, time-honored as the locus of revelation, however negative or unavailing, even down through Conrad.

It is fitting that in the last major review Forster was to publish, almost four decades after he had stopped writing fiction, he praises Lampedusa's *The Leopard* precisely for its restraint in the handling of a deathbed scene: "What a tribute to the urbanity of death! . . . There is no summing up, nor moral balancing, though before his consciousness weakens the dying man thinks what has happened to him and employs himself in separating the good from the bad."[6] Even this last, however, Forster usually denies to his own dying characters, in case meditation should invite a false sense of visionary trespass. And just as vigilantly do his books attempt to exclude the deeply preordained death, aptness pushed to orchestrated epitome. Forster knew the formula but thought it in pure form mostly comic. During the First World War he took a job as cataloguer and fire watcher at the National Gallery after the most important paintings had been stored away, telling his friends that "if he were killed by bombs, he would die, appropriately, among second-rate masterpieces."[7] Death should not, in the less facetious world of his major fiction, be looked to for its suitedness, whether by onlooker, by reader, or especially by a doomed self. Death, by definition as surcease, is more likely to end the chance for clarity than lay the soul open to new modes of knowing. Forsterian death scenes thus gather import from their often violent irrelevance, redirecting the need for vision back into our allotted life in time.

Forster's fiction carves out in this way an iconoclastic place in the line of descent (often dissent and redirection, to be sure) which this study has been following. As much as in Conrad or the Victorians, Forster uses the vocabulary of the grave to estimate the spiritual depletion of his characters. Yet his metaphors of fatality do not drive toward a literalizing moment in the familiar way. Death in Forster differs from the quality of spiritual deadness as a matter not merely of degree but of kind. Furthermore, though Forster is fully aware of the increasing relevance of death's finality for considerations of textual form and closure, as alluded to in *A Passage to India*, for instance, he does not by and large (though with a notable exception in *Howards End*) let his books indulge in the kind of metatextual recognitions, even allegories, which we have come upon so often from Dickens through Hardy to Conrad. True, the hero's memory in *The Longest Journey* is preserved in a volume of his stories called *Pan Pipes*, published posthumously, yet this elegiac gesture does not reflect with much force on the closure and posterity of the quite different text that includes it. In this downplayed metanarrative emphasis, Forster points toward Lawrence. Death for both these authors is too vast and erratic a fact for formalist parallels. In Forster, that is, death is a phenomenon too specific and on the surface too senseless to afford narrative or scriptive analogues. In Lawrence death is too inevitable a metaphor for the extremity of sexual encounters to be expended on mere textual parables, except insofar as the contemplated corpse tends to become, often for a former lover, a readable embodiment of the self in final isolation. Though Forster and Lawrence break more dramatically with the received treatment of death in fiction than perhaps any single novelist before them, they nevertheless do so more in the service of life's urgencies than of form's strategies. The twentieth-century novel must wait until Virginia Woolf for this very distinction between life and text to begin that disappearing act which is at the crux of late modernism. In the meantime, we may watch Forster and Lawrence, for the most part uninterested in or resistant to the attractions of textual self-enactment, arrange for their stories to respect the existential enormity of death by holding it largely to the level of moral philosophy in the one case and erotic psychology in the other.

This sense of Forsterian fiction, however, can too easily pass unqualified. When Forster was at work on his next book after *The Longest*

Journey, he noted in his journal that he was "grinding out my novel into a contrast between money and death."[8] The novel is *Howards End* (1910), and the scene in which this contrast comes fully to voice is well along in it. Helen Schlegel is indoctrinating the misguided Leonard Bast in the mysteries of spirit, after his cynical outburst to the effect that "the real thing's money and all the rest is a dream." Helen answers, "You've forgotten Death," a "real thing" that limits but also illuminates other realities, including that of the self.

> "If we lived forever, what you say would be true. But we have to die, we have to leave life presently. Injustice and greed would be the real thing if we lived forever. As it is, we must hold to other things, because Death is coming. I love Death—not morbidly, but because He explains. He shows me the emptiness of Money. Death and Money are the eternal foes. Not Death and Life. Never mind what lies behind Death, Mr. Bast, but be sure that the poet and the musician and the tramp will be happier in it than the man who has never learnt to say 'I am I.' " (p. 238)

So goes, in sum, Forster's ethic of Thanatos, death personified as a deity rivaling the false idols of materialism. Helen's speech brings the language of being so long associated with death in British fiction squarely into the modernist period, where predications of selfhood are to be gauged, in new and more problematical ways, by death's grammar of negation. Then, too, Helen as Forsterian representative is held back from a commitment to personal immortality, to any "I" beyond the secular circle of its self-definition, by the ambiguity of "happier in it," referring as much to the moment of death as to any realm that "lies behind." It is precisely in these terms from *Howards End* that the philosophy of death "behind" Forsterian plotting serves to recuperate—after all is said and seemingly undone—the formal utility of death within his plots. The "I am I" makes its own inevitable demands on the structural and even stylistic elucidations of (and by) dying. Death seems at first dialectical in Forster, all but contradictory, even paradoxical; it shifts its perspective between the thesis of salvation by the knowledge of an end in view and the insisted-upon antithesis of all knowing in death's rendered moment. Yet even this last is a rule honored in *Howards End* no more in the observance than in the breach: the ironically entered breach of death itself.

Forster's early modernist humanism tends to reverse the Victorian trauma in *In Memoriam* by which Tennyson's persona is rendered "Half-dead to know that I shall die" (35). Forster's "idea of death" throbs instead with the pulse of life. The novelist gives into Helen's voice Michelangelo's formulation[9] of a "paradox" that "became clearer and clearer" to her as she talked: " 'Death destroys a man: the idea of Death saves him.' Behind the coffins and the skeletons that stay the vulgar mind lies something so immense that all that is great in us responds to it. Men of the world may recoil from the charnel-house that they will one day enter, but Love knows better" (p. 239). Especially on immediate encounter, the verb "stay" will not quite stay put at either "stop" or "prop," the vulgar mind halted at the idea of burial and decay, blocked from finer contemplation, but also, in the very charnel from which the mind recoils, stayed *against* an abyss of impersonal oblivion by these memorials and remnants of the physical self.

There is the death that ends life, and so defines its limits, and there is also the lesser death that is definitive of life along the way. This second permeating and insidious death, which Forster half-feared for himself early on, is a variant of the Coleridgian conception of "life-in-death." It is that same figurative extinction willed to Forster's morality from such nineteenth-century writers as Dickens, Eliot, Hardy, and Conrad, whose pages are burdened with posthumous impulse, the emotional zombieism of the unburied dead at heart. Forster, however, must negotiate an all-but-revolutionary separation between the metaphoric death of spirit and death in the flesh so as to maximize the prolonged knowable tragedy of the former as compared with the impenetrable bluntness of the latter. As distinguished from the equally bleak if not so ironically swift deaths in such naturalistic writers as Zola and George Moore, or from the Chekhov of the stories, even from the Thackeray who sent George Osborne to his death in *Vanity Fair*, the absence of spirituality at the moment of death registers in Forster not so much as a cruel fact of the human condition but rather as an aesthetic betrayal of felt expectations. It becomes the calculated tossing away of a narrative opportunity. Forster's books are so assertively literary, so dramatically paced and richly figured, in all but this one last fact of rendered life, and even here, as against the noncommittal clinical accuracy of naturalistic treatment, they protest too much their own pointlessness. After all the British tradition's experiments in momentous dying, and Conrad's ironic revisionism, death in Forster is usually checked off with indifference or acrid dispatch in the voice of a third-person narrator whose omniscience on this subject is like fate's, dismissive and unflappable. Death is thus actively dethroned, its epiphanies defeated by a realism that insists on life's chances for revelation ending with that life, not bettered by death. Refusing to die even under the virulent irony of Forster's pen, British fiction's by-now canonical death scene nevertheless surrenders its moment. Nothing turns on it. Or at least nothing for the hero, however climactic a role death may be assigned in the formal structure of the plot.

Whether as felt consummation or ironic capstone, nineteenth-century fictional dying subscribes widely, as we have seen, to the psychological, if not religious, teleology that underscores the *end* in *tendency*, whether emotional, moral, or sexual. Such schematic death scenes meet their nemesis in Forster—or so he would often have us think, despite the unavoidable dictates of form and prefiguration. Death in short—and there is no long view for the self to take at the instant—neither saves nor damns but merely cancels. Yet Forster knew as well as his characters what it means to pine for the personal immortality death so rudely rules out of consideration, and what meanings such a myth may engender. He saw as part of his fictional mission, while denying all validation of this nostalgic religious urge to the actual death scene of fiction, still to show characters living by such faith as a saving fiction. "One must behave," Foster declared, "as if one is immortal, and as if civilization is eternal. Both statements are false—I shall not survive, no more will the great globe itself— both of them must be assumed to be true if we are to go on eating and working and travelling, and keep open a few breathing holes for the human spirit."[10]

In Forster's view we do not, in cold fact, outlive our bodies, but if our lives embody only this terminal fact they are dead at heart with that letter of mortality which kills the spirit. "If Death were seen / At first as Death," wrote Tennyson in *In Memoriam* (35), a notion reprised later by Forster, then "Love had not been." Death must be faced off and seen through, if only by illusion, else nature mocks the soul, as Tennyson has her do by feminine personification when answering back to man with unmitigated biological precision and a killing rhyme, "I bring to life, I bring to death: / The spirit does but mean the breath" (56). It is the same familiar play on spirit not only as breath, animal function, but also as soul which Forster wants in his image of the spirit's more than respiratory "breathing holes." This sentiment, caught in transition from vestigial religiosity to modernist agnosticism, can be found not only in Forster but notably too in Wallace Stevens, whose famous "Death is the mother of beauty" from *Sunday Morning* is rephrased in a later, equally cryptic line by the apothegm "We should die except for Death."[11] The existential moment of death does not, in Forster's novels, prolong our nature into synopsis, placate our demons, lull our furious delusions into lucidity. It does not in itself sum up or unblind or corroborate. But finally in any narrative, and this is especially clear at the absurd but structurally purposive death of Leonard Bast in *Howards End*, even Forsterian dying cannot help but aspire to a certain surety of form. In the words of that novel's famous epigraph, death can "only connect" with life after all.

□   □   □

And so we return to the explicit thematic center of *Howards End*, to the "I am I" for which death alone is guarantor. It is this novel above all in Forster's work that illustrates on the one hand his theory of death as secular corrective and on the other the countering poverty of any narrative dying, if it remains true to life, in making conscious redemptive connections in either a temporal or a transcendental plane. What is withheld, however, from the rendered act is not denied to the anticipated fact of death, for as a certainty in prospect, rather than a moment endured, death is of crucial rhetorical use. It is just here that the stylistic opportunities of the mortal interval—the whole range of verbal linkages and elisions, puns and doublings, that enable, accentuate, and ramify the traditional scene of death—are recovered by Forster for its forecast and also its aftermath. The death that is nothing to story, everything to exposition, is the one not enacted but reacted to. The off-stage death of a heroine, Mrs. Wilcox in *Howards End*, is that novel's case in point. The spiritual life for which she stands, in a well-known formulation from the novel, is celebrated in a metaphor of the very materialism to which it is an antidote, the life of moral idealism championed as a thing that "pays" (p. 195). But the payoff cannot be in but only in view of death. To make the point that no death, even slow death, can be looked to for certified spiritual remuneration, adding life up at last and so compensating it for transience, style itself at the early death of Mrs. Wilcox seems altogether displaced. For all the ardor and sonority of Forster's prose, where without irony in *Howards End* a simple kiss can be claimed as one of the agents through which "the doors of heaven may be shaken open" (p. 25), death is merely an exit without access. Once more, as in *The Longest Journey*, death boasts no sounding phrases, no resonance or spiritual asseveration, only severance. Its finality perverse, curt, and unconsultable, dying in Forster is starved for the ambivalence that might vibrate open the "doors" or thresholds of even dubious significance. Instead, they are bolted closed by understatement, or in the case of Mrs. Wilcox, bypassed altogether.

Beyond the constraints on plotted decease in Forster, his exorcism of all its familiar rhetoric, still death exercises its control over the trajectory of plot. What is nearly mute in the event comes to articulate the containing structure. Though death may not "select" people in Forsterian fiction, the novel itself has to choose their deaths for them, situate these moments in some sequence, if not shape them rhetorically from within. All that the modernist death scene, on-stage or off, elaborated or curtailed, could hope to do against the grain of this artificially unified sense of the dying moment in context is to lend itself to such overall coherence without borrowing from it any internal cohesion of its own, any spiritual coloration. Yet resonances excluded from the portrayed world of the novel are nevertheless demanded of its work, and so the organizing power of death, even when suppressed as representation, subtends the whole enterprise of fiction, Forster's no less than Dickens's or Eliot's. In narrative, if (and especially because) not in life, even in the dying life it dramatically renders, death transforms lapsed being to pure bearing.

In formal terms, that is, the novel as genre cannot help becoming what Helen Schlegel insists life ought to be: haunted and enhanced by the "idea of death." Such death is *ordered*, in both senses, by fictional form, an imperative of narration as well as a test of its shaping devices, however reduced they may be. This is the narratological hold death has over any text. The idea of death, otherwise known as the sense of an ending, becomes the inevitable incarnation of plot in the world of sheer story, the imposition of discourse on the course of random account, of form on the amorphousness not of death but of life without it. Texts are in this sense "judged" by their own as well as a character's "last words." If *The Longest Journey* and *A Passage to India* both imply by their titles some ultimately mortal transit, then *Howards End* can be taken to entitle its very closure as story in the light of its climactic death scene. Even when not a symbolic moment, and even in Forster's sparest ironic manner, subduing all death's immediate narrative fertility, the idea of death pervades story as an immanence and a limit. I stress this tension within the aesthetic premises of a Forsterian death sentence—a verbal unit all too easily manipulated toward undue symbolism, yet one having been by definition not only molded by but modeled upon the closural implications of all form—because Forster might otherwise seem to exempt himself from the claims of the present study about death as the tutelary genius of narrative. For all his dodges and protestations, Forster's fiction knows the death sentence as homologous with the delimited logic of all story. He is merely determined to inflect this fact with the minimum of rhetorical distortion.

Returning to these formal latencies as educed by the blatant deflection of Mrs. Wilcox's death, we note that the last we hear of Ruth Wilcox alive shows her incarnating the novel's epigraph, "Only connect . . ." The conduit of her love and attentiveness unites the generations as she "walked out of King's Cross between her husband and her daughter, listening to both of them" (p. 87). The next sentence starts the next chapter, with no apparent connection to what has preceded: "The funeral was over." Mention that it is a woman's funeral soon follows, that Mr. Wilcox is in charge (but then he takes charge of so much), that Mrs. Wilcox was looking strange of late; yet nothing grows explicit in this opening passage until a change in tense that clinches our suspicions. We hear from a local woodcutter's mother in indirect discourse that Mrs. Wilcox "had been a kind lady" (p. 88), the entire death scene elided within that almost invisible shift into the pluperfect. At one level we know how to take this, instructed by structure itself. To "connect" the one chapter with the next is to overarch the very chasm of death's discontinuity. Off-stage where it belongs, death has no drama for a spiritual presence who persists as a "welcome ghost" (p. 166) in the hearts of her survivors.

Only the funeral, not the death—and then only to those who did not know Mrs. Wilcox intimately, the local poor—seems momentous: "The funeral of a rich person was to them what the funeral of Alcestis, of Ophelia, is to the educated. It was Art; though remote from life, it enhanced life's values" (p. 88). The passage thus anticipates as a theory of death in art, removed but improving, that later philosophic proposition of Helen's about the "I" enhanced by the contemplation of its own effacement. From the manuscript variants of this passage, without allusions to Alcestis or Ophelia, it is clear that Forster originally had in mind not artistic distance in general, nor the gap between classic stage and audience, but specifically the remove a reader has from a written text, from the death of (in one of the draft versions) "a main character in a book."[12] Even with the specific tragedic emphasis of the printed version, Forster wants us to see our own relation to the mortal hiatus of Ruth Wilcox's off-stage death as an additional displacement of the reaction within the text of those onlookers who take it as art rather than life. To suggest this further, and in rather an exceptional turn for Forster toward scriptive self-consciousness, there is the strategic description of these funereal bystanders as themselves constituted by textual art—mere inked shapes, as against our separate bodied life as readers, coming to words as we do from our real world beyond them: "They thrilled with the excitement of a death, and of a rapid death, and stood in groups or moved between the graves, like drops of ink" (p. 88). For the reader too, at a further remove, these very inked traces are part of that ritual of extinction and elegy in a written work which can bestow the remote envigoration of a surrogate death. By calling rare attention to the textuality of his text, Forster calls more important attention to the narrative and metaphysical liberties of its subtracted death scene. With no stylistic transposition whatever to ease the dying woman's presence out of this world, the very elision of such verbal drama—with both internal spectators and external readers looking on after the fact—calls upon the dropped beat of plot to provide its own deathbed epitome. In line with the transcendental vitalism of which Mrs. Wilcox is the vessel, such unnoted death is of a piece with the seamlessness of her continuing effect on others.

So deflected is Mrs. Wilcox's end that it is not even until a chapter after the surprise funeral that we have Forster's summary of her personal approach to death. The memory of it passes in retrospect through the mind of her spiritual inheritor, Margaret Schlegel, taking the shape there of the younger woman's metaphors for the temporal self. Margaret felt about Mrs. Wilcox that she was a "great wave" that "had flowed into her life and ebbed out of it forever," strewing at her feet "fragments torn from the unknown" (p. 102). As the "wave" metaphor for Mrs. Wilcox shifts to "seafarer," we recognize the suggestion that in her approach to death she has briefly internalized the very medium of her own drowning and dissolution, an achieved feat kept in balanced motion by the antithetical structure of the whole passage. With phrase clanging sonorous against contrastive phrase, what we hear is Forster's best ruminative tone coaching the implicit indirect discourse (note the focusing "she believed") of Margaret's meditation on her dead friend. The young heroine

> stood for a while at the verge of the sea that tells so little, but tells a little, and watched the outgoing of this last tremendous tide. Her friend had vanished in agony, but not, she believed, in degradation. Her withdrawal had hinted at other things besides disease and pain. Some leave our life with tears, others with insane frigidity; Mrs Wilcox had taken the middle course, which only rarer natures can pursue. She had kept proportion. She had told a little of her grim secret to her friends, but not too much; she had shut up her heart—almost, but not entirely. It is thus, if there is any rule, that we ought to die—neither as victim nor as fanatic, but as the seafarer who can greet with an equal eye the deep that he is entering, and the shore that he must leave. (p. 102)

Prose embodies, or at least makes bold to attempt, the proportion it celebrates, anticipating exactly the balance Mrs. Moore is to lose in *A Passage to India*, when the "twilight of the double vision" (p. 208) dims her vision to something more like the gray "frigidity" Mrs. Wilcox manages to avoid. Ruth Wilcox has, as everything in the textual suture that covers over (and heals) her death scene serves to assure, "gone out of life vividly" (p. 103). She has, that is to say in Forsterian paradox, died livingly. And by style alone is her death linked, through its own internal connectives, to the receiving mind of Margaret, the spiritual heir.

This rightly admired[13] passage of conciliated extremes is therefore not simply what it may at first appear: expository rhetoric entirely replacing the narrative style of dying. Many of the same motives, even the same lexical and syntactic motifs, are borrowed here from Victorian fiction's disposal of a life for the spiritual disposition of that life instead. As the only explicit prescription in Forster's novels for how "we ought to die," the passage is installed in part to prepare for a similar reconciliation of opposing or discordant impulses, less symphonic and confident, at the enacted death of the hero, Leonard Bast, late in the novel. In the antithetical finesse of this early passage about Mrs. Wilcox's venture in dying, style becomes not so much a means of momentary transposition as a medium of inclusive mentality. With Margaret absorbing this spiritual poise from Ruth Wilcox, her own indirect style turns back upon the absent death scene to fill its void with rescued emphasis, a hole woven over, raveled up, by prose. The classic interval of the death moment, reworked in this elegiac retrospect, takes its coordinates from the instructive lag between the advance knowledge and the act of death instead of from finite and infinite poles of the latter's extreme breach. When narrative prose thus charts the approach to rather than the negotiation of a death moment, the style of dying becomes less ambiguous impetus than equilibration, latitude more than interval. Such a style is carried here by a widening correlative grammar ("a little . . . but not too much," "neither . . . nor") remodeling the sliding syntax of transposition into a connective logic in a different key, nexus less than exonerated contrariety, not transit so much as antithesis set to rest.

This pattern of a clarifying approach to death followed by an evaded revelation in its moment is repeated for Leonard Bast as he nears the blank doom of his last scene. The most dramatically elided death in Forster, that of Ruth Wilcox, is thus matched at the end, according to the symbolic agenda of the book's mortal economy, by the novelist's most closely and inwardly monitored death, however spiritually immobilized it turns out to be. As much as with Mrs. Wilcox, Leonard's destiny is also a testing of the proposition that the "I am I" is authenticated under the shadow of the self's mortal limit. Toward this fate, staged as complementary to that of a woman he has never met,

Leonard makes his way in the book's climax, intending to apologize to the namesake for Mrs. Wilcox which Margaret has become by marrying the widowed Henry. Leonard's brief affair with Margaret's sister, Helen, seems to him a violation of the world of culture he holds sacred, when in fact the son he unknowingly produces stands at the novel's end as the symbolic salvation of the family. En route to his apology, however, Leonard knows only his guilt. "He did not suppose that confession would bring him happiness. It was rather that he yearned to get clear of the tangle. So does the suicide yearn. The impulses are akin" (p. 319). What a confessing self and a suicide have most deeply in common is that each would abrogate the integrity of the "I am I."

Stephen Wonham, the hero's brother in *The Longest Journey*, is the character in that novel who can say "I am I," or almost say it, and his balked syntax of self-identification is instructive. In Stephen's first conversation with Ansell, a Cambridge philosophy student, the doctoral candidate tells the shepherd that "it interests me to class people, and up to now I have failed with you" (p. 231). Stephen tries to oblige: " 'I——' He stopped. Ansell reflected that there are worse answers. 'I really don't know what I am.' " Even such a minimal and inarticulate version of self-enunciation is a claim on the real. When Stephen later inflects into italics his personal pronoun in objecting to Rickie's reductive identification of him with their dead mother— "*I* haven't risen from the dead"—he then "stutters" out only a further "I'm," implying again the self-sufficiency of a verb of being suspended without necessary attribute. Failing to relax into his own "I am I" in *Howards End*, Leonard Bast, by contrast, is seriously in danger of never getting beyond Jude's negatively circular "I am as I was." In the process Leonard develops a definitional stutter superficially similar to Stephen's, though without even the contracted vestige of "am." Margaret means to congratulate Leonard on a walk out of London to see the dawn, but he would retreat from his romantic adventure into timid definitions of his decent clerk's selfhood: "Now, take me on the whole, I'm a quiet fellow: I'm law abiding" (p. 142). She wants precisely to take him "on the whole," to make connections between his disparate aspirations, but he insists on those neutralizing nouns and adjectives to complete the grammar of his identity. He goes on haltingly: " 'I don't wish any unpleasantness; but I——I——.' "

Margaret interrupts with an assertion that would return his identity to him as the gift of empathy and understanding: " 'You,' said Margaret——'you——you—— . . . You saw the sunrise . . . You tried to gets away from the fogs that are stifling us all' " (pp. 142–143). His quest was, in the Schlegel view, for that "I am I" which Helen later explains to him must always come into freeing relief against the ground of death.

Even before the equative clause of self-posited identity is introduced in Helen's central speech about the redemptive "knowledge of death," her sister, Margaret, has embodied it in a verbal ellipsis that is, in emotional force, a temporal elision. Mistaken by the housekeeper of Howards End at one point, she "stammered," like Stephen Wonham and Leonard Bast before her, but this time with a designated alter ego filling the space of predication and thus subsuming it: " 'I—— Mrs. Wilcox——I?' " (p. 202). In a single contracted syntax, the past tense of the dead woman slides into the present of her surrogate, verbless in a secured being beyond tense. It is against the backdrop of this twofold consolidation of selfhood that the trauma of Leonard's fractured identity is played out as he journeys fatefully to Howards End. The hero is "rent into two people who held dialogues" (p. 316); in the throes of these "disintegrating dialogues" (p. 321) Leonard becomes the true precursor of the modern identity crisis in such characters as Paul Morel, holding second-person debate with himself at the end of *Sons and Lovers*, and of Septimus Smith in *Mrs. Dalloway*.

Before setting out on his expiating journey to Howards End, Leonard had gone to St. Paul's to "see a picture that had educated him in former years. But the light was bad, the picture ill placed, and Time and Judgment were inside him now. Death alone still charmed him" (p. 319).[14] Since in his suicidal despair both time and punitive judgment have been internalized, it is death alone that remains other and still coming. By separating death off from this prophetic triumvirate, Leonard is also fastening upon a lesson previously offered him in Helen's peroration about mortality. During the climactic rite of passage to Howards End, the hero's mind reverts to that "rather paradoxical axiom" of Helen's, "Death destroys man, but the idea of death saves him—that is the best account of it that has yet been given" (p. 324). Between an idea of sacrificial reparation, akin to death or suicide, and the act of death itself stretches the distance that Leonard is now traversing in this last and longest journey.

Though long bowed low by worry, the hero is now lifted free of it, of the whole burden of troubled self-consciousness, by the very repeal of reason in an access to the heart's truth: "As he approached the house, all thought stopped." Reason discriminates, laments what is not. Under inspiration from Helen's "rather paradoxical" axiom of death, Leonard moves instead into a realm of yoked and solacing contraries, a relaxation into chaos after a lifelong struggle against it: "Contradictory notions stood side by side in his mind. He was terrified but happy, ashamed but had done no sin." Just before his death, that is, Leonard has achieved for the first time that "proportion" which we were asked to read back into the temper of Mrs. Wilcox's death, a liberation from extremity itself. He seems to enact in a darker mode what is excluded from the earlier deflected death, and to do so with the very idea of "Mrs. Wilcox," her heir and double rather than the original dead woman, on his mind. "He knew the confession: 'Mrs. Wilcox, I have done wrong,' but sunrise had robbed its meaning, and he felt rather on a supreme adventure" (p. 324), recalling Eliot's and Conrad's repeated use of "supreme" for the "moment" of death. When he soon utters out loud these penitential words, his spiritual confession thereby reaches across the mortal threshold he himself will momentarily overstep. On the verge of death, though he doesn't know it, he is speaking of instincts and natural harmonies embodied in the first Mrs. Wilcox, a woman whose spiritual aura has never left the ancestral home she loved.

It is to this incarnation of domestic love and pastoral affinity that Leonard offers his now meaningless (because morally irrelevant) confession. He is struck down in the process with the flat side of the Schlegel family's sword by the irate brother-in-law of the pregnant Helen, in one of Forster's most precipitously perfect death scenes: "The man took him by the collar and cried: 'Bring me a stick.' Women were screaming. A stick, very bright, descended. It hurt him, not where it decended, but in the heart. Books fell over him in a shower. Nothing had sense" (p. 324). Forster does not write "Looking like a very bright stick, it was in fact a sword that descended." These last instants of subjective vision are instead internalized, the hurried adjectival intrusion of "very bright" measuring the swift interval of the sword's descent in the peripheral sight of the victim. This is also true of the hurt that ensues, registering on the inside of Leonard's consciousness in a complex symbol of pathology, capitulation, and repair, a failure of the heart that finally touches the hero to the quick with feeling. So too is the very death sentence diverted to an inner yield of reference. Once we notice that the arguably omniscient shrug, "Nothing had sense," clipped and dismissive as it seems, is at the same time a deft inward turn of indirect discourse, tied into a simulation of the dying mind, we realize this fleeting scene's full departure from the avowed Forsterian stance of understatement and avoided drama. His general rule, as we know, is that death is too important to be made portentous, too crucial to serve as a sign or symbol for anything beyond itself. But in *Howards End*, Leonard's murder does after all complete the book's organizing pair of fatalities, committing death, that ultimate form of inevitability, to the inner inevitabilities of form.

The same death sentence that would signal its own insignificance grows tellingly ambiguous as we read. In the polyvalent splaying of both subject and object, "Nothing had sense" inscribes in an explicit fashion the typical Forsterian absurdity of death, while at the same time weighting it with multiple import. Whereas physical sensation is canceled by death, it is some kind of other, better sense which may at last be made, be had. Both leveling and overdetermined, gratuitous and parabolic, fictional death yet again sentences contingency to significance. At the death of Mrs. Wilcox, Forster had taken all the ambiguity and paradox associated with the deathbed intervals of previous narratives and brought them to bear not on the moment of death but on the mood of dying. Yet his novel's pervasive emphasis on mortality as the validation of identity seems still to require the enacted scene of death as well as its considered anticipation. This need, suggested early, is answered by displacement in Leonard's end. Structural as well as ethical imperatives thus lead Forster straight to that classic testing ground of identity which he has tried elsewhere to suppress or satirize in his novels, the scene of signifying death. Form itself enforces its own logic: such is death's staying power in modern fiction. What is evicted from representation earlier with Mrs. Wilcox must be evinced with Leonard in order to move the novel to closure.

In preparing for this climax with the metaphoric "knife" of remorse that "plunged deeper into his heart" (p. 323) as Leonard disembarked from the train near Howards End—after his second symbolic sunrise journey in the novel—Forster is thus found acceding to his own version of the transformation of figurative image to mortal fact, the technique that structures so many funereal conceits down through Conrad. When the Schlegel sword completes its sudden "knifing" descent, we realize that the requisites of form have once again brought prefiguration to bear even on a death that would at some level resist all immediate metaphor. This resistance, however, cannot stem the tide of full-scale symbolism. Murdered by a Wilcox, as he has previously been financially ruined by the young man's father, Leonard also seems knighted by the Schlegel spirit and its gleaming instrument. No sooner is this implied than the symbolism takes a different turn. As against an earlier draft's dully literal "Down fell a bookcase,"[15] here the man of books is metaphorically inundated by their "shower," drowning in body as before in spirit beneath their simulations of reality. After a life of sensation and meaning siphoned off from literature, "sense," as both reason and mere sensory response, emerges as an attribute only of the void.

Then too, "nothing" can be not only pronoun but noun, there being no sense now except that made by merciful oblivion, at last arrived. The genius of Forster's passage rests, uneasily perhaps, with its modulating compound of depletion and fervid assurance, for which the symbols are precise, ripe, complicit. A straight ironic reading would show us Leonard done in by his own weakness of heart as it must meet the world's hardness in a few square inches of steel. For all the Forsterian brevity and tonal dampening, the scene tells—or pays. Summation at one level of a "senseless" life, Leonard's death is also a pathetic apotheosis, nihilism enthralled by the hint of catharsis. Leonard dies of feeling, painless but intense, an attack of heart to which the books pouring down are numbingly redundant, as they should all along have been seen to be. Buried under literature as always, nevertheless he is, as so seldom before, struck to the quick. The forgiving clarity of spirit that comes over Leonard at the end, beyond the contradictions that have so long preyed upon him, could hardly be more powerfully glossed than by a famous passage from Thoreau's *Walden* that invokes the image of a lustrous but potentially fatal blade slicing away obscurities from the moment of recognition: "If you stand right fronting and face to face with a fact, you will see the sun glimmer on both of its surfaces, as if it were a scimiter, and feel its sweet edge dividing you through the heart and the marrow, and so you will happily conclude your mortal career. Be it life or death, we crave only reality."[16]

The deflationary ironies of Leonard Bast's death scene are somehow more serene, more stately than in other Forsterian death scenes, and through the tedium and meanness struggles something like Emily Dickinson's formal feeling after great pain. The whole scene as a narrative vaunt, poised dubiously as it is between "squalor and tragedy" (p. 324), between farce and fearsome vision, the absurd and the sublime, a scene by turns melodramatic and rhetorically bland, attempts to triumph over these contradictory tones, to set them in proportion. The vitalizing tension of the antithetical has found both locus and resolution. Forster's general defection from the tradition of the momentous death scene, here ambiguously qualified by the grammatical and tonal balancings of the passage, once more proves the larger rule—the hegemony of death in fictional form. Despite Forster's systematic and inventive restraint, as his novel draws toward closure in a major onslaught of literary symbolism, his hero dies by the book(s) after all.

Even in the moments that follow—or prolong—the scene of his dying, there is a reticent and deeply secreted instance of a half-bitter, half-remitting epitome that takes Leonard over the "threshold" into Conrad's "invisible" death. Preparing a way for the reparations to come, this effect actually transpires in the dawning interval of the self's own posthumousness. If the actual death sentence of this passage is not the one precipitated by that slippage between pronoun and noun in "Nothing had sense," then we would have to locate the fatal moment somewhere just before an equally brief clause, redrafted from an earlier version, which also nominates itself as the terminal quintessence of the protagonist's being in time. The unrevised manuscript offers this coda to Leonard's story: "They laid the corpse on the gravel, and Helen poured water over it."[17] By this draft of the text, Leonard's identity is conclusively understood to have departed with the sentence "Nothing had sense." In the revised phrasing we feel an instant's aftermath of the loss of consciousness which sustains his frail identity, though not his life, into a final tenacity: "They laid Leonard, who was dead, on the gravel; Helen poured water over him" (p. 324). In the final version "the corpse" is still, or perhaps for the first time genuinely, a man named Leonard, dead, the personal pronoun "who" replacing the neuter "it." With the "shower" metaphor for his burial by books already in our mind, the futile gesture of revival by water falls into place as not only a ceremonial cleansing but a second ironic baptism in the "I am I," the original sin of unconnectedness washed clean in a confession coterminous with its final penance. In this return of the hero's body to the novel's heroic earth, there is also the hint, with his ludicrous dousing by Helen, of a grotesque but still reverent irrigation that cures its own black comedy by connecting forward to the organic imagery that closes the novel. There, at the start of the last chapter, death's sword, scythe, or sickle has become the "whirring blades" (p. 335) of the harvester laying low the seasonal hay, part of the vegetative cycle to which that earlier absurdity of the drenched corpse may now be seen to allude. Once more, however, Forsterian irony divides any symbolic option of this sort against itself, for Leonard is laid to rest not in the ancestral garden of the first Mrs. Wilcox but quite decidedly on that harsh "gravel." Only in view of such a redemptive possibility as that held out tentatively here, though, would we note the modeling of that confirming clause, "who was dead," on the novel's matrix of identity in the "I am I." That awful watering is done to one Leonard Bast, *who was himself* now, though dead. The aura of presence and identity graces the subordinate clause even as, by death's ultimate subordination of self, the reflexive pronoun must, though implied, remain forever suspended.

One has only to look forward to the death of Mrs. Moore in *A Passage to India*, as reported after the fact by omniscient narrative, to feel the full insinuating force of the "who was dead" clause in *Howards End*. With the insistent twist of inversion and the subsequent play on *commitment* within a funereal cliché for burial at sea, Forster writes of Mrs. Moore, "Dead she was—committed to the deep" (p. 256). Knowing what we do about the Indian people's denial of her death through the reincarnation of her spirit as the goddess Esmiss Esmoor, we cannot but hear the idiomatic oxymoron "being dead" that obtains as well, if less obviously, at Leonard's death. With more than merely vernacular reemphasis, death comes just in time, given Mrs. Moore's disillusionment, to lend permanence to her being. Dead, perhaps only dead, could she continue to be what she had been to others. So too with Leonard, committed to the earth. Tentative, defensive, fatigued, the seeker after sunrises had finally dawned upon himself: dead, he was at last. Between the "I am I" tacitly achieved on this last journey toward death and the "Leonard, who was dead"— dead of an external blow that wounded him straight to the center of feeling—between the extremes of these copulative predications, one implied, one recorded, opens the brief space of emotional ratification. "Never mind what lies behind Death, Mr. Bast," but be sure that those who have lived by the spirit will be "happier in it than the man who has never learnt to say 'I am I' " (p. 238). The ambiguity of that prepositional phrase "in it," denoting death as either infinite futurity or isolated moment, is never more quietly resolved in Forster. Spiritually awakened for the second and last time, again by the quickening of a symbolic sunrise, Leonard is thus "happier in it," in dying, than he ever was in life. The sheer "nothing" of which he is sensible cements a negative epitome meliorated at once by the burst of momentary self-determination.

□　　□　　□

Meeting his "end" at the titular destination of the whole novel, Leonard recalls for us, and further precipitates, some crucial and illuminating plays on the book's title which effect the displacement of his death, as living deadness, onto the emotional culprits of his exclusion from society—as well as onto the heroine in the form of her own renewal. The hint of terminus as death in the title is scarcely accidental, although fair game for ridicule when trivialized. Dolly Wilcox has alluded at one point to a story about the last male of the Howard line, who " 'went out and was killed . . . I say! Howards End—Howard's Ended!' cried Dolly. 'I'm rather on the spot this evening, eh?' " (p. 203). The fates of the great antagonists of the novel, the gross materialist, Henry, and the extreme idealist, Helen, both ultimately converge around this bon mot grown ominous. Hearing that his son, Charles, will be imprisoned for the murder of Leonard, Henry says "I'm ended" (p. 334), and in the next and last chapter Helen repeats these exact words (p. 337) about her abdication from all passional life. A figure of speech drawn from closure thus twice guarantees the book's own sense of retributive justice, as it must now be turned poetic by Margaret.

For all the rhetorical irony incurred or radiated by Leonard's death scene, it is instead his preceding approach to death, like Mrs. Wilcox's—because so much like—that gives the strongest rhetorical evidence of the passage's cathartic intent. As with Rickie Elliot's before him, Leonard's is literally the longest journey to a rural End. Shortly before Leonard's "supreme adventure," there is a passage that has little other point in the novel except to connect the earlier off-stage death of Ruth Wilcox forward to the actual death scene of the man who dies virtually with her name on his lips. The passage is there to join these scenes even as it would seem to enjoin against the dream of utility or illumination in such a connective act of imagination. The passage in question details Margaret's summoning to the threatened death of her Aunt Juley, the novel's heroine "confronted again by the senselessness of death" (p. 276). Yet this is death in the flesh, not its reflective anticipation, and so, unlike Leonard's spiritually readied end, its determined attempt at senselessness on Forster's part does indeed deliver no sense. The novel moves here into a mode of rhetorical travesty for the narrator's capitalized remark that Aunt Juley's "was an average approach to the Great Gate" (p. 276). Here is a Conradian threshold which for Forster in his normal tone is of course only the gate of negation. This metaphor of the portal is all the more ironic because Juley recovers, like Marlow after Kurtz's death, and returns intact to her world. The aunt, "incapable of tragedy," could not relax into "the great mystery which all agree," as Forster sarcastically has it, "must await her." So continues that tone of vox populi so often parodistic in Forster, especially on the issue of last things. And yet in the flexible potentiality of ambiguous diction, the narrator asserts that Juley could not "realize the mystery." Even negated, it is a perfectly double-edged phrase for the distance— the stylistically simulated interval—between the acknowledgment of an end coming and the actualizing of an arrived death met halfway by the prepared identity. Mrs. Wilcox, years before, had seemed capable of that contributory poise, that "realizing," as will Leonard too not long after this scene of Margaret's deathbed vigil. At Aunt Juley's side, "Margaret saw Death stripped of any false romance;

whatever the idea may contain, the process can be trivial and hideous" (p. 277). It is again the distinction between the contemplation of and the immediate encounter with death.

There is one apparent lesson of Aunt Juley's skirted decease that must first be unlearned by Forster's readers. Knowing of Mrs. Wilcox's end, we may be led by this scene to expect no connective complement for it after all in the novel's awaited climax, especially once we are made privy to Margaret's belief that "one death may explain itself, but it throws no light upon another: the groping inquiry must begin anew" (p. 276). Yet in art, enhancing life's values as it was claimed to do at Mrs. Wilcox's funeral, this certainly cannot be true. Even in that human mood of coherence that approaches to art, connections are bound, once brought to light, also to shed it. Though Forster is writing out of an entirely different rhetorical tradition, all legato strings to Beckett's percussive understatement, still *Howards End* anticipates the hero's impacted idiomatic irony in *Malone Dies* that, "when weary to death one is almost resigned to—I was going to say to the immortality of the soul, but I don't see the connexion" (p. 229). The hyperbolic "weary to death" is literalized by Malone's terminal debility, while his use of "connexion" for the mere transitions in a dark line of reasoning bespeaks a metaphysical incapacity in its other than logical usage. In *Howards End* it is partly because the metaphysical "connexion" between life and death is not available that the other structural connections between one end-stopped death and another must come into play. It is precisely "light" that the anticipated and balanced death of Mrs. Wilcox, in an illustration of how we "ought to die," is meant to "throw" forward upon the complementary fate of Leonard. The hero now negotiates that interval of evacuation which, though unenacted for Mrs. Wilcox, was restructured in retrospect as a seafaring balance on the tide of the unknown. We come to see that the novel's two deaths, the first off-stage, the second on, are not so much sequential as concentric, the latter the inexorable voiding crisis inside the former. The invisible dying of Mrs. Wilcox sustains the momentum of a world uninterrupted by the rent of death; Leonard's then gives us the felt advent of that vacancy as well as completing the effect of Mrs. Wilcox's death on the mission of her spiritual heir, Margaret, and on the continuing vitality of the family home.

With respect (or apparent disrespect) to the Victorian ascendency of death as touchstone of character, twentieth-century revisionism has already passed through its first decade, completed its first great phase, when, six years after Martin Decoud, mortally wounded, drowns in the gulf, Leonard Bast, also mortally wounded, drowns under that shower of books. The bardic Lawrence will go on to rename death as sexual consummation, the lyric Woolf as psychological communion, but in the meantime the ironists Conrad and Forster have deeply unsettled, each in his own way, the premises of fictional demise. Inheriting in the form of the symbolic death scene a narrative option whose power and centrality could scarcely be denied, yet whose detonated charge could no longer honestly be located in a private moment of "revelation" (Conrad mocks the very word), both Conrad and Forster recoup to an equal degree the utility of the death scene, despite the apparent discrepancy between the elaborate rhetorical structure of Decoud's end, for instance, and the stinted, cryptic finish of Leonard Bast.

Given the diversion of so much stylistic energy away from the moment of fatal transit, or the conversion to irony of its vestigial rhetorical patterns, it follows for modern writers that some mode of displacement, not necessarily metanarrative yet, would remain the most potent and adaptable of the three mortal functions in the post-Romantic mode of dying. The mechanics of transposition, for instance, have been contracted by Forster into the mere gap between the ambivalent qualities of "nothing" in Leonard's last instant, after having been stretched by Conrad's *Nostromo* into the grammatical vacuum just past "They looked———." Without interior representation, with only the blunt fact of fatality either dilated by anaphora in Conrad or yanked tight by a single verbal twist in Forster, the style of dying tends to offer up—to the reader only, at best, not to the characters themselves in any introspective breakthrough—a compressed epitome of their narrated lives. While satirizing even the diction of epiphanic clarity, however, both Conrad and Forster still manage to renew the structural utility of mortal displacement in underground alignments more ingenious than any devised, or required, by the Victorians.

The delayed and then climactically enacted death scenes of both Decoud and Leonard fill a void widened by narrative chronology and left gaping in wait for them. Numerous death moments in *Nostromo* are deflected off-stage until Decoud's own get locked into retrospective place, incarnating upon arrival the very principle of human cancellation with his mock-Messianic "It is done." The serenely epitomizing approach to death of Mrs. Wilcox in *Howards End*, displacing indeed its immediate fatal scene—which is shunted aside by the momentum of continuance—is returned to full narrative force at Leonard's death, bearing by then both the whole truth of death's transcendental futility and the entire mystery of its secular grace. Further, the equally displaced ache for some "knowledge of death" (Forster's phrase) felt by Nostromo in the paragraph adjacent to the flashback of his ironic double's death—"And he wondered how Decoud had died"—comes to eerily spiritual rather than satiric issue in *Howard's End*, for Margaret's wonder at Leonard's death brings the heroine to her own spiritual rest. With less faith yet than Conrad in the *scene* of death as an occasion of discovery, Forster rescues the contemplated *idea* of death, before or after the fact, as a redeeming influx of "the unseen."

Hence those restorative displacements in *Howards End* not merely between isolated deaths but forward to continuance. These style itself, departing from the severer ironies of Conrad, is meant to elicit. About Mrs. Wilcox's brand of spirituality we learn early that "she and daily life were out of focus: one or the other must show blurred" (p. 76). When her elided death scene further blurs her over from dailiness into enduring myth, from matron to the softened outlines of a domestic specter, then that death is quite openly taken to epitomize her essential relation to the living world from which it removes her. What is fitting, inspiriting, about this death is then gradually displaced upon Margaret, first through the indirect discourse of its contemplation in that passage where Margaret intuits how we "ought to die," then later in her ruminations after Leonard's death. In this recuperative denouement, the damage already done and Leonard buried, the imagery familiar to us from the wispy aura of Mrs. Wilcox is fully inherited by Margaret in a reprise of the earlier vocabulary. The heroine now "alters her focus until trivial things are blurred. Margaret had been tending this way all winter." Yet the secondary sacrificial displacement of Leonard has still been needed to finish the trajectory: "Leonard's death brought her to that goal" (p. 332).

In the long run, Margaret gains upon this transfiguring goal through a crisis of introspection whose style traverses a cascade of lyrical cadences indebted to the panoramic portrayal of mortal contemplation at the conjectured deathbed of Mrs. Wilcox. After Leonard's fatal accident, in the discordant, crass "jangle of cause and effects," Margaret wonders "what had become of their true selves?" (p. 329), the wasted capacities of their individual living "I"s. The paratactic prose of internal monologue suddenly overshoots itself, buckles, succumbs, then pushes on again: "Leonard lay dead in the garden, from natural causes; yet life was a deep deep river, death a blue sky, life was a house, death a wisp of hay, a flower, a tower, life and death were anything and everything, except this ordered insanity" (p. 330). There is no prose of this sort anywhere else in the novel. Risking chaos in attempting a contrast to demented conformity, growing an archie even within its own antitheses, the logic of answering synecdoches (or are they sometimes metaphors?) for life versus death, peaking at the echo of those early associations for Mrs. Wilcox, "a wisp of hay, a flower" (p. 74), then breaks loose into a dizzy unstrung rhyming on "tower," only for death to reassert itself with the sweep of the rhetorical pendulum. If death is a "sky," it may be, for Margaret if not for Forster, a heaven, but life can also be a "deep river" on this reverie's own secular terms, as in the stream of consciousness from which this sentence itself wells and undulates. The "ripple and great wave" (p. 102) which Margaret earlier confronted in Ruth Wilcox is hereby reshaped, by rhythm as well as explicit comment, as a private flow of mind anticipating both the general imagery of Virginia Woolf's subjective style and the particular symbolism of "communion" in *Mrs. Dalloway*. "At such moments the soul retires within," writes Forster, "to float upon the bosom of a deeper stream, and has communion with the dead."

From Mrs. Wilcox's balance of "agony, but not . . . degradation," through the edging of Leonard's "squalor" toward "tragedy," to the moment when contradictions "stood side by side" in the mind of this man "terrified but happy," where sublimity seems internalized as a neurotic balm—across each of these stages has the narrative charted its rhetorical subtext of linked deaths as they become the thematic increments of displacement. Style has first spun forth the balanced cadences of Mrs. Wilcox's approach to death, subjunctive in the mind of Margaret, and afterwards has worked through again the rescinded contradictions of Leonard's approach to death in the vertiginous, slowly ordered polarities of Margaret's ordeal, smoothed over by the syntax of consciousness to renewed duration and endurance. The novel has thus demanded as much from style as the traditional rhetoric of mortality it works to disenfranchise. To vary the Dickensian formulation, there is in Forster no traversable distance at death, only a stance versed in the lucidities of some intuitive peace of soul. What tragedy did for the Greeks, Mrs. Wilcox's funeral for the poor, the effacement of this novel's hero does for its heroine at the close, and presumably for the reader in turn. For all his evasions and revisions of the Victorian deathbed tradition, Forster devolves upon Margaret Schlegel, every bit as much as Gaskell did upon Margaret Hale, the capacity to be "afresh taught by death what life should be."

We should not finally be surprised to discover that it is exactly in view of the most crucial Forsterian point of contast between classic fiction and life—in view, that is, of the narrated death scene which is supposedly to refuse in Forster the standard blandishments of inordinate because deceptive form—that Forster's fiction releases its narrative to moments of unusual reflexive scrutiny. We have already noted this at the funeral of Mrs. Wilcox. Having worked forward from this earlier scene toward his own last sentence, Forster there has Helen say, in a metatextual exit line that echoes while redirecting her own earlier "I'm ended," that "we've seen to the very end, and it'll be such a crop of hay as never!" Leonard's death has brought her too, and the novel that displaces his tragedy through catharsis into art, straight to this closural goal. Helen's "the very end" implicitly inflects the seasonal in the direction of the apocalyptic. Style, in the shape of a single turn of phrase, has thus guided the book toward the recognition of its own destined end, whose power for us is undimmed, indeed amplified, because its corpses, like all its living characters as well, are only "drops of ink" on the pages of a fiction.

In an age of declining mimetic confidence after the great epoch of realism—fiction still sorting out its possible tones from the chill rigor of naturalism—the novel was taken up by Forster while yet in metamorphosis toward internal consciousness and its monologues, toward relativism of perspective, and finally toward textual self-involution. Always essential to the representation of death as absence, the isolated power of pure style is brought all the more obviously to the fore in such a transitional enterprise, even a style as dated in its studied aplomb as Forster's. Rhetorical tactics in his novels come to carry the ethical weight of his fiction, which often pressures the enacted death scene into resonance and remonstration with the marginal existence of those characters whose lives are only half lived. In a sense Forster was to ask this much of his prose—that it validate the faltering self—not only within his individual fictions but in the never quite assured career he tried to make of them. It was not only his insecurity that communicated itself in person but also his rather heroic labors to stabilize a wavering "I am I." Writing in 1915 to Bertrand Russell about a visit Forster had paid him, D. H. Lawrence was gratified to find that Forster "is not dead yet. I hope to see him pregnant with his own soul . . . there is something very real in him, if he will not cause it to die."[18] That baroque, entirely typical metaphor of spiritual self-insemination, in counterpoint to figurative death, gives us a ready point of rhetorical comparison in the historical advance from Forster into the allegory of dying and arrival in Lawrence. It is with the innovations of Lawrence, and of Woolf after him, that Forster's style and themes, despite their comparative reticence, can only connect.

6

Rites of Trespass

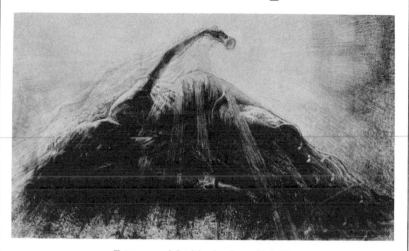

Tristan and Isolde, by Jean Delville
Courtesy Musées Royaux des Beaux-Arts, Brussels

And the dawn blazed in them, their new life came to pass, it
was beyond all conceiving good, it was so good, that it was
almost a passing-away, a trespass.

D. H. LAWRENCE
The Rainbow

6

Build then the ship of death, for you must take
the longest journey, to oblivion . . .

We are dying, we are dying, we are all of us dying
and nothing will stay the death-flood rising within us
and soon it will rise on the world, on the outside world

D. H. LAWRENCE, "The Ship of Death"

ONRAD'S SEA FABLES and river journeys map for the modern
novel a rich archetypal topography. Character after character in
post-Victorian fiction moves as outcast within the confines of his or
her own islanded but shifting identity, struggling to make connection,
often willing to immerse in the destructive element in order to take
the measure of the human will and its mortal limits. The soul's
"longest journey," across the Indian Ocean or otherwise, is often
metaphorically floated in Forster upon a wide sea or fathomless river
able to sustain the vigilant, the equilibrated identity in a transit
beyond the seen. Lawrence's ship of death, ark of all renewal, must
set forth upon either of those two notorious rivers from *Women in
Love*, the inviting bright current of life or the truer black rush of
dissolution (pp. 163–165). Nothing marks Lawrence's unhesitant recourse to Romantic themes and their rhetoric, however much under
revision, nothing records his harking back past the ironic restraint
of Conrad and Forster, more clearly than his complex recovery of the
Flood motif from such post-Romantic elegists in prose as Dickens
and Eliot. Then, in Woolf's novels, time itself becomes the river, in
certain places the waved sea, flowing in rhythm, or not, with the
stream of consciousness her style is designed to chart. Evoked frequently in modern fiction, as in Victorian, drowning in any such
waters is the doom of failed heroic venture. In Lawrence the inimical
force is spelled out metaphorically as desire's "corrosive flood of
death" (*Women in Love*, p. 337) while being externalized, in that
novel and elsewhere, through the multiplied scenes of actual drown-

ing. That deathly flood can be rendered creative only through an exploration of the most subterranean estuaries of will and desire. Drowning in this redemptive sense is not the opposite of life but part of its cycle. One moves through oblivion to keep living. To make this point, Lawrence must, unlike Forster before or Woolf after him, strenuously enact the scene of real and lethal drowning by contrast to its figurative manifestations.

As much as in the Victorian period, or in a transitional writer such as Conrad, the now-familiar rhetoric of the mortal interval organizes the modernist death scene, although the "untraversable distance" to be negotiated by style is variously defined for Forster, Lawrence, and Woolf. Since the relevant interval for Forster, as we have seen, is the deathly gulf between selves, or sides of oneself, rather than between self and some revelatory annihilation, its widening gap can be arched over only by the connectives of empathy and insight. The interval serves instead in Lawrence to figure the more violent erotic fissures between self and other. By becoming in Woolf a temporal gap in the fabric of continuity itself, the potentially rending interval must be bridged by the suspensive filaments of inner consciousness apart from the outer-directedness of either empathy or desire. As a result, each writer's mode of negotiating the deadly gap, not between here and hereafter but within and between selves, has its inherent grammar. The ethic of rescued antithesis and coordinated polarities in Forster assigns to his balanced prose a predominant syntax of *conjunction*; the incremental repetition and erotic heightenings of the Lawrencian style a cumulative structure of *apposition*; the reaching for continuity in Woolf a *periodic syntax* of rupture, interruption, and delayed repair. Following upon the experiments of Hardy in the circularity of the self's predication ("I am as I was") and of Conrad in the grammar and psychology of "how to be," all three of these twentieth-century novelists are also variously preoccupied with the verb of being, its linking and intransitive syntax, its faculties for conjugating vital energy, for defying or redefining the contrary idea of death.

There is nonetheless a more basic motive for the close concentration on Lawrence's style in this chapter. In its most rudimentary shapes his language generates a rhetoric of trespassed limits, of diction and grammar in transgression against their own semantic containment.

What Lawrence characterizes in the foreword to *Women in Love* as the "continual, slightly modified repetition" of his writing, that "pulsing, frictional to-and-fro which works up to culmination," is a habit he defends as fitting for the representation of any "natural crisis." The manifestly erotic give and take of such rhythmic prose is also suited in another sense to the give, the yielding and breakthrough, of that ultimate natural crisis, death itself. As in Lawrence's metaphysic, so in the climacterics of his style: fatality is the obverse face of sexuality.

So far in this study we have been exploring major writers in their various encounters with the subject of death, and this through a verbal analysis meant to shed light on that deeper narrative encounter yet between writing and absence. The particularities of a given author's style, however, have tended to remain, at least after Dickens, a largely variable function in any specific reading of a drowning or a deathbed scene. While George Eliot and Joseph Conrad, for instance, are the most rhetorically adept narrators in the rendering of last moments since Dickens, each commands a style expert in death without seeming in any way to have been fashioned inevitably for it. By contrast, the paradoxically fluid friction of Lawrence's prose—one is tempted to add, the abrasion and leakage—is related, for all the difference in tone, to Dickensian deathbed punning, each style appropriate in its essence to the pivotal transit of mortality. For one thing, Lawrence himself is also quick to implant an ambiguity of diction in his flexible death sentences. Moreover, his most typical device, the slippery apposition of an impacted, mounting syntax—graded through precarious clarifications toward an ineffable threshold of consciousness—honors the eroded exactitude of dying as if appositive restatements were the grammatical equivalent of punning diction, each mode reluctant to narrow death's wavering closure to a single fixed phrase. Together, the mortal double-entendre of a phrase or single word and the wavering appositive series (the latter frequently involved in Lawrence with what Empson calls "double grammar") can serve in the bordering approximation of life's ambivalent last transition. The entire Lawrencian aesthetic of layered statement and cumulative repetition may thus be found compressed into fiction's recurrent mortal interval, where it becomes thematized as a rhetoric not only of verbal increment but of metaphysical encroachment.

Annihilation's sliding continuity with being thereby defines death in Lawrence as a metamorphosis of identity, a transformed phase of character in some new definition of the integral self.[1] After the stylistic experiments of *Sons and Lovers* (1913) in the vocabulary and syntax of predicated identity—in its contrast (or continuity) with death scenes, now figurative, now clinical—Lawrence had established an idiom responsive enough for such parables of drowning and displaced renewal as we find in *The Rainbow* (1915) and *Women in Love* (1920). When the hero of Lawrence's first major novel, *Sons and Lovers*, passes through the early stages of a sexual relationship with the passionless Miriam, we may recognize close parallels between her character and Hardy's Sue Bridehead in *Jude the Obscure*. To borrow Lawrence's own words about Sue, Miriam too seems to have pushed the "clarity of her mental being" to the point where it "was in itself a form of death."[2] It is an infectious deficiency; after intercourse with Miriam, Paul too "wished he were sexless or dead" (p. 29), feeling as Lawrence thought Jude must have, "something like the Frenchman who lay with a corpse."[3] The French allusion can scarcely help but evoke that reviving *petite mort* which contrasts so utterly in Lawrence with such a depleted necrophiliac encounter—that good death in miniature which serves to reanimate identity, the only death from which there is any coming to.

It is during this null episode with Miriam that the halting, exploratory rhythms of indirect discourse further reveal to us Paul's detachment from vitality. We may think of Margaret Schlegel's vision of life as "a deep river, death a blue sky" when we encounter the cadenced inching forward of Lawrence's tentative syntax on the subject of his enervated hero: "To him now, life seemed a shadow, day a white shadow; night, and death, and stillness, and inaction, this seemed like *being*" (p. 287). The paradox of a death somehow not antithetical to "being" is at the root of Lawrence's psychology and its elusive style, but the note of "inaction" here gives pause. The hero, and indirect discourse with him, are blocked at the stage of naming as recognition, stalled in a no more than faintly appositive grammar (the demonstrative recapitulation of "this seemed") without a syntax of advance. Further, in the fourfold noun series that supplies synonyms for this insentient "being," grammatical logic demands plurality—"these seemed"—and is contravened. The unorthodox syntax appears at once reductive and just the opposite, for it begins to insist on the mutual inherence of these nouns in what the passage goes on to designate as the "great Being." Attributes of a unity, they are therefore, even collectively, singular. Yet their stasis, emotional and grammatical, is a warning of the moribund at the heart of the hero's yearning, his revealingly phrased ache to be "identified with" them.

The hero of *Sons and Lovers* may come by default to this frustrated and partial glimpse of the Lawrencian ideal of self-transcendence, but he gets there at an early stage in the development of his author's prose. He thus anticipates the revitalizing death that characterizes the passionate bondings of the Lawrencian hero and heroine from here on. But Paul is desperately alone here, and that is the trouble. Even his sexually satisfying relation with Clara later leaves him emotionally unfulfilled. What we have in this psychologically premature passage from *Sons and Lovers* is an unusually well articulated instance of the Lawrencian style of mortal detachment, self-annihilation, and transcendence which, given the erotic disappointments of its early fictional representative, is inevitably thrown into doubt, made to look defensive, escapist, even suicidal. It is the heroic vision in search of its authentic occasion. The true goal is a love that takes the self out of its life for a time, not just the life out of the self.

The Lawrencian vision is still seeking its proper scene by the close of the novel, a conclusion whose several verbal ambiguities include Paul's recognition on the last page that "in the country all was dead still." That final idiom of stasis carries an aura both subjective and retrospective in its second sense of "still" as "yet," looking back as it does to the "inaction" of Paul's prolonged brooding crisis. Until now the hero's life has been a deadlock of energies from which he is only ready to work free, as hinted by another pun, in the book's very last sentence: "He walked toward the faintly humming, glowing town, quickly." As sparked by diction itself,[4] the biblical "quick" in him has momentarily conquered all that was "dead still." This is no small victory, having been won by breaking the Oedipal blockage that threatens the hero from early in the novel. Emancipation comes only with the death of Paul's mother from cancer, a fate speeded at the end by a morphine overdose administered by the son himself in a chapter called "The Release." The multiple suggestiveness of that title would seem to cover the mother's release both of her tenacious

will to live and so from her dying agonies, even as, in a third implication, its freeing violence sees the hero through the throes of his
own death by association and proxy, a wrenching from maternal
stranglehold into adult possibilities.

The prominence given to the gruesome cancerous death of Mrs.
Morel, its climactic station in the erotic *Bildungsroman* of *Sons and
Lovers*, suggests something else at large about Lawrence's habitual
displacement of death to erotic conceit. The forbidding darkness of
Thanatos is certainly approached with a blend of prophetic fervor and
trepidation equal to that with which the taboo of Eros is transgressed
in Lawrence's works. The explicit and extended death scene, more
frequent and more clinically detailed than in any previous British
writer, answers to, without for a moment subserving, the erotic passages set in counterpoint to it. Death is not reduced to a mere figuring
of sexuality but stressed rather as the greatest threat—in another
sense, challenge—to the continuous momentum of erotic drive. Analogy only carries forward that challenge. If ecstasy can somehow be
seen to resemble the awesome mystery of extinction, even its pain
and annihilation, then whatever else may be learned about sexuality
in the process, and about the deep fear of it that so often turns to
defensive violence, the specter of death itself has been partly de-
contaminated by this erotic comparison. Far from either mere metaphor or aphrodisiac, the Lawrencian death scene is so traumatizing
that eroticism, the very will to vitality, must be made analogically to
fuse with—and so defuse—the violence of death's discontinuity.
Metaphor defines a mode of power. Death becomes a name for sex
so that sex can make a claim on death.

Before Paul Morel's reanimated, latently passional self engages
life again, the dying of the mother, so hideously detailed in advance,
transpires in an elided off-stage moment offered up to plot as a
euphemistic report. Here Lawrencian syntax, without enacting the
appositional elisions of on-stage death or emotional regeneration, still
manages to complement the semantic doublings that help shape the
conclusion. Introducing a set of syntactic ambiguities of tense, compound clause structure, ellipsis, linking predication, and antecedence, prose turns a grammar of mortal transition into a rhetoric of
transformation. To begin with, the common Victorian figure of speech
employed by Paul's sister to announce their mother's death, "Paul—

Paul—she's gone!" (p. 398), is affirmed when her death is further imaged as an end that rejects the sequential grammar of negation: "Who could say his mother had lived and did not live?" This very shift in tense is transcended by the thought that "there was no Time, only Space." There is a sudden unmeasurable, we might say again "untraversable," distance between Paul and his mother, but no fatal temporal divide—only an eternity in which to keep coming near. There is, in short, only the status she would have for Paul, as she does for us, if at death she had become fictional, displaced from a life in time into the spatialized form of art or memory. This is, as we are later to see, an achievement in keeping with the very aura of her corpse as a reembodiment of lapsed youth. Once more in the British novel, if seldom with less formal fanfare, fiction becomes in its own right the model of perpetuation for the losses it chronicles.

To make it through to this point of reconciled grief, as prose is further able to demonstrate at the level of its own minute syntactic adjustments, Paul Morel is forced to enter upon Forsterian "disintegrating dialogues" between conflicting impulses that beset him from within. "What am I doing?" he asks. "And out of the semi-intoxicated trance came the answer," the two words, "Destroying myself" (p. 411). As if to embody this reflexive construction in which suicide or confession must be described, the entire narrative is torn between halves of an inner spiritual debate. In an almost Spenserian allegory of Vitality versus Despair, "the conversation began again inside him." Insisting to himself, "She's dead," he knows this as the voice of "his depair wanting to go after her." In a rapid stichomythia suggesting some warring inner chorus, we overhear "You're alive," then "She's not," then "She is—in you." As if the psychological cleaving of the scene runs so deep as to divide not only voice but verbal structure as well, there is a movement toward ambiguity in this exchange from patterns of clear attribution ("She's dead," "You're alive") through an elliptical format, with "alive" understood, that takes a deceptively parallel track into pure prediction as the verb of being breaks out from its contracted form ("She's not," "She is"). There is no contradiction, just a double perspective. Death, confronted in the flesh, has brought the hero past the facile "non-being" of that vitiated reverie with which we began this exploration of Lawrencian style. Granted that Paul's mother is not alive, she can still be, exist, in him. This is the triumph and the burden of immortality through love. Hesitant, transitional, Paul's "She is—in you" recalls in its saving hiatus the typical deathbed interval of transposition—here across the sliding width of an ellipsis—from one key of being to another. Finally, this elided grammar of presence without identity, subsuming oneself to enlarge and energize another, lends a subliminal possibility to the hero's resolved confidence on the last page of the novel. Thinking her "gone," not dead, he believes that she "had been in one place, and was in another." The logical force of antithesis is not enough to keep the last pronoun from having its own antecedence tentatively displaced from an impersonal locus toward the inhabited "other" of her surviving son.

As Paul is quickened rather than extinguished at the close, "released" to autonomy from the corpse of his origin in a world otherwise "dead still," what he must set his momentum against on the last page are those temporarily becalmed "flood-waters" that are part of the "vastness and terror of the immense night." It is in such a heaving darkness where Paul's spiritual inheritor, first hero of *The Rainbow*, is symbolically to drown in the most extraordinary narrative passage of Lawrence's next novel. It is again the obscure vastness of the other, of the world and of woman, to which in a crisis of selfhood Tom Brangwen not only submits but blindly succumbs. The waters of a great flood, the Lawrencian Genesis at the stage of arrest and purge, provide for *The Rainbow*, in setting and rhetoric, the overwhelming objective correlative Lawrence needs for figuring that kind of literal death from which no rebirth can be worked.

□ □ □

Revelation as the franchise of death had been under assault by modernism, as we know, long before Lawrence arrived on the scene. Conrad's pessimism is strategically camouflaged by the familiar structures of deathbed vision even as they are vacated of meaning, while Forster more openly sabotages the whole expectation of visionary dying. Yet both authors, and Lawrence after them, sustain the Victorian distinction between death as event and as figure. Within the analogical rather than biological perspective on death, however, there is in Lawrence a further distinction to be made: between the dying from and the dying into, mere passing and erotic trespass. Lawrence's revisionary death scene is the passional loss of self that wakes to mutual revelation. Like no novelist before him, not even Emily Brontë, Lawrence matures the seasoned trope of death for orgasm from Metaphysical poetry, the link between libido and oblivion, into a full-scale metaphysics of erotic resurrection.[5] The will's surrender need not become moribund but instead metamorphic, searing the self not only to ash but to phoenix. It is only when the scalding flood and abatement of passion consumes and so dooms a given character that Lawrence tends, like Conrad before him in his nonerotic fatalities, to literalize the metaphor of lethal defeat in an external effacement. After so much aimless swimming against the tide, such a defeat will define the lone death by drowning at the center of *The Rainbow*.

Conrad may gently eroticize the idea of mortal epiphany with that Eastern bride who is just possibly unveiled to Jim in the instant of his apotheosis, but there sexuality is at most a vehicle to death's tenor. In Lawrence, the deathlike vessel of revelation for his heroes is always the unveiled body of love, the "threshold of the invisible" now the orifice of desire and discovery. The hell harrowed by the Lawrencian hero, or the heaven achieved and returned from, is the unseen territory of the libido. In one of the most trenchant and succinct remarks ever made about Lawrence's eroticism, his relation to the epistemology of dying is explained by the fact that in his novels "the psychopomp is the phallus."[6] Sex is the paradoxical death *in* while not *of* the body. Again, such metaphoric dying cannot hope to minimize the irreversible oblivion of the thing itself but only to colonize it momentarily. *The Rainbow* is the first of Lawrence's novels to orchestrate this Orphism of the erotic with the full grammar of appositional trespass commanded by Lawrence as his most confidently experimental.

"The Brangwens had lived for generations on the Marsh Farm," goes the first clause of *The Rainbow*. In retrospect the preposition seems as much purposive as temporal: for breeding they lived, ultimately for the begetting upon themselves of their own latent identities. The hero of the book's first phase, Tom Brangwen, begins where Paul Morel left off, after the shock of a mother's death and in the wake of unsatisfactory sex. It is not until his meeting with Lydia Lensky that the chance for a fully responsive adult love affair begins to recall a mortuary world to life. "Things had all been stark, unreal, barren, mere nullities before. Now they were actualities that he could handle" (p. 26), with "handle" there an idiom drawn in part from the world of touch. When Lydia accepts Tom's offer of marriage, their first passionate embrace is a dying from "extreme oblivion" into new life attended by the grammatical increments of Lawrence's metamorphic prose: "He returned gradually, but newly created, as after a gestation, a new birth, in the womb of darkness. Aerial and light everything was, new as a morning, fresh and newly-begun" (p. 41). The actual moment of metamorphosis is signaled by that pivotal grammar of being which transforms the germ statement "Everything was aerial and light" into its curiously inverted form. The unidiomatic inflection of the resulting clause lands an odd accent on the verb of being, dislodging it from its equative status into a verb of simple predication, simple presence, as if to say that only by being so transmuted into the aerial and the bright can reality honestly be said to have come into being at all. As at the death of Leonard Bast in *Howards End*, Mrs. Moore's subsequent apotheosis in *A Passage to India* knows a similar license with the copulative verb under stress of inversion: "Dead she was." In Lawrencian terms "being" is thereby retrieved from the leveling nihilism of an ended "existence."

To convey further Tom's and Lydia's access to each other, syntax is loosened in the following paragraph, so that the increments of serial grammar overlie each other in a series of fluid fulfillments impossible to mark off precisely: "And he bent down and kissed her on the lips. And the dawn blazed in them, their new life came to pass, it was beyond all conceiving good, it was so good, that it was almost like a passing-away, a trespass" (p. 41). As style's graded transformation glides past us in a paratactic sequence deliberately interknit and elided (not a, b, c, but ab, bc, cd), we are made to wonder whether the pivotal understatement "It was so good" attaches backwards or forwards. Was it "so good that it was beyond all conceiving" or "so good as to be like a passing-away"? Both, of course, especially when we recognize the calculated demolition of idiom taking place along with the syntactic detachments. The experience is "beyond all conceiving" in part because it follows from conception as the birth throes of a new life, a life which "came to pass" both as an occurrence and a "passing-away." This ingenuity of grammar and vocabulary reaches a climax in the appositional "trespass." In connection with Lawrence's first novel, *The Trespasser*, Frank Kermode alludes to the noun *trespass* as one of "Lawrence's favorite French puns."[7] The French *trépas* is "death," and what Lawrence has come upon, and made to seem a profound linguistic coincidence, is a single set of letters, approximately, that covers the central ambiguity in his sexual encounters: the transport that is a passing away, the ex-stasis that becomes a crossing to the unknown; thus is the verbal interval of the classic deathbed graduated by apposition to erotic epiphany. It is not easy to sustain this renovated state, as the still-oscillating grammar of being serves to indicate: "And if his wife were heavy, separated from him, extinguished, then, let her be, let him remain himself" (p. 68). On the face of it, Tom can accept Lydia's isolation—as if it were a separate predication of "being"—because it is reciprocated by a reflexive grammar that undoes his own relativism and dependency. It is just such an instinct for liberated identity that comes to the rescue of the next Brangwen generation, when after a lull in his marriage to Anna, Tom's nephew, Will, discovers that he "could sleep with her, and let her be" (p. 187).

But being, isolated, can wear thin, as Jude discovered in his stalled, powerless "I am as I was." Though in one sense described as having "died out from hot life" (p. 123), Tom Brangwen asks of himself at the wedding of Will and Anna, "Did one never get old, never die?" (p. 131). Tom wonders "what difference was there . . . between him now and him at his own wedding?" (p. 131). With the second generation's ceremonial passage marking by contrast the rut of duration for the progenitor, Tom can find his release only in a more drastic rite of transit. The death of Tom bursts upon us with Forsterian bluntness—"Then suddenly the father died" (p. 240)—and the prose must backtrack to catch up with plot, pacing itself over eight pages of the drowning scene with the stark iterations of fatality. Again the appositive grammar of heroic trespass degenerates to impasse and mere repetition. There has seemed recently for Tom "no end, no finish, only this roaring vast space" (p. 131), the same impersonal universe that was so threatening to Paul Morel at the end of *Sons and Lovers*. But those latent "flood-waters" of the earlier novel are now on the rise. In Tom's drunken confusion when caught out in the storm, "there was a curious roar in the night which seemed to be made in the darkness of his own intoxication" (p. 243). The figurative "roaring" in the hero's earlier tumult of consciousness has turned literal, just as "darkness" now becomes a metaphor for emotional benightedness. Earlier yet in the novel, Tom worries about whether he will "sink or swim," given that the "terror of the night of heaving, overwhelming flood . . . was his vision of life" without his wife (p. 183). In the later allegory of drowning, such troubled subjectivity itself is about to dissolve into the objective flux of things. Despite its terror, it is at the same time the fulfillment of an undeniable if partial death wish on Tom's part, his sense that it would be an "infinite relief to drown" (p. 186). In the difficult times with Anna a "vagueness had come over everything, like a drowning" (p. 186), and in this context "come over" emerges as a suppressed metaphor serving to complement "vagueness" in its etymological relation to the waves that would pull him under.

When Tom stumbles now upon the actual scene of his drowning, two further idiomatic usages emerge ambiguously, each one a prepositional phrase hovering between the locus and the subjective recognition of his death. "In his soul, he knew he would fall" (p. 243). Tom's fatality is anticipated not by reason, not in the mind, but at the seat of spiritual life, which is at the same time, with the other force of "in," the very scene of the collapse and allegorical drowning. A comparable interchange between inner and outer across the eddy of a single prepositional slippage now marks the onset of the hero's dying. Capped by the ironically overruled connotation of renewed life in the repetition of "borne," Tom's actual death sentence, at least the closest to one we have, seems to be comprised by the sinking grammar of "He fought in a black *horror of suffocation*, fighting, wrestling, but always borne down, borne inevitably down" (p. 243, my emphasis). The specific interval of the death moment seems hinged about the darkly gauged preposition in the phrase "horror of suffocation." If the first noun is meant to register Brangwen's terror over the fate that is upon him, then he is still subject to painful awareness—still, that is, a subject—if only for the vanishing seconds until the flood engulfs all consciousness. At which point any horrified recoil has ceded, in the equative sense of the genitive, to the horror that *is* suffocation.

What is now unleashed upon the remaining paragraphs of the death scene are the rigidly channeled and leveling iterations, themselves rigidifying, of the phrase "the unconscious, drowning body." With an evocative ferocity of style, unflinchingly repetitive, we are thus made continuously present at the "stripped moment of transit from life into death" (p. 248). Just before the storm overpowers the hero and he goes under to suffocation, he seems "almost without consciousness . . . a sleepwalker, waiting only for the moment of activity to stop" (p. 242). Since this drunken spiritual daze only sums up Brangwen's life of late, waiting as we know him to be for some sense of an ending, the actual suffocation comes upon him as an elaborately prolonged instance of death by epitome. The legendary drowning replay of life which we think we are not getting is there ironically in the very lack of reflection and review. During this distended "stripped moment," the already twice-tolled phrase "unconscious, drowning body" returns leadenly on the next page after the mention of the "transit of death," and once more on the page after that. The formulaic words not only pursue a graded sinking past insensibility toward certifiable death but also grow in themselves, by numbing recurrence, increasingly inert, stiffening to meaningless ciphers in an unnerving linguistic decomposition. Prose thus signals what has for so long been true about Tom's unchanging existence, what psychoanalysis since Freud has seen in repetition itself: the very work of death.

The epitomizing death is thereby embedded in style's own rhythm. Progressive participles, in their unvaried repetition, convey the paradoxical feel of Tom's belated time serving as a momentum locked within monotony. The flood is as much an externalization of something in the self as was Maggie Tulliver's; but here style in its own right becomes a macabre correlative for Lawrence's theme of the inarticulate, the amorphous. *The Rainbow*'s rhetoric of incremental repetitions seems snagged in its own imitative deadlock, bringing to articulation only the cruel routine of death, fixated by the fact it is there to interpret. The Lawrencian hero's lifelong coming to utterance is choked shut on a single reiterated phrase, rhetoric itself caught in an encapsulating surrender to the uninflected, the inexpressive, the deadened. Whereas in *Howards End*, despite Forster's laconic restraint in the handling of death, the antithetical poise of spiritual connection manages to dispose the poles of squalor and tragedy into a balanced calm before the transit to cancellation, in *The Rainbow* the whole style of measured trespass, with its grammar of apposition, seems to stumble here upon the impasse of mere repetition. Yet by language's inevitable difference from death, the fact of style's mediated representation, it is always an *interpretive* mimesis, never that complete abdication of consciousness it evokes.

Once this "stripped . . . transit" across the untraversable distance of extinction is complete, we realize why we have not actually been privy to the biological moment of death, only to its insentient drift. With Tom's wife, Lydia, looking on at dawn after her night's vigil, we get the coronary verdict: "the body was dead" (p. 247). There is no one named Tom left to pronounce it upon, only the unconscious, long-drowning mass from which Brangwen's spirit had hours before, or even some considerable time before that, begun evacuating. Dilated and deliberately anticlimactic, so that in every sense we know to expect death as we watch it take over silently from unconsciousness, the distended moment(um) of this death scene inscribes the deluge of the unformed self by formlessness, the still inchoate by the chaotic. This epitomizing scene awaits the hero's funereal witness by the heroine, however, to certify once and for all its—and his—finality. Worried about never arriving at a finished selfhood, Tom Brangwen, as his wife notices over his corpse, has come to himself at last in the only way still possible to him. By dying, he has in one existentialist sense—and Lawrence's prose rarely shows this philosophic potential more clearly—come irreversibly into whatever fixity of being he was to achieve, even as that being is obliterated. "He was beyond change or knowledge, absolute" (p. 248). When he is further said to be "inaccessibly himself," his arrival at self-validation is thus disclosed at the same time as a kind of eradication, a removal even from his own access to himself. This quintessential Lawrencian moment of cadaver as epitome anticipates an axiom of deconstruction; as one commentator has recently put it, in a comparison of Adorno and Derrida as readers of Heidegger: "Both see pure identity as death."[8]

Now that Lawrence's symbolic flood has served to transpose the metaphors of erotic turbulence and subsiding will into a readable figure of finality, itself epitomizing Tom's quest for an end, the mechanisms of displacement for the next generation, as before in *Sons and Lovers* and soon to come in *Women in Love,* are ready to be set in motion. The first reaction after Lydia's to the black tide of this dying is that of Tom Brangwen the son, direct heir to the lethal scene as a deadening of desire, followed immediately by a surge of restitution in the nephew, Will. Displaced in Will's direction, the epitomizing death may be purified to renewal; displaced in the direction of Tom's son and namesake, however, this drowning becomes the accusation of a worse finality. The second-generation bearer of Tom's name is a creature of sly surrender to his own moribundity and corruption, though this we only begin suspecting at the time of his father's death by premature finality. As "quiet and controlled as ever," Tom went mechanically through the funeral rituals until the final shock of double recognition when confronted with the coffin's engraved nameplate: "Tom Brangwen, of the Marsh Farm. Born——. Died——" (p. 248). Rarely in *The Rainbow* are we encouraged to guess exactly where we are in historical time; Lawrence wants the Brangwen chronology left vague, suspended in some generalized communal past, but his rewards are multiple here. We recognize the ellipsis but read it also as both a symbolic overlap between the generations and a blighting elision of the present life line. Bred, wedded, bedded, dead, Lawrence's doomed characters have no room for the verbs of being or becoming. In Lawrence's epitaphic irony we see the living Tom before his father's memorial, a son not finally distinguished from his origin in death but virtually extinguished with the father. The dateless inscription, whether incomplete as yet within the plot or left blank only for the reader, slurs birth with death in the effacement of all vitality: Born . . . Died. The poles of being are too close for comfort, its chances as narrow as a coffin. Nothing could be farther in spirit from Tom's spasmodic episode before his own apparent grave marker than the newspaper office esprit de corps(e) a few years later in *Ulysses*, where reading your own obituary notice gives you a renewed "lease on life." Instead, Tom feels his mortgage on vitality being mortally foreclosed before his eyes. Displacement becomes an introjection of death and so an ejection from life.

That nothing but a blank in the space of inscription separates Tom's being born from his becoming dead is the allegory that causes his galvanic start of recognition before the coffin. It further seems to induce the double death he subsequently undergoes, first before our eyes, then as an implicit admonition before those of Ursula, heroine of the book's second half. "The good-looking, still face of the young man crinkled up for a moment in a terrible grimace, then resumed its stillness" (p. 248). What is portrayed here is more than simply discomfiture and recovery. There is an agony, then a deathly grin, then the ensuing stillness not of return so much as of finality—or the former seen under the aspect of the latter, mechanical self-suppression as a stasis unto death. Already dead in a sense, Tom the second, belated and effaced, shortly becomes a corpse standing in state for another to gaze upon, as he had gazed on the body and then the coffin of his father. His niece, Ursula, a young girl looking for models of being, soon comes upon her dead-spirited uncle already decaying toward the admonishing specter of a death's-head, "his face distorted, his lips curled back from his teeth in a horrible grin, like an animal which grimaces with torment . . . the teeth all showing, the nose wrinkled up, the eyes, unseeing, fixed" (p. 249).

It is by deliberate contrast, two short paragraphs later, that we are shown Will Brangwen's revivification through death. Just before the chapter where his uncle dies suddenly in the flood, Will has been reborn to and upon the body of his wife through an experience of "ultimate beauty, to know which was almost death in itself" (p. 234). The stress on the acceptance of shame and the probable play on "fundament" for "bottom" in "heavy, fundamental gratification" (p. 235) suggest that he and Anna have entered an anal stage in their lovemaking, a scouring and restorative "sensuality" that seems "violent and extreme as death" (p. 234). It is this sensuality to which they return at the end of the death chapter. "The death had shaken" Will, but it "seemed to gather in him into a mad, overwhelming passion for his wife" (p. 249), where the participial adjective participates in the language of the same flood or "whelming" it assuages. Out of all this death and partial rejuvenation, the heroine of the book's third and final generation, Will's and Anna's daughter, Ursula, must make her way—and from *The Rainbow* into her central role in the next novel as well, *Women in Love*. She does so by taking heart from the symbolic rainbow that forms over the colliery landscape in her first book's last paragraphs. I have dwelt on the coming to crisis of those symbolic "flood-waters" from the end of *Sons and Lovers* in *The Rainbow*'s central chapter, "The Marsh and the Flood," not just because it is the plot's one literal death scene, touchstone of all rhetorical and erotic counterparts, but because in more ways than one it is the definitive episode for the final heroine too. Ursula's closing rainbow is after and before all an encompassing symbol rooted in Tom's earlier death scene, overarching it on either side and so containing it as archetypal base, a symbol consequent upon though glimmering above its most powerful narrative occasion. As out of death new life, so above the flood of destruction bursts the arc of erotic covenants unbegun, threshold of hopeful trespass.

□　　□　　□

Turning to Lawrence's next novel, *Women in Love*, we find again how the habitual fluctuations of his diction and syntax—the varieties of recurrence, cumulative or not, the tapping of Romance etymology and dead metaphor, the sliding emphases of prepositional phrasing, inversion, ellipsis, conjunctive grammar, or suspended antecedence, the mounting pressure and release of appositional structure—how all these verbal features and more can be used to approximate the ambiguous encroachments upon death as symbolic moment. Style lends definition in this way to every aspect of Lawrencian death, whether in the form of its metaphoric anticipation only, its enacted scene, its emotional displacement as grieving and assimilation, or its erotic counterpart in transfiguration and violent renewal. After various figurative preparations, the first actual death scene in *Women in Love* is another drowning, this time of a woman and man together. Its epitomizing force is then transferred to a secondary recognition in itself equivalent to death. The industrialist figure Gerald Crich, magnetized by this dying, is a continuation from Tom Brangwen the younger in Lawrence's critique of the automatized and unmalleable modern soul. Himself a tense, fearless, too perfect and secure "diver" (in the early chapter by that name) into the cold depths of impersonality, Gerald must oversee the drowning of his sister Diana— indeed as the end of something in himself that can never return to the warm surface of life. The drowning scene is the first sustained narrative marvel of *Women in Love*, the most awesome run of sheer storytelling power since the death of the elder Brangwen in *The Rainbow*. It is also slyly established to reflect some deficiency not only in the antihero Gerald but in the Lawrencian spokesman, Rupert Birkin.

Characteristically intoxicated by paradox, Birkin has been holding forth with Ursula about death and decay as positive and progressive—

a new version of Forster's ethic of Thanatos in which the "I am I" emerges from a knowledge of death—until a perfectly timed, fittingly ambivalent interruption. " 'You only want us to know death,' " accuses Ursula. " 'You're quite right,' said the soft voice of Gerald, out of the dusk behind" (p. 165). There is nothing in what follows to indicate which of the two second persons Gerald's penumbral "You're quite right" is meant to address. His brusque assent seems given both to Ursula's resentful interpretation of Birkin's position and to the substance of Birkin's point as she angrily formulates it. As he is often to do, Gerald mistakes Birkin's philosophy for a simplified brand of death worship, and makes the worse error, as his "You're quite right" at least partly implies, of mistaking it for the truth. Birkin, by contrast, is the neo-Forsterian hero who can say, "I myself, who am myself" (p. 96), without rigidifying like Gerald into pure will.

Within a few pages an actual death has struck. Gerald has one of his few moments of repose in the novel blasted by the piercing cries from his sister Winifred about Diana's disappearance. He and Gudrun have been rowing together on the water, drifting into intimacy and sensing its menace. The sudden terror of death by water is a grief they take personally. Someone is drowning on the Crich property, and the master, the God of the Crich machine, must resume his incarnation, awake from his human peace and return to mechanical efficacy: "He was looking fixedly into the darkness, very keen and alert, and single in himself, instrumental" (p. 171). As the last adjective implies, and all the more by its syntactic isolation and fixity, this modern creature of industry dies back now into automatism and soulless instrumentation. At the simultaneous vision of this transformation and the external threat of death—they are hardly to be distinguished—Gudrun too "seemed to die a death." Almost at once we hear across the waters the terrible reiterations of "a girl's high, piercing shriek" calling out one of Lawrence's most direct homophonic puns, "Di—Di—Di—Di—Oh Di—Oh Di" (p. 171). Heard in the darkness, Winifred's obsessive monosyllable is both a nickname and a verb in the imperative mood, a girl's pleading summons to her sister that simultaneously (however unintentionally) commands her death. Falling on the ears of the newly intimate couple, Gerald and Gudrun, it might well remind them of the love that is both supplication and repulsion, the beckoning destruction of their own deadly sexuality.

If Tom Brangwen died in a predominantly symbolic flood, at least the symbols were meant in part for him. Yet when two young people about whom we know nothing, and learn nothing from their deaths, drown together in the allegorically charged pages of "Water-Party," we sense that much is yet to come before the meaning of this demise will be fully disclosed. A young man dives to save a girl from drowning, and in trying to cling to the chance of life he offers, she accidentally strangles and suffocates him, dragging them both down to their doom. On the face of it, nothing could seem more simply pitiful. But long after the idea of a stranglehold has become erotic and voluntary in Gerald's passion with Gudrun, hundreds of pages later, Gerald stammers out to the mate of his stale sex and violent enmity: " 'Why must you repeat it so often, that there is no love?' . . . in a voice strangled with rage" (p. 433). When he tries to make breathing room for himself by strangling Gudrun instead, he fails—and goes off to freeze to death in the snow, the long-delayed culmination of his aborted attempt to save the drowning couple in that current "as cold as hell" (p. 176). When "the bodies of the dead" in that early tragedy were recovered toward dawn, it was found that "Diana had her arms tight round the neck of the young man, choking him," and Gerald is appropriately (we later see) the first one to speak: "She killed him" (p. 181). Way beneath consciousness, in the colder currents of being, Gerald glimpses his own destiny. When the novel's last "body of the dead" is recovered after the doomsday finale of "Snowed Up," that prefigurative death by water sixteen chapters before has frozen to the fate of a world ended in ice.

Shortly after the double drowning, the hero, Birkin, like Will with Anna after the drowning of Tom Brangwen, braves the embrace of a sexual death with Ursula. Their first intercourse thus becomes the yielding to "an extreme desire that seemed inevitable as death" (p. 179), leaving the self in a paradox of disintegration, "satisfied and shattered, fulfilled and destroyed" (p. 180). "I was becoming quite dead-alive," admits Birkin to himself, a functional corpse who displaces his deadness onto the drowned couple and fires what is still alive in him in the clutches of a different kind of death. The new birth achieved out of the released cramp of such passion does not, cannot, last long for either partner, unless it is renewed. Diana has drowned at night on Saturday, and by the next evening, having waited in vain for Birkin the entire day, Ursula realizes that her "passion seemed to bleed to death" (p. 183). Thirty times in the first three pages of this chapter, "Sunday Evening," variations on "death," "dead," and "die" are roped into service, until the prose reads like a jotting of apothegms tethered to an *idée fixe*. "The knowledge of the imminence of death was like a drug." "Death . . . is beyond our sullying." "One might come to fruit in death." "The only window was death." "Death is a great consummation, a consummating experience" (pp. 183–185). Prose is not just a record but an instance of fixation, tending again toward that repetition unto death. By the time Ursula and Birkin are reunited in the "Moony" chapter, however, Ursula has realized that only those "who are timed for destruction . . . must die now" (p. 237), and it is this knowledge, rather than her very being, that "reached a finality, a finishing in her." Just as Birkin, "dead-alive" before their lovemaking, came back to himself in her arms, so now, after her own purgatorial death-in-life, she is ready to seek union again in his embrace. Their axis of the plot has reached a psychological clearing, beyond which lie further erotic and emotional prospects. Together they proceed for the rest of the book to sustain and constantly remake their union. At this point the plot's own interest shifts to those characters, Gerald and Gudrun primarily, who are in fact "timed for destruction," whether it be libidinal, literal, or both.

This second phase of the novel begins with the imminent death of Mr. Crich, standing in relation to his son's defeated finality as did Tom Brangwen's drowning to the terminal fixity of his son and name-sake in *The Rainbow*. Leaving Birkin and Ursula on the "threshold" of their engagement, we move into a chapter by that name concerned ironically with the portal of oblivion. Unlike in Conrad, it is a "threshold" with no "invisible" mystery beyond it. Thomas Crich is overseen dying a slow and resentful death, while Gerald stands appalled before this spectacle of an unaccepted end that grotesquely exaggerates his own deadened energies. The son's life functions are indeed arrested at one remove, for Gerald finally "could not breathe in his father's presence," the presence of "visible and audible death" (p. 276). Mortality becomes an unspeakable mortification of Mr. Crich's as well as his son's ego, and the book's language of terminal trespass, of thresholds broached and tentatively negotiated, of beginnings bred of endings—all of it perversely festers in this sketch of the old man's refusal to acknowledge and relax into death. The writing has the temper and edge of Lawrence's most incisive prose, and the second edge (anticipating Beckett) of his most subversive: "He never admitted that he was going to die . . . He hated the fact, mortally" (p. 277). Through idiomatic hyperbole, fear of dying becomes itself a mortal wound. And into the embrace of this despair Gerald is also snared, "convulsed in the clasp of this death of his father's" (p. 277), where the obdurately unnatural prose is knotted over itself in a mesh of grammatical dependence, odd by ominous prodding.

The style never lets up. "For to realise this death that he was dying was a death beyond death, never to be borne. It was an admission never to be made" (p. 277). The sound pun on "born," the play on "admission" are traces of a lost and better possibility glimpsed only as they are swept away. It is one of the passages in Lawrence where stylistic ambiguity exists only as the shadow of itself. The effect has a rare power, calling up the dynamics of mortal trespass only to expose them as inoperable. Punning and redundancy in Lawrence's style are often an investigation by variant, an attempt to erase mistaken contrarieties, to find the subsuming commonness in a tension of opposites. But in these two sentences negation aggravates into dichotomy the alternate meanings, stiffens them into unyielding contrast. One potential pun per sentence straddles the mortal divide, and negation petrifies them there; Crich is on the "threshold" of sheer nothing, never to be born out of death, never to be admitted into renewed life—and this is, in the only senses of the two words here in place, what he cannot *bear* to *admit*. Even the verb phrase "to realise this death" suggests the whole rhetoric of fruitful ambivalence on the wane. For the himself "unrealized" Thomas Crich, the acts of "recognizing," "effecting," and "making real" are all equally intolerable efforts when the object of such psychological exertion is death. The fragments of ambiguity in this passage are never reconvened as transformed versions of a more deeply achieved common denominator. The great "threshold" passage in *The Rainbow* was an erotic opening up between Tom and Lydia worked through by incremental apposition: "At last they had thrown open the doors, each to the other . . . it was the transfiguration, glorification, the admission" (p. 91). Acceding to the fact of otherness, they gained access to it. Such is the simultaneous "admission" of and into a new interplay of being where even the syntactic contraction of a reiterative ellipsis in "She was the doorway to him, *he to her*" (my emphasis) distills their mutuality down to a pure sexual vector. But Thomas Crich cannot acknowledge the ultimate otherness even of death, and so the threshold to revelation, or even to an accepted sense of the inevitable, is walled up and morbidly forbidding.

As with Tom Brangwen, the death of the elder patriarch in *Women in Love* is a degeneration in the processes of his becoming. Mocking the whole idea of maturity and arrival, the idiom of beginning is ironically enlisted to describe a regression visible in Mr. Crich's "inchoate dark eyes" (p. 313). And if the father is not yet become, what of his half-begotten son? It is on the same page that Lawrence reveals Crich's terror of his son's only "imminent being," and on the next we find Gerald governing the reflexive pronoun *own* in this unexpected sentence: "The real activity was this ghastly wrestling for death in his own soul" (p. 314). Why "for"? Death itself would seem to loom as the unacknowledged spoil of victory in this self-divisive clash of ego and suicidal will. Gerald phrases his resolution to stay by the father's deathbed as an effort to "see it through" (rather than the restorative, hopeful sense of "see him through"), saying this often enough to implicate the very preposition in a fatal trespass upon which the son will, in effect, accompany the father.

To fend off the caving in of his very will to exist, Gerald now reaches out to Gudrun as a sexual prop for his inner void. "He would have to find something to make good the equilibrium . . . and so equalize the pressure within to the pressure without" (p. 314). The literal-minded mechanical terminology of "equilibrium" is an unconscious burlesque of Birkin's mystical "star-equilibrium" (p. 311) formulated three pages before at the end of "Excurse," the erotic ideal of absolute selves in an orbit or field of vitalizing relativity. As Gerald engineers Gudrun into a position of mechanical support for his undermined identity, the result is, by the laws of mechanics, that he transfers to her buttressing consciousness the deathly stress of his own spirit, and for the second time with this man—here sexually, while before it was in fear of Diana's drowning—Gudrun "died a little death" (p. 321). It is fatality prolonged across five pages that remorselessly overturns the imagery associated with Birkin's and Ursula's sexual rebirth in the preceding chapter. In a redundancy of mortal idioms Gudrun is said to be "passed away and gone" in Gerald, while he was "perfected" (p. 325), finished fatally in the dark manner of Tom Brangwen the younger. Such sexual passing away between Gerald and Gudrun is a trespass this time in the sense of a violent transgression, a balancing against each other in mortal antagonism. This chapter is called "Death and Love," and it has not two topics but one. Gerald returns from Gudrun directly to the death chamber, within range of his father's dying groan: "The faint voice filtered to extinction." The son is overcome more by contamination than lament, feeling that "his own heart would perish if this went on much longer" (p. 326). There is a "strange noise" now which breaks the silence, and then one last wordless sound, an abortive mortal interrogative which would seem struggling vainly to understand the "what" of death: " 'Wha-a-ah-h-h!' came a horrible choking rattle from his father's throat, the fearful, frenzied eye . . . passed blindly over Gerald, then up came the dark blood and mess pumping over the face of the agonized being." The seat of suffering at the last is not a "man," or the generalized animal form "creature," but "being" abstracted into pure agony. When the death rattle becomes a bawling cry like a baby's on first entering the world, and when Gerald's equally "imminent" self is then left "echoing in horror," we have the final signs of displacement: the son's whole being locked into rhyme with this dying, a soul undelivered and resonating to vacancy.

That appalling sight of blood and vomit "pumping over the face" finds it equivalent two years later in the unsuppressable memory of the death of Stephen's mother that comes to him in a dream near the start of *Ulysses*. It stands as the nightmare of the hero's prehistory from which this new novel must awake. The vile, involuntary details of this recollection include the "bowl of white china" that "had stood beside her deathbed" holding "the green sluggish bile which she had torn up from her rotting liver by fits of loud groaning vomiting" (p. 5), where participial adjective and gerund spill over into each other in that last immitigably ugly phrase. Imploring a respite from this inset memory, as if to get his own story going, Stephen speaks in a vocative that is also an elliptical negation: "No mother." He then adds a sentence that is half plea, half reflexive fiat of self-annunciation—in a grammar that recalls the ironies of freedom as sheer predication from *The Rainbow*: "Let me be and let me live" (p. 10). Only left alone by this exorcised specter of original death can the hero be let free to become himself. If domestic death scenes like those of Mrs. Dedalus, Mrs. Morel, or Mr. Crich, despite their violent rejection of all Victorian euphemism, are nevertheless, as one critic has recently suggested, "determinedly and self-consciously anachronistic,"[9] with their familial locus and their attempt at articulate disposition, then it is only fitting that their vestigial targets should be progenitors born well back in the last century. Only in death can these parental figures release their children to the dilemmas of a modern life line. In appropriate chronological order, *Sons and Lovers* works this "dated" domestic deathbed scene out of its system only on the last page, *Women in Love* somewhere midway along, *Ulysses* almost at (and as) its very inception.

None of these deaths is more systematically displaced onto the next generation than that of Mr. Crich. So insistent is Lawrence in transferring the epitomizing death of the still spiritually incipient father to the inchoate form of the son's soul that he takes Gerald from the scene of death to Gudrun's bedroom for a regressive escape not only from this death but from the adult life it seems to threaten. There the "corrosive flood of death" becomes metaphoric for the "effluence" and "ebbing" (p. 337) of their loveless sexuality, a scalding stream of need mistaken for the amniotic "flow of life." It is "as if he were bathed in the womb again," as if the feminine other were "Mother and substance of all life" for him. The "terrible frictional violence of death" with which Gerald now "filled her" (p. 337) is an etymological travesty of anything like sexual or emotional "fulfillment." At the beginning of this "Death and Love" chapter, just before the father's death, Gudrun felt "she would pass away" (p. 333) in Gerald's arms, an extinction without the ecstatic trespass and accession. Now Gerald's *petite mort* with her, imaged as the return to the womb, is also another drowning like that which exploded their peace in "Water-Party," in which Gerald feels himself "dissolving and sinking to rest in the bath of her living strength" (p. 337).

Once the two couples, Birkin and Ursula along with Gerald and Gudrun, have journeyed to the ski resort on the Continent for the last phase of the novel, Gudrun extricates herself from this regressive relationship with Gerald by a sinister liaison with the decadent artist and polyglot wit, Loerke. While they are isolating themselves in a sickly private world of linguistic indulgence and perverse verbal "intercourse," an embittered Gerald is reduced to bafflement over the simplest items of English vocabulary. He worries the ordinary in language, not the ornate. Asked by Birkin if he is "all right," Gerald answers, "I never know what those common words mean. All right and all wrong, don't they become synonymous somewhere?" (p. 430). Gerald has driven himself to the point where, at some glacial pole of experience, apparent antonyms meet and freeze. There is, he realizes, a potential for tragic self-delusion in such standard parlance as the idiom "all right," a perversion of "all" as a gesture at wholeness, the minimal tricked up as a sufficiency. When Birkin asks Gerald at the end of this parting conversation why he continues to "work an old wound" with Gudrun, Gerald replies abstractedly, "Oh, I don't know. It's not finished" (p. 431). Confronted in the next chapter with Gudrun's "It is over between me and you," a phrase giving unidiomatic prominence to her own pronoun, Gerald retreats into another of modern fiction's inner dialogues in which he distinguishes again, as with "all right" versus "all wrong," between the simplest integers of English idiom: "Over, is it? I believe it is over. But it hasn't finished. Remember, it isn't finished" (p. 452). Though "aloud he said nothing whatever," he goes on speaking "to himself" in the first-person plural, including in the implied web of his address not only Gudrun but also that deadly will in himself that strives all but posthumously for some depth of nonbeing more satisfying than just having things over: "We must put some sort of a finish on it. There must be a conclusion, there must be finality" (p. 452). Gerald the man becomes a character in his own collapsed life, groping blindly for a finis.

It is precisely this rhetoric of finality that marks his point of no return in the snow. As Gerald approaches with homicidal intent both Gudrun and her new partner, it is Loerke who enunciates one of the ruling motifs of the novel's conclusion: "*Maria!* you come like a ghost" (p. 462). The hero, Birkin, has also made the journey abroad "like a *revenant* himself" (p. 381), one of the many characters in Lawrence who must sojourn awhile as their own ghosts in order to reorganize their true beings. It is Gerald's tragedy simply that he never wants to come back alive. When Gerald now grabs Gudrun violently by the throat and begins "watching the unconsciousness come into her swollen face" (p. 463), the murder is interrupted by the mock solicitude of Loerke's interjected French: " 'Monsieur,' he said, in his thin, roused voice: 'Quand vous aurez fini——' " (p. 464). In the novel's most striking instance of polyglot irony, for once perhaps unconscious on Loerke's part, this ambiguous address implies either a straightforward plural or the sarcastic politeness of the formal French singular—either, "Sir, when you two are finished" or, more likely, "When you, sir, are finished." Ultimately this battle to the death must be rendered in the singular, a warring not so much between Gerald and Gudrun as between Gerald and his own will to a Hardyesque finis. What Loerke anticipates for Lawrence's silent antihero is rather like Decoud's "It is done," or more to the point Helen Schlegel's hyperbolic "I'm ended," without her opportunity to see "through to the end" with what actually remains of herself. Gerald's too is a closure by abdication, but with no reprieve.

Lawrence's character nevertheless remains afraid of his misunderstood suicidal desire: "Somebody was going to murder him. He had a great dread of being murdered" (p. 465). The second half of his disintegrated self has taken over beyond dialogue or debate, the self-effacing threat externally embodied, and very soon he "could feel the blow descending: he knew he was murdered." Gerald's tortured being thus commits itself to oblivion in a virtual revelation of its own nature after the fact, as suggested by the epitomizing, almost definitional copula "was murdered" rather than the passive "had been murdered." Birkin claimed early on that "a man who is murderable is a man who in a profound if hidden lust desires to be murdered" (p. 27), and Gerald thought it "pure nonsense." Yet what we are now watching is the only successful "murder" in the novel, the only crime which can genuinely exemplify Birkin's formula, because in Gerald's death the willful murderer and the willing murderee are the same disjoint mentality. The personification is entirely proleptic when Gerald experiences a "dread of being murdered . . . which stood outside him like his own ghost." Once again in this novel, the antihero is haunted by the specter of himself as unwilling revenant, here both as a prophecy of the ghostly shadow he will have shortly become and also as a prelude to his expiration.

If fear of death is a ghost, then his mortal dread itself has died, and there is nothing left to hold off the convergence of murderer and victim within the perished will to live. This voiding collision is matter-of-factly rendered in the narrative with a stark accreting grammar unlike anything else in this novel, a crisp precision of sequence going nowhere: "But he wandered unconsciously, till he slipped and fell down, and as he fell something broke in his soul, and immediately he went to sleep" (p. 446). Decoud's cord of silence breaks at last. This death in the snow is also a literalization of an earlier metaphor as explicit as any such figurative transpositions in Dickens, Hardy, or Conrad. In the "Death of Love" chapter, rather than conceiving himself as disintegrated from without by the death of his father, Gerald "knew how destroyed he was, like a plant whose tissue is burst from inwards by a frost" (p. 338). When the figure comes to actuality in the Alps, what is registered is precisely that burst or broken will to live. It is not that Lawrence's narrative fades out before the death scene to the report of its outcome. This *is* death: something irreparably snapped in the desire for consciousness.

The elided interval of the actual death moment, a conjunctive syntax covering over the fatal disjuncture, is, as often in fiction's ironic death scenes, a minimizing tactic that in and of itself epitomizes the victim's living effacement. There is a similar suggestion, by title and subsequent enjambment, in Thomas Hardy's poem "Dead Man Walking." Hardy anticipates by negation that common Lawrencian metaphor of transit. "There was no tragic transit," writes his "iced" persona, "When silent seasons inched me / On to this death."[10] In Lawrence's version of this lethal chill from within, Gerald's freezing to death sums up not only his life but the complete threefold structure of the death scene as fiction so frequently articulates it. Gerald's lust for unconsciousness is metaphorically transposed in the snow from torpor to mortal finality even as his freezing of the blood from within epitomizes the unyielding waste of his entire emotional life. By lateral displacement, through a kind of osmosis of iciness, the death also chills Gudrun to the marrow of her indifference, while threatening further displacement upon his friend Birkin. When Gerald's corpse is retrieved from the snowbank, even "the life breath" of his last moments is "frozen into a block of ice beneath the silent nostrils" (pp. 468–469). The corpse emits an almost Gorgon-like spell, for staring at it Birkin wonders "if he himself were freezing too, freezing from the inside."

It is just this lateral transference of death that must be reversed to a vision of prophetic continuance in the adjacent self in order to afford the novel the tone of unmet possibility on which it will close. Gerald is the failed exemplum for a theory of secular transcendence and communal immortality shared by Birkin with his author, Lawrence, with Conrad, and more directly yet with Forster and Woolf. Gerald collapsing midstep into the frozen locus of his end debases the passionate dream of trespass and admission which Lawrence's style is always lying in wait to engage. Only afterwards can such rhetoric enter, through indirect discourse, into the meditation by Birkin on the squandered eternity of his dead friend. Even as the afterimage of an excluded spiritual triumph, the prose is still an instance of apposition as a traversing of the mortal interval, death's "stripped transit" calibrated beyond temporality itself: "Gerald . . . even after death . . . might have lived with his friend, a further life" (p. 470). Such is the consolation of modernism at large, its answer to death's blankness. No one but Lawrence, though, would have said it this way. Like the doubling of a pun harnessed to the uncertainty of the death moment, the phrase "a further life" is set off by a comma to encourage its reading both as a cognate object governed by "lived" and also as an appositive phrase that redefines the living friend, in his own person, as the extended being of the dead beyond the grave: displacement in a single ambivalence of phrase. Even as the rhythm of amplification is tuned to metamorphosis, it is a syntax of salvation unachieved by plot; despite the appositional grammar of immortal displacement, trespass, and completion, this is rhetoric in a final vacuum. Lawrence thus closes *Women in Love* with the style of dying as survival gone into mourning for its own denied moment.

The Victorian masters of rhetorical demise wanted death to do the last work of life—clarify, adjudicate, conclude, encapsulate. They were also fascinated by death for the way it could be made to catch the flickering light of what might (or might not) lie beyond it. Except in his last poems, Lawrence wanted death opaque to myths of heaven, yet he became a major strategist of its secular drama in part to command its analogous range of terrestrial transcendence—not ascension but sexual access, not resurrection but rebirth. In this way Lawrence's most revolutionary innovation, the erotic good death, comes into sharpest focus against the contrasting ground of actual demise. Whereas Forster precipitously exiles the old-fashioned modes of death to make room for a visionary humanism unruled by momentous dying, its spurious symbols and epiphanies, Lawrence is more directly in touch with the tradition. Unable to avert his imagination from the extended death scene, he reactivates the structural formulas of narrative fatality in order to maneuver them into metaphoric congruity with the new and unheard of. Forster's fiction banishes the revelatory death scene; Lawrence's novels recover death as a name for visionary trespass. Lawrence thus leaves the scene of death exactly where Woolf takes it up: as the locus for intuitive extensions of being that serve us in this world.

□   □   □

It is too soon to leave Lawrence without giving fuller account of a motif that cuts across, and deep into, most of his major fiction, and that culminates in a strange, late work in which the erotic good death and the ordinary throes of mortality coincide in an explicit myth. The motif is that of the contemplated corpse, and the 1928 novel is the retelling of Christ's Passion and Resurrection in *The Man Who Died*, otherwise titled *The Escaped Cock*. For the first time in Lawrence a corpse rises to new power from its own scrutiny, transforming the pattern of displacement to pure miracle.

The first pangs of this new Messiah's resurrection are a deceptive renewal that lapses once more to insentience. "And again it was finished" (p. 165) is Lawrence's ironic rendering of Christ's last words. Looking back over his days of self-scourging fleshly existence, this suffering Christ realizes that what he had offered to others was only "the corpse of my love" (p. 205). The cadaver into which he for a second time degenerates after the tremors of resurrection thus literalizes his condition in so-called life. The Man Who Died is forced still, we hear, to suffer "pain, unknowable, pain like utter bodily disillusion" (p. 166). The corporeal effect of a spiritual cause is at work even within the fluctuations of that single word "disillusion," signaling again that this mythic hero has died a symbolic death not unlike that of Tom Brangwen, Gerald Crich, or the countless secular protagonists before them in English fiction, characters whose ends are metaphoric reformulations of their living wills. The noun *disil-*

lusion effects a mock incarnation of the abstract in the concrete, especially when one hears shuddering within it the implied and far more likely near-homonym *dissolution*. It is through just such a disillusionment of false faith, the diction insinuates, that this literal disintegration now racks the hero. Style itself not only presents but submits to the onset of decomposition in its own wavering syllables.

As if by suspended compensation, a similar slippage of syllabic weight later marks the most articulately realized moment of the new Christ's restoration in the arms of the priestess of Isis. Released from the "corpse" of his festering celibacy, given over to "another sort of death: but full of magnificence" (p. 206), asserting his true Passion in an erection rather than resurrection with the punning bravado of "I am risen!" (p. 207) as his astonished *"Consummatum est,"* the Man Who Died puns twice further on the near-homonym of "atonement"—for a religious expiation become erotic chiming. With again an adjacent vowelizing in mind, as in "disillusion," he speaks of an "atonement with" (p. 207) Isis in the prepositional sense, that is, of a rhythmic attunement. This phonic oscillation is compounded with a syntactic fluctuation as well the second time around. "This is the great atonement," sings the risen Lord, "the being in touch" (p. 208). The grammar of "being" in this context is both nominal (for the state thereof, conditional upon flesh as its very definition) and more casually gerundive (for that idiomatic touch with otherness that lives upon such palpability and closeness).

It is essential to recognize how this myth of the risen corpse, through "another kind of death" known as sexuality, fulfills a major drive of Lawrencian symbolism throughout his work. It is also crucial to see how the scrutinized corpse contemplated in novel after novel in scenes of empathy or explicit displacement, by lover or double, though never before reborn in this way, has in another eerie sense, by an almost ghoulish rejuvenation, seldom failed to renew itself—or at least to evidence anew the previous self of which it is an inert fulfillment. Some of the novels already considered exemplify this recurrent motif, and to them I will return. But there is one famous story comprising little else. In "The Odour of Chrysanthemums" a husband's corpse is brought home from a mining accident to his wife in a state that crystalizes the distance between them in life. "She saw him, how utterly inviolable he lay in himself," summarizing that "intact separateness" for so long "obscured by the heat of living" (pp. 299–300). Confronting his own post-Romantic crisis in the imagination of otherness and its inaccessible privacies, Dickens wrote in *A Tale of Two Cities* that "something of the awfulness, even of Death itself, is referable to" the fact that a dead body, the self as corpse, is only "the inexorable consolidation and perpetuation of the secret that was always in that individuality" (I, ch. 3). The awful abstraction of a capitalized Death finds its truest point of "reference," that is, in the epitomizing isolation of every cadaver. In "The Odour of Chrysanthemums," once the "heat of living" has dissipated from the body of the dead husband, and before any embalmer's cosmetics have gone to work on the body, the man's separateness is symbolized by a return to a state well before the possibilities of connectedness or sexuality. "Not a mark on him," mumbles his aged mother, "clear and clean and white, beautiful as ever a child was made" (p. 300). This reclaimed and fixated innocence further isolates the corpse from the living wife, inducing in her an identity crisis at one remove. This recognition is couched in the sort of severed inner dialogue familiar in Lawrence ever since the aftermath of Mrs. Morel's death in *Sons and Lovers*. As the miner's wife "looked at the dead man," the rigor mortis of the contemplated corpse displaced upon her sense of self, "her mind, cold and detached, said clearly: 'Who am I?' " (p. 300).

The cadaverous reversion to youthful bloom, to a kind of prelapsarian innocence, a virginity of the ego, intact and distinct and resistant, is also stressed by implication at the death of Mrs. Morel: "She lay like a maiden asleep . . . like a girl asleep and dreaming of her love . . . her face was young, her brow clear and white as if life had never touched it" (p. 399). The last subjunctive, an idiomatic hyperbole turning on "life" when meant as mature experience, also implies that life has in another sense never "touched" the innocent self, by never having moved it to self-consciousness. Yet there is more to the phrasing, a sense that life truncated by death is not only an arrest but a wiping clean of the slate, less being over than starting over: that repetition which is again the work of death. Repeatedly in such scenes death emerges as the point of all return. It is worth recalling here a comparable buried metaphor in *David Copperfield*, in line with the textual analogies throughout that chronicled "life." In the eyes of the hero authoring into shape his own past, the death of David's mother somehow "canceled," as in a virtually textual excision, all the cares that had visibly worn her down since "her calm and untroubled youth." This recovery of the mother's bloom in death is only complicated for Lawrence in *Sons and Lovers,* of course, by the hero's Oedipal confusion. Confronted with the smiting maidenhood of his mother's corpse, Paul "bent and kissed her passionately. But there was coldness against his mouth" (p. 399). The emotional idiom gone literal, and thus mortuary, this is still the chill rejection of a forbidden love, a love in turn which too easily forbids all others. Here we find suggested a further strategic use of the rejuvenated cadaver as inert avatar of a former self. The matron reembodied by death as her virginal self lies there as the corpse of her son's innocence as well, while symbolizing further a desire which, if consummated, would have been entirely fixating, and so fatal, for the maturing son.

In *Women in Love,* it is another reversion of a corpse to a state of innocence that outrages Mrs. Crich over the body of her husband. In a one-way dialogue typical of their relationship she rails about his being "beautiful as if life had never touched you—never touched you" (p. 327). An exact paraphrase of the narrator's words over Mrs. Morel, that "never touched you" boasts again the same idiomatic ambiguity. Once more a shock wave is sent out from the corpse that seems to implicate attendant lives in both its fatality and its denial; the disturbance is registered here upon the sounding board of a homophonic pun on the pronoun *I* in the wife's first words to the corpse, "Ay . . . you're dead." It is this ironic negation of an on-looking self in the proximity of a death that was also dramatized with Tom Brangwen before the coffin plate of his father. Yet his was a denial by proxy in the absence of the physical body, symbolized by the emptiness of its mere wooden repository. It is continuous with this symbol that in the next (Ursula's) phase of the novel the idea of the figuratively risen corpse must first be planted in metaphor, when the heroine "knew the corpse of her young, loving self, she knew its grave" (p.356). The recovered will to love that impels her forward into the next novel is, in these terms, a resurrection. The actual contemplation of a corpse in *The Rainbow,* however, is Lydia's over the body of Tom. As we have already seen in part, it is one of the most moving and suggestive passages in all Lawrence. There is a moment when the lifeblood seems to drain from her: "She went pale, seeing death" (p. 248). She realizes that the corpse still inhabits somehow the threshold between death and its previous warm life. "Neither the living nor the dead could claim him," she thinks, and then in a subtly ambiguous phrasing Lawrence adds, "He was both the one and the other, inviolable, inaccessibly himself." That phrase, "the other," not only takes definition from the antecedent contrast of life versus death but cannot help edging over to an independent meaning as the ineradicable otherness of man to woman in his oneness and singleness, even of man to wife in their supposed "one." Through the mystery of the dead body Lawrence has set about to sacralize the corpse in honor of the sanctity of living flesh, in all its attempts at erotic bonding.[11]

In *The Rainbow*, even a vision of Eros immortalized is born from the very contemplation of Tom's corpse and the introspective rituals of genuine mourning. Brangwen's death, it seems, has made Lydia immortal, through a "knowledge" in both the biblical and the emotional sense: "So she had her place here, in life, and in immortality. For he had taken his knowledge of her into death, so that she had her place in death" (p. 256). Even access to the beyond is mutual. Secure in the memory of Tom's love in death as well as in life, Lydia is translated to something beyond mortality along with her husband, as Birkin promises Ursula at the end of *Women in Love* if either of them were to die. This passage in *The Rainbow* is followed by a gratefully acknowledged displacement even more explicitly couched in terms that reverse and cure Brangwen's stalled identity. Looking back over her days with him from the vantage of their end and his, Lydia yields up her thoughts to indirect discourse with a typical Lawrencian turn, first of etymology, then of idiom. "She was established . . . in this stretch of life," a "stability" of which his corpse is the mirroring inverse, for "she had come to her self," with the sense there of awakening as arrival. The incremental emphasis a sentence later skews the idiom in the service of the explicit: "She was very glad she had come to her own self." And so she "reached out to him in gratitude, into death." Much as Leonard's mortal end brings Margaret to her "goal" in *Howards End*, Tom's death seems to lift Lydia at last to the recognition of such a destined point of rest. Once more in Lawrencian fiction the trespassed taboos of Eros and Thanatos console, remodel, and vivify each other.

Tom's buffeting and mystification by the endless roaring of the outer world have been summed up in the flood as if it were a drowning reprise of his identity projected onto the landscape and then sealed up in the stiffened symbol of his separateness as a corpse. That effigy, become available to his wife as the readable essence of the man, begins finally to suggest how corpses serve Lawrence where other writers look to epitaphs or textual memorials. The corpse Dickens waited upon in the Paris morgue had to wait in turn for its own "identification"; in Lawrence a corpse alone tends to identify the self. Defying time and abridging human duration, this arrest of life as pure retrospective form replicates in little the operations of the fiction that contains it. For Lawrence, that is, the contemplation of a corpse seems to replace the variously implied strategies in other novelists for the invocation of a text within the text, establishing a pattern of corporeal empathy in lieu of verbal epitaph. Like a memorial record elsewhere, the stared-upon corpse is identity entirely objectified, the irreversibly realized sine qua non of human selfhood yielded altogether to an interpreting consciousness. The corpse thus occupies the paradoxical space held by metanarrative strategies both before Lawrence and after him in Woolf and the postmodern novelists: the locus of life perfected by finality, human content not evacuated so much as wholly externalized. What is implied by such moments, for all their existential directness and vocabulary, is a virtually "narrative" incarnation of lapsed—that is, elapsed—identity, the breathing self converted to readable tableau. If, finally, the horror of a corpse—where before there was a husband or lover or parent—can be made more than brute mass, can be seen still to matter, to mean something, then once more the fear of death has been partly subdued and neutralized by (or by analogy with) a narrative text.

Over Tom Brangwen's body Lydia thinks, "He was a majestic Abstraction, made visible now for a moment, inviolate, absolute" (p. 248), that last adjective bringing with it an etymological shadow of "absolution," of virtually sacred purification. Tom's corpse is for Lydia the divination of eternity in the body of time. This comes dangerously close to that debased and all but paradoxical abstraction of the merely material in Gerald's corpse, the "cold" capitalized "Matter." Seeming to objectify some majestic significance, however, the manifest substance of Tom's corpse lends concrete shape to the abstract, becomes a transubstantiation, as it were, of being into palpable meaning. This embodied "Abstraction" of Tom's body, as of so many scrutinized cadavers in Lawrence's work, thus anticipates the resurrection of the Man Who Died out of the self-contemplated body of his own living death, as well as Ursula's mourning for the "corpse of her young, loving self" farther along in *The Rainbow*. Redeemed by erotic recognition in himself, the later passional Messiah of *The Man Who Died* rises from his grave as the Abstraction of desire made flesh, true Incarnation of erotic impulse. Many of the dead bodies earlier in the novels are only secular versions of this doctrinal miracle in Lawrence, types to the antitype and fulfillment of the Man Who Died. Like the novels that house and then entomb them, the plots tracking their lives to epitaph, these corpses, repeatedly stationed to evince the finality of achieved form, are Lawrence's version of meaning fated to pure flesh: the Logos of the "I" on view as Other.[12]

Just as Lawrence's baroque equations of sex and death turn out to be as much an attempt to domesticate the latter as to escalate the stakes of the former, so does the apparent refusal of textual self-consciousness in death allow for its oblique confession. Offering up its fixated body as trace, indelibly revealing the self in its final and definitive lineaments, the Lawrencian corpse can become the open book of another's fate. It is no accident that books like *Sons and Lovers* and *Women in Love* are rapidly propelled to their deliberately unstable conclusions from the scene of meditation over a corpse. For all the open-endedness of Lawrence's concluding strategies, the resistance set up by his fictions to rigidifying closure, their attempted emphasis on temporal rather than spatial form, still the Lawrencian novel yearns, like many of its characters, for the condition of being not only over but finished. His plots often achieve this state by some dialectical tension and then resolution between the fixed point of a readable corpse and the briefly sustained textual momentum restituted from it as a deferral of finality itself. In a sense the entire stylistic experiment of Lawrencian fiction, like a hero's corpse, is an embodiment of the Abstract in the concrete, the legible. More perhaps than his actual death scenes, the ruminated-upon corpse may thereby supply the ultimate displacement of the novelist's terminal imagination. As is true for Woolf in a different but deeply commensurate way, the aftermath of fatality, whether in a contemplated corpse or reimagined death scene, offers a model of fictional form at large as a closed structure of significance. The narrating word in Lawrence, incarnate in the body of a novel as story, as in the effigy of a corpse as history, anticipates Woolf by being transfigured there to an interpretable text.

Effigy and Transfiguration

Death in the Sick-Room, by Edvard Munch
Courtesy Munch-museet, Oslo

Death was an attempt to communicate.

VIRGINIA WOOLF
Mrs. Dalloway

A current under sea
Picked his bones in whispers. As he rose and fell
He passed the stages of his age and youth
Entering the whirlpool.

T. S. ELIOT, "Death by Water,"
The Waste Land

RUMINATING IN BRIEF about the "test of great poetry," Virginia
Woolf's heroine Clarissa Dalloway thinks to herself how the
"moderns . . . had never written anything one wanted to read about
death."[1] This regret passes through her mind in an early sketch for
the famous novel, a story called "Mrs. Dalloway in Bond Street"
(1923). The itch to take dying at second hand, from a text or otherwise,
is still with Clarissa in the later plot, allegorized there by her relation
to the suicide of Septimus Smith, a hero introduced by Woolf to
rectify this deficiency of modernism by himself becoming the new
psychotic bard of death.

At about the time of this seed sketch for *Mrs. Dalloway*, Woolf
published *Jacob's Room* (1922), a book that climaxes in the death in
absentia of its hero. The novel includes early in its course a scene
in which the merest good-bye from this young man has for a female
character the "taste" of finality disinfected of the funereal, namely
"the sweetness of death in effigy" (p. 68). This is a local notion
broadly suggestive for any reading of Woolf's fiction as a whole, since
"death in effigy" can evoke more than some transitional event, like
valediction, that stands by analogy for the act of dying. It can also
imply the single, even solitary death that stands in for another, as
does Septimus's for Clarissa, any hero's for us. So dies Jacob in the
long run, an event off-stage and undetailed that touches the novel
with mortality at the remove of absence itself, the one evacuation
from plot a metaphor for the other.

In *A Room of One's Own* (1929) Woolf allows that great books "continue each other, in spite of our habit of judging them sepa-rately."[2] This is no less true of her own career than of the tradition out of which it emerges. Indeed the (re)generational plot of *Orlando* (1928) does in this light offer us, in its structure of sexual mutation over the centuries, a perhaps not unduly fanciful model for the shape of Woolf's whole career. *Orlando* is an epic of the psyche stretched to an epochal evolution of the androgynous spirit. With Woolf's most important novels tentatively strung together into a similarly extended crisis of consciousness, we might say that Rachel Vinrace dies in *The Voyage Out* (1915) in order to live on unviolated in and through her fiancé, Terence, who disappears and resurfaces, named Jacob Flanders, eight years later, only through sudden death to vacate *Jacob's Room* and be reborn again, sexually realigned, as the title character of *Mrs. Dalloway* (1925). It is she, Clarissa, for whom Septimus Smith kills himself so that she might live on long enough to die under the name of Mrs. Ramsay in *To the Lighthouse* (1927), of natural causes, and later yet as Rhoda in *The Waves* (1931), of her long-repressed suicidal impulses. She finally outlives herself briefly in that same book, as Rachel originally did through Terence, by undergoing yet another sex change and emerging into her ultimate destiny as a novelist. So incarnated, the central Woolfian protagonist becomes a metaphysical hero named Bernard who flings himself in the book's last paragraph against that capitalized Death which has taken such an oddly modulated toll of his predecessors.

Woolf asks rather ominously in *Orlando*, "Has the finger of death to be laid on the tumult of life from time to time lest it rend us asunder?" (p. 67). The answer is found threading through the deaths at the center of her fictions, especially of the three on which this chapter concentrates—*The Voyage Out, Mrs. Dalloway,* and *The Waves*—in a pattern of tacit narrative allegory that is in its own way "continued" from habits in Dickens, Eliot, Hardy, Conrad, and Law-rence: the drowning that, by doing the self in (or under), sums it up. In Woolf the "tumult" that must be stilled momentarily by death is the turbulent rush of consciousness itself that, once disturbed, can whelm the very mentality through which it courses. Death rests its hand upon such troubled waters so that the tempest should become again the beneficent co-motion of self and world. Here Woolf's novels are steering their course into well-charted waters, yet sounding them to a new depth. As troped toward sheer psychology in some of the major texts of the English tradition, drowning consciously endured is the self as pure subject intersecting, sunk in, the world as pure object. Drowning provides in this way the spectacle of identity reviewing itself as it is given over, given back, to the realm of insentience.

Though none of her main characters actually drowns, Woolf remains, with Lawrence, the modern novelist who most seriously explores the post-Romantic prerogatives and ironies of death by water, if only as a psychological figure for some submergence of private will in the horizonless reaches of the life in time. Her largest subject is the crisis of Eros adrift in Chronos. The titles of both the earliest and latest novels we will be taking up in detail, *The Voyage Out* and *The Waves*, give evidence of, while dividing, the scope of Woolf's preoccupations with such matters. On the one hand there is the wayfaring modern psyche, all voyages launched at varying peril upon the shoreless oceans of identity. On the other hand there is that impersonal universe unmappable by mind, indifferent and bewildering, toward and sometimes against which the islanded identity turns in its urge for order. Roiling or at rest, formless, enormous, and unknowable, Wordsworth's immortal sea, like Whitman's after it, swirls churning round the human universe in Woolf, lapping or lashing its borders. Death in her novels, often delineated in metaphor as a drowning, discovers its agenda and its emblems within a symbolic program of plummet and dissolution.

Without a drop of water christening her fate in the name of the literal, Rachel in *The Voyage Out* founders and drowns even more obviously than Maggie Tulliver in the immeasurable depth of her resistance to the reduced world of maturity offered her. Septimus Smith is already a "drowned sailor" when we meet him in *Mrs. Dalloway*, dredged from his dementia to inscribe, in poems rescued from time, the secret depths of this temporality. Rhoda in *The Waves* dreams of watery death in a leap from a precipice that would release her from time; after a suicidal jump to approximate this dream, her dying lends strength to her friend Bernard's acceptance of time in his final defiance of the waves' symbolic attrition and effacement. In their heft and heave, invisible depth and eternal return, the waves in Woolf's imagery encircle and sustain the self, now threaten it, here buoy and there upset it, all in their symbolic role as the very (s)pace of duration, of being in time. What makes Woolf so incontestably a master of this Romantic motif, well before her own drowning suicide, is the original urgency by which the symbolism of water, waves, and drowning is assimilated into grammar and analogy, the articulating rhythm and figural texture of her fluid prose style, the alternating solvency and viscosity of syllabic patterns, the rich precipitancy of its conceits.

As the intersection of vertical mortality with horizontal continuance, drowning provides an extreme test case for Woolf's experiments with the stream of consciousness in its role as the interior monologue of mortal impasse and transmission. This is so if for no other reason than that the ultimate transmission looked for, and increasingly by the characters themselves, is the transcription of life's fluidity as text's flourish. Movement, translucency, flux, with the drowning that plunges into them in order to sum them up, all harbor urges toward that finality which the self both yearns for and fears. The transparent race and play of consciousness beneath the surface tension of Woolf's words becomes, in certain of the minds it is there to reveal, a desire for the fixed opacity of aesthetic text, for phrases shaped and tabled, poems left, stories wrested and set down, pageants drafted or staged, a mark made. This is the desire for what Bernard the novelist calls in *The Waves*, seeming to describe the mystery of otherness when in fact symbolizing the incisiveness of that human inscription meant to chart it, a "fin in a waste of waters." What we are beginning to touch on here is the gradual postmodernizing of Woolf's revisionary Romanticism. *The Voyage Out* is headed in this respect entirely toward *The Waves*. Together with *Mrs. Dalloway* these three novels, each and in sequence, demonstrate how fictional identity is eased by that applied "finger of death" in just the way such illuminating finality is most often brought to bear on our lives—though the metaphoric extension of death's pointed work in the impress of the writer's pen. Calling us in book after book to the perusal of our doom in the death of a surrogate, Woolf summons us at the same time to that death in effigy which is any book.

□   □   □

One of the most densely imaged and artfully dilated scenes of drowning in the English novel since that of Maggie Tulliver in Eliot's deluge is that which takes the life of a young woman in *The Voyage Out*, a heroine who never for the duration leaves the scrubbed, decorous order of her sickroom. But though death in Woolf has its hygiene and etiquette, it has also its mystery and its metaphysic. Surrounded by doctors, friends, and fiancé, nursed in the aura of their concern and attendance, Rachel Vinrace nevertheless dies submerged in the abject solitude of her own terrors, in the desperate, until at length relaxed, integrity of her singleness. As with Woolf's suicidal characters to come in *Mrs. Dalloway* and *The Waves*, Rachel dies to preserve the self that cannot sustain her alive. Though it goes against the grain of his ironic method, Forster was among the earliest to perceive Rachel's fate as "not an interruption" of narrative "but a fulfillment," indeed a climax "as poignant as anything in modern fiction."[3] For "fulfillment" read "epitome": Rachel's flight from time as the ultimate symptom of her sexual trepidation.

The title of the novel figures forth Rachel's maiden voyage into the unmarked waters of emotional exploration. Shortly after becoming engaged to be married on a tour of South America, the heroine contracts the fever that is to kill her. The burning forehead of desire, or even its expectation, symbolically besets her as the fatal thing she is afraid it will have to be. What she fears in marriage and its sexual intensity, what death conveniently releases her from, is the puny fusion which passion insists on idealizing between hopelessly separate selves. "Am I Rachel, are you Terence?" (p. 289) she asks in one of her rare moments of happiness. It is her hope there that personal transcendence has been achieved by gentle, affectionate contiguity rather than by some more violent means, either sex or death; but her question is only a holding action against the inevitable. Repelled by passional intimacy, Rachel's identity can relax its hold on self only in death. Sex would swamp the will in passionate aggression without dissolving it back to oneness with the universe. Rachel craves instead that fuller drowning.

The heroine is put in mind of such a fate, just at the onset of her feverish headache, by lines being read to her at the time from Milton's *Comus*, lines about a heroine's endangered undersea retreat beneath the "glassy, cool, translucent wave" (p. 329). Stricken by a raging fever, Rachel at first seems to clutch at the solace of hallucinatory drowning as a palliative, couched in images drawn from Woolf's own early bouts of madness. Yet the waters that bear Rachel down to final solitude and dissolution offer a metaphoric wish-fulfillment of her overheated brain at another level. "To be flung into the sea," the heroine yearns at one point (in the detached infinitive grammar of such a longed-for abrogation of finitude and time), "to be washed hither and thither, and driven about the roots of the world—the idea was incoherently delightful" (p. 298). To disengage from the rigors of relatedness, to disintegrate in an undersea release: this is the delight of incoherence itself, a flight from the very centeredness of the self. Drowning thus figures both the remission of her present pain and the persistent drift of her deepest impulses.

The text from Milton about magical preservation beneath the waters of nature now loses even its own opacity of phrase to become an all but "translucent" access to the thing itself behind the iambic swell and dip of language: "The glassy, cool, translucent wave was almost visible before her, curling up at the end of the bed" (p. 329). With this massing of sibilance and assonance reified as fact, Rachel has begun yielding herself to a drowning in the soul. It is a transference from living peril into a poetically conceived myth of redemption by submergence. The most revealing hallucination to which she must submit before that of actual drowning is the apparition of "a tunnel under a river" (p. 331) reminiscent of the dream that followed her first sexual encounter in the novel, the unexpected kiss from Mr. Dalloway onboard ship. She was repulsed there by his unreciprocated lunge of desire, sending her "down a long tunnel" with "damp bricks on either side" (p. 79). In that imaginary episode endured in the mind's submarine depths she was forced through a passageway or corridor that emptied into a "vault." Hers was an unconscious journey toward womblike retreat serving to reverse the trauma of passage through the original birth canal, with the whole ordeal encoding her need to flee the enforced maturity of sexual embrace. Now, bedridden and faithfully tended, Rachel nevertheless drowns beneath waves swollen over her from that enunciated text of *Comus*. She "fell into a deep pool of sticky water," hearing only "the sound of the sea rolling over her head," the sound, as it were, of those lines from Milton. The encoffining glass transparency of the cool wave that once lay "curling" before her in fantasy becomes the very shape of her fate in a shift from present to past participle, for at this point "she was not dead, but curled up at the bottom of the sea" (p. 341). Achieved through a dangerous incarnation of the Miltonic rhythm as real wave, then through a deadly incorporation into it, this is the return to fetal peace she has been seeking. Long before Rachel's "incoherently delightful" vision of drowning, she had been pleased to imagine herself "different from anything else, unmergeable, like the sea or the wind, . . . and she became profoundly excited at the thought of living" (p. 84). Added in ink above the line in Woolf's second typescript of *The Voyage Out*, that adjective *unmergeable* is a key to the impervious, virginal crisis to come.[4] When living on as woman seems to require the sexual merger of marriage, Rachel reverts to the amorphous wavelike integrity of insentience, embodying the curl of the wave by which she had hoped to be cooled and swept free. Rather than giving herself over to erotic otherness, she blends instead with the immemorial sea, while offering another kind of requital to Terence, the *petite mort* without the passion.

For Rachel, first in the heated, repellent clench of Mr. Dalloway, then in the feverish relaxation of her will in dying, metaphors of drowning are repeatedly meant to image both the fear of sexuality and the flight from it. Woolf is drawing here on one of the reigning tropes of eroticism in the British novel, the surrender to another that feels like submergence and extermination. Thinking herself lulled into melodious inundation within the sexual will of Stephen Guest, Maggie Tulliver was only succumbing to tides of desire in her own fantasy life; yet the metaphor of drowning was still operable, opening the floodgates of allegory later. Harking further back in the English tradition to a male passion that would sublimate all sexual energy in religious fervor, there is the fluvial topography of St. John Rivers's psyche in *Jane Eyre:* "I was tempted to cease struggling with him— to rush down the torrent of his will into the gulf of his existence, and there lose my own" (p. 35). Drowning submergence is a form of submission. The last pages of Henry James's *The Portrait of a Lady* (1881) further illustrate the ambivalence of this metaphor as between death wish and mortal threat. In the passionate embrace of Gaspar Goodwood, Isabel Archer is dizzied by the oblivion inching over her. The whole scene seems churned from the idiomatic description of her "swimming head," immediately projected outward as "the noise of waters" bearing down upon her, again the "rushing torrent" of male desire. The "world . . . seemed to open out, all round her, to take the form of a mighty sea, where she floated in fathomless waters . . . in which she felt herself sink and sink" (ch. 55). That closing, plunging cadence of repetition is the indirect discourse of a stream of consciousness style which Woolf would later pursue in her own experiments. Pressured by Goodwood, James's heroine literalizes the idea of the *petite mort* in believing that "to let him take her in his arms would be the next best thing to her dying." Though the heroine is almost willfully sinking into this extinction of self, still "she seemed to beat with her feet," fighting off the drowning rush of another's need. The passage is so explicit about its controlling metaphor that Isabel now compares the nature of her racing brain with the received opinion about death by water: "So had she heard of those wrecked and under water following a train of images before they sink." Yet it is precisely this thought, this thinking, which, because the encounter is a merely figurative inundation, grows capable of saving her. Given a second to reflect, she is gone from Goodwood's arms, swimming free of the libidinal pull.

Rethinking the traditional formulas of symbolic drowning in her heroine's virginal trial by symbolic fever, Woolf instead has Rachel Vinrace search the farthest depths of her own "swimming brain" for the lethal relief of unconsciousness. The transmission of imagery and syntactic rhythm which now links the psyche of the dying girl with her simultaneously denied and embraced lover is so complete, ruling out as it does all severance and so all grieving, that one is tempted to call this initial instance of mortal displacement in Woolf's fiction a "communicable decease." The very euphemism for death is purified into the assuagement of that contagious peace Terence shares with Rachel, when all the anguish "pressing on him" suddenly "passed away" (p. 342). Figurative transference and synesthesia now wash over the indirect discourse, unmooring its references in a confluence of effect and affect. Hearing how the "waves beat on the shore far away," Terence finds his peace shaped to their distant murmur, for like a sea swell it seems "to lap his body in a fine cool sheet" (p. 343). The last word here is appropriately not "wave" but that noun "sheet," which can serve both for fluid surface and for cloth become shroud. Terence is bedded in metaphor with Rachel after all.

The rainstorm raging outside "washed profoundly between the sky

and the sea" (p. 345), recalling an earlier moment of closeness between the couple when "darkness poured down profusely," an inundation that "left them with scarcely any feeling of life" (p. 289).
Not following Rachel in her drowning reversion to the womb, Terence
can still be bathed in the peace she radiates. In the growing silence
of her slowing breath, "they seemed to be thinking together" (p. 353)
without and beyond words, until the apparent negation of "No, she
had ceased to breathe." What does this "no" cancel? Rachel's death
can be detected only through Terence's breathless, attentive reciprocation of it, and in the oneness of their held breaths lies its consolation, its very redefinition. Putting us back in mind of that phrasal
wavering between corpse and its softened recognition for the heroine
in Gaskell's *North and South* (the exclamation bonding the dead Bessy
to the becalmed spirit of her friend, Margaret, "And that was death!"),
Woolf writes, "So much the better—this was death." In a rapt transformation of phrase hit upon by Woolf in her revisions of the novel,
Terence realizes, "It was nothing; it was to cease to breathe."[5] The
noun of negation is purged by vernacular wording in the split second
of its recognition, as a similar play on "nothing" was put to ironic
use in *Howards End*. Woolf's calculated flux of diction and syntax
in the rendering of the death moment comes to climax in the simultaneously phrased interval between absence and its reabsorption as
presence through love. Cheated of its severence, death is demoted
in the name of closeness.

Woolf thus sends into play the threefold functions of the literary
death scene across an elusive verbal interval that closes in final
ambivalence. The figural logic of transposition in the distended scene
as a whole, where the early metaphors of watery death as ecstatic
disintegration have risen to engulf an entire psyche, now precipitate
out by symbolic epitome the self's fears of sexual union. Though
Rachel dies virginal and unmerged, Terence's empathy then cleanses
her terrible drowning to a new reciprocation floated upon the displaced
metaphors of wavelike sustenance. Her dying words shortly before
had been, "Hullo, Terence" (p. 353), a willed recognition from her
watery abyss. It is at this point that the "curtain which had been
drawn between them for so long vanished immediately," removing
all mediation. Sealed up in her fear of sexuality, Rachel could not
previously acknowledge Terence as the intimate other, the one who

would burst through that "curtain" and claim her. Now, in dying, safely beyond desire as act, this vanishing of the curtain is the removal of the veil or membrane that begins the long rhythmic consummation of the death scene. It is a dying neither privative nor violent but revisionary. Once the "nothing" of death is recognized by Terence, he can rename it as "happiness . . . perfect happiness." Though "impossible while they lived," their "complete union" now "filled the room with rings eddying more and more widely" (p. 353). In place of the wedding band and bond there are these looped, concentric ripples of the unifying water imagery emphasized by Woolf's eddying style. The room now being "filled" with the couple's mutuality, Terence in the next incremental clause "had no wish in the world left unfulfilled" (p. 354). The death scene that began with the fluted beauty of Milton's assonant iambs, deepened to psychodrama, now smoothes off into the sonic repletion of this filling full of syllables.

Terence has all along intended to become a writer, a novelist, one with ambitions something like Woolf's—to intercede for speechlessness in the crevices between articulation. "I want to write a novel about Silence," he explains, "the things people don't say" (p. 216). After his engagement to Rachel he realizes that the "book called *Silence* would not now be the same book that it would have been" (p. 291). This is a realization that can only be thought renewed by the communicable silence and peace of her death beside him. Terence's fiction would thus, broken free of Woolf's, still enroll itself immediately after hers on the list of such modernist titles as *Heart of Darkness, The Longest Journey, Howards End,* and *Victory,* before them *The Wings of the Dove, Our Mutual Friend,* even *The Return of the Native.* These are titles which, whatever else they may designate, personify, or allegorize, seem also covert periphrases for death. Rachel Vinrace knew early in Woolf's novel that her life was only "the short season between two silences" (p. 82)—even before she knew exactly how short it was to be. It is no accident either, for the novelist who would go on to write *The Waves,* that this symmetrically framed temporal space is, among other things, a textual model for life. Narrative or plot line is understood as the articulation of a life line between preceding silence and ultimate closure. In psychological rather than textual terms, or using the one so as to inform the other, this image of a life margined by silence predicts the interchanged hush of heroine and hero at the end. Terence's novel, if he goes on to write it, must inevitably be altered by Woolf's final synonymy between death and the silence that lies between and falls after all words.

The importance of Terence as survivor—moving past the death scene into its latent transcription, however metaphoric, in a novel of his own devising—is only emphasized by the allusion just before Rachel's death to another novel about death, Balzac's *Cousine Bette*. Though her uncle originally feels it "too horrible" (p. 172) for her to read, Rachel still keeps it near her, almost for its totemic function, "as some medieval monk kept a skull, or a crucifix to remind him of the frailty of the body" (p. 301). The most painful identification she has with this novel as latter-day memento mori is with a scene where "women die with bugs crawling across their faces" (p. 301). To encourage her, Terence suggests that "we so seldom think of anything but ourselves that an occasional twinge," the recognition in art of those terrors our life may try to deny or at least suspend, "is really rather pleasant." So he may eventually want to say about a book named *Silence* that may well, like *The Voyage Out*, come upon its epitomizing title scene in the death of a woman no less terrible in its way than the treatment of dying in Balzac's realism.

In the same year that *The Voyage Out* saw publication, the Hogarth Press, under the direction of Woolf's husband, Leonard, published those remarks by Freud, discussed in Chapter 1, about the distance at which modern life and modern warfare keep the human psyche from the fact of death. It is a distance requiring "compensation" in the "plurality of lives" available in literature and theater, where we can "survive" the dying hero "with whom we have identified ourselves." Freud's notion amounts to the Medieval skull as memento mori updating itself to the psychoanalytic object of transference. So might Rachel healthily have used her Balzac, seeking that "twinge" which purges and rejuvenates. Since within Woolf's treatment of death, as in many of the novelists who preceded her, mortal epiphany aspires to the condition of the transmissible fiction that contains it, so also is Terence able to die safely with Rachel, his later readers of *Silence* with whatever he may have to say in turn of that death, Woolf's readers in any case with the deathbed tour de force she now closes.

What mainly remains, for us as for Woolf in the novel, is the specification of Rachel's achieved stasis, freed from time, as a stillness akin to textuality itself. One of the female choric voices in the aftermath of the death wants also to redefine the fact of mortality so as to banish its standard diction: "I'm positive Rachel's not dead," positive that "she's still somewhere" (p. 362). In the conflated adjectival and adverbial senses of *still* as both "at rest" and "yet," the one defines the other: a still being and a being even still. Whether or not Terence will ultimately produce that fictional text named for the very death whose terror his participation in Rachel's has inoculated him against, surely the further sense of "silent" whispers along one face of the phrase "still somewhere." It reminds us of the heroine's mute but powerful continuance in a book by Woolf, speaking to us even after its mortal climax. As Keats demonstrated with his synecdochic urn, Woolf's novel is itself, like all texts, wed to silence in its very portrayal of the dying bride thereof.

☐ ☐ ☐

In *Mrs. Dalloway* a decade later, first crowning achievement of Woolf's mature period, Septimus Smith returns as a kind of neo-Keatsian poet more than half in love with easeful death. Reversing the relation of Terence to the dying Rachel, Septimus's own erotic fulfillment in annihilation provides the motive for continuance in the heroine, Clarissa Dalloway, who partakes of his death in order to take new heart for living. Between Rachel's posthumous predication in the faith that "she's still somewhere" and the famous last line of *Mrs. Dalloway*, adverbially determined and returned to the world, "For there she was," lies the elaborated mechanism of displacement in the later novel. Plot is thereby designed to transmit the epitomizing death at an even deeper level of telepathic participation.

It can scarcely rest with coincidence that in Woolf's first time out as a novelist she dramatized for her hypersensitive heroine—as feverish ordeal, indeed as a fatal surrender of identity—the very modes of knowing in prose which would characterize Woolf's own later experiments as a beleaguered innovator in the novel form. In subsequent comments on her art Woolf would describe that "tunnelling process" which gets her, like Rachel drowning, beneath the temporal surfaces of life into "the deep water of my own thoughts navigating the underworld"[6]—and so into the cavernous depths of her characters, into (as she phrases it elsewhere) the "pools" and "dark places"[7] of consciousness which have gone unplumbed, unsung. Rachel's fatal plummet to the cold deeps of her own repression, anticipating the reiterated imagery of the "plunge" in *Mrs. Dalloway*, is a way of figuring in part what the author must brave herself in order to dramatize it. Rachel's death, layered by Terence's participation, thus composes a symbolic anatomy of the artist who, living through the death she imagines, sacrifices something of herself for the reader. What may sound impressionistic in the phrasing of it becomes in fact a structural principle. In the mortal role reversal of *Mrs. Dalloway*, with the hero dying on behalf of the woman who will give that death expression, the allegory of Woolf's own artistic achievement becomes all the clearer. I mean nothing more sentimental by this than what Freud had in mind. I do not mean that great novelists suffer for their art but that they suffer *in* it, pluralized, as Freud might say, by their own plots. Sacrificial male victim offering up a revelation netted in the mesh of phrase; the heroine's interior monologue inheriting from the bard of darkness the immortal poem of survival: this is the composite portrait of the elegiac artist in the novel *Mrs. Dalloway*. The efficacy of such art is finally embodied in the woman with whom the novel's name is identical and whose survival of a double's death, as an effigy of her own, is taken up in the indirect discourse of the book's own continuance.

Woolf would wait two years after the artistic breakthrough of *Mrs. Dalloway* for an explicit allusion to an early Romantic text of death by water so instructive for the mechanisms of psychological and textual displacement in her work. Beginning a saddened refrain at the close of *To the Lighthouse*, Mr. Ramsay lets pass his lips those unidentified "mournful words" from the last stanza of William Cowper's "The Castaway" (1799)—"But I beneath a rougher sea / Was whelmed in deeper gulfs than he" (p. 248)—and seems about to do so again later when he and his boating party hear about three men previously drowned in the same spot (p. 305). Woolf's identification with Cowper, given his own bouts of madness alternating with periods of lucid artistry, must have run deep. Like Melville's drifting Pip, withered seed of the human condition fallen overboard in anticipation of the "thrownness" of the existential fate, we seem in Cowper to be all of us mortal castaways from cradle to grave endlessly rocking, our anchorless lives as if cast natally away from oneness. By the close of the poem Cowper has managed to suggest that the former sailor's watery grave is not just the sea in which he sank but the tear-stained memoir by Lord Anson in which he has come down to renown: "No poet wept him; but the page / Of narrative sincere" that describes him "is wet with Anson's tear." Whether "by bards or heroes shed," such tears "alike immortalize the dead"—especially when, as a narrator's tears, they dry themselves as inked impressions. Cowper knows no more of the sailor through report than Clarissa Dalloway knows of the "drowned sailor" Septimus Smith through rumor at her party. But the heroine like the bard can immortalize him in that text comprising her last internal monologue, Septimus's own tortured poetry indirectly setting her life in rhyme. Art needs the sacrifice of its subjects because, as "The Castaway" puts it, "misery still delights to trace / Its semblance in another's case." This sweetening of death by the effigy of language as mortal "trace," uttered to oneself or actually transcribed, is Woolf's deepest theme in *Mrs. Dalloway* and *The Waves*.

We know from her famous Modern Library introduction to the novel that in the original plans for *Mrs. Dalloway*, Clarissa was ultimately to die, presumably of her weak heart, or to commit suicide. The character of Septimus Smith was subsequently conceived and inserted into plot to take this fate upon himself as, in Woolf's own term, Clarissa's "double." This psychotic young veteran, shell-shocked in the war, is terrified of the return from the grave of the dead officer, Evans, he loved too much to dare mourn.[8] He has married in flight from this emptiness, yet is now repulsed by sexuality, sublimating his blocked passion by scribbling notes to himself intended to transcribe his insistent visions of melioration and community. He is called a "border case" (p. 129) by his doctors, knocking as it were on the madhouse door, but among the portals he is meant by Woolf to straddle is the far threshold between life and death, limning in his demented insight the thin line between psychosis and Orphic power. He occupies also as bordering principle the space between the sane endurance of a woman he has never met and her succumbing to a death, whether suicide or not, meant to diagnose her frail hold on life. One of this double's bardic cryptograms, the repeated bromides of his madness, is "How there is no death" (pp. 36, 212). His own death is there in the novel to check what is in one sense this transcendental claptrap as well as to prove his perpetuity across death in a different key. For a heroine who is herself given to thinking how "unbelievable death was!" (p. 185), his violent end must then be acknowledged by empathetic proxy.

It is also true that with a contrary tug of their minds, even from the first, both Septimus and Clarissa are drawn to a feeling for death as the presiding dark genius of life. We have just met Septimus for the first time in the London streets; a hearselike gray car of state passes, arresting traffic in the way death halts the flow of life. This passing then activates within the hiatus it has created a detached yet not extractable meditation, unidentified with any single consciousness on the scene, about the graveyard oblivion to which all normal flesh is heir. Whether it is queen, prince, or prime minister in the ominous limousine, majesty itself as "enduring symbol" throws into relief the mutability and sure doom of the common man. This particularized moment in time seems eerily to telescope all history into an epochal long view, propelling the anxious mind outside its own decaying body and across time. What ensues is thus an elegiac forecast of a period when "all those hurrying along the pavement this Wednesday morning are but bones with a few wedding rings mixed up in their dust" (p. 23). Each Wednesday is Ash Wednesday in this plot of resurrection.

Couched in an idiom neither decidedly that of Septimus nor of Clarissa but wedged between their most nearly abutted internal monologues so far, this paragraph explores the very role of prose as mediator between the characters, carrier at once of their privacy and their mutuality. The man who often thinks of his own body as a fleshed corpse, Septimus has just before mechanically extended his arm to his wife as a "piece of bone," an obvious associative link forward to the prophetic pessimism of the subsequent passage. And immediately after the passage we commute to the resumed monologue of Clarissa's indirect discourse: "It is probably the Queen, thought Mrs. Dalloway," gender-identified with the dream of endurance despite the facts of her time-bound female body. Yet neither connection, forward to Clarissa nor back to Septimus, secures a confident ascription of this passage to the heroine or her double. One of the very few stretches in the novel whose discourse is so indirect as to escape all definite subliminal links to a single mentality, this passage seems to serve two psychological functions at once through the workings of form. First, it is both an emotional as well as a narrative bridge between the two characters at just the point of their nearest textual coincidence. The fascination with death, however bracketed off and abstracted, becomes appropriately enough the true interface between the doubled protagonists. What they have between them (in both senses of the preposition) is the articulated consciousness of finality contained by phrase. Second, this veering from the innovative decorum of the stream of consciousness into a digressive exercise in both narrative and temporal omniscience, foregrounding itself as a technical as well as a psychological departure from the rule of inner monologue, seems to enter Woolf's claim as narrator upon the very fictional tradition she is at work revising. This uncharacteristic paragraph appears conversant with that particular aspect of traditional omniscient commentary whose perspective, regardless of its given content, might always have been seen as a knowingness about evolving finality, about form and closure, about last things—a long view akin to eternity and thus complicit with death.

In a chain of attribution that becomes a crucial nexus, Septimus Warren Smith is later announced, shortly before his leap to death, as "the most exalted of mankind; the criminal who faced his judges; the victim exposed on the heights; the fugitive; the drowned sailor; the poet of the immortal ode; the Lord who had gone from life to death" (pp. 146–147). These jostling epithets are so deeply apposite as to rephrase, one after the other, the ramified fact of Septimus's position as surrogate for the heroine. He is each of these things by turns, but also by antithesis, and finally by gathering synthesis: cynosure and pariah, pinioned victim and escapee, drowned corpse and poet, and all this in the sense of a risen Lord who has harrowed the hell of his own annihilation and come back to tell of it—all this, that is, in the sense of hero as vessel of the Orphic vision. Not only do saviors, martyrs, and messiahs die for us, but our fictional heroes too, and so too the poet or novelist who gives us them, gives them up to us as vicars of our own mortal recognitions. It is important that, even before Septimus leaps upon the railings of his London boarding house, he has "gone from life to death." This sense of having "crossed" the Conradian threshold is repeatedly worked at in the novel's first draft in connection with drowning and magic salvage.[9] Dying is for

Septimus already metaphoric, resurrective, even before his death. Its intuitive absorption by the heroine, as analogous to a recuperation of her own spirit, is therefore only in keeping with his bordering, mediatory status from the start.

Even on his second appearance in the book, long before those pounding appositives seem tabulated in the recesses of his own interior discourse, Septimus is portentously described as having been "taken from life to death" (p. 37), his presence before us by virtue already of mortal return. This "Lord who had come to renew society" is for us and for Clarissa in particular "the scapegoat, the eternal sufferer." In that later description he is therefore not the sinking but the already "drowned" prophet, his death leap held in wait as just one more plummet to the underworld. Though he feels "condemned to death" for not having "cared" when Evans was killed, there is a more telling phrasing of his fate that discomfits legal terminology, offering a "verdict" determined where we would expect the resulting sentence. "The verdict of human nature on such a wretch was death" (p. 138). In the daily disposition of Septimus's prolonged trial, as itself a vicious circle of expiation, living death sentences the soul to suspended animation.

There is more to the image of deranged soldier as drowned sailor than the emphasis on depth, penetration, and unscarred retrieval. The hero's gift for language having turned to curse, with all too many words for his terrors, Septimus lives his life at the pitch of the archetypal drowning vision, flooded by retrospect, all his days and their betrayals replayed, all time telescoped into the single convulsive instant of perception, one and then another, intolerable. He is the self submerged in its own dream life, with so total and unwilled an access to past loss and lost past, not only to his own memories but to the whole history of the time, the war, the unmourned end of his friend—an access irruptive and dis-integrating—that he dies each minute only and in order to survive. Drowning is another way of naming the nature of his "border case," a terrorizing consignment to the interval between violent death and revelatory renewal. Measured on the lateral axis between "doubles," this is the distance between that "drowned sailor on the shore of the world" (p. 140) and the heroine who, through him, reasserts her faith in the "waves of that divine vitality which Clarissa loved" (p. 9).

A bordering within Woolf's own dubious, elusive wording makes a related point by a warding off of syntactic clarity when Septimus's wife is said to resent his desire "to talk to himself, to talk to a dead man, on the seat over there" (p. 98). The interval between Septimus alive and dead is located in the very slippage between sequence and equivalence in that ambiguously appositive grammar. He thinks he is speaking to Evans, his superior officer, but of course is talking only to himself; yet what is such mania in the first place but a death of the autonomous mind? A similar liminal irony colors our sense of those jotted funerary aphorisms that are called this tortured poet's "messages from the dead"—messages from *his* death as well as from those who have gone before, the risen Lord at once origin and mere scribe of their disclosure. Chief among these messages are the sacred phrases that burst out in a sybilline litany as the "supreme secret" won from death (George Eliot's adjective too, and Conrad's), including most prominently, as abbreviated and reiterated, "no crime; love" (p. 102). This sacrificial poet as "border case" erodes the grammatical boundaries of his own oracular monosyllables in a prophecy of tolerance and lifted interdict: "no crime love," not his for Evans, not Clarissa's for Sally Seton.

In reiterating to his own ear this implicit sanction against all sense of the sexually illicit, Septimus finds himself "fumbling for a card and pencil" (p. 102) to enroll the cryptic insight among his Delphic fragments and mortal missives. When we first hear of his compulsion for transcribing these oracular flashes, Woolf notes in her own symbolically communicative shorthand that "he notes such revelations on the backs of envelopes" (p. 35). In his psychotic closed circuit these cryptograms seem already, and only, return addressed. Just before his death, he instructs his wife, Rezia, to burn all these "messages from the dead" (p. 224), including his "odes to Time." Knowing they are too eerily beautiful to lose, she instead decides to "tie them up (for she had no envelope) with a piece of silk" (p. 224). In this way the messages are preserved unforwarded by the one soul with whom they have managed, if dimly, to communicate.

Most resonant among these productions, though we hear nothing from it, is Septimus's "immortal Ode to time." Here is a paradox about temporality under the aspect of the infinite that serves also for a gesture at the deathlessness of all creative enterprise. Though enacted in the finally drowned and resurfaced hero's conclusive death leap, a suicide fugitive from the same world of time his text would somehow transfigure to permanence, time's transcendent peace had earlier descended upon Septimus in the thrall of a crazed grace. Before he decides to escape at any cost the normalizing asylum his doctors have in mind, Septimus has achieved a rare moment of transport by glimpsing for an instant how "beauty . . . was the truth now" (p. 105). In this Keatsian confidence, he thinks to himself that "beauty was everywhere," and as if in answer comes a remark from Rezia that is actually meant to recall him from this rhapsody to a more Prufrockian diurnal purpose. Though merely a "general voice" in the first draft,[10] it is now his rejected wife who intercedes with "It is time"—time to go now. For a vanishing second, however, beauty is the truth of time, time the medium of all loveliness. It is a second distended until it bursts. The intended meaning, the meaning that would retrieve him for the world of normal intentionality, peels away from the word *time* with the self-shucking brusqueness of a pun. The poet of unscheduled "time" can only hear the inner echo of the noun. Introspection then waxes explosive: "The word 'time' split its husk; poured its riches over him" (p. 105), an epiphanic surge that floods this drowned sailor once again, this time from the springs of surety.

The moment is for the hero sublime, by direct precedent a sexual sublimation, and in the long run a violent prophecy. It is not just that this splitting of time's skin prefigures Septimus's own rending escape from temporality, in its most brutal and dehumanizing form, when he leaps down upon his landlady's iron railings. The metaphors of his temporal epiphany are lent in the first place from the notorious earlier passage about Clarissa's lesbian ecstasy, a swelling of self toward another, "some pressure of rapture, which split its thin skin and gushed and poured with an extraordinary alleviation" (p. 47). The "swollen" moment, elation as erotic inflation, relies on and relishes an imagery unrestrained by gender in part so as to link itself forward not only to the splitting of time's "husk" as a poetic balm but to Septimus's actual suicide, when the exquisite rift is transposed to death wound. There on the house railings, legal boundary of domestic privacy, Septimus's own temporal body is ruptured by a hideous phallic penetration—at once paranoid homosexual nightmare and the lethal release from it. The poetic "border case" thus undergoes, so that Clarissa can move onward in empathy without doing so, a forbidding trespass across the spiked, fatal demarcation between private space and the sphere of otherness in which he finds no comfort, splitting his own thinnest of skins in a final alleviation, replacing both visionary and sexual longings together with the consummation of death.

It is through the structural doubling of hero for heroine, implemented by style, that the full import of the death scene comes forward. The sacrifice of Septimus is disclosed as essentially a poetic act, not only visionary in its final implications but verbal. The anticipatory pairing of Mrs. Dalloway's rapture with Septimus's violent closure announces its meaning, as in the water imagery of *The Voyage Out*, by analogy with Woolf's own language, that mimetic registration of a deep consciousness streaming through and across themselves in the medium of what *The Waves* calls "warm soluble words" (p. 69). Such a liquidity and run of syllables, undulant, protean, directly accords with Woolf's achievement in that passage about Clarissa's expansive libido. Some phonic "pressure" within the very echoing phrase "pressure of rapture" seems to push the inscribed "rapture" over toward that unsaid, unsettling, but linguistically implicit "rupture" as it immediately "pours and gushes" upon the sentence out of a cleft of pure inflection. Here is style matched to the stretched, frail ache of desire in an interval akin to those negotiated gaps of mortal trespass we have previously considered. At risk is the same surrender of discrete identity, the same sundering by otherness, to which Septimus is soon to submit in his bludgeoning jump. That even Clarissa's ecstasy of distention is equivalent to the splitting of time's husk as well as identity's shell is hinted by another taut syntactic play, this time with an interval explicitly temporal, that closes her erotic vision: "It was over—the moment" (p.47). To what does the ineffable "it" succeed as the sentence snaps shut: idiomatic adverb or familiar Woolfian noun in an appositional use? It is only true to the compressed, indeed pressurized and explosive, nature of this "moment of vision"—and a single phrase must spread and rend itself to make this point—that, like death gone through, such an epiphany is over the moment it has passed into denomination. So too with Septimus's "Ode."

Rezia's anxious, catalytic "It is time," then, unaware of the beauty Septimus was trying at the very moment to construe from time, is indeed the voice of his most relentless devil, the demon of duty, routine, and conformity. With time's limitless possibility reduced thus to the merely punctual, it must be punctured to freedom again by a fatal leap. So Septimus the poet of the "Ode," Orphic sojourner among hours and days in a novel whose first draft had the working title *The Hours,* wringing out from grief his hymns to time, becomes Mr. Smith as all but anonymous everyman. He is the hero risen to unwilling Lord and broken on the rack of his own incapacity for dailiness. Septimus dies to redeem the spent promise of infinite blessing from the rent shell of temporality. That odic redemption is fittingly attested to, even as we are deflected from the actual scene of the poet's death and its knifing finality, by its reification again as verbal energy, verbal effigy. Stylistic testimony to this appears in the flow of the heroine's own inner language after she has taken time out from her party to stare into the hole in time tunneled out by her double's jump. It is through the inner articulation of will to which his death has helped her that she is able to recover her very self from the charnel recess or interval of her undefended identification with the maiming detail of his death. It would seem that she has been sent after all, all the way across town, one of his unsigned and otherwise undelivered messages from the dead.

Recovering in effacement his own access to the split, spilt ecstasies of time, Clarissa's double, in his death on the railings, nailed to his own private suffering, is the double or replica of a greater and ageless sacrifice too. Dying as if he were the corporeal word of time itself slain into eternity, a monosyllabic poem rather than poet, Septimus Smith is the Word incarnate, embodied and finally bloodied Logos, man made Lord only so that he might rendingly surrender himself back to the eternity out of which his numinous but mute Word was first differentiated into temporal flesh. Abusing language, Conrad's cynical writer, Decoud, canceled himself from within it. Revering the Word, the truer poet Septimus dies *into* it. Which is ultimately to suggest that as symbol of crucifixion, Septimus's suicide is all the more an allegory of poetry won from the iron and bloodied teeth of death. The hero pierced to extinction at the surface of the earth that gives him birth is, as much as in his role as "drowned sailor," not only a typical Woolfian symbol but a figure out of Lawrencian myth as well. In Lawrence's poem about humanity's mass drowning and the ship of death that might spirit us free of deluge, "Already our bodies are fallen, bruised, badly bruised, / already our souls are oozing through the exit / of the cruel bruise" (where enjambment is the implied mimesis of a mortal seepage.).[11] As Woolf's version of the Lawrencian Man Who Died, Septimus Smith redeems this slow torture by time through his willed rejection of it, his replacement of atrophy by epiphany even at the cost of death.

Mrs. Dalloway's resistance, along with that of Septimus, to a real belief in mortal closure has to do with her refusal of that straitening characterization of the self that would readily delimit it by annihilation. Rejecting the idea that "I am this, I am that" (p. 11), able to keep the predication of her identity untethered from definition, she gravitates toward a "transcendental theory" of immortality that circumvents her private "horror of death" (p. 230). Prose rhythm becomes a microcosm early in the novel for the medium of this continuance. Despite the heroine's knowledge that, in one sense, "death ended absolutely" (p. 12), still "on the ebb and flow of things, here, there, she survived, Peter survived, lived in each other" (p. 12). Phrase oscillates with phrase in a linguistic sway that brooks no impasse. Clarissa's recoil from "I am this" or "that" includes her within the Forsterian ethos of impersonal immortality. Transferring such falsely narrowing demonstratives outward to the whole field of otherness, Clarissa feels that the "unseen" in identity "might survive, be recovered somehow attached to *this* person or *that* . . . after death" (p. 232, my emphasis). Septimus's death stands as external proof, his sacrifice attached "somehow" to a woman for whom everything about him is "unseen."

Her double has somehow gotten through to her, and so reached, through her, to his own perpetuity. Partly it is the "this" or "that" she consciously fled from becoming that meets its complement in his own search for a grammar of the "I" that will complete without having to define and defeat his being. Near death he interrogates himself as follows: "But if he confessed? If he communicated? Would they let him off then, his torturers?" (p. 148). He makes the attempt: " 'I— I—' he stammered." Yet, "What was his crime? He could not remember it." Casting about for some confessional message, he can only stammer again, as if it were a real assertion, "I—I—." It is an enunciation of presence which, tragically enough, can on its own terms sustain no continued *am* to go with it, but which nonetheless, heroically enough, requires no such prolonged life to have successfully rescued essence from flux and guarded it against violation. I am what I am, even if I can no longer continue to be, it or otherwise. The Forsterian hairsbreadth between "confession" and "suicide" in Leonard Bast's disintegrating dialogue from *Howards End* will shortly be traversed by Septimus. In the meantime, his fourfold repetition of identity becomes another extemporaneous ode to the self in time. Recalling the clausal ironies of self-predication in *Jude the Obscure*, with verbs of being camouflaging a void; the death-vouchsafed "I am I" of *Howards End*; Birkin's "I am that I am"; Rachel Vinrace's merger-querying "Am I Rachel, are you Terence?"; in *Jacob's Room* the title character's insistence that "I am what I am, and intend to be it" (p. 36); and paralleling most closely the unconscious self-confidence of Stephen Wonham's "I'm——," Septimus stumbles in syntactically detached self-declaration ("I—I—— I—I ") upon the cryptic mystery of his own "message," that he has regained and momentarily reintegrated the central self which is the necessary ground of any meaning that might outlast him. The "I—I—," scarcely disintegrating after all, reads like a visual bracket erected to contain and guarantee the autonomous space of identity.

Septimus cannot in his desired sense really confess, he can only begin communicating. And he can only do this by a communion of some sort with the woman who will survive in the name of his offended body, his spirit, and his offered blood, what she is able to intuit of them. "Communication," Septimus mumbles early on, "is health; communication is happiness; communication——" (p. 141). He breaks off with a dash, balked in his attempt at approximating such redemption with synonyms. After hearing of his death in the middle of her party, the mere mention of a young man jumping from a window tossed off as a cocktail anecdote by the presiding psychiatrist, Clarissa, inverting her double's elliptical maxim, fills in its blank through a participatory understanding. "Death," she recognizes, "was an attempt to communicate" (p. 280), a going out of self even at the expense, the final expenditure, of that self.[12]

It is no easy task, either, on the receiving end. Marlow did little more than peek over the "threshold of the invisible" at the death of his double, and this at the side of the dying man himself, in the presence of his last words. Miles across town, nowhere in sight of the sacrifice of her own double, Clarissa must now reinvent the facts of that sacrifice and through them its invisible truth. They must be simulated along the connective channels of a mutual stream of consciousness that cannot be dammed up by a lone dying. She must, in a word, improvise his oblivion in her own words: "He had killed himself—but how? . . . He had thrown himself from a window. Up had flashed the ground; through him, blundering, bruising, went the rusty spikes. There he lay with a thud, thud, thud in his brain, and then a suffocation of blackness. So she saw it" (p. 280). The woman in whom Peter Walsh, in his phallic imagination, sensed "an impenetrability" (p. 71) now submits voluntarily to a stabbing worse than any she could otherwise have known. The adverbial inversion of "up had flashed" takes cognizance of direction and momentum even before denoting the destination of the plunge. So too with the inverted grammar of impalement in that next clause ("through him . . . the spikes"), impact recognized before agent of death in a simulation gruesomely prolonged by the tripled "thud" of the brain's dying pulse. The inverted syntactic span *is* the rehearsed interval of the death plunge itself. It is the ugliness, the horror of this internalized prose that grants its full heuristic utility for the heroine during her desperate respite from identity. Hers is the heroic, the perilous and appalling version of that complacent feeling of Peter Walsh's about the "communal spirit" of civilization when he sees the ambulance summoned to Mrs. Filmer's boarding house. His language domesticates, when it is not actually inverting, the whole tone of the book's "communal" mortality. Thinking it "morbid, sentimental, directly one began conjuring up doctors, dead bodies . . . a sort of lust over the visual impression" (p. 229), he would seem to be criticizing Clarissa in advance. This sickly inquisitiveness into the details of death, as he sees it, risks being infected with the deadliness itself (as his own metaphors indicate) and so becoming "fatal to art, fatal to friendship." It would do so by casting the shadows of a wordless and silencing horror over the "communal" nature of both. Yet Woolf's own "art" conjures the "fatal" to explore that need deeper even than friendship, the mortal bond reached for by the human creature in extremis.

Woolf the narrator has, as we know, stepped out of Septimus's mind just before the instant of death to render the scene from without—

a window, a vanishing body, an awful drop—giving us all anyone but the corpse could have known: the sheer fact of his leap. Yet only if Clarissa can reinvest the dying mind with presence will the suicide be rescued from fictional statistic to emotional revelation. Taking up Septimus's role as one who "interpreted . . . to mankind" (p. 103)— a transitive phrase suggestively free of object, as if the text were himself and his secrets from the other side of life's border—Mrs. Dalloway becomes, in the registrations of her own rushed vision, the authentic reader of the only death scene of Septimus Warren Smith worth having, a felt version, deciphered into significance. Whatever happened, of course, she was nowhere near, any more than were we. What in the final analysis *Mrs. Dalloway*, the artifact, has arranged to allegorize is not just the way all deaths we care about from the outside minister to us in their dramatic displacement like theater, fiction, or poetry. The book also encodes the more fundamental fact that such deaths must always be made up out of thin, in fact evac-uated, air. They are conjured either by the original author of the death scene (be it in poetry or prose), a scene for which there is never full documentary evidence, or by the sympathetic investment in such a scene by the receiving consciousness. By inventing the texture of a dying in the inevitable absence of testimony, Clarissa Dalloway recovers the original energy not so much of reading but of authorship itself in this dark mode. In the fullest possible doubling and indebtedness, she reincarnates Septimus's fleshed Word—the split husk of his life in time—and does so as in her own renewed person the internal narrator of a fictional elegy, an ode in prose to endurance. In the double sense of morbid conception, as Peter would have it, and receptive ordering, Clarissa's meditation on Septimus is her own "message from the dead," both as expressive spirit and exegete, a talking of her way back to the world in the summoned and understood visions of her double's plunge.

One way of characterizing this process so as to defend it against charges of callousness or inauthenticity is to name its displacement of death as a kind of mourning, an intuitive method of death by effigy and life by transfiguration. Mark Spilka has recently argued that Virginia Woolf's documented failure to grieve sufficiently for the deaths that came her way, beginning with her mother's, is the first and efficient cause of a prevailing imaginative failure in such novels as *Mrs. Dalloway,* where death may seem dismissed too readily.[13] Woolf's stance toward mourning rites, however, appears in structural terms more a wrestle than a quarrel, engagement rather than antagonism. Scarcely rebuking the necessities of grief or refusing its insights, she transmutes them to parable in her novels. Let us allow that blocked grief may be Septimus's trouble, but how in the same way can it be Clarissa's? The hero knew and loved Evans in life; the heroine never hears of the hero until after his death, yet of course, against all odds, she does feel for him grievously, if briefly. What then is the quality of her grief, or more to the point its phase? Workable grief might be defined in this context as the inclination (but only temporary, transitional) to risk thinking of death as more than a discrete event, not just something that has happened to another, something outside the self. If not gained upon by insight and purgation, some new mode of knowing and going on, however, grief may take the living with it; mourning is nothing if not passing, for otherwise it is only more death. Septimus joins with the dead in a grief ironized to defiance so that Clarissa can rejoin the living, not because she must evade or betray the identification with him she has felt, but because she must get it over with, get over it. If Clarissa's magnetic attraction toward death could not aspire to transfiguration, then Septimus would have been redundant, instead of what he is, symbolic: an embodied phase of grief, the fatal one, the one that requires drastic containment and then renewal—if not ordinarily in another, then in another phase of the self's sorrow and restitution.

In novel after novel, but most fully in *Mrs. Dalloway,* Woolf engages with grief by allegorizing the recovery of self as the displaced resurrection of a second self. If for this theme we seek a set of biographical coordinates, it would appear as important as any reaction, or lack of it, on Woolf's part following her mother's death to recognize that Virginia's own early suicide attempt in the manner of Septimus, a leap from a third-story window,[14] is in *Mrs. Dalloway* survived into middle age by the figure of a female heroine. In fiction, as in life, this survival is perhaps made possible only by the poetic or fictional double, the artistic consciousness incarnate in Septimus and cousin to Woolf's own writerly self, whose encounters with mortal grief have been sacrificed to meaning—and outlasted. Before the doubling of Septimus for Clarissa, there was Terence joining Rachel in the in-

terstices of respiration, only to inherit that silence as the theme of
his writing; dying a little with her, his grief grew into its own succession. With the parable of Septimus and Clarissa, it is not that there
are those of us who overreact to death and those who underreact, nor
that there are those who overreact so that some of the rest of us can
underreact, but rather that there is that in each of us which must
first suffer so that the rest of our consciousness can be released to
peace. The minute the double is introduced into the scheme of *Mrs.
Dalloway*, psychology is dispersed—not necessarily spread thin—
to allegory, and Septimus stands to Clarissa as one phase of the
psyche to another. When it is clear that he also stands as deranged
poet to his audience, and so finally as incarnate word of death to its
empathetic reception, then the scheme is itself doubled. The next
clear stage of the allegory follows in *The Waves*. The working through
of grief is arrayed there across three characters similar to those in
Mrs. Dalloway, a never-met soldier, a grieving suicide, and a participating consciousness and survivor; but the genders and energies
are realigned so that the ongoing hero is now a writer, who imagines
all the lives with which he empathizes, or whose ends he laments,
to be stories or texts in the first place. Loss and memorial become
one and the same, grieving and elegy both achievements in verbal
narrative.

Without such direct metanarrative plotting, *Mrs. Dalloway's* closure
reincorporates death into the very body of its indirect discourse,
Septimus's psychotic poetry become Woolf's psychic prose. The conclusion of the novel is as much an experiment in the grammar of
maintained being and adverbial inflection as the metaphysically elliptical "She is—in you" at the end of *Sons and Lovers* or the aftermath
of Rachel's death in *The Voyage Out*. Septimus was never able to
complete that confessional syntax four times launched with the first-
person pronoun. Yet, through the tunneling of consciousness at the
core of Woolf's exploratory style, the author reclaims for her heroine
the fleeting trace of the hero's identifying pronoun and attaches it
implicitly to a declaration of presence comparable to Colonel Newcome's variant of the Old Testament "Here am I," at least in its
secular taking. Because Septimus is willing to die just possibly to
communicate rather than certainly to censor his vision, his message
can be posthumously relayed to a hostess who, by merely returning

to her party from the contemplation of his death, radiates so intensely that determination still to *be* somewhere, as "I" rather than "that" or "this" specified thing, that her faith in identity conveys itself as stylistic and emotional aura to the free-floating indirect discourse of the narrative's finish, "For there she was." Building toward this ringing closural restraint, Woolf's language is again found enacting the very achievement of a reinflected reality it has set out to name. This last sentence is spun from a context that has put increasing pressure on idiomatic language toward the finish, as if probing the ordinary for its transforming potential. The power of these conclusive monosyllables rests both with their adverbial inversion and the final torque given the verb of being. Diction and syntax are elsewhere complicit in this way as the novel drives toward closure. Thinking that the communal festivities have fixed something forever, summing it all up in the moment as it passed, and implicitly relating this sense of well-being to her "transcendental theory" of mortal transience redeemed by community and the preservation of love, Clarissa assures herself, about the two most passionate relationships in her life, that "a part of this Sally must always be; Peter must always be" (p. 277). The framework of inversion loses ground to the mystical twist of the supposedly parallel clause, loosened as it is from restrictive status into the unconditioned realm of pure being. By being a part of this, now and here, Peter will exist forever, and by association Sally too. The copulative verb specifies a grammatical linkage only to release itself to the celebration of a spiritual bonding cemented beyond all tense.

It is in the very next sentence that Clarissa notices the arrival of Sir William Bradshaw, the psychiatrist come to gossip about the dead young man. She quickly retreats with the news into an empty room adjacent to the party and enters upon the precincts of Septimus's death with that desperate precision we have already examined. In response to his imagined drop, her party's "splendour fell to the floor" (p. 280). She decides finally that his heroism consists in having "flung it away" in order to save it. But what is the "it"? Though we cannot yet say, we have begun to understand the full reach—across the metropolis and its sea of anonymity—of Septimus's last words at the very moment of his jump. The dying double's blurted final utterance has found at last a grammar answering to the suspended impetus of its headlong neuter pronoun. In his "I'll give it you" (p. 226), the "it" is of course partly meant, taken as vernacular filler rather than oracular fling, as an idiomatic jab at revenge against doctors so blind to the interiority of Septimus's pain that they suggest at one point, "Throw yourself into outside interests" (p. 138). With the results of such therapy travestied in a thrown corpse, there is another sense of "give it you" which transvalues the absurd brutality of this death. It is the sacramental sense more openly experimented with in the first draft, where "the window sill was an altar" and Septimus's jump, in his own muttered word, an "offering."[15] Though very much in keeping with the book's themes of communication and mortal communion, this liturgical force—of fatality as offertory—is revised to the published text's idiom of defiance. The grammatical accusative in "I'll give it you" loses its accusatory charge as Clarissa becomes its indirect, its displaced object. When what the hero "gives" is intuitively received in its finer terms, the legacy of his plunge is thus transferred to the heroine's own "gift" for continuance, in and as herself. Septimus's psychosis can go into final remission only as transmission, pathology cured by telepathy, communication at last achieved.

Guessing that he had "plunged holding his treasure" (p. 281), Clarissa can rationalize—or emotionalize—this further example of the drownings she so often discovers in the very waters upon which she succeeds in keeping afloat: "It was her punishment to see sink and disappear here a man, there a woman, in this profound darkness" (p. 282). It is not a "punishment" she has taken lightly, yet it is suffered in the name of deliverance. Though in this "darkness" of a Conradian "destructive element" Clarissa has been willing to "immerse" herself, she has gone through her symbolic plunge and undoing for the sake of those "waves of divine vitality" that alone console her. And so, without having earned any extraordinary heroic status, she has secured her enduring presence.

Discounting earlier in the novel any feeling for Clarissa as "striking," "beautiful," "picturesque," or "clever," Peter adds, "There she was, however; there she was" (p. 115). Her very existence seems to substitute for attribution. By the end of the novel such presence is still tribute enough, for the celebratory grammar of Peter's early monologue becomes the novel's own: "For there she was," half merely adverbial, half reincarnating, positing the self as well as positioning it. No finis could be more superbly tuned to the rhythms of continuance. Clarissa's earlier version of carpe diem about the passing "moment," an imaginative "plunge" that "transfixed it, there" (p. 59), becomes now, after the memento mori of Septimus's plunge, the inverted but equally transfixed "there . . . was" that retrieves her into being. Only paraphrase can approach it, and of course can't touch it. There and only then she had reentered the space of community. In being there again, back with the others, she had come from the dead and again could *be*, so that there and only there could her being thereafter, and elsewhere, be reaffirmed.

Forster the year before seems to have wanted some of the same doubleness with the confirmation (in both senses) of Mrs. Moore's end, "Dead she was." It has everything to do with the power of Woolf's closure, as a sacrificial death scene transfigured through effigy to renewal, to realize that it echoes—Woolf might say "continues," even purges—some of the greatest such scenes in the English novel, from Thackeray to Forster, and through them, of that greatest text in Western culture. Even Leonard Bast, "who was dead," takes his place in this tradition, trying in his heart to say a quasibiblical *"Adsum"* to the woman he would have as his judge. Before him, Jude the Obscure serves as his own spiritual executioner in the middle of his last biblical peroration. With his wheezing "And I here," he can neither get beyond Septimus's "I—I . . . I—I" nor open the hope for a complementary verb of being, like that inscribed by displacement in the last monosyllable of Clarissa's secured gift for going forward. It is only true to Woolf's growing rigor about the metaphysics of identity, however, that exactly this vocabulary of presence should come into question in *The Waves*, tested there, even more strenuously, by death.

□ □ □

"Oh! thought Clarissa, in the middle of my party, here's death" (p. 279). The party in the first section of *To the Lighthouse*, in which the guests think themselves partaking of "eternity," is also impinged upon by a memento mori like the monk's skull alluded to in *The Voyage Out*. This is that boar's-head skeleton in the room of the heroine's children, which it is one of Mrs. Ramsay's last acts in the novel to shroud with her shawl. "Let sanguine healthy mindedness do its best with its strange power of living in the present and ignoring and forgetting," wrote William James in a strikingly parallel metaphor, "still . . . the skull will grin in at the banquet."[16] It is from the interior monologue of Lily Briscoe, the character who lives on in Mrs. Ramsay's stead in much the way Clarissa does for Septimus, that we hear an extended figure for that intrusion of death upon life which brings existence to epitome, life's massing to essence as well as to disintegration. Lily realizes that "life, from being made up of little separate incidents which one lived one by one, became curled and whole like a wave which bore one up with it and threw one down with it, there, with a dash on the beach" (p. 73). It is the master metaphor in embryo of Woolf's later novel, *The Waves*, which refers by title both to the individuated rhythms that coalesce finally to a single life and also to that impersonal universe of flux and destruction which defines in its vastness the very absence of self which is death.

Part of the movement toward *The Waves* already visible in *To the Lighthouse* can be detected in the closural emphasis on Lily's abstract painting as an artifact analogous to the formal narrative entity which its completion serves in turn to complete. The "stroke" of "luck" that threw the "odd-shaped triangular shadow over the step" (p. 299), itself the ghostly trace of an unseen original form, seems to anticipate, by playing upon, the brush "stroke" that will complete her picture. This conversion of contingency to technique within the meaning of a single phrase is then compounded by a different ambiguity in that gesture of technique which is common to both painting and to the literary art which here includes it: that finishing "line" in the book's penultimate sentence that sets right the whole composition, both picture and text.

This formalist complexity in *To the Lighthouse* also manages to attract to its concerns Woolf's recurrent symbolism of drowning, in a way that further prefigures *The Waves*. While reaching out to her dead friend, Mrs. Ramsay, so that she risks a plunge into the "waters of annihilation" (p. 269), Lily cannot put the finishing touches on her canvas until Mr. Ramsay, himself preoccupied with the drowning refrain from "The Castaway," makes his way across these same waters to the lighthouse. It is at just this point that the mythic dimensions marked out by the double accomplishment of trek and artifact come to voice in Lily's utterance, "It is finished." And in the very next sentence these archetypal overtones of death and resurrection are referred even farther back from Christian sacrifice into antiquity: "Then, surging up . . . old Mr. Carmichael stood beside her, looking like an old pagan god, shaggy, with weeds in his hair and the trident (it was only a French novel) in his hand." The poet figure Carmichael is not so much the "guilty-river god" of Rilke's third *Duino Elegy*, "Neptune of the blood" with his "terrible trident,"[17] as he is the emergent figure of literary art itself in a context where drowning is the ruling metaphor of annihilation, figure for all that is formless and forgetful. Symbolically "surging" up here as if from the depths of Lily's own meditation on the whelming gulfs that threaten separately herself and Mr. Ramsay, that invincible trident takes modernist shape in what might have been another painted canvas but is in fact a narrative text, "a French novel," recalling Rachel's copy of Balzac in *The Voyage Out*. Indeed, as symbol rescued from flux into articulate utterance, a symbol in the form of an object or instrument retrieved from effacing waters into textual efficacy, that brandished and empowering novel is Queequeg's inscribed coffin in a readable tongue. In *The Waves* its place is taken by a closural soliloquy in the voice of a novelist-hero whose alternative to articulation is engulfment by the very waves of the book's title.

Artistry aside, it is a female character in that later novel with whom Woolf as attempted (and eventual) suicide most closely identifies, and with whom she in fact shares explicitly, as we are to see, some of her own childhood traumas. Without the creative bent or vent of a Lily Briscoe, the neurotic Rhoda is a woman even more terrified of time than is Septimus Smith, for she is a self without any power to poeticize it as eternity inside out. Rhoda is in a sense the title victim of the novel. Fearing the natural beat of the waves with which she cannot synchronize herself, the metaphoric tread and contour of time, Rhoda lives with the strain of anticipated catastrophe, waiting to be dashed and dissipated "like the foam that races over the beach" (p. 130). Worse than drowning, this is the self as medium of its own dissolution, annihilated by its inherent inaptitude for being. Rhoda's is a terror of the temporal that is refracted and in some cases corrected in the other main characters of this novel—if characters are what we decide to call them, or novel their collage of soliloquies. It is finally by a twofold effort of displacement that the writer Bernard (playing Clarissa to Rhoda's Septimus, as well as to the absent hero, Percival) succeeds as novelist in overcoming that temporal impasse of discontinuous selfhood which threatens the loss of the only thing these characters have to call their own: the wavelike rhythms of their curled, unfurling, their furiously earnest utterance.

The whole fiction can be read as the abridged *Bildungsroman* of the psyche, told six times over. It is divided between italicized interchapters of omniscient description, in which the principal characters are never mentioned, and the soliloquies that make up the main body of the novel. These are the monologues of three men and three women never pointed to by narration except for such unvaried filler as "said Rhoda," "said Bernard." In this most unflinching experiment in the stream of consciousness, character for Woolf has become *only* inner voice, identity its own articulation to itself. This is merely a first way, then, of hinting at the privileged hold the idea of narrative form will gain on the question of death and on those metaphors transposed from living idiom to approximate it. Beginning with birth, the six characters (the seventh, Percival, never directly heard from) embark upon the manifold demands of perception itself, assault their schoolroom lessons, quarrel, kiss, fear, love, weaken, weary, face death, in one case (Percival's) stumble to it, in another (Rhoda's) leap to embrace it, in yet another (Bernard's) charge forward to defy it. It is this incremental mortality ordering itself to hierarchy that tests Woolf's rhetoric of effigy as never before.

The first death comes to the much-lamented soldier Percival, never met by us, who dies in a riding accident in India before he even sees combat. His end is the end of an epoch, the death scene of the atavistic chevalier. Typically for Woolf, the bare facts of his death come by telegram, as if unauthored, unmediated. By an act of sympathetic projection somewhat less graphic than Mrs. Dalloway's, the poet of the group, Neville, extrapolates from the telegraphic message a full-scale staccato death scene. It is the first of many mortal displacements through monologue in the novel. At just the point where the italicized interludes have reached the sun's zenith in their charting of a diurnal arc, the waves of the evoked seascape are *"steeped"* like dashing steeds, *"rippled as the backs of great horses ripple,"* and these *"waves fell, withdrew and fell again, like the thud of a great beast stamping"* (p. 150). It is the "thud" of Percival's death fall too. Neville begins addressing the tragedy by saying as objectively as possible,

"This is the fact. His horse stumbled; he was thrown" (p. 151). But facts are themselves thrown over by an involuntary imagination like Clarissa's: "The flashing trees and white rails went up in a shower. There was a surge; a drumming in his ears." Outer is now subsumed by inner at the instant when death removes externality forever: "Then the blow; the world crashed; he breathed heavily. He died where he fell." Beneath the unsorted spate of subjective impressions gathers Woolf's central archetype; the "flash" and "shower" of forms green and white, the surge, then drumming blow, then crash and expiration—all of it takes the covert curve of the waves. Neville now surrenders to the displaced temporal finality of death in a pun turning on the taunting, anarchic tense of his own surviving words in "all now lies in the unreal world which is gone." A potentially present-tense verb seems subversively dismissed by a plural noun (the other sense of "lies") in an evacuated present that also decimates memory, reducing the "unreal" past not only to dust but to delusion.

Neville the poet is a manipulator of phrase prepared by his earliest experiences in this novel to invest death and its displacements with verbal shape. He is the first to give voice to a potentially (and quite literally) paralyzing fear of death to which his fellow characters, being mortal, are also prone. The violent idea of any death, including, of course, a violent one, has to make way for meditation upon it. Its shock can only then be imaginatively absorbed, if not abated, through the medium of language, the incipient poet's phrase making. When still a young child Neville was inducted into the knowledge of death at so unforgettable a moment that it is the halted instant in the time of recognition, not the actual rupture of death, by which his memory is riveted. He never forgets how "I felt when I heard about the dead man through the swing-door last night" (p. 24), the fact of death symbolically screened by language to begin with. "His blood gurgled down the gutter. His jowl was white as a dead codfish. I shall call this stricture, this rigidity, 'death among the apple trees' for ever." By his thought alone the child's mind is stricken, his body struck still at the center of a suddenly petrified universe: "He was found with his throat cut. The apple-tree leaves became fixed in the sky; the moon glared; I was unable to lift my foot up the stair." Inner and outer are frozen by the fact of a death that suspends temporal flow not only for the corpse but by displacement for the participating consciousness. The repeated demonstrative *this* in the compound phrase "this stricture, this rigidity" points disconcertingly not to the stiffening corpse but to the boy's own arrested progress up the stairs. And the appositional clotting of the demonstrative phrases is language's own impacted response to this fixation, the speechless cadaver with its severed throat evoked in the effigy of a poet's phrase. Through a sliding implication within a single noun, in fact, the whole process of displacement is enacted in the sense of death's fixture internalized as emotional "stricture."

The deathless Eden of childhood is thus violated by a symbolic tree revised from a poplar to the biblical apple in the novel's second draft.[18] It is not, therefore, the mutilated cadaver that is denominated as "death among the apple trees" but rather the knowledge of that death—abstraction detached from its occasion—as it intrudes for Neville upon a pastoral scene both then and "for ever." No quarrel here for Woolf with the generalized grieving of the mortal state, since even her poet's phrasing has fallen upon (or sought solace in) another pun at the imagined sight of the tree's "greaved" silver bark. Language is under sway of mortal acknowledgement, almost stunned by it, as before in the blurted intuitions of Septimus Smith. The natural motives for the transposition of death into accessible speech tap something so deep in Woolf's delegated verbal imagination that they seem to have telescoped the functions of mortal rhetoric as we have been exploring them. The struggle to utterance about dying becomes its own verbal (and so affective) displacement of that death upon the very effort of its recognition and reference, once formatively for the child, then again at the death of Percival, then in a more complex way for Bernard, the novelist, at the close.

Rhoda's demons, by contrast, do not take readily to displacement or catharsis in the single phrase. Unlike her predecessor Mrs. Dalloway, Rhoda cannot find in the death of the Other that which would healthily precipitate, crystallize, and expel her own terrors of finality. Dying as a termination does not address the more nauseating fears of her existence, her terror of the death no one can die for you because it is synonymous with your life, moment by moment. Since Rhoda cannot make without terror the transit from one instant to the next, each one seems to slam her headfirst against the *thought*—a tiny but unremitting version of the fact itself—of violent annihilation. Where

Neville keeps the impassable in its place, Rhoda, the other character along with Bernard most obsessed with temporality and death, knows as time goes on little else but the immitigible rigor of frustrated sequentiality: "I cannot make one moment merge in the next. To me they are all violent, all separate" (p. 130). She adds in the next sentence, with that unwitting ambivalence of phrase that often seems to trip her up, "I have no end in view." No purpose, perhaps, yet there is that "end" as violent rupture which she cannot keep from view in the yawning gulf between moments. She wants a wavelike continuity and gets only pummeling and dispersal: "I do not know how to run minute to minute and hour to hour, solving them by some natural force until they make the whole and indivisible mass that you call life." Her participial meaning is halfway between the two derivatives of "solution," a problem solved or resolved on the one hand and on the other a discreteness dissolved into unity. She also says on this page that she is "whirled down caverns," a violent version of Woolfian introspection or tunneling that reminds us of Rachel Vinrace and her traumas of temporality.

Again, the wavelike cresting of prose style serves as register—and offers review. In the early stages of Rachel's fever in *The Voyage Out*, her break with sanative continuity is signaled by a delusory spatialization of time bent to the curve of Woolf's periodic syntax: "There were immense intervals or chasms, for things still had the power to appear visibly before her, between one moment and the next" (p. 347). Predicating, pulling back for explanation, then dropping the preposition into place; thrust, parenthesis, thud. With that second comma (which introduces the syntactic ambiguity) inserted after the first typescript of the novel,[19] the prose opens its own temporal "interval" to the span of an imitative spatial delay, suspending its grammar over the gap in logical sequence that Rachel's thoughts struggle haltingly to describe. The wavelike inflection of a comparable periodicity assists Clarissa Dalloway later in capturing that "indescribable pause" in her pulse before the chiming of Big Ben, a hiatus at the heart of the very advance and resumption of time, "a suspense (but that might be her heart, affected, they said, by influenza) before Big Ben strikes" (pp. 4–5). These suspensions, hovering intervals, necessitated leaps, and all the paranoia to which they are prey, are Rhoda's disorienting lot. For all three heroines such intervals are evinced through the discontinuous lurchings of that inner monologue by which the specter of fatal lapse must be raised in the first place. Hence Rhoda's later scriptive model for disjuncture. Apostrophizing her deprived life in retrospect, she blames it for having "snatched from me the white spaces that lie between hour and hour" (p. 204), those interstices of being's inexorable text that have been "tossed . . . into the wastebasket" (p. 204). Yet it is her besetting paranoia which has rendered these spaces intolerable, Rhoda thereby declared as a postmodern victim of the deconstructive imagination. Articulation's mark on the blankness of the unvoiced world is so precarious for her because, in the characterization of Derrida's typical metaphoric melodrama, "death strolls between letters."[20] This is akin to the death in Woolf that isolates and paralyzes, not the communicable dying that unites.

Louis strikes a keynote of this late book, of Woolf's novels generally, and of the whole tradition of transference and catharsis out of which they come, when he says, "All deaths are one death" (p. 170). Beginning the pattern of double displacement in *The Waves*—which transfers the death in absentia of Percival along the channels of intuited consciousness through the off-stage suicide of Rhoda into the mind of the novelist hero—Bernard is himself given the penultimate response to Percival's death in the memorial chapter, "This is my funeral service" (p. 197). He then yields place to Rhoda, who, making it her funeral too, closes the section less collectedly. She is suspicious of all such elegiac pungency of expression, especially the molded and modulated effusions of the wordsmith Bernard: "He will have out his notebook; under D, he will enter 'Phrases to be used on the deaths of friends' " (p. 161). This is for Rhoda too studied, too mannered. Instead she begins her section with an involuntary start of metaphor to mark her wrenching arrest by the contemplation of death. Here she borrows directly from one of Woolf's own vividly remembered terrors: " 'There is the puddle,' said Rhoda, 'and I cannot cross it' " (p. 158).[21] It is a homely obstacle, an illogical impediment, the merest lacuna in continuity yawning as an "enormous gulf." Within two paragraphs Rhoda has implicitly referred this "puddle" outward to the encompassing conceit of the novel as a whole, saying of the fluid shock waves sent out from the sudden vacuum of Percival's death and its resulting whirlpool, "I ride rough waters and shall sink with no one to save me." Unable to transpose Percival's death into understanding or even fine phrase, Rhoda seems to fall victim to a virulent subversive punning outside her control. Saying in various forms in this soliloquy that "Percival, by his death, has made me this gift, let me see the thing" (p. 163), she means the deathly essence under the surface and within the clefts of time, nothing like the gift for endurance of Septimus's "I'll give it you." In her most devastated, ambivalent phrasing of this dilemma—the pun as punishment—she puts it this way: "Percival, by his death, has made me this present, has revealed this terror" (pp. 159–160). The "present," the given, is received into the mind in all its cruel insistency, time itself tortured by loss.

Rhoda closes this requiem monologue for Percival by fantasizing the delivery of an elegiac bouquet in images that anticipate the novelist Bernard's galloping charge against oceanic death at the end of the novel: "We will gallop together over desert hills . . . Into the wave that dashes upon the shore, into the wave that flings its white foam to the uttermost corners of the earth I throw my violets, my offering to Percival" (p. 164). But the tossed flowers for the dead seem not enough of an offering. She must reinscribe their arc in suicidal fantasy with the trajectory of her own thrown body, over the edge of the world into the waves beneath. The hyperbole (in the root sense) of her identification with the hero's fall is literalized as the "casting beyond" of her soliloquized death fling. The very texture of this articulated plunge takes on a momentum and plasticity of its own, not figuring the death leap so much as enacting it and finally incarnating its destination in the irregularities and ridged divisions of its own verbal surface: "We launch out now over the precipice. Beneath us lie the lights of the herring fleet. The cliffs vanish. Rippling small, rippling grey, innumerable waves spread beneath us. I touch nothing. I see nothing" (p. 206). The corrugated simulation of participial grammar gives way to that last verb's spreading like the watery destination it predicates, its two senses diverging into view with the instantaneousness of Rhoda's free fall. The waves not only "lay spread" beneath but, their rippled pattern broadening as she drops towards it, they also "spread open" rapidly before her vision just as it is about to be canceled. A single verb thus conveys both the vista and its accelerated eventuation as a fatal impact. "There was a surge; a drumming in his ears," conjectured Neville upon receiving news of Percival's death. Rhoda's "The sea will drum in my ears" now is the echo that connects this imagined elegiac plunge with the hero's fall whose lethal momentum it would seem moved to lament and anatomize, replicate and then redirect.

Instead, rebuking all attempts at sublimation, this imagined leap anticipates the scene of Rhoda's own death. Just as Septimus's jump was reduplicated in Clarissa's mind as, for the reader, its only rendered scene—given narrative space only through psychological displacement—so too is Rhoda's death in the exclusive keep of the hero, Bernard. His narrative hold on it is, of course, all the more explicit because of his role as a novelist, inventive memorialist in prose. The approximate method of Rhoda's death in the printed version of the novel is suggested primarily by Bernard's later passing clause, "when she leapt" (p. 281), whereas the second draft had specified the death through his voice as a fall like Percival's, though probably begun by a jump: "And Rhoda had taken her own short cut, falling, by accident it was said, from a window."[22] In all of the draft versions it is nonetheless her own foreshadowing of descent from the precipice, out past the threshold of the earth into the drumming flood of primal waters, that remains definitive. In her last set of speeches, before the actual death leap is incorporated into Bernard's closing soliloquy, Rhoda recurs to that visionary premonition as a communal destiny. Her friends walk slowly from her "towards the lake," and for her this march bodes their own loss to the waters of oblivion, an external engulfment answering to the deathward stream of their inner consciousness: "The tide in the soul, tipped, flows that way; they cannot help deserting us. The dark has closed over their bodies" (pp. 229–230). The whole Romantic juncture between psyche and landscape is there in disrepair. It is a metaphoric lapse of waning self to dark waves of effacement, of Chronos to Chaos, human duration to erasure in the ebbing tides of temporality. This wish for drowning in a world that cannot sustain her—for a removal by fusion familiar to us from Rachel's requiemlike rather than epithalamic merger with the world in *The Voyage Out*—is here, near Rhoda's end, displaced temporarily onto other characters as the involuntary fate of all lives in time.

Before we close in upon the actual words by which Bernard, in the book's last soliloquy, transvalues fatality to renovating phrase, more needs saying about the relation of death to expressive continuance. Whatever may be thought lost in drama and psychological charge with the pastiche of soliloquies that makes up *The Waves* is returned amply to it from biographical quarters. It becomes Woolf's riskiest admission yet of the poverty of phrase in sublimating and fending off death—and this by a novelist whose own suicide by drowning seems in retrospect to have been postponed over the years only by the outlet and anodyne of art. Genders reversed, Woolf is Bernard, professional novelist driven to the wave-lashed shore of a fading confidence in phrase. She has made it to this point with him, as he has, only through the deaths of alter egos undergone and overcome as "stories," her entered and published phrases for death after death not yet her own. We may be angling at last into position to address one of the most persistent questions about Woolf's career in fiction: why so many of the verbal artists she portrays in her novels, whether frustrated poets, amateur or professional novelists, are male figures, male voices. This question seems especially vexing for being asked of a creative world fashioned by that modernist female writer who above all, with a preeminent temerity of experiment, wrested fictional style from the patrilineage of English letters. Answers seem to lie along a path littered with symbolic corpses, and so in turn inform our largest inquiry into the role of the death scene in Woolf's fiction, whose mortal parables include not only the relation of trauma to perseverance but of art's labors to those of life. Indeed one comes to suspect that the figural displacement of death by phrase may contain a paradigm for the gender deflection of authorial (not to say creative) impulse in Woolf's female characters.

Beginning with *The Voyage Out*, it is the would-be novelist Terence, legatee of death as subject or at least titular aspect of his novel, *Silence*, who brings the impetus to prose fiction into alignment with the inertia of female death. Well in advance of Septimus Smith, scribbling poet and messenger of annihilation in *Mrs. Dalloway*, and Bernard, the dying writer in *The Waves*, Woolf's earliest fictional stand-in thus sets the pattern for the rest. Terence establishes the death-tested relation of verbal art to the female consciousness it would in part inscribe, whether the recording imagination be that of doomed lover, surviving double, or suicidal counterpart. It might in other words be said, this late in the fictional tradition, that the death scene's long-standing rhetorical and psychological function of displacement is itself being reified and allegorized by Woolf. The continuity so often difficult to achieve within selves is sometimes managed between them, the unbalanced heroine frequently evened and completed by some masculine extension—through articulation—of her identity. Difference, or again displacement, is thus installed by plot, often actually embodied, as a symbolic model: some alternative mode of being; some disjunctive and so surviving face of an otherwise failed identity; transference itself given flesh; a palpable and powerful ceding to otherness. *Orlando* overlaps this creative necessity upon the androgynous stages of a single self. For the female psyche in crisis, maleness is only one name for this essential difference, deferred death another, aesthetic distance another, with authorship in each case a potential manifestation. Despite the long years of mastered intimacy with her own talent and her own style, and despite her passionate quest for the true woman's voice in art, it would seem that the writing self, with its allegiances to order and authority, its continuities won from ruin, appeared to Woolf so strange an otherness within her— though making, as it were, all the difference—that it might have been an alternate self altogether, indeed projected into plot as a male opposite. This would have little to do—or nothing except by way of disabused mythology—with sexist platitudes about creative productivity as a masculine virtue, but rather with Woolf's sense of something cool, removed, and oddly assured, something forever estranged and undomesticated, alien even as it alienates the self's worst frailties, about the powers summoned by her in the never quite familiarized mood of art.

Taken in this way, the gender allegory of Woolf's writer figures is intriguingly sequential. In *The Voyage Out,* the fragile truth about the female libido can be intuited by the male mind only if that mind is willing to die from itself into the abyss of a woman's very retreat from the male. By the same token, this feminine reality can be shaped into verbal conception only by a second self so lucidly released from these same psychic dilemmas that it might as well be an expressive alter ego of a different sex entirely. The articulate self as Other—so Woolf seems to be enciphering with this first of her parabolic death scenes—is all that has survived intact from the adolescent ordeal of her own sexual withdrawal. And yet years later in Woolf's fictional tracking of the feminine mind, *Mrs. Dalloway* suggests that the demands made upon the clarifying power of art are so extensive and extreme as to have sacrificed the artist entirely, bled the expressive double to emptiness. The Septimus in both Clarissa and Virginia, the disturbed and bisexual artist of painful phrase, has many times been asked to endure deathly recognitions for the woman, herself bisexual, who would keep up her being in time. Such an autobiographical allegory of adjusted genders now passes into its third, climactic stage. The sacrificial auspices of art are not in the long run enough for the Rhoda-like aspects of Woolf's or any invalided woman's psyche. It must have felt to the troubled Virginia more and more clear in her career as the writer Woolf that the woman in her was doomed, no matter what ministrations were performed by either the isolated homosexual poet in her or the workably married novelist, by the Neville or the Bernard—or, say, by the androgynous genius of her own poetic prose. In her role as Viginia Woolf, half of a renowned literary couple and major novelist in her own person, she was farther removed by the act of writing from her Rhoda-like demons than any latitude within her own gender would have given room to illustrate. Twice over in *The Waves*, therefore, this creative self is cast by default as a masculine consciousness steeped in the keen isolation of aesthetic language. It is this aspect of the creative mentality, difference reified, otherness incarnate, that lives on bravely in *The Waves*, invoking in the closural role of Bernard the worn forms of masculine heroism with revisionary panache. This novelist becomes, like Percival, the anachronistic horseman of his own apocalypse, facing the waters of his end with authenticity and wit. So too survives the public Woolf. Novelist in a man's world, contained and prevailing master of prose style, she makes do with language until the waters of the Ouse River take her down to her own long-deferred silence.

Two exceptions to this pattern of female death alternated with male artistry suggest themselves on either side of *The Waves*—exceptions centering on the aesthetic functions of Lily Briscoe, the painter in *To the Lighthouse*, and Miss La Trobe, the playwright in *Between the Acts*. Lily's painting is inspired by the death of a woman, her beloved Mrs. Ramsay, and it is not Lily after all but Mr. Carmichael, the renowned male poet, who stands as the representative of specifically literary art. At the end of Woolf's career, Miss La Trobe comes closest to a Woolfian artist of words, and yet her status as historical dramatist and pageant maker associates her with the Woolf of *Orlando* in particular rather than with the later stream of consiousness experiments, of which *Between the Acts* is the final examplar. A revealing division of labor occurs in this regard in *To the Lighthouse*. After years of controlled dissonance between Lily the painter and Mr. Carmichael the poet, we hear his defense of the aesthetic act sieved through her indirect discourse: "That would have been his answer, presumably—how 'you' and 'I' and 'she' pass and vanish; nothing stays; all changes; but not words, not paint" (p. 267). It is a deconstruction of the very declensions of pronominal identity while at the same time a celebration of their rescued expression in artifact or text. Though Lily "had never read a line of his poetry," she understood it to be "extremely impersonal; it said something about death; it said very little about love" (p. 290). It thus passes, in Woolf's own terms, that "test of great poetry" which the moderns, in her view, so often fail. So too does Lily's canvas pass this test in its way. Since she requires for the completion of her painting, besides a kindled sympathy for the widowed Mr. Ramsay, also a renewal of feeling for the dead heroine, that canvas, even in an abstraction that renders it as impersonal as any poetry could possibly be, still manages to say something about death and perpetuation—just as does the fiction by Virginia Woolf with which it is simultaneously brought to a finish.

Imagining her new play at the end of *Between the Acts*, Miss La Trobe thinks that its first words gradually "rose to the surface" from the mired landscape around her. Her "words of one syllable sank down into the mud. She drowsed; she nodded." Not drowning with them, instead she dreams or "drowses" them into new being: "The mud became fertile. Words rose . . . Words without meaning—wonderful words" (p. 212). Illustrating the modes of recurrence in fiction, and various structural renewals through them, J. Hillis Miller has compared this moment to the earlier death by water of the Lady Ermyntrude, who is mentioned in passing to have "drowned herself for love" in a mud-bottomed hollow, a tragic retrospect intruded much earlier into the text: "It was in that deep centre, in that black heart, that the lady had drowned herself" (p. 44). This is clearly a salient if brief allusion for the novelist who will have drowned herself as well before the publication of this very novel; any fleeting dream of human or aesthetic renewal must indeed be rescued from such a fate. Considering death as "the event which cannot be presented directly," Miller writes, "The drowning of the Lady Ermyntrude is a mirror of Miss La Trobe's new play. One descends into the pool. The other rises from its mud." Between them is Woolf's own "web of words," suspended "not from the known to the known but from the unknown to the unknown."[23] As anticipated by the title metaphors and symbolic hallucinations of *The Voyage Out* and *The Waves*, here for the first time it is literally the drowning of a woman that seems to transfer fatality into some mysterious fluidity of expression. No displacement from existential finish to textual reincarnation could be more explicit, from muddied end to primordial utterance. At the very end of Woolf's life in letters, we have the woman drowned and the woman of words encountering and thereby balancing each other in the same text. It is only to the point that for so long the terms of this threatened convergence had to go forth in disguise, allegorized in fables of creative sacrifice and fatality divided between men and women.

Still, however much this gender-coded silhouette of Woolf's career may obtain in the relation of Bernard's closing articulation in *The Waves* to Rhoda's preceding death, it is the aging writer's insouciant and searching way with phrase, at least as much as the sexual displacements it may facilitate, which comes forward for celebration in Bernard's last soliloquy. To the extent that Bernard shares in the fatality of Rhoda's terminal visions, this novelist-hero must salvage himself, along with what meaning he can, from the backwash of ennui and formlessness before tossing himself forward at the waves in the novel's last paragraph. His final cumulative soliloquy, which must among other work report, incorporate, and transfigure the fact of Rhoda's death (as a further function of Percival's fall), begins as if with the retrospective vision of a man drowning in that dark "tide of the soul" which Rhoda last spoke about: "Now to sum up . . . Now to explain to you the meaning of my life" (p. 238). But meaning and being are at odds, every narrative *sum* ("I am") to be tallied as summation only at the point where experience passes from ongoing to foregone time. By replaying now in his own refashioned words the phases and cycles through which the novel has already passed, as T. S. Eliot would say the "stages of his age and youth," Bernard is only doing what he has always craved as narrative mentality to achieve.

In this distended closural moment, his language not only transposes into new similes and conceits the pending specter of final silence; in so doing, it also epitomizes his life as compassionate and comprehensive phrase maker, summing up always as he goes, a stylist of the mutable and fugitive.

Bernard is himself a linguistic master of that vanishing interval which is the secret genius of the death scene from Dickens forward. Just before his final soliloquy, as if precipitating those last words we have from Rhoda about drowning, he evokes the transience of life as a whole in a craftily judged and nuanced burst of accentual prose. Existence is thrown into relief against the symbolic vegetation of the graveyard: "Let it blaze against the yew trees. One life. There. It is over. Gone out" (p. 229). The monosyllabic fragment flung between others almost as slight—"there," ambivalently adverb or expletive—teeters from referential side to side with the tentativeness and fragility of life itself. "One life there—then it is over," or "One life—there, it is over." The split second of our perceptual double take is the relative duration being described. Life, and the phrases invented to tell its story, form, flash, and vanish to the same rhythm, for in the largest sense they are in this novel one and the same. Bernard's evocation seems to recruit the full stylistic ingenuity of a death scene because even as statement, in this novel of pure statement, it has the contour of a drastic transitional event. Verging toward a kind of reflexive adverb enunciating only itself as speech act, "there" punctuates the phrasing in swift simulation of the elusive presence it alone, as language, can be thought to constitute. Hermeticizing the tradition of fictional dying, life is distilled to passing grammatical fragment, a truncated narrative in little, with death merely a particular disposition of its rhythm, a transposition of emphasis, a verbal pivot into the irreversible.

Here we arrive at the root of Bernard's imminent crisis, his perplexing death of self. The novelist-hero, the self as novelizing hero, lives, or would live, in his phrases, and they fail him; they too know death. In this final soliloquy he seems grievously attenuated to their mere fluency, no longer even the embodied vessel of his own speech. By being from the first a self in both senses "composed" (p. 30), made of phrase, he is prey to that frailty against which no speech can guarantee. Remarks Neville, the poet, "Bernard says there is always a story. I am a story. Louis is a story" (p. 37). When in the final soliloquy Bernard puts ironic quotes around "characters of our friends" (p. 243), he seems to be signaling a similar sense of narrative shape as well as psychological essence. Bernard, the inveterate note taker, thus admits to more than might at first appear when declaring "I shall enter my phrases" (p. 36)—as if he means not only them into a notebook but he into them. The crisis coming for Bernard has to do with the lost confidence not only in the interior monologues of autonomy but in the inscription that would sift, purify, and fix them in their full expressiveness.

The textualizing of Bernard's already verbally involuted imagination can be seen in a metaphor like "the margin of my mind" (p. 189), bracketing the space where notes toward that definitive summary of his life are being amassed. He ventures that conceit in a soliloquy just before Rhoda's fantasy of fall and drowning, and he too is imagining a "waste of waters" in which a single "fin turns," a "bare visual impression—unattached to any line of reason" (p. 189). Suggested instead is the "line," the physical impression, scored by a stylus in making its mark across the waste of blankness that is his life's unwritten text or its margin. "I note under F., therefore, 'Fin in a waste of waters.' " It is toward some "final" statement that he inscribes this "mark," and the jotted notation itself implies the "fin" at the root of *final*, the emblem that, even as mere sign or set of letters, spells its own terminal relevance. It does so in those innocent "words of one syllable" (pp. 287, 295) for which Bernard more than once yearns in the last soliloquy. It is with them that he might find an answer to the question "By what name are we to call death?" (p. 295), where the double sense of his verb *call* suggests that summoning which is at one with denomination. The novelist and phrase maker who comes down to the close of the novel fearing that his life has been an "unfinished phrase" (p. 283) may thus have forgotten that lone syllable filed under *F*. Yet in retrospect this notation may well suggest itself to the reader as the premonitory symbol of that finis (to borrow from Conrad's allusion to death at sea) achieved amid another such waste of waters in Rhoda's fantasized leap, to be followed at the end by its revivifying effigy in Bernard's phrases.

Well along in the extant draft of *Mrs. Dalloway*, Woolf temporarily altered the name of Septimus to Bernard Warren Smith. Recovering that first name for *The Waves*, she gives the character a new version of the rent identity which tortured Septimus. The self-conscious alter ego of Bernard, his "biographer, dead long since" (p. 259), seems to represent a superintending verbal consciousness formerly responsible for Bernard's reverberant phrases and then disappeared somewhere behind them, so that now "no echo comes when I speak" (p. 284). When Bernard later amplifies this mourned loss of a conscious, self-phrasing identity—"All this little affair of 'being' is over" (p. 288)—we recognize that it is over precisely (and paradoxically enough) because, once it has quotation marks around it, its continuous breathing has been given up (shaped up) as the spoken breath not of life but of the voiced definition of life. The second draft of *The Waves* is more explicit on this score, yet when Bernard remarks there that " 'I' had died,"[24] it is again because the quotation of self is the swathing of it as a finished thing.

As Bernard moves toward that final confrontation with the waves of nonentity, he is thus passing through a crisis similar to the one which the drowning of "Water-Party" in *Women in Love* serves to displace for Birkin. Lawrence's hero was becoming "quite dead alive, nothing but a word-bag" (p. 180) because of his persistent "Hamletizing" over the very question of being and nonentity that now obsesses Bernard. Once conceived of as all words, the "I" loses even the self that used to channel and shape those words, becomes only the flow of language, not even its articulated conduit. Bernard's crisis as sacrificial fiction maker moves toward the postmodern dilemma outlined by Roland Barthes in "The Death of the Author," the emptying out of presence from text that leaves only a "subject," not a "person."[25] A scriptive "I" remains, but in Bernard's terms no fleshed-out autobiographical overseer—or oversayer. Bernard as articulate agent, articulate animal, has become a "man without a self." This metamorphosis is genuine trial by abnegation: the severance of self from its voiced effluence. Gone is the confidence with which Bernard as master of language was earlier able to say to himself as subject "I recall you" (p. 189) to a new "chapter" of identity, where the verb meant not only "remember" but, in the performative sense, "call up"—invoke, that is, in the very language of reference as manifestation. By now, inscription is no longer the space of inhabitation; the "entered" phrase no longer gives access.

Such a gradually inoperable pun on "recall" underlines the fact that the whole last summarizing soliloquy must struggle to regain just this lost opportunity for punning or doubling between memory and voice, recollection and inflection, scriptive depletion and elegiac empowerment. In so doing, Bernard's closing monologue sums up for us, by superimposing one last time, the two chief mediations of death in fiction with which this whole study has been concerned: empathy and textuality. Bernard's last speeches—alert to the deathlike displacement from identity which is any summing up, any epitomizing statement of the sort he has embarked upon—still reach again for that healing displacement of death which may follow from its contemplation in the corpse of another. The evacuation of self into mere words must be endured, indeed verbalized in its own right, possibly cured, through the enactment in words of those previous deaths first outlived by the memorializing mind, then "recalled" there by phrase. Enter again, for recapitulated exit, the dying Percival and the dying Rhoda. The writer's nearing death gives hearing again to the deaths that precede it, even as the language asked to transcribe this repetition seems to mourn its own removal from originality. Empathy *in articulo mortis* tries to rehabilitate articulation through the mysteries of feeling. Yet how, finally, is the figurative death of self through utterance related to the nonmetaphorical dying of others summoned by that utterance?

Bernard's last soliloquy becomes a eulogy to style overriding its own elegy for the world's content. Into the chronological reconstitution of his life as retrospective summation intrudes the first of the two displaced fatalities to be beguiled and alchemized by style, beginning with a muted simulation of Percival's fall through inverted grammar: "Into this crashed death—Percival's" (p. 263). Bernard recognizes the Clarissa-like penchant for reenactment as catharsis: "There should be cries, cracks, fissures . . . interference with the sense of time, of space . . . flesh being gashed and blood spurting, a joint suddenly twisted." But dying is instead transposed into stylistic cadences by a narrating consciousness who believes all lives, and so all deaths, to be only "stories" in the first place. "Was this then," he has earlier asked, "this streaming away mixed with Susan, Jinny, Neville, Rhoda, Louis, a sort of death?" (p. 279). If so, then physical death, by a compensatory logic, should be susceptible to empathy as its redefinition, death transfigured to the effigy of phrase and its felt inflections.

Such transfiguration we encounter in a retrospective catechism which one critic finds "a passage perhaps as moving as any in fiction"[26]: "Here on my brow is the blow I got when Percival fell. I see far away . . . the pillar Rhoda saw, and feel the rush of the wind of her flight when she leapt" (p. 228). The sonic bond between "brow" and "blow" catches in a reverse temporal sequence of effect returned to cause the displacement of death's force; physical impact passes through psychological impress to stylistic stroke in the interval, right "here," of verbal transference. With Rhoda's concentrated elegy in that second sentence, the play of "flight" as both a fleeing and a flying to her obliteration caps the imitative prepositional cadence of her fall in the push and rush of the doubled "of." Bernard's emphathetic phrases again enact, or "evoke," what by conjecturing they project into and reflect upon. The conjoined predicates cadenced to describe Percival's fall and Rhoda's leap seem part of the same fatal trajectory, the same falling rhythm—a single prolonged, two-stage descent through the surface of inexorable time.

After abbreviating his simulation of Percival's death, Bernard enters the first mention anywhere of Rhoda's actual (rather than previously fantasized) suicide. So has Clarissa Dalloway served in the earlier novel as the locus of the true dramatized scene of Septimus's jump. Bernard explains how he "evoked to serve as opposite to myself the figure of Rhoda," who "had gone . . . had killed herself" (p. 281). As if to "evoke" is an exclusively verbal act that comprises all we are to hear, all there is, of her demise—so that her death transfers her to "figure" in rhetorical terms as well—Bernard speaks of her as a serviceable "opposite" in the sense both of contrasting with and completing his own endangered selfhood. As "figure" for self-annihilation, Rhoda is a psychotic antithesis to Bernard's sanity while also the true voided counterpart of his present pessimism about identity. She is situated in his imagination to "serve" him not in the cool avoidance of grief but precisely to keep both these sides of his mind in balance, so that empathy for her fate need not be suppressed, with all the self-knowledge it flows from and reinvigorates, in the guarded name of self-preservation. It is through his animating memory of her that he keeps time moving long enough to sum itself up in a run of valedictory enunciation, deferring his own death by conferring upon it through phrases an imaginable shape. In so doing, Bernard can plunge back into his verbal life—even if this means lunging at death—rather than shuffle off the vestiges of his phrases and drop straight out of identity.

The shifting ground of Bernard's selfhood in articulation is wittily hinted by the suspensive and effectually twofold syntax of the sentence immediately following his internalization of the two deaths. Along with the ordeals of his other friends, these deaths are bound into and round out the text that is Bernard: "Thus when I come to shape here at the table"—we hear the clause as a grammatical and emotional sufficiency for this self-made man as self-transcribed voice, at least until its completion (or supplementation) by "between my hands the story of my life and set it before you as a completed thing" (p. 289). Satisfied with the grammar of his coming into "shape" or verbal presence, we can only equate it, not entirely recast it, with the additional sense of his proceeding to shape up his "story." In Woolf's typical periodic syntax, the noun of her hero's being cannot be distinguished, that is, from the predicating verb of his autobiographical soliloquy.

For all its energy, however, style can no longer authorize the hero's existence: "No echo comes when I speak, no varied words. This is more truly death than the death of friends, than the death of youth" (p. 284). It is the death, that is, of those friends whose fatalities he has been attempting to incorporate as symbolic of his own lost youth. There may be speech still, but it has no "echo," no resonance against a personal reality apart from, outside of, or containing it. The obsessive biographical mutter must proceed without the biographer, who is no longer its premise or even a presumption from it. This is a fate worse than death, the death of others or one's past, because it is the continual annihilation of the present as defined by one's own presence in it. Bernard summarizes the dilemma to himself this way, knowing that his recovery will have to come through the very words that seem to have emptied him out: "But how describe the world seen without a self?" (p. 287). In any but the autobiographical mode, this is of course the very license of omniscient narrative. It is in fact a novelistic enterprise which Woolf has carried to its extreme in the italicized interchapters of *The Waves,* where there are human selves occasionally but no personalized consciousness as filter of the vision—just words summoned miraculously to evoke a visible but unseen universe. Bernard, in other words, and still in words, is moving as monologist toward a style that would match Woolf's in these interludes, pure saying without conscious seeing or focal consciousness. Toward this end Bernard has one last soliloquy to negotiate, in which he must once more transpose metaphors from the deaths of Percival and Rhoda, as previously mediated and remade by his own phrases, to epitomize now the drift, pitch, and fling of his own resistance to death as silence.

Very near the end Bernard musters a triple pun, sequestered but regenerative, which sums up the motives of the whole last soliloquy. Five paragraphs from the close of *The Waves*—meaning his declaration, it would seem, only dismissively in context—Bernard announces, "I have done with phrases" (p. 295). Not (we want to say) at least as long as this phrase is being spoken or noted. Bernard would appear to mean mainly "I have finished with phrases," while he might also admit that all he has accomplished, finished, perfected, whether as storyteller or himself as story, has been "done with phrases" alone. There is no object of the verb *done* in this transitive sense of the grammar, because there is no object in mind but the phrases themselves that are both cause and effect of Bernard's life in narrative. We quickly realize, therefore, that phrases are still his almost prodigally to command. Then too, beyond the nostalgic and the dispensing senses (having done it with phrases until having done with them), there lies waiting that present preterite of declaration and progressive intentionality done up in this knot of denotation (the *OED*'s definition, after "desist from," as "make an end with").[27] In this paradoxical salute to banished eloquence, his meaning is heard as a faintly archaic, strained, florid, and entirely appropriate high-toned turn. Freed up within the rich ambivalence of the English language, in the vitalizing interval between the two retrospective tenses of the phrase and the shift into the textually self-reflexive and sustaining present (I now make do with phrases to conclude), the space of verbal restoration and final triumph is widened into view. The phrases that have long served, yet recently seem to have failed the hero, rescued from within by word play itself, lend momentum to a defiance of death, of being too soon "done," that grows possible only through their agency and grace.

Early in the novel, Neville expresses his literary vocation to himself in these terms: "Now begins to rise in me the familiar rhythm; words that have lain dormant now lift, now toss their crests, and fall and rise, and fall and rise again. I am a poet, yes" (p. 82). So too Bernard in his last paragraph alive: "And in me too the wave rises" (p. 297). When Bernard utters his determination to charge oceanward against death the way Percival "galloped in India," we may also recall Neville's "words and words and words, how they gallop—how they lash their long manes and tails" (p. 83). The deathly last foray of Bernard's is constituted by a purely verbal "charge," gallop, or gambit—a figural "recharging" of the verbal self as a resurrection from autobiographic nonentity. His own language has been regaining its malleable finesse even as it laments what is lost. The verbal artist who has recently internalized the flux of the world's waves within the syllabic undulation of his own prose in portraying the communal "moment" in dissipation—the way gathered friends "as a wave breaks, burst asunder, surrendered" (p. 278), where there is a sundering and spread, a breaking and dilation within the assonant interval of the last two words themselves—this artist, facing death, is still making space for himself in speech. Bernard even flourishes near the end a harmonizing pun on "mane" for watery "main" (p. 267), which Woolf borrows from Byron.[28] In a single bonding syllable it captures the animal body of the organic world fused in death's intensity of perception with the nonliving universe of lashing waters.

Combining both the fatal accident on horseback of Percival and the rushing flight of Rhoda, knowing his own end in terms he has learned from others, pitting himself against eternity in a spirit of acceptance somewhere between fatalism and fervor, Bernard spins out the conceit of his heroic gallop against negation. It is as if he must mortally depart this world in order to answer his vexing question about the description of that world seen without self. His heroic charge against oblivion in the last sentence is followed by a blank space, and in turn by one last six-word section of italics, an idea that occurred to Woolf far along in the process of redrafting:

"I strike spurs into my horse. Against you will I fling myself, unvanquished and unyielding, O Death!"

The waves broke on the shore.

Bernard has wanted since early in the novel to hit upon "some perfect phrase that fits this very moment exactly" (p. 69). In any normal temporal sense, his problem is of course that the moment "this very moment" is said or inscribed in a demonstrative phrase, it has passed to "that." The only moment so fixable, as hinted in the etymological suggestion of "finished" in Bernard's "perfect," is the one to which no further time succeeds.

There is nonetheless a redemptive loophole—or call it a disclosed interval—here, a breathing space where in fact much of Beckett's and Nabokov's fiction stakes out its narrative territory. If "I" is a fiction whose very declaration is a distancing of self from the inscription that would embody it, then so is the equally conjectural personification in the apostrophe "O Death!"—every naming of death being in the same space, and for the same space of time, the secured deferral of its real advent. Noting how in the second draft the last phrases were jotted down as if in verse,

> & like him I will
> fling myself against you,
> unvanquished and unyielding
> O death

we see even more clearly in the third line's enjambment (itself a prosodic "yielding") how the detachment which loosens to ambiguity the compound phrase of undefeated force, "unvanquished and unyielding," is thus taken to describe in the moment of their mutual exclusion both "I" and its end, both self and the principle of its sure effacement. This sentence brings to compressed perfection Woolf's experiments with periodic syntax in the evocation of the death moment. Mutually invincible, however soon to be indivisible, Bernard and Death yield nothing to each other except recognition across that adjectival hedge and hinge. It is a salvation by (and within) a stylistic interval as timely and finely judged as any such rhetorical elision in the British novels we have had under investigation.

The cutting edge of this climax is certainly honed by the textual abutting of "I" against its death. If every saying is in grammatological terms a kind of slaying, then "O Death!" loses its sting in the very teeth of signification. Woolf thus anticipates and detoxifies the mortuary undertone—or here undertow—of the entire deconstructive critique. The last italicized sentence, *"The waves broke on the shore,"* hovers halfway between a symbol for Bernard's death and a synecdoche for the world that extends past him in space and also in time. In that hovering, that resistance and give, stretches the free space of verbal play, a tribute to the phrase maker even as it may exclude him or figure his end. It is the classic interval of the death scene coded both as typographical gap and referential ambiguity. In linguistic terms, the hinted, merely conceivable shift from the axis of contiguity to the axis of figuration, from the metonymical to the metaphorical sense of breaking waves,[29] might itself signal and inscribe the dying away from unmediated presence. Nevertheless, washing across the blanched space of silence in all their angled raggedness, these choppy italics are also the slanted text of continuance, at least of the world as text. The long-coveted "words of one syllable" at last provided, they turn self-consciously scriptive even in their own half-mimetic typography, tilted on the line, cursive, curled. With them, if not in them, death as closure is discovered to be nothing more or less or worse than the world suddenly without self, voiced in those omniscient, almost corporealized and autonomous italics into which the novelist's own phrases—Bernard's, Virginia's—seem to have been merged, subsumed. The world "seen without a self" is now recognized not only as the deathless reality of a universe recorded without percipient source in any personal consciousness but, in the other sense of "without," the seen world that lies inalienably outside the self, vast and forever.

Insofar as the death which the novelist is willing to encounter in the waves is one, like Rhoda's equally predictive and figural end, imaged as a drowning in primal waters, it is only so imaged by a countervailing fountain of new and fluent phrases welling from within—the epitome, indeed the apotheosis, of the man of words. Bernard has earlier asked rhetorically, "Should this be the end of the story? a kind of sigh? a last ripple of the wave? A trickle of water?" (p. 267). To make it otherwise he must tap, draw on, pump up to utterance that dormant verbal self, his essential being, that "lies deep, tideless, immune, now that he is dead, the man I called 'Bernard' " (p. 291). When he does so, as we have seen in the last paragraph, it is a wave as shimmering and flamboyant as any the sea can send forth to swamp it. When "in me too the wave rises" (p. 297), sweeping Bernard toward a further metaphor of chivalric incorporation, he adds, "It swells; it arches its back." Here is the curve, the very archness, of phrase when self-consciously inscribed, uppity, impulsive, and proud. As a way of gathering up in a last threnody and catharsis the three functions of death we have been concerned with from the first, we can hear in Bernard's last words the novelist's own self-epitomizing transposition of verbal essence into the cessation of one last splash. We hear it as the stylistic yield of his earlier ventures in the displacement of fatality by effigy and (trans)figuration. Even the world "without" him, to which he thus cedes, is there before us in his own saving play on the preposition.

Only Lawrence among the major writers we have studied tends to abstain from any explicit interest in the relation of death to textuality,[30] except as the latter finds its equivalent in a readable cadaver. As bright book of life,[31] the novel asks of death mostly that it throw further light on the contours of being by its contrasting shadows; the corpse rather than the elegiac text carries the burden of what remains. Most of the previous novelists since Dickens in the British tradition let their texts more openly claim kin with the work of death—not only its cathartic operations but its displacement of presence. Dickens follows out the implications of prose as an "embalming" in *Little Dorrit*, an extended exercise in epitaphic commemoration in *David Copperfield*, a dying glimpse of posthumous retelling in *A Tale of Two Cities*. The multiple narrative framework of *Wuthering Heights* allows for a sardonic travesty on the function of fiction as mortal containment and catharsis. Thackeray invokes an Orphic prototype for the ushering of his plot to the otherworld of finality. George Eliot's binding of inscribed biblical epitaph to carved epitaph is another way into the issue, or around it in the sense of its framing, as in Jude's capitulation to biblical precedent when in Hardy the existential is surrendered back to the textual. Conrad searches the moment of demise, that moment compacted to disclosure *in articulo mortis*, for those instants of seeing when the mortal turning point turns articulate, and then in *Nostromo*, with Decoud's inscribed record and the deaths it includes or anticipates, imagines death itself by analogy with the conversion of identity to text. Even Forster, among the major novelists before Lawrence the least preoccupied with metanarrative questions, still textualizes the elided funeral of Mrs. Wilcox as art, its participants inked into presence as the reader's stand-ins.

Bernard's summing up then retraces the shape of Woolf's fictional

career in this regard. A few years later in her own life, Woolf was
to inscribe—as indeed a reflexive inscription, textually conceived—
the kind of verbally rehearsed death scene Bernard lives through
again for Rhoda and for Percival, and Clarissa before them for Septimus. What Woolf records is war's very real terror frozen in a prose
of unflinching participation. In this remarkable passage from *A Writer's Diary* she spells out her gruesome conjectures about death by a
German bomb: "The crushing of my bone shade in on my very active
eye and brain: the process of putting out the light—painful? Yes.
Terrifying. I suppose so." Yet the moment of closure in this passage
of fantasy—as in the analogy fashioned from it for any death scene
as life's last sentence—breaks off with a typical metatextual irony,
fatality the ultimate ellipsis: "Then a swoon; a drain; two or three
gulps attempting consciousness—then dot dot dot."[32] The German
for "death" spelled backwards or not, those fading named signs of
finality as softened "period" give us the scriptive effigy of death
through a word play that relieves death's very anticipation. It is death
domesticated for the writer in and as a textual option.

Lawrence asks in *Women in Love* how anyone can settle for life
lived in such an aimless, uninflected way that it becomes like an
outmoded "picaresque novel" (p. 294). Woolf's experiments in consciousness eschew old forms of mental structuring for what can be
thought of as the text of a new subjective picaresque, streaming,
freeform, but avid for revelation. And her characters know this,
sensing a Conradian double bind. Bernard sums up the danger implicit in the relation of textuality to mortality: that the very search
for form in life makes flux too anxious for fixity, nudges the transient
toward the cumulative, the immutable, the moribund. Language comes
to encroach on felt engagement, record on experience, style on vitality. And so the pressure increases upon verbal articulation for a
mode of interior speech that will be true both to the phenomena
received by the mind and to the transformations of consciousness
they must undergo. Lawrence strove to simulate not so much the
mind's self-narrating language for its desire as the pulse of desire
itself. Any modernist sense of syllables and phrases articulating in
part their own dubious purchase on the world is burned away in the
heat of this mysterious approximation. Not so in Woolf's novels, for
in manipulating the "lava flow" of language (*The Waves*, p. 79) she

is well aware of its linguistic nature—and so of its remove from the warmth of original life.

Some of Woolf's major characters, alert in this way to the language that mediates their reception of the world, cannot keep their sense of loss or alienation from growing to crisis or from using the stream of artificial speech to float them away from the adamant muteness of the world. The death scene as linguistic scenario, the very scene of articulation, tests this extremity in either direction. The traditional strategies called up by Woolf for enacted and relayed, displaced and assimilated dying lend weight and revelation both to the ordeals of the main figures and to the role of language in enunciating the nuance, gloom, and promise of such mortal labor. Rachel finds her escape from life in the unfurled translucency of Milton's wavelike verse and ends up curled into herself in finished shape at the bottom of an imagined sea; her "silence" is then memorialized in a novel by that name gestating in the brain of her lover. Clarissa turns a terrible rumor into the mental text of death, interpreting within her own shuddering transliteration of it the "immortal Ode" to time it was meant to inscribe in blood; such a finite sequence of sacrifice, displacement, and private interpretation is all the while being rendered perpetual in a novel named for the elegist and exegete of that death. Rachel and Septimus, that is, both drown in those very depths of self upon which the risen Clarissa might still delight. Replicating the fall of Percival which she could not otherwise assimilate, so does Rhoda imagine her own drowning in the tideless, treacherous caves of her nature; this suffering in turn provides, in structural terms, that the surviving protagonist of the novel, an accomplished novelist this time, will have the courage to keep articulating himself until he can score "fin" or "finis" athwart the wasting waves of his own death. Early in the novel, as Bernard determines to "pass from the service for the man who was drowned" (p. 78), he adds in parenthesis, "I have a phrase for that." Language alone is still serving him at the end to mediate the confrontation with death, by water or otherwise, to provide another way to "pass" on, an alternate kind of passage.

Formal issues are by this point in the British novel so problematical as to become psychic crises—or is it the other way around? In Bernard's search for that word of "one syllable" to name the knowing convergence of self and its effacement, his implied heroic version of the biblical, then Thackerayan "Here am I"—tossed at the waves in that last ejaculation—turns back upon the asserted circumscription of its own speech act. It suggests that Bernard exists for and to himself, as always but no less so now, here in his present phrases: in the flash and waver, the mount, turn, and roll of his own words about the waves, about himself and the loss of being, about death, fins, and finalities. Summing up or otherwise, he can properly claim *"Adsum"* only in the border realm between speech and blankness, on the shore of his own willingness either to drown in otherness or summon it from within. The private wave that rises to meet its outer crash in Bernard's baroquely rhetorical death sentence rises through that novelist's own still-swelling will to speech. It is the wave that could not sustain Rachel, that folded and flattened itself within the waters of her withdrawal, the wave that remained always beyond Rhoda, which she could never address or internalize, only dash herself against in imagination. The novelizing impulse surviving her is that uprush of words which has by the miracle of willed speech enabled the hero to transubstantiate the waters of annihilation to his own still coursing blood. With the waves waiting at the ridged shoreline of their own italics, Bernard, done in by phrases yet still having done with them, goes to his fictional finis making even silence listen, dying in style.

Afterwords

Death Bequeathed

Death of Chatterton, by Henry Wallis
Courtesy The Tate Gallery, London

A Poet's death is, after all
A question of technique, a neat
Enjambment, a melodic fall.

VLADIMIR NABOKOV
Poems and Problems

And then somewhere in midspace other waves, other on-
slaughts, gather and break, whence I suppose the faint sound
of aerial surf that is my silence. Or else it is the sudden
storm, analogous to those outside, rising and drowning the
cries of the children, the dying, the lovers, so that in my innocence I say they cease, whereas in reality they never cease.

BECKETT, *Malone Dies*

And suddenly Pnin (was he dying?) found himself sliding
back into his own childhood. This sensation had the sharp-
ness of retrospective detail that is said to be the dramatic
privilege of drowning individuals . . . a phenomenon of suffocation that a veteran psychoanalyst, whose name escapes me,
has explained as being the subconsciously evoked shock of
one's baptism which causes an explosion of intervening recollections between the first immersion and the last. It all happened in a flash but there is no way of rendering it in less
than so many consecutive words.

NABOKOV, *Pnin*

A FTER THE "death of the novel"[1] and the deconstruction of its
fictive language, how does the human fact of death retain its
power in narrative art? Losing ground as subject, death tends to renew
itself as formal issue, modality of narration as much as motif. Formal
anxieties in Virginia Woolf's *The Waves* arrive at the point in British
fictional history where they not only intersect and clarify psychological
dilemmas but seem interchangeable with them. Postmodernism draws
much of its charge from this short-circuitry. In Beckett and Nabokov—those exemplary masters to whom we now turn after the previous
British lineage of this study—death thematizes itself as the means
to its own narrative end, the heretofore (if sometimes thinly) masked
fact about the verbal medium in which any death sentence or scene
must be couched. The expatriate stylists Beckett and Nabokov, writ-

ing their most important work in a language not natively their own, lend special force to any such linguistic disclosure; theirs are eccentric or displaced texts that may seem distanced at inception from their natural grammar and vocabulary, all enunciations as if dying away from original voice.[2] Since the rise and decline of the traditional novel, the phenomenon of death remains among the few fictional beneficiaries of a decentered vision. Death fills the power vacuum at the center by shifting emphasis from its formerly glimpsed function as sheer terminus to its role as the disclosed ground of all figuration, the void beneath every device. In this way death underwrites all utterance without becoming party to any new lease on presence which speech might wish to inscribe and secure.

To update Yeats, the postmodernist "center" that "cannot hold" results from a surrender, variously conditional in the novels of Beckett and Nabokov, of death's metaphysical bearings to its purely metatextual ones. The stylistic interval of the post-Romantic death sentence, Dickens's "untraversable distance" of temporal rupture, becomes in Beckett and Nabokov the very duration of all utterance *over* time— in both prepositional senses implicitly worried by Rhoda in *The Waves:* spread neutrally *across* time while also stretched self-consciously *above* its abyss. The threefold rhetorical functions of the death scene as bequeathed from Victorian fiction can consequently be seen as the interlocking mechanisms of textuality itself. In reviewing them we can watch them pursued by postmodernist prose to a rudimentary level, defining the ontology of writing as much as the psychology of dying. As the retrospective inscription of an imagined, never-present world in imaging words, the always elegiac work of traditional narrative is disclosed in its own right as a transposition into legible script; this very fact offers an epitome of the deathlike fixity of any text, providing in other words the displacement of temporal duration and fatality into the closed form of story. Factored down to the work of inscription itself, the three terms thus collapse upon each other. More indissolubly than ever before, thanatology is married to narratology, the postmodern novel engraving from cover to cover an oblique mourning for mimesis itself. From this union of death and narrative there issues for the novel as story the renewed birthright of a genre in exhaustion.

With death now the metanarrative scene par excellence, many

individual stories continue to localize and enact it by becoming in themselves manifest emblems of terminal form. In the novel's new hermetically closed circle, death remains the muse of metaphor. But what privileged figures retain or renew their utility? There is one in particular, the metaphor of drowning, in which this study has developed a special stake. Yet even by the time of *The Waves* there was nothing left to drown in but the same words with which one had ordinarily thought to keep afloat on the random flood of impressions. As a previously recurrent trope for the relation of self to nature, ego to externality in death, drowning becomes in postmodern fiction the surrender of the myth of articulate individuation to the bath of mute language, the virtual collapse of *parole* back to *langue*. Hence the formal reverberations—in the second epigraph to this chapter (*Pnin*, p. 21)—of Nabokov's lampoon about baptism telescoped with death in the compressed seconds of drowning; for it is indeed the "so many consecutive words" of fiction which lend to any retrospect (not just a mortal one) its verbal force. Dying in narrative must always open a stylistic interval with which to declare the end of time in the inevitably temporal medium of language; yet because narrative, unlike revelation, can never be simultaneous with event, as Woolf's Bernard had to learn, story may seem to lack precisely that immediacy of rendering which it seeks, to find itself always just a shade posthumous.

Certainly Beckett's first-person fiction reads like one long expiration of the drowning breath before sinking and asphyxiation in the "aerial surf" of silence, as Malone puts it in the epigraph to this chapter (*Malone Dies*, pp. 221–222). There the phrase "whence I suppose" is either elliptical for "from which comes," followed by an inserted statement of supposition, or else verbal conjecture is itself the agent of an only supposed "surf," traced in the undulations of scripted speech like Woolf's waves of utterance. The narrator's may be a breath transcribed as soon as it escapes, but never soon enough for the sign to be identical with the thing—to be, that is, identity. In Beckett's *Malone Dies*, ending in every sense "at sea," the narrator-hero holds out promise early on that he will have time to "frolic, ashore" (p. 193) in his phrases before the end, preserved from the "vast main" (p. 186) of effacement within that very flow of speech which will define his final Woolfian plunge. Only then could he contentedly "go down with" his "refuge" (p. 193), where that last noun seems an obsolete verbal composite of the "refuse" of his life and the storage hold of its collection. The jetsam of identity is rescued in a pun on its own safekeeping. That formally maintained balance between the fatal and the vital plunge of the moment in *Mrs. Dalloway* is in Beckett the purely linguistic balancing act, somewhere in "midspace," of vanishing voice over the gulf of silence. Even the invocation of death by water in this epigraph—"drowning the cries of the children"—is diluted to a mere figure of speech for the exclusion of all other voices but that of the narrator whose dead metaphor it is: a swamping of the heard world rather than a submergence in it.

At certain critical junctures in its English literary history the death scene tends to polarize its practitioners. Thackeray is to Dickens rather as Forster to Conrad: parodist of epiphany to elaborator of revelatory options even when they go unratified. Beckett stands in a comparable respect to Nabokov: grim satirist of the death scene to its revisionary ironist, colonist of closure to habitué of ambiguous thresholds as they become border states. What of course also unites these last two authors from their seemingly antipodal positions, besides their self-conscious transmutation of death into a function of form, is that they are each in the process tirelessly funny. For all the treacherous satiric tone attending the end of his villains, for instance, Dickens was deadly serious about the death scene, while Beckett and Nabokov, polar opposites in actual style, are its first notable comedians. The humor is brutal on the one hand, luminous on the other. Endlessly wrestled with in Beckett for the least shred of sense, death often seems necessitated in Nabokov as the voucher of aesthetic transcendence, an apparition of portent, a lightning flash from the realms of surprise. Late in the tradition, its solemnities worn bare, black comedy nonetheless prevails in both authors—a macabre gaiety, to paraphrase Yeats again, unabashedly transfiguring all that dread.

The sustained soliloquizing of *The Waves* was of course a considerable move toward the postmodern involution of all plot as fragile articulation, all character as evanescent trace rather than psychological trajectory. If Bernard were, at the end of *The Waves*, either too arthritic or too cynical to mount the steed of identity, to couch his spear and take heart from heroic precedent, to shout death down with style, then he might linger in his last disgruntled soliloquy forever, his biographical self long since dead of narrative inanition. We might then mistake him for Beckett's Malone dying. Yet if Bernard were to pick up a pen rather than a spear and write another novel, this time defying death's vulgar nagging with ethereal flourishes of wit, we might take him for a Nabokovian narrator. Beckett and Nabokov effect the ascendance of style over plot with an equal but opposite conviction, the one writer by default, the other by inventive vaunt, the one in cruel lieu of plot, the other in the name of the novel's renovation through sheer verbal will. With the glum humor of the moribund, acerbic, absurd, purposeful, Beckett appears on the fictional scene to throttle plot entirely in a stalled but insistent dying that foists off all action onto voice. It is left to Nabokov to administer unorthodox resuscitation to the novel as an admitted artifice of sheer style, all narrative the very fiction of a plot.

□ □ □

Appearing two decades after *The Waves*, and Woolf's vision there of the verbal self as its own biographer, was Beckett's postwar trilogy, *Molloy* (1955), *Malone Dies* (1956), on which this section will concentrate, and *The Unnamable* (1958). Taken together, these books ironically revise the ideal of developmental selfhood, and its attendant grammar of being, ironic leagues beyond the transfigurative rituals and restitutions of *The Rainbow* or *Orlando*. In Beckett the sequential heroes die repeatedly not to a new life but to a new phase of death. Metamorphosis becomes a sloughing off without inward refashioning, identity slowly molted without being remade. In his ailing book-length monologue, Malone might ask, with Robert Browning's Bishop at St. Praxed's, "dying by degrees" in that earlier dramatic monologue as an eccentric voice suspended somewhere between selfhood and effacement, "Do I live, am I dead?"

In a characteristic contortion of language, Beckett's Malone does indeed admit a "possibility" that "does not escape me, . . . and that is that I am dead already and that all continues more or less as when I was not" (p. 219). The purposefully awkward "that is that" of the explanatory clause obtrudes itself for a sly second as an idiom of finality rather than a formula of relative grammar. More startling yet is the debunking in the last four-word clause of the entire rhetoric of being in the English death scene. Climaxed in Woolf, with her

supple undulations between verbs of predication and attribution, es-
sences and characteristics, that mode is here sabotaged at its core.
The aura of "For there she was" in *Mrs. Dalloway* is nowhere to be
found in the vicious circular wit of "more or less as when I was not,"
half elliptical (for "was not dead"), half absolute negation of existence
(as in "was not and never had been"). If Bernard comes only at the
end of *The Waves* to feel that he is a man without a self, subject
without person, Malone seems to realize right from the start that he
is not so much a man as a denatured *manus* making its way across
the blank pages of a life with a pencil where a crutch should be.
Beckett's Malone dwells from the first in that referential Hades to
which Thackeray's characters and narrators are consigned only at the
end of *The Newcomes*—and for Malone it *is* hell, the excruciation of
a man without self taking down in longhand the drone of his own
soliloquies turning to obsequies.

A putative "I" closeted off somewhere in a squalid space as claus-
trophobic as the interior of his own brain, a man maimed but seedily
gallant, crippled but never bitter, takes notes all day and all night,
not that he knows the difference, on the random humiliations and
discomforts of his bedridden misery, all duly in view of the death his
limbs give promise of, what there is left of them. This is Malone.
This is the solo groan of the self as its own elegiac scribe. It is also
in embryo and in parody the deconstructed "scriptor" anatomized by
Roland Barthes in "The Death of the Author," a speaking voice "in
no way equipped with a being preceding or exceeding the writing,"
a voice "born simultaneously with the text" and so dying cotermi-
nously with it.[3] Malone becomes the very principle of postmodern
articulation, whose every "so there I am" (p. 235), referring inevitably
to the scribbled utterance just transpired, is the ultimate textual
reduction of any metaphysical *"Adsum."*

Beckett writes from France in the mid-fifties with a voice, about
voice, increasingly familiar to us in the French accent ever since.
He describes at one point the speech of Malone's alter ego, Lemuel,
whose "cries were of two kinds, those having no other cause than
moral anguish and those, similar in every respect, by means of which
he hoped to forestall same" (p. 267). Syllable by syllable, utterance
is a holding action against the void it is there to bewail. Earlier
Malone has admitted, "I did not want to write, but I had to resign

myself to it in the end" (p. 207). The idiom "in the end" does not just smile, it grimaces from that line, along with the etymological irony of (re)signed script. Traceable signs are a hedge against forgetting, privileged over speech in this way. "At first I did not write, I just said the thing. Then I forgot what I had said." Thus the narrator's writing "is in order to know where I have got to, where he has got to" (p. 207). The adverbial parallelism is actually apposition, for the "he" is at best one of the speaker's confected second selves, displaced into text as a third-person character in a manner reminiscent of the valedictory recessional that closes *The Newcomes*. It is this that Malone, dying, finally speaks forth when he stops in his tracks, or traces, for this metanotation: "But my notes have a curious tendency, as I realize at last, to annihilate all they purport to record" (p. 259). Conversely, then, here is the answer to a death that can be conquered simply by being so ceaselessly conjured, obliterated by iteration. Or put the other way round again. the postmodern narrative act, not only diverting the very terrors it would vest with expression but absenting all essence whatsoever by the mere act of reference, has no other subject but that immanent death it is linguistically equipped to tame only by naming.

If the ironies of modernism from Hardy and Conrad onward can be read at times as a repressed yearning for the spiritual sureties of a Victorian deathbed, then Beckett's fictions can be characterized by a sardonic nostalgia for the death scene itself as closural satisfaction. This vain craving takes the inverted form of a metaphysical send-up expelling from the confines of narrative all the familiar prescriptions for dramatized demise in literature. *Malone Dies* thus supplies us in retrospect with a handy compendium of the ploys and *topoi* of the classic death scene in the whole tradition we have been tracing. The narrator plays fast and lose with the idea of death as an absolute in the very first sentence, the mortally mincing "quite" a preposterous adverbial modification: "I shall soon be quite dead at last in spite of all" (p. 179). Later he repeats this notion with a further illogical nudge: "Soon, I shall be quite dead at last, and so on" (p. 209). Some idioms simply perjure themselves in such a context. Back on that first page we find an additional phrasal parody of fiction's ordinary formulas of life, death, and judgment: "Indeed I would not put it past me to pant on to the Transfiguration, not to speak of the Assumption."

In this context of Christian entelechy, the idiom "put it past me" is trying to put one over on us, with the logical as well as doctrinal "assumption" of further life ruled out. The parading and then betraying of both verbal and narrative expectations continues in this same first paragraph: "Yes, I shall be natural at last, I shall suffer more, then less, without drawing any conclusions." Death is "natural" to the species, yet in Beckett there is no illuminating teleology leading us to an end that lends clarity to an individual life. Striking down the whole tradition of epitomizing death, the only "conclusion" drawn is the one the deceased is drawn *to* in the single sense of an end.

As the speaker's last splutters of salvaged vitality, such word play mocks the formulas of death and orthodox spirituality even as it invokes their urgency. Redundancy, paradox, figures fallen into disuse—these are the playthings of decease when all other pleasures are denied, populating the vacuum left by a vanishing plot. In *Malone Dies*, for instance, the narrator interrupts a particularly uncompelling deathbed anecdote about the Lamberts with this self-chastising comment about his own maunderings: "Mortal tedium" (p. 217). With Dickens's Lady Dedlock he might complain that he is "bored to death." Language, by being a piece with death at the referential level, an evanescent ghost of presence, is matched at the figurative level by a post-Joycean addiction to metaphors and formulaic phrases neither entirely dead nor confidently alive.[4] There is this, for instance: "Scrupulous to the last, finical to a fault, that's Malone, all over" (p. 233). It amounts to a parody of mortal epitome at the idiomatic level that a vernacular equivalent for an expression like "in a nutshell" should be synonymous with the phrase for completion: that's Malone, in other words, through and through. One begins to suspect a consistent drift to this verbal flippancy, pointing toward a new, mutant rhetoric of death. The one italicized sentence in the novel, highlighted beyond all the rest as self-conscious verbal construct, is introduced as follows: "I know those little phrases that seem so innocuous and, once you let them in, pollute the whole of speech. *Nothing is more real than nothing*. They rise up out of the pit and know no rest until they drag you down into its dark" (p. 192). This is the grammar of the abyss, as anticipated by Forster and Woolf, where noun of void yawns in the very jaws of pronominal negation. Yet word play itself can shortly somersault to contentment along the reverse face of this very trick of diction, in a turn of phrase about the end of all phrase: "Then that silence of which, knowing what I know, I shall merely say that there is nothing, how shall I merely say, nothing negative about it" (p. 221).

Describing his climactic fantasy of a feet-first birth into death from the womb of time, as if to image a numbness rising from his lower extremities to his brain, Malone is sure that his head will be the last thing free, cranium and consciousness together. "That is the end of me" (p. 282), the mortal extremity as it were. Beckett seems in this way to have returned to the rhetorical motives of the traditional death scene for a sustained inversion of its purposes. The punning appropriate to mortal ambiguities, the ambivalent interval of death bridged by a single spread of designation, has turned inside out to become the funereal tenor of all metaphor. The least corner gets lifted on the fabric of idiom in Beckett's black-comic masque of verbal ambiguities, and the skull grins beneath. If in earlier writers the pun comes naturally to the death scene, in Beckett death comes mordantly to almost every pun, undergirding the linguistic tissue of narrative with the reductive skeleton of finality.

The stylistic aura of the death scene, its straddling ambiguities, its elided idioms, its inherent doubling of vision now imbues an entire text with funereal duplicities. The flight from obdurate temporality is made by Malone in his repeated punning fondness for "pasttimes." He not only harbors a sense of himself as a being in extremis but, with a paradoxical stretching of the superlative as if to a farther reach of crisis, he comforts his last hours by thinking that "rectifications in extremis, in extremissimis, are always possible after all" (p. 251), where "after all" appropriately locates his hope in a destination beyond the temporal gist of its idiom. Yet mostly he knows better. Describing what rigor mortis does to our "mortal remains," he manipulates a terminal pun less heartily, noting how the blood is drained from us "in the long run" (p. 223). Asking about the reputed "death rattle" to which he is looking forward, he suspects in a related graveyard pun from the dead language Latin, buried in the present French idiom, that "perhaps it is not de rigueur after all" (p. 249). Twenty more pages along in this relentless dying, he is still congratulating himself on his narrative progress: "That's the idea, rattle on" (p. 268). Our sense that the whole book-long enunciation is a continuous death rattle is only brought to direct point by such word play, the notion being implicit everywhere else. The thought that "perhaps I'm going" at last is even called at one dour turn, by euphemistic redundancy, a "passing weakness" (p. 252).

Beneath the vernacular skein of punning phrase there is, however, a deeper structuring yet of narrative by death which a book by the name of *Malone Dies* is bent on demonstrating. This can be illustrated by a single suggestive coinage, "defunge," working in tandem with the mortuary punning. Such a verb is an assault by and against language to which at least one critic has taken objection.[5] Yet what must be noted about this coinage is the temporal implications of its perpetual entrapment between frittered past and the unmaterialized future, in its own right a psychic more than a verbal barbarism: "But let us leave these morbid matters and get on with that of my demise . . . unless it goes on beyond the grave. But sufficient unto the day, let us first *defunge*, then we'll see" (p. 236, my italics). It is a dreary "day" he takes perverse delight elsewhere in calling "the livelong day" (p. 220), with an idiomatic hint of its lifelong ordeal. In that etymological dovetailing of "defunge," then, we have the novel's central paradox packed into a single baroque invention. The portmanteau collapse of "defunct," in all its past-participial finality, upon the transitive echo of "expunge," made passive of course by the drained vitality of context, does necessary violence to the language in order to name the terrible innovation of Beckett's plot, prolonging as it does the instant of demise to an interminable torpor. It is a tedium alleviated only by the kind of verbal play that here designates it, all speech in *Malone Dies* a bereavement over the very void it tries to fill.

This is by no means in Beckett to take facile comfort from some existential certainty about death as congenital, abiding, encased in us and our speech as the seed of our eventuation. Rather, Beckett's work is a rigorously witty recoil from such philosophical relaxation into death. Not just a premise to rest on but a feat to achieve, the personalized and authentic death in Beckett is an even more heroic endeavor than some branches of existentialism would suggest. The black and rankling jokes of Malone's word play serve this metaphysical turn not only by never letting death's metaphors die peacefully but by tinging all language with hues of the tomb. Demise of course permeates being as it does meaning, waiting both here in space, inside me, as well as there in time, somewhere, sooner or later, patient, ineluctable. To recall that Shelley said as much a century before Sartre, in the first stanza of his poem "Death," is only to return this study to its point of origin in those radical definitions of death incident to Romantic agnosticism. Shelley's rhyme itself serves to universalize a death echoing through the world of organic phenomena. "Death is here and death is there / Death is busy everywhere," he writes, and in a burst of prepositional dispersion, "All around, within, beneath, / Above is death—and *we are death*." Beyond this acknowledged ubiquity, and even beyond the local play in Beckett with puns and metaphors of death, it is the whole act of novelizing the encounter with death that provides a formal parable of the novel's own attitude toward that dying. The paradox of death for Beckett, at once inner and outer, here and coming, inherent and unarrived, is at last and at large the paradox of narrative art as spatialized temporality. Story, a shape as well as a duration, is present to us as a defined whole even as it moves, or we through it, toward the completion of itself as form. A book is all there before us at once even when taken a sentence at a time, just as death is no more ours when it is over with than when it is on its way. Like death, therefore, narrative structure is a determinate shape as well as a determined labor toward it. In this same way death stands to life not only as a contrary fact but also as an unfolding and an integral finishing. Such, then, is the formal equivalent for *Malone Dies*, as a novel, of that manifold view of death articulated within it. Beckett more than any British novelist before him espouses the intimate bond between prose and corpse, for fiction is to its raw materials as death to life, variously and at once a presence, a process, and a product.

To isolate death as the third of these, to contain it as closed subject within the formal limits of story, Malone the narrator must turn death's plot into the narrative of someone other than himself. He thus invents a series of fictional doubles in his vacuum of real community and propels them through a virtual drowning retrospect of his own life in parable, with names changed to extenuate the blame of the defenseless. The first double is, halfway through the novel, transformed into the second, and the cast thickens near the end, when the primary narrator seems intent on killing off these projections for his own edification, the deflection of his own fatality. The two most important of the narrated alter egos—the one metamorphosing into the other, at midpoint, as if dying away into his future self—are the strategically named Sapo and Macmann. Widely recognized as a derogatory verbal condensation of *Homo sapiens* and a familial code for "son of man" respectively—word play substituting for, or generating, character as well as plot—these cryptic nicknames also reflect on their author, Malone. His name thereby emerges, one may speculate, as a contraction of "I'm alone" in which the "I" has been squeezed out along with the verb of being under the numbing pressure of demise. "On the threshold of being no more I succeed in being another" (p. 194), Malone congratulates himself, with the pun on a willed succession as well as a success. Along with Conrad's portal of latent revelation, Malone's "threshold" reminds us again of the receding linear bar in Thackeray's conversion of speaking presence to the sequential avatars of its narration.

A curious anticipation of such storytelling as a reflexive ratification of the narrating self occurs in Ford Madox Ford's *The Good Soldier* (1915). With an unwitting double-entendre that witnesses a Malone-like collapse of biology into biography, Ford's narrator, Dowell, says of his doomed characters, not only as erstwhile comrades but as counters in his own struggle for retrospective coherence, "It is so difficult to keep all these people going" (p. 222), moving against torpor, that is, toward their several deaths and suicides. Yet he must keep it and them up, partly because, as he confesses earlier, "we all so need from the outside the assurance of our own worthiness to exist" (p. 115). In that limp periodic phrasing, the clinging infinitive at the end not only depends grammatically upon "worthiness" but also implies an elliptical "in order," which makes existence itself conditional upon the whole preceding grammar. Ford's narrator, for one, desperately needs his very right to exist mirrored and confirmed in others, even if only in the characters about whom he writes. As in Woolf and Beckett later, the least turn of suspensive grammar in such a context can open utterance to its own abyss.

The postmodernist Malone, concerned less with validating than

with ending his life, finally personifies a bitter, violent side of himself
in the bloodthirsty Lemuel, a suicidal deputy commissioned to kill
off Malone's other narrated alter egos. By providing something (someone) entirely external as the agent of a death entirely other, and by
plotting to act this out at a desperate pitch of butchery, Malone
appears to exorcise that mortal anxiety which haunts him from the
start. Malone forges other selves so as to become the author, not just
the victim, of his own effacement. If he can utter it, maybe he can
suffer it without inordinate pain. Perhaps if he is able to write about
his own death so near at hand, in the person of Macmann, say, he
will even miraculously have outlived that death. "My story ended I'll
be living yet. Promising lag" (p. 283). The promise of this lag,
however, does not seem at first glance to be borne out by the end of
Malone Dies, which trails off in grammarless and dangling shards,
as if the named narrator, and also the book named for his death, is
expiring as his pencil slows to a halt.

Disappointed earlier with the rhythms of his narration, Malone
berates himself, "I have missed the ebb" (p. 253). To prevent this
at the end, he turns the metaphor literal and has his subsidiary cast
set sail on a frail bark toward an inhospitable island and then brings
them back at his whim, according to the erratic tides of his inner
desire. "Gurgles of outflow" (p. 287), we hear said of the track of
the boat through the water, connoting also the garbled utterance, a
virtual death rattle, that serves to impel Malone's craft, as it were,
toward a quite literal turning point in the piloting of plot. Lemuel
seems about to slaughter Macmann with his hatchet when the violence
of this invention fails Malone. It is as if he would release his created
counterparts to their own living autonomy on his deathbed in order
to double his chances for that "promising lag." Perhaps they, who
are only Malone in mask, might outlast him whose time is up, rather
than he them. Instead of the mutilation of Macmann, Malone's
own continuity as narrative voice is itself hacked to fragments. Lemuel is ordered, or at least declared, to do no more violence, no more
hitting

with it [his hatchet] or with his hammer or with his stick or with
his fist or in thought in dream I mean never he will never

or with his pencil or with his stick or
or light light I mean
never there he will never
never anything
there
any more (p. 288)

Aimless locatives and severed negatives win out over the grammar
of being in this "defunging" of copulative predication itself. It is
straight to the point that Lemuel's weaponry, evoked by those hacking
iterations—both chopping and coughed out—includes in its arsenal
the same pencil by which this violence has all along been made to
seem textually pending and is now forever suspended in a final negation of everything: never will he or anything (be) there any more.
It is a prophetic fact so final that the very verb of being seems
redundant and, to Malone's fading mind, unrecoverable, in any of
the blurted clauses it might serve to complete. We are indeed a far
cry, a deranged *cri de coeur*, from the celebratory verb of being that
threads its incarnating way through the pages of *Mrs. Dalloway* down
to its last invulnerable declaration, "For there she was." Beckett once
said that by the end of his trilogy "there's complete disintegration.
No 'I,' no 'have,' no 'being.' "[6] Indeed, for many of its final pages
The Unnamable, sequel to *Malone Dies*, is one long paratactic death
sentence. At one point in the preceding volume too, Malone's dozing
off predicts not only this final disintegration but also the deathly loss
of consciousness imparted by the syntactic fracturings and evacuated
predications in the last pages of his novel. Simple sleep is there
described as a fainting away from presence when "subject falls far
from the verb and the object lands somewhere in the void" (p. 234).
This might be a perfect linguistic exegesis of Decoud's death moment
in *Nostromo*, "They looked—," but is in context a more subversive
undoing of narrative itself. The dwindling voice's "never anything
there any more" at the end is just such a falling away of all verbs
and a complete voiding of their possible objects. Among the corpses
of those alter egos who have lent Malone surrogate presence, never
will there be anything there that has "being" any more, or that stands
in need of its locutions. It is the rhetoric of fiat in effacement.
   There is nonetheless a catch, a narratological loophole or, as Ma-

lone has phrased it, a "promising lag," and it becomes Beckett's equivalent of the sometimes redemptive, sometimes merely terminal interval so frequently revealed in the style of the fictional death scene. The autobiographic paradox of a first-person death scene running down to the instant of closure is opened up as a narrative possibility deep within that pun on the subjective versus objective genitive in "My story ended I'll be living yet": the storytelling that requires "me" as signifying subject or the story that takes "me" as signified object, the story by me or of me. Malone discoursing on the deaths of himselves, so to speak, in Sapo become Macmann is this doubleness returned toward unity. The interval is there just in time, but not in real time, only in the spatialized temporality of the fiction as a construct of deferral or displacement. Better to think of the term "lag" in its spatial rather than its temporal sense, gap more than lapse. It can stand for the ontological "distance" between voiced self and its conversion to trace rather than a split second's reprieve from void. It is useful, in other words, to sense the probable etymological source of "lag" in *lack*, becoming that interval of absence which is the space of inscription in any representation of the self's own life or death— even when the textual crisis is as extreme as it seems here. For at the narrative level, Beckett's novel is not a book *about* Malone's death, but a text that *is*, that constitutes, both by title and content, the proposition *Malone Dies*. The very text, dropping off at the end, seems to drop dead as we read, without such an italicized and ontologically independent sentence as *"The waves broke on the shore."* At the end of *Malone Dies*, Lemuel and the others left at sea, there are never any waves anymore either. After over two centuries of experiment in the fictional death scene, this is the unprecedented death of an entire novel.

A later version of this climactic episode brings the narrator himself to his own watery death in Beckett's story "The End" (or "La Fin").[7] Embarked in a small craft like a coffin in a parody of all those Romantic settings-out on the seas of eternity, borne darkly but not afar, dragged soon and fearfully to death, the narrator turns this story into a study in closure itself—as suggested blatantly enough by its title. The drowning not only provides the plot's last move but frames there in metanarrative fashion the whole notion of terminal retrospect. On the way to this fate the narrator describes his lapsing from physical

containment into the wash of waters with an ambivalent and discon-
certing syntactic interval that serves to mark the beginning of his
death: "I too, when I moved, felt less boat than wave, or so it seemed
to me" (p. 69). In this main clause of feeling, objective and subjective
registers, palpability and fantasy, seem to merge in a grammar wavering between predicate object and predicate nominative—felt more
of as well as more *like* the wave: either Malone's registration of these
waters as sheer otherness or his linking identification with them. It
is within just this interval of lapsing out from contained self to external
phenomena that dying is not only begun but defined. It has been said
before in a more hopeful way: in the destructive element immerse,
where that element is the very medium of being.

In *The Unnamable*, with a textual play on the "coma" of oblivion,
the narrator knows his fate as a disappearance somewhere between
his own words, when "the comma will come where I'll drown for good,
then the silence" (p. 409)—punctuation as final rupture. The drowning in "The End" begins when, after the narrator has "drifted with
the currents and the tides" awhile longer, he quite literally pulls out
the plug of his sinking craft and so of his life. Instead of the fatal
waters, he swallows a "calmative." At once, "the sea, the sky, the
mountains and the islands closed in and crushed me in a mighty
systole, then scattered to the uttermost confines of space" (p. 72).
Completing the pattern of previous externalizations, the metaphor of
a fading heartbeat is transferred to render the contractions of the
outer world in this penultimate moment of drowning consciousness.
One more sentence and the narrative has reached "The End" with a
vaporous reprise of all the "mighty never": "The memory came faint
and cold of the story I might have told, a story in the likeness of my
life, I mean without the courage to end or the strength to go on." The
subjunctive "might" opens the interval between enervation and brave
closure, trapped within which the vanishing plot fades to its own
receding "likeness." The retrospective compression of the drowning
victim, what Bergson and Poulet after him discuss as the "panoramic
vision of the dying," is all but explicitly analogized by Beckett to the
narrative act—but as a story here twice deferred, life at two removes
from itself. The speaker's is a latent story which might have been
told but is instead feebly recalled in its merely conjectural status as
a lost opportunity. The exhausted rhetorical and structural devices

of the consequential death scene, even at the metanarrative level, could hardly be more thoroughly laid to waste—and to rest. Worse than Bernard feared in *The Waves*, this is the ultimate "Fin" in a waste of waters.

□   □   □

From the suffering rut of Malone's monologue we return in the novels of Vladimir Nabokov to that ultimately metanarrative formula evinced by George Eliot in *The Mill on the Floss* for "the transition of death, without its agony." Beckett's heroes are trapped in a travail without freeing traversal. Nabokov's meet death as an epiphany liberated from pain, a transition which connects across its own threshold to revelatory trespass and textual transfiguration. The momentary balance which Terence, Clarissa, and Bernard—for, and so with, the reader—are able to secure by displacement or phrasal daring in the closural moments of Woolf's fictions, without quite the final toll of fatality, is comparable to what several of Nabokov's heroes achieve at the point of coincidence between their own deaths and the close of the text that has engendered only to elegize them.

In his penultimate novel, *Transparent Things* (1972), Nabokov puts into the words of a mental patient a notion Nabokov himself shares with Beckett. This is his understanding of the widespread mistake in thinking that the question of "survival after death," once settled, would go far toward solving "the riddle of Being. Alas, the two problems do not necessarily overlap or blend" (p. 93). Nabokov repeatedly courts the "blended" moment in rhetoric only to expose its metaphysical elusiveness. His is a style of elision and overlap exempt from the pressure of explanation, a hymn to the mystery of the textual intervals it enacts. Ending the first verse line with a nagging idiom straight out of Beckett, Nabokov elsewhere writes, "A Poet's death is, after all / A question of technique, a neat / Enjambment, a melodic fall."[8] The assonant "neat" is slanted off from an internal near rhyme with "-nique" toward the neatly timed run-on, and eased from there into the cannily unsaid "dying cadence" for "melodic fall." Existential death seems at times in Nabokov not only a dead but a decomposed metaphor in the stylistics of closure.

The comparably prominent relation between textuality and mortality in Beckett and Nabokov turns out in many ways to be contrastive, measuring their divergence on the postmodernist spectrum. Death in Beckett lays claim to its full viciousness and intimidation, however much palliated by word play and gentled in the event by equivocation. In Nabokov style tends to elide death into mere figure, all terminus merely a transposition of terms. Beckett channels his obsession with death as absence and negation so as to deconstruct progressively the whole play of signification that shapes the referential gestures of narrative. Nabokov never stops this play and this playing; the fantasy of presence incarnated by text is no sooner seen through than put back into play as heuristic illusion. Where Beckett succumbs to the textual status of the narrative endeavor, Nabokov summons the specter of exclusive textuality only to model all narratology on some new verbal cosmology. With Beckett deploying the full range of verbal effects at his disposal to approximate the intractable fact of death, we find Nabokov's style contriving to talk its way out (the other side) of dying. A single instance might help elucidate the difference between them. The closed rectangle of the fictional page is only intermittently projected by Beckett as a three-dimensional world, and at that only as the cramped world of a single book's dimensions. He has his hero Malone decline toward death at the voided center of a space defined by "these eight, no, six, these six planes that enclose me" (*Malone Dies*, p. 221). They are, among other things, the six sides of the narrative volume that describes them, a geometrical containment that gradually erodes as its sustaining consciousness breaks down. By contrast, Nabokov closes *Transparent Things* by imagining death's "ultimate vision" centered on a kindred but distinct geometry, the three-dimensional "incandescence of a book or box"— read: its capacity for illumination—"grown completely transparent and hollow" (p. 104). It is a transparent coffin perhaps, but also the shape of fiction itself. The barely habitable cell of signifiers which Beckett manufactures and then dismantles burns to become in Nabokov a space lit from within and delimited by magic margins, invisible limits.

If in Nabokov a poet's death is only "a neat / enjambment," let us turn to the death of a poet's own issue, his daughter rather than his poetry. Such a death, by drowning, occurs at the exact enjambed midpoint of the poem called "Pale Fire" at the heart of the novel by that name, a poem which is a long meditation on the death that centers it: "A blurry shape stepped off the reedy bank / Into a crackly, gulping swamp, and sank" (ll. 499–500). The metrics step off their own tread across the run-on at the pivotal turn of the entire poem, proceeding then to the dying cadence of the final rhyme, "and sank," with any further momentum toward chaos or void belied by the orderly heroic couplet. The human victim is relegated to a "shape," the swamp personified as "gulping," yet the fine tuning of the whole transition betrays a stylistic finesse at odds with the blank event. Drowning as a yielding of identity to materiality, a swallowing of self by the impersonal, is carried by the metaphors of the passage without being transported to new meaning by them. The rather amorphously defined daughter of the great poet, Haze(l) to his Shade, is in a sense epitomized as a "blurry shape" in death. Yet the interest of the passage rests not with the metaphysics of drowning it might evoke but with the verbal transition, the multiple enjambment as it were, through which the human story achieves its displacement into pure style. In this sense the couplet is a microcosm for the whole textual allegory of death in *Pale Fire*, as in Nabokov's fiction both before and after it.

Death, Nabokov closes *Bend Sinister* (1947) by saying, is "but a question of style . . . a question of rhythm" (p. 241). He then glosses as well as enlarges the thought in his 1963 preface, insisting that "death is but a question of style, a mere literary device, a musical resolution" (pp. xii–xiii). Such a claim could stand as motto for this book, especially when Nabokov's point is seen not to rarefy so much as clarify death as a novelist's challenge. Less the aestheticizing sidestep than it at first appears, Nabokov's remark would acknowledge that inevitable stylizing of death whose consideration began these chapters. Death again stands forth as that absolutely elusive narrative moment which, all words and no action, is always lettered rather than lived, a figure or specter of sheer speech—always, that is, less evidenced in words than "devised" creatively by them. Later in *Pale Fire*, between the drowning of his daughter and his own death in midrhyme, falls the poet's near encounter with death after a heart attack. Again enjambment manages to bridge the interval it cannot wholly portray: "I did know that I had crossed / The border" (ll. 699–700). Meter itself becomes the measure of eternity. At one level of generality this is the familiar myth of immortality through art. But this is not a level at which the novel *Pale Fire* has much abstract business. It is rather within the syntax and prosody, the lexical pliability and high varnish of style itself that the trangressed limit of temporality takes its definition. Style in Beckett, enfeebled to a lone cry as the whole bottom drops out of the novel as genre, falls through in Nabokov to a wilder freedom yet, autonomous and autotelic in an opportunism of pure beauty. His rhetoric abdicates from the reality it then refabricates, and death becomes a touchstone of strange centrality. Since mimesis has always bowed at death to the freely imagined, the death moment becomes more than ever before paradigmatic. It is an instant of undeniable fictive will. Yet if death is only a "question of style," what about life? Such a rhetorical question, animated by the lambent play of his language, is the extravagant gambit that valorizes the maze and dazzle of Nabokov's fictions. Though not always the focal subject, death remains the vantage of all such stylistic elaborations.

This was true from early in Nabokov's career, long before *Pale Fire* or his later novel *Transparent Things*. We may begin by looking at *The Real Life of Sebastian Knight* (1941), appearing only a decade after *The Waves*. The title figure is a famous novelist, recently deceased, whose last novel is described in minute detail by the narrator as the Beckett-like death scene of a text itself. As with Beckett's glamorless and vulgarized version of the Woolfian stream of consciousness in "gurgles of outflow," nominally describing the sea which threatens to reclaim his characters, so in *Sebastian Knight* it is the welter, surge, and abatement of prose in its own right that becomes the medium of finality. The novel is "itself . . . heaving and dying" along with the hero, who is "sinking throughout the book . . . now rolling up this image, now that, letting it ride in the wind, or even tossing it out on the shore, where it seems to move and live for a minute on its own and presently is drawn back again by grey seas where it sinks or is strangely transfigured" (p. 175). The unulant conjunctive grammar of this sentence eddies, even in the retelling, with its own congruence between subject and descriptive mode.

Beyond the metaphors associated with this death as a wavering delineation at the "shore of consciousness" (p. 175), the rhythms of build and dip also attach specifically to "the swell and fall of uneven breathing," and in turn to the breath of utterance in the contours of its own inscription. But psychological mimesis is still firmly in office. The dying man comes to realize what the deathbed tradition in literature might have taught him: how interval and rehearsal rather than prophetic vision delimit the capacities for representation at death. He knows "that only one half of the notion of death can be said really to exist: *this* side of the question, the wrench, the parting, the quay of life gently moving away . . . the beach receding" (p. 177). It is from within this interval of withdrawal that revelation, such as it is, must unfold. Only by "an incredible feat of suggestive wording" can the author infer without referential directness "that he knows the truth about death and that he is going to tell it" (p. 178). Since this can only be the truth about life seen from the point of view of finality, it amounts to the textualization of the world as a suddenly legible narrative. Prose style becomes the very model of order and cogency. The world's topography is now like "the page in a book where these mountains and forests, and fields, and rivers are disposed in such a way as to form a coherent sentence: the vowel of a lake fusing with the consonant of a sibilant slope" (pp. 178–179). The last is a self-exampling sibilance followed by the alliteration and assonance of another case in point: "the windings of a road writing its message in a round hand, as clear as that of one's father" (pp. 178–179), an original and authorizing speech. Here is the exaggerated legibility of the given.[9] Death in fiction, as well as the death of fiction in the sense of its closure, is the stuff of elusive artifice converted to revelatory pattern.

As in most novels, so in *Sebastian Knight* the revelation is entirely retrospective, addressing this side of last things. It italicizes the texture of life at the verge of unconsciousness. What Nabokov sets about to suggest later in his career is that the very discovery of pattern within the process of life's story or text is the uncovering not of life's truth in the act of death but of death's finality in the work of a summarized life. Every "coherent sentence" thus seems gathered from flux into an orderly death sentence of a sort. *Pale Fire* not only suggests this but allegorizes it at every level of its manifold fantasy. When the waters into which Hazel's figure vanishes, in the interval of enjambment, are given their true geographical coordinates, they do not provide a mappable path of meaning rendered legible at death so much as a linguistic parable of death itself as the gaping interstices of language. As if she emerges out of one of Rhoda's nightmares in *The Waves*, the introverted and neurotic Hazel Shade takes her life in an icy lake (or lacuna) between "Exe and Wye" (l. 490), between two consecutive letters of a punning alphabet where there is no scriptive footing, only void. Rhoda too, we recall, feared those same "white spaces" where Derrida perceives annihilation in the gap(e) between all letters, death a manifested function of difference.

Charted as if the lay of reality's land were merely the surface of a poem, Hazel's ironically textualized death is thus a linguistic counterpart to the stalking of her father by the assassin, Gradus, until the last line of Shade's fatally truncated poem. Devious incarnation of the gradual, this personification of fatality in the name Gradus seems to lurk between letters, words, and lines, which is not to say in the absence of text but within the scriptive differentiations from absence that make text possible. The annihiliating Gradus thus makes his way "through the entire length of the poem, following the road of its rhythm, riding past in a rhyme," even "hiding between two words" and "breathing with the caesura" (p. 78) as an aspect of cancellation en route rather than merely *ad quem*.[10] "Steadily marching nearer in iambic motion" on the "escalator of the pentameter," Gradus is seen "stepping off" in a double sense—both marking and departing—the metrical unit into the next line's "new train of thought." He is secreted there within the pun on "train" as vehicle, gaining on whatever final word will double for the onset of silence.

The formal allegory of *Pale Fire* has to do with the way it dramatizes the inherence of death in writing itself, drives death out of hiding into a visible condition of all textuality. For a sense of this we need to stand back and consider the organizing structure of the book's self-embedding nest of texts. Nabokov's novel, so-called, once introduced to us through a foreword by Charles Kinbote, emigré pedant from a mythical European state of mind called Zembla, is then primarily composed of an unfinished poem in four cantos, one line short of its five hundred rhyming couplets, by American poet John Shade, followed by Kinbote's extensive, testy, and fanatical annotations. But this is only as it seems. Between the lines of poem and prose we begin to perceive that Charles Kinbote, who fancies himself the exiled King Charles of Zembla—as we are always exiled from the glories of our daydreams—may be in fractured fact the mad Professor Botkin, colleague of Shade's at Wordsmith College and editor of his post-humous verses. If we can suppose with many critics, indeed the majority, that Shade has invented the character of Kinbote to explicate his own poem for him, we should also be able just as readily to imagine Kinbote as a maestro of prose puzzles who has projected himself into the persona of a doomed poet in an ingrown game of mouse and cat. [11]

The latter role is closer, for one thing, to Nabokov's in writing the book, at least as close as the two names, Kinbote and Nabokov, approach to anagram. Kinbote emerges from such a recognition as a feverish fabulator who has devised his alter ego's accidental assassination so as to give irrevocable finality to his (their) text. Shade (as *his* name would adumbrate) is devised simply to be annihilated, a subhuman assassin's bullet taking him forever beyond Kinbote's reach: "I felt—I still feel—John's hand fumbling at mine, seeking my fingertips, finding them, only to abandon them at once as if passing to me, in a sublime relay race, the baton of life" (p. 294). Akin to Malone's pencil, the imagined baton is ultimately the pen of art which has given Shade what life he has in the first place. It is the penned art of the poem itself, putatively by Shade, as well as of the appended and deviously preemptive endnotes by Kinbote. Every character seeks his or her continued life at the "fingertips" of the author, which might suggest, of course, Kinbote's receiving not just better expression but life itself from Shade, rather than the other way around. Yet, conversely, every maker of texts may feel the artist he knows he has in him fumbling at his fingertips to get free, to become immortal—and so to give himself over in turn, as Thackeray has hinted, to the holding hand of the reader. As Kinbote says in the final sentence of his foreword, again recalling the editorial parable at the end of *The Newcomes*, "For better or worse, it is the commentator who has the last word" (p. 29). In a later "stage play" which Kinbote has in mind to create out of this death scene, the poet hero will perish in the "line of fire" (p. 301) between two lunatics, returning us by another pun to the death lurking from line to line, just waiting to be dramatized, in the present state and status of the text.

To tell of his Zemblan adventures of power and dispossession, otherwise understood as his wildest dreams, Kinbote creates Shade as a poetic offshoot who should be able to transmute them to beauty, but who does so only by fitful glimpses here and there in a poetic text otherwise engaged. A novel, Nabokov suggests, is not just prose compared to poetry but some coalition, some composite form, that goes forward both at the pace of narrative and with the charge of poetic symbol. By the defiantly hybrid shape of the book bound under the title *Pale Fire*—half elegant verse, half prose gloss, to be read interchangeably as per instructions, the one after and in the light of the other—Nabokov's creation, though seemingly not a novel at all, announces itself as both the quintessence of the genre and an exegesis upon it. Bringing the rhapsodic and the prosaic into commentary on each other, the beautiful and the mimetically dutiful (however deranged the latter's "reality"), *Pale Fire* becomes in essence every great novel's transparent imposition of verbal harmony upon the frustrations of identity, song upon quest for self, mastered creation upon the degrading record of loss, attrition, deposition, exile. The condensation of elegiac verse faces off the rawer material of supposed gloss, undigested nostalgia, and obsession to define in their very interchange the genius of fiction as life under pressure of art, art of life.

Kinbote, without his voiced fantasies of Shade and other shadows, might be only a diarist dying, another version of the Beckett persona. But if Malone, all alone, could really believe in his Sapo and Macmann, could release his own wit to them, liberating rue into amusement, then he would come at least a little closer to the confidence of Nabokov's narrators and their easy way with finalities. We may recall here the typifying exit of Conmal, the Russian translator in *Pale Fire*, whose "last words in his last delirium" were, *"Comment dit-on 'mourir' en anglais?"*—"a beautiful and touching end" (p. 285). This linguist's epitomizing wish to end in a transaction between spheres of purely textual reference may even suggest a motive for the close of *Malone Dies*, the hero's secondary creations left adrift somewhere between the mainland, their fatherland, and an unspecified island—as if between their native French and their English incarnations, dead of the very idea of transposition into another set of terms.

To return to *Pale Fire* and that plot's largest argument, it would seem to be Nabokov's point that any persona, whether musing aloud at his desk or being hunted down by a mad assassin, as Kinbote thinks he too is at the end—that any first person in fiction is always caught halfway between an autonomous "I" and the murderous impulse of all art to enshrine identity in permanence. For days after the shooting, Kinbote "wore" Shade's poetic draft about his person in the form of "ninety-two index cards," feeling himself "armoured with rhyme" (pp. 299–300). It is this same draft that he had tried with allegorical futility to hold up as a protection for Shade in the moment of the assassination. Shade stands all along for that aspect of genius which inevitably dies out of life into text, while Kinbote, still talking at the end, represents that deathproof aspect of art as the displacement of self and voice into book. Fiction cannot save, it can only preserve. William Burroughs has made much this same postmodernist point. Asked in an interview if it were possible to suggest "in your own writing where your death is reflected," Burroughs replied, "I would say in every sentence."[12] For Kinbote, every line of Shade's poem sentences to death that half of the creative self willing to delve into the realm of elegy. In Melville's phrase "an author from the dead," in other terms the sacrificial agent in the Orphic recovery of all narrative poetry (all the poetry of narrative), Shade bears as his very name an anagram of that Hades which metaphorically designates in Thackeray, for instance, the entire region of retrospective plot. The art of this Shade (in the dictionary sense of his name as a dweller among the dead) having been willed either by or to Kinbote— or in some sense both—is raised from the very death which is the native domain of commemoration. Shade's text is thus the record of descent into some more openly visionary configuration not so much of his name as of his identity and his dreams.

In the first paragraph of *Transparent Things* (1972), the most provocative speculation on death and textuality in Nabokov's work following *Pale Fire*, it is Hugh Person whom we hear hailed by the narrator, a character whose first name identifies him by near-homonym as the almost (but not quite) second person of any fictional address. Hugh, all but "you," stands between the "I" of the narrator and the reader thus indirectly addressed, half within the plot as character, half identified with the recipient of plot. As sacrificial victim of the death destined to close the novel, he is thus, in Woolf's terms, a perfect "border case" for the illustration of death's transactive style in the interval, both invisible and atemporal, between the scene of annihilation and the scene of reading. As hero, "You" Person is always equidistant from the author who pens him and the reader whose silent voice enunciates him as a cathartic second self. When he is later called by the narrator "our Person" (p. 75), the triangulation of author, character, and reader is complete in an editorial as well as regal plural. It is through just this sacrificial surrogate, standing in for the author (almost as his own person) by way of creative empathy, that death is brought to life for the receiving consciousness of the reader.

Transparent Things can be seen to reverse only so as to restate the allegory of *Pale Fire*. Here Hugh Person is the humble proofreader assigned to edit the later works—including the posthumous novel—of the renowned author R., an obvious avatar of the Nabokovian style. Shade is to Kinbote as R. is finally to Hugh, an already dead writer who is nevertheless (indeed therefore) the guarantor of his satellite's immortality. This is true in *Pale Fire* because Shade has supposedly imported Kinbote's story into his capacious and memorable art, or at least seems to have evoked it there as coded undersong. In *Transparent Things*, as we shall see, R. lifts Hugh beyond mortality by actually appearing at his death, in the last paragraph of the novel, as confessed omniscient overvoice, easing the decedent across the stylistic and metaphysical interval to disembodiment, reembodiment, or call it textual finality. As much as R. shares in the thematic and stylistic preoccupations of Nabokov, so does Hugh, in his undeveloped talents, fantasies, even lovers, share too in the rich biography of the novelist whose aesthetic dreams in fiction he is assigned to proof—to prove true. When the deathless voice of narration, apparently R.'s own from beyond the grave, hails Hugh at the end, we hear the perfected artist inviting the fallible human (side of himself) to rest. The narrator of *Transparent Things* at one point uses a suggestive textual metaphor for the relation of dreams to life, calling them the "anagrams of diurnal reality" (p. 80). Hugh's wild dreams are also the anagrams of that transmutation of reality known as R.'s art. They are as Kinbote's fantasies to Shade's poem, or say as Shade to Hades, and so in one of Hugh's wildest nightmares we find an early version of some recurrent dream motif called a "first rough draft" (p. 59). The ambiguous, repetitive nightmare of this dreaming proofreader, within which he dies finally in a hotel fire, goes, the tables turned, through a final redrafting in R.'s own voice at the end.

On our way to this last scene of the novel, we must pause over the inset text, comparable to Shade's posthumous published poem, which prepares for the redefined terms of the novel's closural fatality. This is the posthumously received last letter written by R. to his publisher, which, as much as Decoud's last letter to his sister in *Nostromo*, is a concerted study in the relationship of textuality to death. This deathbed letter occupies the whole twenty-first chapter of the novel, and more than any other compressed stretch of fiction I know manages to catalogue, investigate, and then divest itself of a whole range of mortal platitudes and textual formulas. R. explains that he expects either to be "proofread by cherubim—or misprinted by devils" (p. 82), the last a pun on typesetting apprentices. It is a tried and tested turn. Authors have frequently enjoyed, by the logic of epitome, thinking of themselves as perfected at death like their own texts in press, redeemed ineffaceably by record from the vicissitudes of experience, *bound* in every sense for remembrance. John Donne offers an early instance of this trope of textual eternity which would be dear to the heart of Nabokov's translator, Conmal: "All mankind is of one author, and in one volume; when man dies, one chapter is not torn out of the book, but translated into a better language . . . some pieces are translated by age, some by sickness, some by war, some by justice; but God's hand is in every translation, and his hand shall bind up all our scattered leaves again, for that library where every book shall lie open to one another."[13] Before he became an autobiographer Benjamin Franklin had as a young printer sketched out his own epitaph in this same mode: "The Body of B. Franklin. Printer; Like the Cover of an Old Book, Its contents torn out, And stript of its Lettering and Gilding, Lies here, Food for Worms. But the Work shall not be wholly Lost; For it will, as he believ'd, appear once more, in a new and more perfect Edition, corrected and amended by the Author."[14] In a quite different agnostic mood, Keats passed on to his publisher this in-joke and double pun just before he died: "Tell Taylor I shall soon be in a second Edition—in sheets—and cold press."[15] The poet is perfected by, and textually displaced into, the paradox of a dead but deathless volume.

R.'s next broadside at the mortuary tradition in his last letter is also a play on the linguistic epitomization in which certain kinds of vocabulary find their true validation only in finalities. Told by an Italian doctor that his *"Operazione* had been *perfetta,"* R. quips that "it had been so in the sense Euler called zero the perfect number" (p. 82). "It is comic," R. continues, but "I used to believe that dying persons saw the vanity of things, the futility of fame, passion, art, and so forth. I believed that treasured memories in a dying man's mind dwindled to rainbow wisps" (p. 84). He had a belief akin to the overarching instincts of Thackeray's *Vanity Fair,* say, "but now I feel just the contrary: my most trivial sentiments and those of all men have acquired gigantic proportions." As time runs out on the living man, the smallest things of this world seem a microcosm of an eternity by which they are no longer dwarfed: "The entire solar system is but a reflection in the crystal of my (or your) wrist watch." Human life ticks to the greater rhythms of the timeless, or vice versa, and even the signifying configurations on a private timepiece wheel in the shape of vaster orbits, infinite renewals.

R. now describes the miracle of his own serenity in death with a writerly play on "composure" (its scriptive overtones of "composition" already familiar from the more obvious punning in *The Waves*) as in particular an author's articulate dispensation at the end: "Total rejection of all religions ever dreamt up by man and total composure in the face of total death!" Would that he could compose it into portable form: "If I could explain this triple totality in one big book, that book would become no doubt a new bible and its author the founder of a new creed." The moment of revelation is, however, deflected by the text, resistant to scripted form, "not merely because a dying man cannot write books but because that particular one would never express in one flash what can only be understood *immediately"* (p. 82). Italicized into prominence, this adverb marks the intensive moment that has no room for extension. It will always in the "mediation" of narrative require that "so many consecutive words" violate or deny in their own verbal duration the attempted paradox of the instantaneous interval. It is a composure, in short, that has no room in which to be composed.

There ends the letter, apparently with no time for subscript or signature, as if that italicized word, *immediately,* was itself tilted forward into the epiphanic instant about which it despaired of speaking. The chapter closes with a "note added by the recipient," followed by this addendum: "Received on the day of the writer's death. File under Repos—R." Redolent of the financial term for "repossessed property," the abbreviation for a repository of correspondence stands also, by scriptive synonymy, for the "repose" of the soul which this writing constitutes. As one might suspect from such verbal dexterity, the supposed recipient's shorthand "—R." seems almost to be the signature of the writer himself posthumously overseeing the disposition of his last written work, in all the anonymity of its masked subscript. Like Decoud's letter offering up the truth of events as he sees them to the vessel of his memory in a loving sister, R. gives himself up to the secular creature upon whom his immortality as writer is fashioned, the "greater Publisher" (p. 82) of eternal reissue and renown. In writing, the novelist R. had always secured his withdrawal from the immediate present—as if all letters, all words, were his last, but also his immortality. By the most elusive reflexive logic of the whole novel, R. outlives himself in any text, fictional or epistolary, at least long enough to sign and seal his fate within that text.

What are the consequences of suspecting R. to have signed off for himself this particular last missive, the internal text of this brief chapter? It might well be that we are helped in this way to imagine him as writing the whole present novel as well as that one posted text, and chapter, within it. His admitted posthumous novel, the one we hear referred to at least, is to appear under the title *Tralatitions*, meaning "metaphors," unless the publisher changes it. Yet what is *Transparent Things* but another name, indeed a metaphor, for metaphors as such, for words translucent to similitude, windows upon likeness? Beginning to suspect at some point that novelist R. may be, by a homonym no more lazy or irrelevant than Hugh for "you," *our* novelist, that he may have written as his last fiction the book we are now reading, we realize why the intonations and sprung idioms in which the narrative voice speaks to the dying Hugh in the last paragraphs of *Transparent Things* seem drawn from the bastard locutions of the naturalized English speaker R. His immortality, proven by the book, can extend as fictive gift to his created hero and proofreader. In the last novel by Nabokov before *Transparent Things* there is a similar conclusion, though not as inventively dramatized. In *Ada*

(1969) it is stated outright of hero and heroine that "if our time-racked, flat-lying couple," supine like an open book, "ever intended to die they would die, as it were, *into* the finished book, into Eden or Hades, into the prose of the book or the poetry of its blurb" (p. 587, Nabokov's emphasis). More recently than *Transparent Things*, in his own devious reversal of the usual figurative relation of ephemeral living author to immortal if phantom character, John Fowles closes *Daniel Martin* (1977) by having the narrator declare himself in the final sentence as the title character's "ill-concealed ghost." That feeble shrouding of the author's status as effectually posthumous—and so in a sense already immortal—is rendered in Nabokov even more deliberately flimsy by the structural "transparency" of his earlier novel.

Earlier yet in Nabokov's work the closural death scene has repeatedly collided with a rescuing confession of fictional artifice. What *Transparent Things* adds to *Ada* and its Nabokovian predecessors in this vein is primarily the dramatized death of the narrator himself. Its plot enacts the inevitable removal of its own articulation from the imagined world of the novel to the scene of its writing, where narrating voice can subsequently be discovered to await coincidence with the hero at his and the novel's own last moment. At the end of *Bend Sinister* the hero, Adam Krug, is spared one kind of "execution" by the confession of another, redeemed from assassination by stylistic assignation. "I felt a pang of pity for Adam," writes the narrator, "and slid towards him along an inclined beam of pale light" (p. 233), a pale fire of transfiguration just before the hero faces the firing squad. Narrator appears to his character through the manifestation of the book's heraldic title in a slant of strange light—that is, in the definitive medium of the text itself that constitutes, presumably along the angle of a moving pen, such an oblique illumination of the world.

This novel's prefacing definition of death as mere style, the rhetoric of sheer "literary device," returns now in a passage which succumbs to a forced periodic interval in the very conception rather than the enactment of death, putting a strain on the prose more violently suspensive than any comparable parallel grammar of overarched discontinuity in Woolf: "I knew that the immortality I had conferred on the poor fellow was a slippery sophism, a play upon words. But the very last lap of his life had been happy and it had been proven to him that death was but a *question of style*. Some tower clock which I could never exactly locate, which, in fact, I never heard in the daytime, struck twice, then hesitated and was left behind by the smooth fast silence that continued to stream through the veins of my aching temples; *a question of rhythm*" (my emphasis). The "question of rhythm" is the very question begged by the disorienting sprung rhythm of this passage. The hero having been put to, and at the same time beyond, death, that dying is now displaced into the narrator's closural metacommentary on the creative pulse of his own performance. Recalling the role of apposition as a primary impetus in the Lawrencian style of trespass, and bearing in mind the threefold appositive phrase from the preface to *Bend Sinister* describing death as "but a question of style, a mere literary device, a musical resolution," one is at least tempted to detect in this closural passage death's appositional redefinition (as italicized) distended across an interval of some forty words in a grammatical test case for the very limits of the apposite, the proximate, the approachable. Pressing the natural rhythms of syntax to the farthest stretch of coherence—across not only stylistic time but the invoked clock-tower symbolism of time as prosodic measure—this prolonged mortal interval, replayed and participated in by the discursive voice, transposes the preceding narrative solution of death toward its "musical resolution" as prose style in extremis. Prose contorts its way inward from the bloodless efficacy of a "literary device" for death to the very lifeblood of the devising mind in the "aching" pulse of its invention. The final cadence of closure then becomes the accepted silence on the other side of creative expenditure. And yet again the apparent aestheticism is held in check, for the very word "question," beneath its meaning as mere "matter," preserves also the suggestion of death's irreducible mystery and its interrogation by narrative.

Even earlier in his career, it is a similar benign annihilation of hero into character to which Nabokov consigns the executed protagonist of *Invitation to a Beheading* (1934; translated 1959). At the moment of his decapitation by the guillotine in a Paris square, the hero is retrieved from this three-dimensional end into a cardboard apocalypse. In this outdoor theater of death, suddenly the "spectators" are "quite transparent now" (p. 222), and the "dust, rags, chips of painted wood," further on the "pasteboard bricks, posters" into which this stage-set world reverts, call up the two-dimensional paper surface of the text upon which this mortal backdrop has after all been rendered. The fate that would level, indeed sever, the hero instead flattens the world to page. The site of execution has thus become the scene of reading, the fated city "square," of which little now "[is] left," being transfigured to the rectangle of its novelistic inscription. In the metatextual economy by which death is rescued and recompensed by style, the encircling trees are said to lie "flat and reliefless," a sculptural as well as vegetative pun (worthy of Hopkins's "Goldengrove unleaving") on the contrasting "relief" of the hero's reprieve from death. As at the end of *Transparent Things* too, it is finally utterance alone, the presumed ventriloqual projection of the narrator, which not only ushers the dying character out but summons him from beyond; in the very last sentence of the *Invitation*, the protagonist makes "his way in that direction where, to judge by the voices, stood beings akin to him."

Like this early hero, invited not only *to* but out *through* a beheading; like the protagonist in *Bend Sinister*, not falling to his death but cadenced to closure; like the "flat-lying" couple in *Ada*, dying into rather than out of the book; like Fowles's Daniel Martin, hero and book by his name, survived by an admitted spectral originator—so too the proven hero of *Transparent Things*, himself a proofer of texts, finds himself resurrected into the transcribed voice of his always and already "ghostly" progenitor and double. As his dutiful proofreader is in the process of being composed and composited, the omniscient R. speaks to him in a fatherly, authorizing tone whose verbal tics we have heard him use before: the paternalistic and patronizing "son" (p. 69), the familiarizing filler "you know" (p. 16), incorporated here into the whole scrambled syntax of the novel's last sentence, "Easy, you know, does it, son." Grammar, like life, is coming apart at the seams. Just before, Hugh is in the middle of an erotic dream of reunion with the wife he accidentally murdered years earlier, also in his sleep, completing now the closed circle of his "uncorrected" dream world, when a hotel fire, mysteriously set, immolates him at the moment of pity and terror while *translating* him into proofread final copy: "Person, *this* person, was on the imagined brink of imagined bliss when Armande's footfalls approached—striking out both 'imagined' in the proof's margin (never too wide for corrections and queries!)"

(p. 102). At this moment authorship tips its hand, retrieves the hero for continued narrative, validates and preserves him, but only as an invention within an epiphany of the book's own formal and formative energy: "This is where the orgasm of art courses through the whole spine with incomparably more force than sexual ecstasy or metaphysical panic" (p. 102). The very pun on the spine of a book bursts with the *jouissance* it asserts. The textualized, corrected Hugh has undergone a transposition from a quoted and qualified "imagined" to the thing itself unhedged, and this in a joint epitome of his prodigious dream life and his profession as corrector of texts. It is fitting that his attempted escape from the flames is blocked by a "fatal draft" (p. 103), a final pun combined of textual revision itself and the afflatus of original inspiration that has motivated it. At the same time, whereas Kinbote in an editorial pun admits his desire to be "bullet-proof at last" (*Pale Fire*, p. 100) by hiding behind Shade's poem, Hugh might paradoxically be seen in the very moment of his narrative immolation to be fireproofed by the text for future readers.

It is at this point that the narrative voice, given a second wind, intervenes with an elaborated language of displacement across an interval from life to text which prose attempts to conjure with an absolute minimum of rhetoric. It is an effort at displacement with no temporal bearings: the deathbed interval become the mere space of differentiation. Calling to "our own Person" across the liminal border of death, narrative in R.'s tone and tongue offers a mere demonstrative, "it," that turns out to be a reflexive self-demonstration, stalled momentarily by the grammatical intrusion of the language of faith or "belief" in lower case. "This is, I believe, *it:* not the crude anguish of physical death but the incomparable pangs of the mysterious mental maneuver needed to pass from one state of being to another" (p. 104). Character partakes in a displacement of state rather than a temporal transition, while that last pronoun, "another," its antecedence determined, could never in any conceivable secular grammar become an adjective shoving off into a new descriptive phrase, there being nothing sayable to which it might refer forward. The style of dying involves not only a rhetoric but a grammar of retrospect. Remembering R.'s emphasis on the *"immediately"* which any consecutive text of death would have to belie, we may well take the italicized *"it"* to stress the simple here and now of the conclusive "this." The text would thus refer in a reflexive manner to the very demonstrative phrase that names the finality of death. After the clobbered grammar at the end of *Malone Dies,* this is the language of fiat revindicated by a specification of the text itself, not Hamlet's "let be," but "let this" (here: this textual moment) "be it." Dying for the hero is no more than the naming of death for him by the narrative voice. And so, though peremptory, how anguishing can it be? For this is his perfection too, a displacement from imagined presence into textual memorial that is the only labor of dying in this fictive universe, epitaph and apotheosis in the same phrase, a dying *into* rather than out of the book.

One six-word monosyllabic sentence after an indentation—"Easy, you know, does it, son"—and this novel, like *The Waves,* comes to an end by ceding its drama to omniscience in its own bizarre, inbred sense. Jauntily choppy, periodic, halting but confident, bordering on a Beckett-like grammatical entropy but suggesting instead an infinite gentleness in the displacement of ended presence into rendered text, this is Nabokov's closure at its most assured. Shade made it possible for Kinbote, and vice versa, the unnamed narrator for the heroes of *Invitation to a Beheading* and *Bend Sinister.* Now the immortal R. secures such closure for his second person, You. Yet it was Malone who said it: "My story ended I'll be living yet. Promising lag." In Nabokov, too, this lag is textually ingrown, atemporal. Its interval is simply the definitive, the inevitable space—mediated but laboring for the power of immediacy—between story and discourse, imagined event and its report when plotted to closure. Besides identifying the voice as R.'s, that garbled vernacular of the death sentence seems also to raise questions about the very capacities of language when confronting a death scene. Tmesis (syntactic cutting) replaces mimesis in an attempt to break open, to discompose the interval long enough for the "flash" of recognition. Such normative syntax as, for instance, "You know, son, easy does it," once transposed (in both the typographical sense and that of the special mortal terminology of this study) becomes the transfiguring truth Hugh knows on his own "I's" behalf, on Ours, on R.'s. "There exists an old rule," writes Nabokov in *Look at the Harlequins!* (1974), "—so old and trite that I blush to mention it. Let me twist it into a jingle—to stylize the staleness: The I of the book / Cannot die in the book" (p. 239). But if the "I" can confer some part of itself upon a dying effigy, and by deferral or deflection name that second self's death without having further to effect it, then that promising lag becomes the work of textuality itself in the ever-suspended scene of death.

The novel that opens in direct address—"Here's the person I want. Hullo person!"—closes upon another jostled apostrophe to the "son." It does so in a language of disarrangement whose balked syntax generates the delays and reemphases of a periodic grammar gone piecemeal. The master stylist renowned for the syllabic brocade and sensuous folds of his syntax ties up this narrative with the simplest of crossed stitches: "Easy, you know, does it, son." With even euphony eschewed, it remains a question what kind of style death is a "question of." In the shuffling vocative register of this last cockeyed apostrophe, such mainstays of the verbal interval as elision and punning, anaphora and apposition are all excluded. Absent is the grammar of Forsterian connection, of Lawrencian trespass, or of Woolfian fluidity, even the syntactic disengagement and disintegration of Beckett's closure. Instead of eased dissipation or transit, there is contortion from within, a transfiguring torque on the idiomatic mold of the language's deep structure. The mortal formula of transposition, by syntax or metaphor, has, as mentioned, become in its other sense the internal flip-flop of language, a slippery grip and spin on utterance, as if by force of will it can be twisted into new writ. It is indeed a "mysterious mental maneuver" in which the mortal interval has grown entirely hermetic: the internal relation of syllables and words. The grammatical metathesis (or syntactic transposition) accords with the rhetorical metastasis (the rapid "remove" from one frame of reference to another discussed in connection with Dickens and phrased by Nabokov as a transit from "one state of being to another"). What results is a metatextual furthering of this elusive "maneuver," a transformation prose both declares and in its own formulation endows.

After more than two centuries of the English-language novel, the fictional death scene has transparently purified itself to a revelation about the very scene of fiction. Against the precedents of postmodernism, the motivating force of transposition in Nabokov has become the writer's epitomizing dream of release from "so many consecutive words" into an undeferred vision of stylistic essence without reference, a displacement from the secondariness of transcribed content to the state of sheer form. If, as suggested in the second chapter, death as a stylistic challenge must in some sense play both sides against the middle, with the far side always inexpressible, here is a whole posthumous text that stands confessed within this limbo and this bliss, holding firm on the paper-thin threshold between imaginative articulation and imagined (re)incarnation.

Not only does this closure sum up the threefold structure and rhetoric of the traditional death scene as an acknowledged textual maneuver, but *Transparent Things* further serves for review here by epitomizing in this passage its own attempted compromise between a phenomenological and a deconstructive imagination of the text. With his fiction conceived now as trace, now habitable space, now the one inscribing our entrance to the other, Nabokovian deconstruction would rebuild our faith in presence within the contours of a story's entirely invented world. For R., for Kinbote before him, for the narrator of *The Real Life of Sebastian Knight* earlier yet, a text is the regally privileged "state of being" where a phenomenal world available somehow through words carries through on its promise and grows noumenal. Unwilling, even or especially in death, to relax his faith in the credibility of such a world, N.'s surrogate specter R. can certify it anew by incorporating into its bordering consciousness a "real" person, his Hugh, at the last instant when character is able to be transfigured from independent figment of the text to an admitted verbal fixture in it.

If as the dying mind approaches the point of revelation the world itself turns to a "coherent sentence," with (again from *Sebastian Knight*) the "windings of a road writing its message in a round hand, as clear as that of one's father," then that inscribed road is also the only route of access to the space it crosses. This is the disclosed topography of the Logos, where every authored world is as clearly turned out as that of any First Cause or Universal Father, indeed as that of the "anthropomorphic deity" (*Bend Sinister*, p. xii) behind the verbal metamorphoses of any text. Speaking *ex nihilo* to his "son," R. in his last utterance offers up the disconnected nonsequiturs of his broken English segued to finis like the "translation" of the dying linguist, Conmal, in *Pale Fire*. These last words testify to an unattributed but indubitable state of being cogently invoked simply by coinciding with the textual security of closure and containment. Brought to limit and illumination by death, and this through the virtuoso opacity of his word play, the phenomenological *jeu d'esprit* of Nabokov's fiction is to render a whole world transparently accessible through the things of the text that openly confect it.

□ □ □

There is scarcely anywhere to go from here but into that inverted paranoid nightmare that constitutes the final page of Thomas Pynchon's *Gravity's Rainbow* (1973). There we as reading audience (you persons) are translated to a cinema audience—"old fans who've always been at the movies (haven't we?)"—singing along with lyrics on a screen as on a "dim page," while outside the long-threatened rocket arcs its way down, screaming faster than sound toward our screechless because instant doom. If just before the close of *The Waves* Woolf renders in Bernard's fate the death of the voiced "I" within a fiction, and if the work of Nabokov and Beckett repeatedly brings the authorial voice of fiction, and thus the novel itself, to its own death scene, Pynchon has driven farther into the realm of the formally inordinate to exact, and enact, the extinction—or just short of it, depending on how fast we slam shut the book—of his own reading public. The standard process of readerly identification with the goings on or giving out of a narrative is stripped here of all its safeguards, the very mechanism of displacement disengaged. Pynchon's seems an attempt to challenge by transgressing the fundamental protective contract of the Hegelian representational sacrifice, even if the annihilation of the reading audience is inevitably past capture by the legible.

If we believe, however, at the end of *Gravity's Rainbow* that we are in fact there at the scene to be slaughtered, we have indeed died away (as to a lesser extent we always do in reading) from our own trusted presence, our own present, into the ghostly world of inscription, past to begin with (this novel is backdated to the Second World War) and always absent. At the close of Gabriel Garcia Marquez's *One Hundred Years of Solitude* (1967), the hero of its phantasmagoric chronicle reads through the magic book of his people until past record overtakes the future by the hairsbreadth of a line inscribing his own death. In *Gravity's Rainbow* novel as form and its enclosed legend as story coincide with even more startling results. We discover not just the hero but ourselves to be written by Pynchon, to be his subjects, doomed to the paranoia which we had thought, at least by the distance of reading, we could banish. Wrong, we are as cruelly wronged by the fate of reading as are any of the characters within the book by the ubiquitous nemesis of the System or Machine which now even fiction has become. Rather than being distilled by art, death spills over. As we sit immobilized within "these walls" of Pynchon's cinematic deathtrap, enclosed by what can also be taken as the plane surfaces of his own coercive book, the actual falling rocket inscribes its both scriptive and ballistic arc through the differential interval of its "last delta-t." Within this interval the final two words of the novel blurt out their truncated invitation to "follow the bouncing ball" of the doomsday sing-along on screen: "Now everybody————." To para- phrase Beckett, predicate falls away from subject and lands some- where in the void, but here the severed subject, scarcely permitted any detachment in the emotional sense, is each and every reader. As in the pivotal transition of a classic death scene, this injunction instantaneously doubles—in the interval of its very utterance—for the general roll call of Armageddon. At this most closed of open- ended terminations, however, we are drawn to fill in the blank with "Now everybody————dead," not only at our obvious peril but by way of a verbal impossibility. The style of dying is always at the point of crisis elliptical, unsayable, in one way or another effaced. Here Pynchon demonstrates quite precisely, by grammatical excision, how the canceling finality that emerges in the vanishing interval of any death sentence has no real verbal form available to it, has momentarily abolished, and here forever, the very text that, monitoring death's arrival, would finally denominate it. Nabokov's closure in *Transparent Things* notwithstanding, dying is easier done than said.

In *Gravity's Rainbow* we take our very life in our hands by holding with them the book that asks us, more directly than we usually notice fiction to be asking, to step out of that life into the finality of art, here a blinding universal "End." The death on which all narrative is founded has found us out at the close; and so in the ultimate maneuver of demise by proxy we stand outside of ourselves, dumb- struck at our own annihilation, not warmed so much as incinerated by the contemplation. After so many English-language novels of death as deflection and catharsis, Thomas Pynchon cuts off the life line of mortal fiction, cancels its sacrificial distance, chokes closed the space of doubling. Collapsing the poles of reader and represented reality, turning the *de te fabula* to ironic ferocity, *Gravity's Rainbow* becomes the very death scene of reading. From modernism to postmodernism is a long fictional distance—from the conclusion of *The Rainbow* to that of *Gravity's Rainbow*, the closural archings of human promise to the ballistic geometry of doom. Pynchon is a long way, too, from Conrad's aesthetic of seeing as a flash of insight before "eternal rest." Ends render up what is intended—or at least hold out, by being held off, a hope that they might. Apocalypse means, of course, revelation as well as doom. Yet the contemporary novel that would end with our own blinding death along with that of the world it portrays enacts a desperate literalization of the analogy between fictional closure and deathbed vision.

In the various senses of a fictional "End" was our beginning, and upon its implications we here close (round). We return to Dickens for the first and the last closural sentences he set down as a novelist, the finish of *Pickwick Papers* (1836) and of the postscript to *Our Mutual Friend* (1864–1865). First,

> Every year, he [Pickwick] repairs to a large family merry-making at Mr. Wardle's; on this, as on all occasions, he is invariably attended by the faithful Sam, between whom and his master there exists a steady and reciprocal attachment which nothing but death will terminate.

THE END

and three decades later,

> I remember with devout thankfulness that I can never be much nearer parting company with my readers for ever, than I was then, until there shall be written against my life, the two words with which I have this day closed this book:—THE END.

September 2nd, 1865

After the wedding breakfast which ends the main body of *Pickwick*, a white hiatus, a gap on the page, conveys us to a coda in which the editorial masquerade of the preceding chronicle is replaced at long last, as at the end of *The Newcomes* later, by the omniscient author's admission of pure fictionality. This candid valedictory voice compares the personal losses attendant on the "course of nature" (a given life line) to those incurred in the "course of art" (the plot line of any fictional discourse). The editorial voice then wistfully salutes his own creations as they take up their places in that enclosed memorial rather than unfolding drama which the novel, ended, comes to be. In that future-looking but still elegiac last sentence about Sam and Pickwick, the tacit echo of the matrimonial liturgy ("till death do us part") lends its vocabulary to an attachment guaranteed in the wake of another actual marriage, though secured now between two men who are unabashedly "real" to us only as characters in a book. The historical preterite of the main novel, shifted to a perpetual present tense for the coda, veers off into a mortal future for that last subordinate clause, "which nothing but death will terminate." Yet the death that must come, presumably first to Mr. Pickwick, is not only postponed but supplanted by the fictional terminus of "THE END." In this "steady and reciprocal attachment which nothing but death will terminate," even the adjective of expected duration and continuance ("steady" for "uninterrupted") seems redefined as a spatial rather than temporal modifier (for "balanced," "stable") as putative biography yields to confessed invention, history to fiction, scriptive sequence to the roundedness of spatial form. For men who are only characters, their narrated deaths deferred or otherwise, "THE END" is the sole finality that applies, preemptive but at the same time redemptive, calling a halt that exalts to permanence, immobilizing but also immortalizing.

Though the specter of death at the end of *Pickwick* is raised only to be aesthetically disarmed, the novel's coda nevertheless gives us an instance of fictional closure seen under the aspect of human mortality. The process seems reversed for that postscript to *Our Mutual Friend,* where, in a more modern and potentially disturbing manner, human life itself and its mortality are viewed under the aspect of textual closure, life more a volume than an event. Such different writers, we have seen, as John Donne, Benjamin Franklin, and John Keats—as well as Thackeray, Hardy, Conrad, and Woolf, to name only the most prominent novelists—have taken up this conceit. Dickens at the end of *Our Mutual Friend,* however, by making death an equivalent threat to himself and his scripted people, achieves something more than this reflexive textual metaphor for the writer's life as a book in press or print. Explaining his close call with death, Dickens writes that "Mr. and Mrs. Boffin (in their manuscript dress of receiving Mr. and Mrs. Lammle at breakfast) were on the South-Eastern Railway with me in a terribly destructive accident." After tending to the injured victims among the human participants in the disaster, Dickens "climbed back into my carriage . . . to extricate the worthy couple. They were much soiled, but otherwise unhurt." This charming notion of characters as fellow travelers with their author soon backfires in the metaphysical surprise that Dickens's own life could be analogized to a text awaiting its final caesura. Closure ("until there shall be written against my life . . . THE END") becomes a gesture of some higher omniscience that matches both life's and literature's originating fiat with a countering finality: so let it be written, so let it be done, achieved and finished.

As noted in the second chapter, this sense of reality as the phenomenal transcription of an originating edict is implicit in the figure of apocalypse at the death of Paul in *Dombey and Son*. All of elapsed history, the whole world of extension in space and time, seems pointed there toward the moment when the universe will be "rolled up like a scroll." What is most intriguing in the postscript to *Our Mutual Friend* is the reciprocal relation of author and his characters that emerges there. If Dickens is ready to figure his own life and death as no more, respectively, than a narrative and its "End," then the characters in his published stories may well derive a corollary advantage from this fact, their complementary natures transferred from a textual to an existential status. Or to put this into reverse order, the order of its unfolding in the postscript after all the narrative's words are over: in some arresting creative economy, the extent to which fictional lives wax authentic is the extent to which authorial presence (when put forward as an "I") formulates itself as a textual fiction. In a dizzying relativism of scriptive incarnation, Mr. and Mrs. Boffin are only as real as, and no less real than, Dickens himself would be if he were a divine aritificer's own invention, which—so Dickens is willing to suggest here—he may well be.

At the textual level, style is one name for the means by which "The End" might find itself "written against" the life of a given character, his or her finis effected in a certain turn of words. Style is of course in any text the material of a story's presentation without being verbally present to its characters. Like death in this way, style is necessarily external to narrated experience; at the moment of a fictional dying, style merely joins and glosses all else in being quintessentially so removed. If those characters from *Our Mutual Friend* should not only have risked textual destruction in that railway transit with their author but have gone on to die in a traversed verbal interval syntactically enacted by narrative itself, the formal implications for death in fiction would have been rounded out within the stylistic microcosm of the death sentence. While such a sentence does its work as a verbal adjudication never pronounced upon characters within their own hearing, always a manifestation of pure discursivity in the realm of story, always in other words a special case of style, narrative discourse at the same time moves to reveal and develop its more comprehensive formal relation to the life outside of story and this side of human closure.

As if it were a postscript to the whole Victorian novel, Dickens verges in that last ending he lived to complete on a model of selfhood that would grow increasingly predominant in the novel's next century—and increasingly problematic. Identity becomes the articulate story of form inside of, or by simile with, the form of story. It is thus that profit comes in fiction from the loss that is death, some gain taken from the toll of the most antique and ubiquitous grief told over. How being, as an end in itself, must paradoxically be forwarded by the knowledge of finality: such is the first and last lesson taught by narrative from the platform of its staged death scenes and their focal death sentences. Conveyed by narrative through its styles of dying under their various rules of closure, the power of such demonstration is less a moral than a morale. The regimen of a fictional text reconciles us to mortality by essaying its possible shapes—by taking them to the limit. So it is that death remains one of the best reasons for seeing our reading through.

Notes
Index

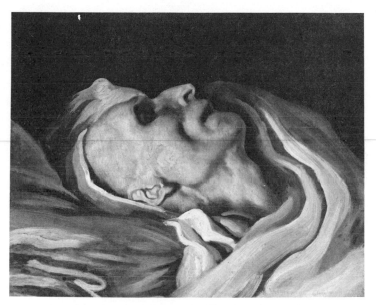

After Death (A Study), by Théodore Géricault
Courtesy The Art Institute of Chicago

Notes

A Note on Texts

Where there are no standard scholarly editions of the Victorian novels under discussion, I have quoted from the best available single text (often a Penguin paperback, for instance) or series, including the *New Oxford Illustrated Dickens*, the Oxford Thackeray, and the New Wessex edition of Hardy (London: Macmillan, 1912). I have used the definitive Clarendon editions of Dickens when they exist for a given novel (with separate notes for manuscript variants), and also of *Jane Eyre*, ed. Jane Jack and Margaret Smith (Oxford: Clarendon, 1969; reprinted with corrections 1975) and of *Wuthering Heights*, ed. Hilda Marsden and Ian Jack (Oxford: Clarendon, 1976). Given the wide range of available Victorian texts, parenthetical citations through Conrad are by chapter numbers (or by roman and arabic numerals together when volume and chapter are required). The one exception is Conrad's *Heart of Darkness*; since its three subdivisions do not facilitate location of a quoted passage, I have cited page rather than chapter numbers from the widely used Norton Critical Edition, ed. Robert Kimbrough (New York: W. W. Norton, 1963). For the fiction of Forster, Lawrence (including his three-volume collected stories), and Woolf I have followed standard practice in citing by page the Vintage (Random House), Viking, and Harvest (Harcourt, Brace, Jovanovich) paperbound printings, respectively, with the exception of the Harvest edition of Forster's *A Passage to India* and the Vintage edition of Lawrence's *The Man Who Died*, jointly printed with *St. Mawr*. References to Woolf's *Jacob's Room* are to its joint issue with *The Waves*, while for the latter novel I have given page numbers from its more recent separate printing (1978). Occasional page references to Joyce's *Ulysses* and Ford Madox Ford's *The Good Soldier* are to the standard Modern Library and Vintage editions, respectively. All Beckett citations are by page from the single-volume edition of the trilogy *Three Novels by Samuel Beckett* (New York: Grove, 1965). I have used the McGraw-Hill editions of Nabokov, where available, for *Bend Sinister*, *Transparent Things*, and *Look at the Harlequins!*, while referring to the standard Putnam's editions of *Invitation to a Beheading* and *Pale Fire*. Grove Press and Avon, respectively, publish the English editions of *The Real Life of Sebastian Knight* and *Pnin*.

1. Points of Departure

1. *The Sense of an Ending: Studies in the Theory of Fiction* (London: Oxford University Press, 1966), Frank Kermode's early experiment in narratological theory under the aspect of closure, is guided at the outset by the question, "What human need can be more profound than to humanize the common death?" If "we survive, we make little images of moments which have seemed like ends; we thrive on epochs" (p. 7); Kermode's focus is less on death's formal "imminence" or enactment, however, than on its dramatic "immanence" (p. 6). The chief studies of death's actual portrayal in fiction are Frederick J. Hoffman, *The Mortal No: Death and the Modern Imagination* (Princeton: Princeton University Press, 1964), an overview that stresses the evolving relation between mortal violence and the self from Dostoevsky through existentialism, and more recently Lawrence L. Langer, *The Age of Atrocity: Death in Modern Literature* (Boston: Beacon Press, 1978), concentrating on Thomas Mann, Albert Camus, Aleksandr Solzhenitsyn, and Charlotte Delbo. Touching on several of the same Continental writers in his chapter "The Metaphysics of Death," in *Dimensions of the Modern Novel: German Texts and European Contexts* (Princeton: Princeton University Press, 1969), pp. 215–257, Theodore Ziolkowski suggests "that the generation of Joyce, Mann, and Proust was enacting in its works a rite of aesthetic sublimation of death"; he then footnotes the "more radical formulation yet" of R. M. Alberes that in formal terms "the novel is a substitute for death" (p. 218).

2. The linguistic as well as psychological extremity of death is given pointed voice in an anecdote of Rilke's narrator in *The Notebooks of Malte Laurids Brigge*, trans. M. D. Herter Norton (New York: W. W. Norton, 1949), who finds in his father's wallet after his death a brief narrative copied out by hand as a memento mori. It details the death and last words of Christian the Fourth, who finally "expressed with his whole face the single word his tongue had been forming for hours, the sole word that still existed: 'Döden,' he said, 'Döden' " (p. 143). Death by any other name, or noun, is naturally the last word to go, because it is the one that takes no living reference with it, taking leave instead of all human meaning.

3. G. W. F. Hegel, *The Phenomenology of Mind*, rev. ed., trans. J. B. Baillie (London: George Allen and Unwin, 1931), p. 605.

4. Leon Edel, *The Life of Henry James*, vol. 2 (New York: Penguin, 1977), p. 800.

5. Addressing this linguistic paradox in commenting on the "dichotomous" universe of Céline's fiction in *Powers of Horror: An Essay on Abjection* (New York: Columbia University Press, 1982), Julia Kristeva detects among

his ruling antinomies "Death and Words, Hell and the Writer, the Impossible and Style" (p. 160). Despite its impossibility, its prohibited and prohibiting blank, death stands prominent among those powers that horrify, those horrors that empower. In terms not too distant from those of Kristeva's own Lacanian bearings, the relationship between the representational impossibility of death and the covering maneuvers of style, between absence and mediating metaphor, is discussed by Irving Massey in *The Gaping Pig: Literature and Metamorphosis* (Berkeley: University of California Press, 1976). Though the "absolute frontier" between the conscious and the unconscious is ordinarily associated in recent psychoanalysis with the sexual swoon, in different terms with the presence or absence of the signifying phallus, "it is also possible," writes Massey, "to speak directly of the connection between the image and the 'absence' called death, without making the detour through the sexual . . . When I will say that images mask the memory of death, I will not be proposing anything irreconcilable with Lacan's idea that images mask a traumatic experience of absence, but the emphasis will be different" (p. 12). See Chapter 6 for the conjoined and mutually adjusted absences of death and sexuality in D. H. Lawrence, where the transpositions (or "maskings") of metaphor are meant to render accessible to each other the adjacent realms of Thanatos and Eros.

6. Woolf, *The Second Common Reader* (New York: Harcourt, Brace, and World, 1932), p. 55.

7. In the second paragraph of *Moll Flanders* the heroine alludes to various associates of hers "having gone out of the world by the steps and the string," and nears the conclusion by escaping the fate of fellow prisoners who by now "were all out of the world." See Modern Library college edition (New York: Random House, 1950), p. 278. Earlier, upon the death of her first husband, Moll notes that it "concerns the story in hand very little" to say more of their conjugal tragedy than "that at the end of five years he died" (p. 51). Death in *Jonathan Wild*, for the reprobate hero, is the removal from "this" rather than "the" world, twice mentioned in the gallows scene as being of narrative interest only for the brutal "conformity . . . of his death to his life" (p. 16).

8. Squire Allworthy in *Tom Jones* "considered his wife as only gone a little before him a Journey which he should most certainly, sooner or later, take after her" (ch. 2), where the last temporal phrase carries the suggestion also of "taking out after" his lost companion. In the first-person report of the Vicar of Wakefield, he transcribes his own deathbed oration in prison just before his surprise recovery (the whole twenty-ninth chapter, as its subtitle has it, being devoted to variations on the vicar's faith that "the wretched must be repaid the balance of their sufferings in the life hereafter").

Goldsmith's hero confers the Enlightenment's emphasis on death as a transformation to pure rationality, the moment when "the good man leaves the body, and is all a glorious mind." Yet the vicar finds that he need not make so soon this far "journey," destined as he is to live for awhile longer in view of its eventual necessity. Similarly, Defoe closes the sequel to *Robinson Crusoe* by showing the hero, in the very last sentence, readying himself "for a longer journey than all these" he has chronicled. Indeed, this postponed but inevitable venture in an unloggable exploration "out of the world" (in Moll's words) seems intended as the *terminus ad quem* of the book's title, *The Farther Adventures of Robinson Crusoe*.

9. "Death" is the unmodified title of lyrics by Shelley, Thomas Hood, and George Darley. Byron's "And Thou Art Dead" gives, from the title on, an explicit emphasis to what Phillipe Ariès has characterized as the crucial shift in Romanticism toward the psychological projections of "the death of the other," *la mort de toi* (see n.12 below), as did Wordsworth's earlier Lucy poems and the "Boy of Winander" episode from *The Prelude*. Thomas Lovell Beddoes has brief lyrics titled "Dirge" and "Song of Thanatos" in this vein, and there is a dirge by George Darley entitled "The Sea-Ritual."

10. Anticipating this study's connection of drowning imagery with parables of visionary death and aesthetic transfiguration (more directly than does Darley's "A Sea-Ritual" or Shelley's *Adonais*) is the "drowned" hero (IV, l. 693) of Keats's *Endymion*, suddenly "spiritualized" (l. 993) out of his living death by the goddess of the moon and so redeemed from his sublunary "bier" (l. 973). Compare too the death into fusion and illumination in Shelley's *Epipsychidion*, where the last clause of its main narrative, "I expire," alludes to the expiration of "winged words" four lines before, words that aspire to "pierce" through "annihilation" to the phrasing and consequent embrace of their desire in a sphere of poetic refulgence "beyond the grave," as the coda phrases it. There is an even more extended narrative death scene, as minutely detailed as any other in the verse or prose of the century, at the end of Shelley's *Alastor* (ll. 626–662), where an elaborate pattern of enjambment eases us from the hero's recognition "that death / Was on him" across "the smooth brink / Of that obscured chasm," both literal and figurative, to a final fading in counterpoint with an actual moonset. The failed quester's "last sight / Was the great moon . . . o'er the western line / Of the wide world," at which transitional moment the play on the poem's own bordering "line" is enlarged to a more crucial poetic parable. Adumbrating my claims for death as a metanarrative reversion (or transcendence) from human content to literary form, the hero is converted from seeker to mere figure, man to image, at the moment of death, as "the murky shades involved / An image, silent, cold, motionless, / As their own voiceless earth and

vacant air." The confirming play at the second enjambment between the "as" of possession or incorporation and the "as" of analogy—that is, figuration—merely highlights Shelley's sense that poetry alone can embody and engrave this doomed heroic venture, however "feeble" (l. 709) the imagery of such elegiac verse.

11. In "Death as Death," Laura Riding writes, "The prophetic eye / Closing upon difficulty, / Opens upon comparison." See *Selected Poems: In Five Sets* (New York: W. W. Norton, 1970), p. 50. Though not in context about poetry or figurative language, the lines might be taken to differentiate the equative from the analogic "as," the latter being the opened "comparison" of metaphor itself.

12. This happens to be the term chosen for a major English translation of a classic death scene in Balzac. In the "deathorama" (the French *mortorama*) of *Père Goriot*, the summarizing expressiveness of the hero's deathbed scene, with the old man deluded into thinking his two heartless daughters have returned to his side, reads, *"Ce soupir fut l'expression de toute sa vie, il se trompait en course."* See Balzac, *La Comèdie humaine* (Paris: Bethune et Plon, 1843), IX, 526. In the Marion Ayton Crawford translation of *Old Goriot* for the Penguin edition (Baltimore, 1951), the French is rendered as follows (my emphasis): "The last sigh of this father was to be a sigh of joy, *a sigh that epitomized the feeling of a lifetime*; he was cheated to the end" (pp. 297–298). This epitomizing compression of a life is of course not new to literature with the nineteenth-century novel. In *Death and Elizabethan Tragedy* (Cambridge, Mass.: Harvard University Press, 1936), Theodore Spencer comments, "The most interesting use of death as part of dramatic technique (if it is correct so to classify it) is the part it plays in the exhibition of character. The brave man, the hero, dies gladly, scorning to fear; the coward dies trembling" (p. 201). Exemplifying this, as Spencer does not, there is the death of Cardinal Beaufort in *Henry VI, Part Two*, striking Warwick as the very affidavit of living ferocity (my emphasis): "So bad a death *argues* a monstrous life" (III.iii.30), while the king speaks as if there were a kind of epitomizing semiotics of death (again my emphasis): "Ah, what a *sign* it is of evil life / Where death's approach is seen so terrible" (III.iii.5–6). Besides the fictional adaptation of this dramaturgic strategy, turned to further introspection in the post-Romantic novel, such correlation between life and dying also colors the treatment of Romantic and Victorian biography. In *Truth to Life: The Art of Biography in the Nineteenth Century* (London: Collins, 1974), A. O. J. Cockshut suggests that the death scene, in little, is an instance of hit title rapport between living duration and its summary, alluding to "the consecrated formula" for the epitomizing biographical death scene: "As in life, so in death" (p. 53). A character within

Balzac's novel actually says about Old Goriot in his typifying obliviousness at the end that "he will die as he has lived" (p. 300). The most widely noted recent study of death from an extraliterary perspective, Phillipe Ariès's *Western Attitudes toward Death: From the Middle Ages to the Present*, trans. Patricia M. Ranum (Baltimore: The Johns Hopkins University Press, 1974), later expanded into *The Hour of Our Death* (New York: Knopf, 1981), explores from a sociological, religious, and cultural point of view the relation of death to shifting historical perspectives of the self and its limits, including an account of the revolutionary effects of Romanticism and its modern aftermath.

13. Burke, "Thanatopsis for Critics: A Brief Thesaurus of Deaths and Dying," *Essays in Criticism*, 2 (1952), 370–375. Further compressed beyond his outline, the following are Burke's categories, with death understood as: a natural culmination of hunger, disease, sorrow and the like; an analogue of corruption; the "dying life" of excessive self-control and "mortification"; dignification; the dialectical opposite, and thus celebration, of life; an image of fulfilment; a surrogate for sexual union; mortal relief; rebellion; rebirth; sexual frigidity or emotional impotence; mental imbalance; and access to the unconditioned realms of oneness or divinity.

14. Freud, *Beyond the Pleasure Principle*, in *The Complete Psychological Works of Sigmund Freud*, trans. James Strachey (London: Hogarth Press, 1955), XVIII (1920–1922), 38. Montaigne's remark that "the continuous task of your life is to build death" and other formulations of this sort are quoted by Jacques Choron, *Death and Western Thought* (New York: Collier, 1963), pp. 220–221. This strand of thought in Western philosophy and psychology seems closer at first glance to the teleological consciousness of death and the plotting toward it in prose fiction than is Wittgenstein's sense in the *Tractatus* (6.4311) that "our life has no end in just the way in which our visual field has no limit," quoted by James Van Evra, "On Death as Limit," in *Language, Metaphysics, and Death*, ed. John Donnelly (New York: Fordham University Press, 1978), p. 24. Freud returns to his point about the "death instinct" farther along in *Beyond the Pleasure Principle*, with a sense of literary precedent as supporting evidence: "We have drawn far-reaching conclusions from the hypothesis that all living substance is bound to die from internal causes . . . We are accustomed to think that such is the fact, and we are strengthened in our thought by the writings of our poets" (pp. 44–45). If Freud meant the phrase "aim of life" in describing death in the two senses of *end* applied by Burke ("purpose" and "cessation," cited above in n.13), then the paradox of life defined by death as "limit" would find an illustration, not unlike Wittgenstein's at that, in an early work by the most philosophically schooled of the Romantic poets. "Resembles

life what once was deem'd of light, / Too ample in itself for human sight?" asks Coleridge in "What is Life?" Related questions follow about whether life can take definition only in relief against its contrary, its "colours" alone "By encroach of darkness made." See Ernest Hartley Coleridge, ed., *Complete Poetical Works* (Oxford: Clarendon Press, 1912), I, 394.

15. In the mock-heroic mode of this novel, Fielding satirizes the death of his condemned criminal in the subtitle to the gallows scene as "the highest consummation of human GREATNESS" (ch. 15), rephrasing this sarcastic accolade at the scaffold with the arch assessment of Wild's execution as "this completion of glory, which was now about to be fulfilled to our hero." When Wild then steals a "bottle-screw" at the last moment from the presiding cleric's pocket, Fielding takes it "to shew the most admirable conservation of character in our hero to his last moment," where "conservation" is a version of "preservation" or persistence within the narrative as well as the moral economy of the hero. After Wild is twice said to have been sent "out of this world," Fielding follows this "conclusion" of the hero's destiny with a concluding chapter of his own assessing the rogue's character from the vantage of his hanging, "in all the conformity above mentioned of his death to his life" (ch. 16), greatness meeting here as elsewhere the "fate adapted to it." As if such retrospect were a formal mandate of closure, the last paragraph of the preceding death chapter has begun to suggest that the fictional utility of epitomizing death is virtually a constitutive need of narrative. Yet, as it might be in a post-Romantic novel, this fact is in no way enacted by Fielding within the dying mind in its last seconds of consciousness at the end of the noose. Wild is seen (from the outside only) to have suffered "a death as glorious as his life had been, and which was so truly agreeable to it, that the latter must have been deplorably maimed and imperfect without the former; a death which hath been alone wanting to complete the characters of several ancient and modern heroes." The play on "agreeable" for such a horrid correlation between life and death joins the metaphor of violence in "maiming," the latter becoming explicit in the last sentence of this chapter, where the author admits that, even though it would sometimes "do violence to truth, to oblige his reader with a page" of epitomizing execution for historical figures, it would still be appropriate to the moral shape of biography. Though this thought, in the early years of prose fiction as genre, prepares for Fielding's concluding chapter of postmortem summation as a crucial narrative ingredient, still his contemptuous assessment of Wild's character is performed so much from the outside as to be very far from the Romantic preoccupation with either the psychological "conservation" of the death scene or with the approach to dying as an eschatology of selfhood. The most obvious exception, on the face of it,

to the rule of rigorously secular dying in eighteenth-century fiction is Fielding's fantastic picaresque *A Journey from this World to the Next* (1743). Although the novel literalizes the figurative motif of the posthumous journey discussed in n.7 above, nevertheless the main ethical destination of this journey turns out to be defined in the manner of a retrospective disclosure at the point of death, since even "in Elysium . . . every soul retained its principle characteristic, being, indeed, its very essence" (ch. 8). For all the supernatural projection that conserves and extends such a mortal concentration of identity forward over the course of an imagined afterlife, the logic here is still primarily that of a death by epitome.

16. At the start of his chapter on "Memory and Death," in *The City of Dickens* (Oxford: Clarendon Press, 1971), Alexander Welsh observes that Dickens, very much like his Victorian peer Tennyson, speaks of supernatural powers in an afterlife "as fervent wishes, statements burdened with the consciousness of what cannot be proved—like the nagging thought, 'we have but faith: we cannot know,' of 'In Memoriam,' " and he quotes Humphry House, from *The Dickens World*, 2nd ed. (London: Oxford University Press, 1961), p. 132, to the effect that "a religion in a state of transition from supernatural belief to humanism is very poorly equipped to face death, and must dwell on it for that very reason." The most serious challenge to this view is to be found in the recent study by Andrew Sanders, *Charles Dickens: Resurrectionist* (New York: St. Martin's Press, 1982), where Welsh's supposedly "too narrow" claim for agnosticism is taken to task (p. 33); though much evidence is brought forward to document Dickens's private lip service to resurrection and immortality, Sanders's critical readings map the resulting biographical argument too singlemindedly upon the death scenes themselves, its transcendental grid obscuring many of their operative ambiguities. See also the extended discussion of George Eliot's wrestle with the Victorian expectations of the death scene, including its potential religious dimension, in Thomas A. Noble, *George Eliot's Scenes of Clerical Life* (New Haven: Yale University Press, 1965), pp. 102–122, and Robert Lee Wolff's comments on the religious inflection and ambivalence of the death scene in fictions specifically about the crisis of faith in *Gains and Losses: Novels of Faith and Doubt in Victorian England* (New York: Garland, 1977), *passim.*

17. Thomas, "Altarwise by Owl-light, II," in *Collected Poems, 1934–1952* (London: J. M. Dent, 1952), p. 71.

18. Ruth Bernard Yeazell, *The Death and Letters of Alice James* (Berkeley: University of California Press, 1981), p. 43, quotes a letter of Alice to William James on July 30, 1891, about death seeming to her "the most

supremely interesting moment in life, the only one in fact, when living seems life."

19. See H. P. Sucksmith, ed., *Little Dorrit* (Oxford: Clarendon, 1979), p. 772.

20. See Alan Horsman, ed., *Dombey and Son* (Oxford: Clarendon, 1974), p. 743.

21. The shift to passive voice at this moment is noted by William F. Axton, *Circle of Fire: Dickens' Vision and Style and the Popular Victorian Theater* (Lexington: University of Kentucky Press, 1966), p. 250.

22. Thomas H. Johnson, ed., "It was not Death, for I stood up," in *The Poems of Emily Dickinson* (Cambridge, Mass.: Belknap Press of Harvard University Press, 1951), p. 391.

23. "I felt a Funeral, in my Brain," in Johnson, p. 199.

24. Brooks, *The Melodramatic Imagination: Balzac, Henry James, Melodrama, and the Mode of Excess* (New Haven: Yale University Press, 1976), p. 9.

25. Brooks, p. 5.

26. It is no accident that some of Brooks's most telling examples come from the context of death and mourning—illustrations ranging from the funeral of Old Goriot attended by the hero, Rastignac, who "buried there his last tear of youth" (p. 139), through the death of Milly Theale in James's *Wings of the Dove* at the start of the next century. In James, indeed, Brooks speaks of the rhetoric of melodrama as a metaphoric "transaction" (his earlier term from I. A. Richards) between the "not directly representable" death of the heroine and those who seek comprehension of it in terms "transposed" (he might have said) from a worldly register; James's metaphors thus suggest the "necessity *of* metaphor in dealing with Milly's abyss: the impossibility of direct confrontation of it, the need to allude to it only through forms that, in their strain, figure its existence" (p. 191).

27. Jacques Derrida uses the repeated last utterance of Poe's Valdemar, *"I am dead,"* as one of his epigraphs for *Speech and Phenomena*, trans. David B. Allison (Evanston, Ill.: Northwestern University Press, 1973). Roland Barthes alludes briefly to Derrida's discussion of any enunciated "I am" in its relation to death (pp. 54—55) in his own essay, "Textual Analysis of Poe's 'Valdemar,' " in Robert A. Young, ed., *Untying the Text: A Post-Structuralist Reader* (Boston: Routledge and Kegan Paul, 1981), p. 160, n. 12. Stressing the "scandal of the enunciation" and its "paradigmatic disorder" (p. 153) as predication, Barthes does not take up the story's clue to the general treatment of death in narrative. For him the chief interest of *"I am dead"* is a linguistic transgression as "performative utterance" beyond anything foreseen by Austin or Benveniste, an "unwarranted

sentence" that, performing itself, "performs an impossibility" (p. 154).

28. Brooks, "Freud's Masterplot," *Yale French Studies*, 55–56 (1977), 281.

29. Coleridge, *Essays and Lectures on Shakespeare* (London: J. M. Dent and Sons, 1907), p. 116, who takes it upon himself to answer the king's subsequent question—"Can sick men play so nicely with their names?"—with the claim that "on a death-bed there is a feeling which may make all things appear but as puns and equivocation. And a passion there is that carries off its own excess by plays on words."

30. In *The Adventures of Peregrine Pickle* (1751) the dying Commodore Trunnion is confident, in his own words, of finding a berth in "the latitude of heaven" as per his "sailing orders," trusting that he may be duly recorded "in the log-book of . . . remembrance" (ch. 79). Other seamen mourn him in just such vocational terms, one apostrophizing his corpse as a "hull fairly laid up," yet still hoping "to set up thy standing rigging in another world." Another character's letter to the hero about his aunt's illness could almost be a direct source (shifting from nautical to highway terms) for Tony Weller's mortuary missive about his wife in *Pickwick Papers:* "I hope you are in a better trim than your aunt, who hath been fast moored to her bed these seven weeks, by several feet of underwater logging in her hold and hollup, whereby I doubt her planks are rotted . . . and she has quite lost the rudder of her understanding" (ch. 94). A later book by this novelist Dickens loved best, Smollett's *Adventures of Ferdinand Count Fathom* (1753), actually employs the "final discharge" metaphor (ch. 60) that Dickens uses in *Pickwick Papers* for the death of the Chancery prisoner. Though in their comic sentimentality rather than mock-heroic irony these figurative finales are more psychologically specific than the symmetries of death and life in Fielding's *Jonathan Wild* (see n. 15 above), they still fall short of the genuine Romantic inwardness of the death of Barkis, for example, in *David Copperfield.*

31. John Clubbe, ed., *Selected Poems of Thomas Hood* (Cambridge, Mass.: Harvard University Press, 1970), pp. 91–93. See also "Sally Simpkin's Lament; or John Jones' Kit-Cat-Astrophe," pp. 98–100, about a man who has "solved death's awful riddle" only by being bitten in half by a shark, at which point he no longer has the necessary breath left to deliver his revelation, "I am doomed / To break off in the middle!" Hood's notorious punning here displays an idiom of mundane discontinuity transposed from defunct to functional metaphor by the violence of an untoward death.

32. Discussing this passage in *American Hieroglyphics: The Symbol of the Egyptian Hieroglyphics in the American Renaissance* (New Haven: Yale University Press, 1980), John T. Irwin doubles the textual with the sexual through a quasiphallic etymology of "chapter" and an emphasis on its "six-

inch" extent, arguing for an emblematic conflation of "phallic coffin / life preserver / book" (p. 349) that connects with his remarks on the phallic upsurge of Queequeg's inscribed coffin at the end of the novel.

33. Charles Feidelson, Jr., ed., *Moby Dick: or the Whale* (Indianapolis: Bobbs-Merrill, 1964), p. 723, n.33.

34. Irwin, *American Hieroglyphics*, p. 161. Though his chief emphasis in on "the transformations of the godlike whale into the book" (p. 315), and on its "pyramidal" bulk as essentially hieroglyphic (pp. 285–286), Irwin takes considerable interest as well in the parallel between the tattoos of Queequeg, covering him "like a second skin" (p. 146), and those on the right arm of Ishmael, where the dimensions of the whale are "copied ver-batim" (p. 162). In keeping with the archetypal explorations of his study, Irwin traces the symbol of Queequeg's tattooing copied out upon the coffin back to the " 'chest' of Osiris that Isis brings back by ship to Buto as part of the scenario of rebirth" (p. 299).

35. This consideration of Bergson on retrospective mortal vision and its connection with his theory of temporal juxtaposition appears in the extensive untranslated appendix to *The Proustian Space*; see Poulet, "Berg-son: Le Thème de la vision panoramique des mourants et la juxtaposition," *L'Espace proustien* (Paris: Gallimard, 1963), pp. 137–177. A perfect fic-tional illustration of Bergson's "panoramic vision of the dying" in the par-ticular case of drowning occurs in William Golding's *Pincher Martin* (New York: Capricorn, 1956), its entire two-hundred page narrative unfolded in a "flood of connected images" (p. 9) during the extended death moment of a wounded and drowning man, as "his consciousness . . . lay suspended between life and death" (p. 8). Focused on death and pursuing the question of juxtaposition and rupture in more linguistically oriented terms than Berg-son's, one of the earliest American attempts to reconcile phenomenology and deconstruction was made by Robert Detweiler in an essay on "The Moment of Death in Modern Fiction," *Contemporary Literature*, 13, no.3 (1972) 269–294, where the structural importance of "interiority" in the first-person portrayal of death is closely explored. Drawing his examples largely from contemporary American fiction, his theoretical bearings from Poulet, Barthes, and Derrida, among others, Detweiler argues that "the death mo-ment can function paradigmatically as the beginning of a structuralist epis-temology" because of the absolute disparity that renders that moment a pure break "with time, with space, with consciousness" (p. 277).

36. Much contemporary work in narrative theory has come to address the question of death in these terms. Tzvetan Todorov, for instance, takes death as central to what he calls in his title *The Poetics of Prose*, trans. Richard Howard (New York: Cornell University Press, 1977), since the

"absence of narrative signifies death" (p. 74). Building upon Todorov, among others, Wendy B. Faris, in "1001 Words: Fiction Against Death," *Georgia Review*, 36 (Winter 1982), 811–830, considers narrative as a Scheherazadian staving off of death through a series of illustrative texts that lead her finally to Nabokov's *Ada*. In his often-cited essay "Freud's Masterplot" (see n.28 above), Peter Brooks pursues Freudian notions from *Beyond the Pleasure Principle* to account for the fictional deferral of the death drive, suggesting that Freud offers "a dynamic model which effectively structures ends (death, quiescence, non-narratability) against beginnings (Eros, stimulation into tension, the desire of narrative) in a manner that necessitates the middle as *détour*, as struggle toward the end under the compulsion of imposed delay, as arabesque in the dilatory space of the text" (p. 295). For other recent thinking along these lines, see Chapter 7, n.30.

37. Benjamin, "The Storyteller: Reflections on the Work of Nikolai Leskov," *Illuminations*, ed. Hannah Arendt, trans. Harry Zohn (New York: Shocken Books, 1969), p. 101.

38. Freud, "Our Attitude Towards Death," in "Thoughts for the Times on War and Death" (1915), *Complete Psychological Works*, XIV, 291. Ionesco makes a similar point in "Experience of the Theater," *Notes and Counter Notes* (New York: Grove Press, 1964), by remarking of *Richard II*, as an example of a central phenomenon of theatrical violence, that "it is I who die with Richard II" (p. 136).

39. Nietzsche, *The Will to Power*, trans. Walter Kaufmann and R. J. Hollingdale (New York: Random House, 1967), b. III, no. 822 (1888).

40. Benjamin, "The Storyteller," p. 94. This is a passage discussed by Peter Brooks in *The Melodramatic Imagination*, p. 51, and also on p. 224, n.50, where Brooks is "led to reflect on the number of deaths enacted in *Comédie Humaine*, and the kind of significance they confer on life, the kind of reflection and judgment that they solicit."

41. Benjamin, "The Storyteller," p. 94. Benjamin, as well as Georges Poulet (see above, note 35), is anticipated in this use of the retrospective death moment as figure for the stylistic intensities and compressions of fiction by the influential German poet and essayist Theodor Däubler, who opened his 1916 essay on "Expressionism" by invoking the "popular wisdom" that "when a man is being hung, he experiences his entire life over again in the last moment. This can only be Expressionism!" The point is then amplified in a way that would allow the inclusion of drowning along with hanging as an occasion of such instantaneous vision: "Quickness, simultaneity, the greatest effort toward the interrelationship of all that has been seen are the preconditions of this style . . . All that has been lived

through peaks in something spiritual. Every event becomes its own type."
See Däubler, *Dichtungen und Schriften* (Munich: Kösel-Verlag, 1956),
p. 853, my translation.

42. Benjamin, "The Work of Art in the Age of Mechanical Reproduction," *Illumination*, p. 221 and passim.

43. These remarks are quoted by Jacques Derrida, *Writing and Difference*, trans. Alan Bass (Chicago: University of Chicago Press, 1978), pp.
257–258. This passage from Bataille is of central use to John Kucich for
his opening chapter on the violent economies of enacted "storytelling" in
Dickensian fiction, in *Excess and Restraint in the Novels of Charles Dickens*
(Athens: University of Georgia Press, 1981), p. 38.

44. Yeats, *Collected Poems* (New York: Macmillan, 1933), p. 264.

45. In Derrida, *Writing and Difference*, p. 258.

46. In an early essay by Blanchot, "Literature and the Right to Death"
(1949), as well as in "The Gaze of Orpheus" (1955), and indeed as a
prevasive idea throughout the recent translation of his essays under that
latter title by Lydia Gray, *The Gaze of Orpheus*, ed. P. Adams Sitney (New
York: Station Hill Press, 1981), Blanchot lays the groundwork for much of
the deconstructive critique of language as presence and literature as incarnation. Elaborating in "Literature and the Right to Death" on the Hegelian notion of every "naming" as an "annihilation" of the "uniquely real"
(p. 42), Blanchot entertains its consequences for the radical absence at the
basis of all designation—"Negation is tied to language" (p. 43), since "when
I speak: death speaks in me" (p. 43)—as well as for the paradoxes of
literature as not only a hollowing out of its very denomination but as enclosure
of its own secured permanence: "But as one realizes the void, one creates
a work, and the work, born of fidelity to death, is in the end no longer
capable of dying; and all it brings to the person who was trying to prepare
an unstoried death for himself is the mockery of immortality" (p. 58).
Mallarmé is repeatedly invoked by Blanchot as an exemplary instance of
such paradoxes, and the most recent American venture in this line of critique
is appropriately Leo Bersani's metaphorically intended *The Death of Sté-
phane Mallarmé* (Cambridge: Cambridge University Press, 1982), with its
three chapters, "The man dies," "Poetry is buried," and "Igitur, the poet
writes." Mallarmé's verse, thus read, seems to deconstruct its own aesthetic
of "subjectivity" so that "what he refers to as his death, far from being
another theme in his writing, is the move which ruins the possibility of
thematic understanding," even as the "themes of a self" linger in the texts
to "memorialize the personality to which they posthumously refer" (p. 19).
Though Blanchot is alluded to by Bersani, there is a further unexplored

connection with Roland Barthes's work on "The Death of the Author" (see below, "Afterwords," n.3).

47. Jarry, *Cesar-Antechrist*, in *Ouevres Completes* (Monte Carlo: Henri Kaeser, 1948), IV, 339, *"Quand on voit son double on meurt."* Notions of doubling, used in a variety of senses, figure prominently in Michel Guiomar's *Principes d'une esthetique de la mort* (Paris: Librairie Jose Corti, 1967), a study that draws its illustrations from music and film as well as from literature. Guiomar's fourth chapter is in fact called "Le Double," and is intended rather in the sense of my term *displacement*, discussed in his introduction as *"transmissions, transferts et échanges"* (p. 19).

2. Traversing the Interval

1. Dickens, "Some Recollections of Mortality," in *The Uncommercial Traveller* (London: Oxford University Press, 1958; orig. publ. 1861), p. 192.

2. Derrida, "Living On," trans. James Hulbert, in *Deconstruction and Criticism* (New York: Seabury Press, 1979), pp. 133–134.

3. T. S. Eliot works for a similar effect within a single comparative phrase in his poem "Whispers of Immortality," in which the plosive designation of John Donne's desire to "penetrate" the sensual mystery of death is echoed immediately in the alliterative phrase "Expert beyond experience," a syllabic pushing beyond in its own right. Eliot, *Collected Poems, 1909–1935* (New York: Harcourt, Brace, 1930), p. 61.

4. Stevens, "To an Old Philosopher in Rome," *Collected Poems of Wallace Stevens* (New York: Alfred A. Knopf, 1978), p. 508.

5. Manuscript of *Our Mutual Friend* at The Pierpont Morgan Library, New York City, I, 119.

6. Manuscript of *The Old Curiosity Shop*, Forster Collection, Victoria and Albert Museum, London, p. 665.

7. I have taken up the thematic effect of this temporal dislocation in the narrative, as it secures the psychological contrast between Quilp and Nell, in *Dickens and the Trials of Imagination* (Cambridge, Mass.: Harvard University Press, 1974), p. 98.

8. *Bleak House*, corrected proofs, the Forster Collection, p. 459.

9. The Forster Collection manuscript changes have been reproduced in George Ford and Sylvère Monod, eds., *Hard Times*, Norton Critical Edition (New York: W. W. Norton, 1966), "Textual Notes," p. 262, 153.18,19.

10. Forster Collection manuscript, vol. II B, p. 164.

11. These include the deaths of Emily's parents and Ham's, the hus-

band of the lone and lorn Mrs. Gummidge, Rosa Dartle's parents, the husband of Mrs. Steerforth, who might have been a steadying influence on her son, the much-grieved Mrs. Wickfield, and the floridly regretted Mr. Pidger of Miss Lavinia Spenlow's past.

12. F. R. and Q. D. Leavis, *Dickens the Novelist* (New York: Pantheon, 1970), p. 50, where the effect is deemed so "perfectly free of sentimentality" that there is "nothing finer in Tolstoy's novels." Not exploring the story's impact on David as an interpretable "narrative," nor its allegorizing of some dead phase of his own innocence, Q. D. Leavis senses that the thematic motive for this avoided death scene is rather that the truest mother of both David and his mother does in fact survive in the figure of Peggotty.

13. It was suggested by Melvyn Haberman, after my 1982 MLA paper in Los Angeles on the Dickensian rhetoric of death, that this overt simile is precisely what brings the moment to the fore as a self-conscious secondary "narration" within the supposedly more cogent, less mediated, more mysteriously intuitive and internalized rendering of standard Dickensian practice. I explore further the idea of the inset deathbed narratives by individual characters, with the additional example of Biddy's story of Mrs. Joe's death in *Great Expectations*, in "The Secret Life of Death in Dickens," *Dickens Studies Annual*, 11 (1983), 195–197. Elsewhere I have considered the relation of symbolic death moments (whether reported by Esther Summerson or by the omniscient narrator) to the sustained identity crisis of the heroine in "The New Mortality of *Bleak House*," *ELH*, 45 (Fall 1978), 443–487, where I attempt to answer Ruskin's attack on the supposedly morbid and irrelevant indulgence of the Dickensian death scene. I failed to stress in that article, however, how directly the overseen deaths of the book contribute to its emotional resolution. When the father figure Jarndyce presents Esther to her destined husband, the doctor Woodcourt, and to her new version of Bleak House, this locus of consolation seems rather cryptically dubbed in honor of the unforgotten dead: "Alan Woodcourt stood beside your father when he lay dead—stood beside your mother. This is Bleak House" (ch. 64).

14. Adjusted from the manuscript's original italicized version, "the little creature *I* had once been" (distinctly positing a diminutive predecessor), the revised reflexive construction "was myself" emphasizes more directly the arrest of time in this mental tableau. See Nina Burgis, ed., *David Copperfield* (Oxford: Clarendon Press, 1981), p. 115. The symbolic embodiment of David's former self suggested by "on her bosom" was also a second thought even before copy went to the printer; for the phrase had originally been set down as the more predictably figurative "in her bosom"

(Forster Collection manuscript, p. 112), heart-held memory rather than embraced corpse.

15. In *Woman and the Demon: The Life of a Victorian Myth* (Cambridge, Mass.: Harvard University Press, 1982), Nina Auerbach develops in passing a similar sense of the Dickensian death scene as a character's essence in arrest. Mentioning that "as with Quilp, Nell dead is Nell alive" (p. 87), Auerbach sees the same internal logic in Steerforth's death: "Like Quilp, he dies the appropriate death of drowning amid a storm's mindless energy. His corpse, too, is an emblem of his essential passivity, evoking most improbably his recurrent motif of placid sleep" (p. 88). It is to this epitomizing sense of Steerforth's stilled body that I would add its displacement of David's adolescent identification with him, become now the corpse of dreams brought low.

16. I am indebted for this insight about David's vocational pun to Elliot L. Gilbert.

17. Forster Collection manuscript, p. 234.

3. Transitions

1. In *The Last Chronicle of Barset* (1867), for instance, Trollope titles a famous chapter "Requiescat in Pace" (ch. 11), referring not only to the death of Mrs. Proudie portrayed there (which Forster was later to praise so highly in *Aspects of the Novel*) but to the peace from nagging interference which descends with that death upon the soul of her husband. A later punning chapter title in this same novel, "Near the Close," refers to Dr. Harding's proximity to his beloved Cathedral "close" (or precincts), while the narrative events of the chapter gradually draw him near to his own human closure. George Eliot reverses the suspensive logic of these doubleply titles with the chapter in *Adam Bede* called "The Last Moment"; we expect Hetty's execution by "deliberately-inflicted sudden death" until, in the penultimate moment, Arthur arrives with a reprieve.

2. J. A. V. Chapple and Arthur Pollard, eds. *The Letters of Mrs. Gaskell* (Cambridge, Mass.: Harvard University Press, 1967), p. 324, where she adds in her letter to Dickens, "There are five deaths, each beautifully suited to the character of the individual."

3. See Jack P. Rawlins, *Thackeray's Novels: A Fiction That Is True* (Berkeley: University of California Press, 1974), pp. 202–215. Since in Thackeray "the basic vanity is a forgetting of one's own mortality" (p. 213), it is important that mention if not demonstration of "old age, decay, exhaustion and death" be repeatedly brought to our attention as future inevitabilities by which "events of the dramatic present are judged" (p. 202).

4. Gordon Haight, ed., *The Mill on the Floss*, Riverside edition (Cambridge, Mass.: Houghton-Mifflin, 1961), p. 455, n.7.

5. Knoepflmacher, *Laughter and Despair* (Berkeley: University of California Press, 1971), p. 133. Without mentioning *The Mill on the Floss*, Mark Schorer in his stylistic approach to *Middlemarch* offers indirectly one of the most considered defenses of Maggie's death in the flood. Stressing the kinetic figuration of consciousness in Eliot as a "stream" or "channel," Schorer quotes Dorothea Brooke's thoughts about "the niceties of inward balance by which man swims . . . or else is carried headlong" into the eventual "gulf of death"; without the former balance, the latter is, of course, the fate of the earlier heroine in *The Mill on the Floss*. See Schorer, "Fiction and the 'Analogical Matrix,' " in Howard Babb, ed., *Essays in Stylistic Analysis* (New York: Harcourt, Brace, Jovanovich, 1972), pp. 346–347; Schorer's essay was originally published as "Fiction and the 'Matrix of Analogy,' " *The Kenyon Review*, 6 (Fall 1949), 539–560. More recently, Nina Auerbach offers a suggestive cultural framework in which to consider Maggie's drowning in *The Mill on the Floss*. Concerned earlier in *Woman and the Demon* (see above, Chapter 2, n.15) with the drowning deaths of two male characters in Dickens, Quilp and Steerforth, Auerbach goes on to explore "the intense popularity of Shakespeare's 'mermaidlike' Ophelia in Victorian iconography," a symbolic "presence" that "infuses such unlikely prose contexts as the ending of George Eliot's *The Mill on the Floss*, transmuting into myth Eliot's obsession with the figure of the drowning Mary Wollstonecraft" (p. 94). Amid her several illustrations of mermaid images and undersea fantasies, Auerbach mentions without reproducing the painting of Ophelia by Millais (p. 94) that appears at the head of this chapter, including instead a reproduction of George F. Watts's "Found Drowned" (p. 163).

6. Thomas Hardy, "The Last Time," *Complete Poems*, New Wessex edition, James Gibson, ed. (New York: Macmillan, 1976), p. 687.

7. This phrase lends itself to the title of Miller's eighth chapter, "Literature as Safeguarding of the Dead," in *Distance and Desire* (Cambridge, Mass.: Belknap Press of Harvard University Press, 1970), where Miller sums up his sense of the exorbitancy of all fictive record in Hardy: "Far from granting his characters the oblivion they desire, his writing cooperates with the impersonal mind of the Void by keeping their fugitive moments of experience alive in the new form his words give them. His writing gives his people that immortality they flee" (p. 239). See also Blanchot, "Literature and the Right to Death," cited in Chapter 1, n.46.

8. The phrasing here is that of A. Alvarez in "Thomas Hardy's 'Jude the Obscure,' " in *Beyond All This Fiddle: Essays, 1955–1967* (New York:

Random House, 1968), p. 187. For Alvarez, what the child represents "was already embodied in fully tragic form in the figure of Jude. There was no way of repeating it without melodrama." Yet the emphasis seems more on what Little Jude's suicide predicts than on what it replicates, and this as a comment not on his expendability, whether psychic or dramatic, so much as on his namesake's.

9. This recurrent Vulgate response to divine invocation appears most notably, in the voices of Abraham and Moses respectively, in Genesis 22.1 and 22.11, and Exodus 3.2.

10. Highlighting the inevitable displacement of narrative act (*I* say) into narrative scene (*he* is, *she* does, *it* so happens), Thackeray's closure looks forward (with, indeed, its allusion to the Orpheus story as a parable of any and all story) to Maurice Blanchot's theory of "The Narrative Voice (the 'he,' the neuter)," closing essay in *The Gaze of Orpheus*, cited in Chapter 1, n.46. Blanchot's commentator in the Afterword, P. Adams Sitney, notes that as early as 1949 Blanchot "seized upon Kafka's definition of literary language as the 'passage du *Ich* au *Er*, du *Ie* au *Il*.' This transformation of *I* to *Ile* reechoes throughout Blanchot's theoretical work" (p. 195), particularly in the last essay of this *Orpheus* volume. There Blanchot writes, "The 'he' of narration in which the neuter speaks is not content to take the place usually occupied by the subject, whether the latter is a stated or implied 'I' or whether it is the event as it takes place in its impersonal signification. The narrative 'he' dismisses all subjects, just as it removes every transitive action or every objective possibility" (p. 140).

4. Thresholds

1. Eloise Knapp Hay has taken Ian Watt to task in a review article for the "flippant" remark "that Conrad here 'inadvertently suggested that his book would die as soon as it had been read.' " See "A Conrad Quintet," *Modern Philology*, 79 (November 1981), 184. Her claim that the requiem mass's "eternal rest" (*requiem aeternam*), in redemptive opposition to its *morte aeterna*, lies behind this line as an intended echo is more in keeping with my own sense of the special grace implied by Conrad's analogy to deathbed illumination.

2. In "Lying as Dying in *Heart of Darkness*," *PMLA*, 95 (May 1980), 319–331, I argue that this morally compromising coda amounts in symbolic effect to the last of the book's many death scenes. What I want to stress here, by extension, is that this first dramatized retelling of Kurtz's story is not only an existential but a textual allegory of death. Not just a cover-up,

it also discloses the always mediated nature of narrative as a belated laying to rest of event, whether real or imagined.

3. I consider the extranarrative link between violent image and its audience at the death of the helmsman in the film version of *Heart of Darkness*, in "Coppola's Conrad: The Repetitions of Complicity," *Critical Inquiry*, 7 (Spring 1981), 462–464, where the filmmaker seems deeply alert, in his own point-of-view strategies, to those tactics of displacement which so frequently double, then universalize, death in Conrad.

4. In "Un Rapport illisible: *Coeur des ténèbres*," trans. Vincent Giroud, *Poetique*, 44 (Winter 1980), 473–489, Peter Brooks relates this question of Marlow's to the "traditional concept" of drowning retrospect, citing Poulet's appendix on Bergson (see Chapter 1, n.35).

5. Conrad, *Heart of Darkness*, ed. Robert Kimbrough (New York: Norton, 1963), ms. citation, p. 70.

6. With Conrad's phrase "all the wisdom," one is certainly put in mind of Benjamin's use of the term so important for Peter Brooks's sense of the melodramatic imagination (see Chapter 1, nn.24,37). Continuing his interest in a poetics of the ineffable at the limits of metaphor, Brooks has given us the most sophisticated reading to date of the frame narratives of *Heart of Darkness* in their relation to the death scene that centers them, in his *Poetique* article, cited in n.4 above. (I am particularly grateful to the author for his unpublished English version of this essay.) Brooks treats Kurtz as a late-comer to the Victorian melodramatic tradition, distant cousin to those many characters who, in the "transmission of wisdom to succeeding generations," virtually "write their own obituaries, to provide the younger protagonists with the material to view the meaning of their own lives retrospectively, as obituary, in terms of the significance that will be brought by the as yet unwritten end" (p. 478 in the published French translation). My argument about *Nostromo* takes the novel to be built around a sequential rejection of just such "transmission" by its doomed characters.

7. Conrad is elsewhere explicit about the relation to fictional form of this human yearning for finality. Including "sudden death" among the satisfying novelistic closures in his "Henry James," from *Notes on Life and Letters* (London: Dent, 1924), pp. 18–19, Conrad extrapolates from this sort of fictional motive to the human condition at large in a statement anticipating Freud's sense of the "death instinct" in *Beyond the Pleasure Principle*. "Perhaps the only real desire of mankind," writes Conrad, "is to be set at rest." The comment specifically illuminates the closural death scene, the metaphor of death for harborage, and the prologue's sense of fictional finis as a laying to rest in *The Nigger of the "Narcissus."* These notes by Conrad

serve Peter Brooks, at the close of "Un Rapport illisible," as an appropriate unification of narrative "last words" (Conrad's phrase for closure) with those of mortal experience.

8. Shelley, preface to *Alastor: or, the Spirit of Solitude*, in Thomas Hutchinson, ed., *Poetical Works* (London: Oxford University Press, 1908), p. 15.

9. In a structuralist reading of Conrad's language for his closing chapter, "Discontinuous Semiotics: Language '*in articulo mortis*,' " in *Thorns & Arabesqus: Contexts for Conrad's Fiction* (Baltimore: The Johns Hopkins University Press, 1980), pp. 195–222, William W. Bonney is especially suggestive on the ironic collapse of Decoud's speech, as climaxed negatively when that "thin cord of silence" removes all ordinary "tenor" from language (p. 206). Bonney then quotes Georges Bataille's *Death and Sensuality* to confirm his point that "in proximity to death language reveals 'the sovereign moment at the farthest point of being where it can no longer act as currency. In the end the articulate man confesses his own impotence' " (p. 207). I would add that Decoud's last words, "It is done," which Bonney does not take up, confirm this point by way of a closural self-consciousness at the "sovereign" threshold of silence.

10. See Geoffrey Hartman, "Virginia's Web," in *Beyond Formalism: Literary Essays (1958–1969)* (New Haven: Yale University Press, 1970), p. 74, for this cryptic suggestion about Lily's last brush stroke and her accompanying words: "Lilly [sic] Briscoe's 'It is finished,' referring in turn to the reaching of the Lighthouse and to her picture, is deeply ironic. It recalls a suffrance greater than the object attained by this last term, by any term. Each artist resists his vision."

11. Derrida's remark, "I believe that the condition for a true act of language is my being able to say 'I am dead' . . . My language signifies, in spite of the lack of object," is quoted by Richard Macksey and Eugenio Donato, eds., *The Languages of Criticism and the Sciences of Man* (Baltimore: The Johns Hopkins University Press, 1970), p. 156.

12. As if his valedictory distance from his own life were as great as that of Thackeray's narrator from the plot of *The Newcomes*, Decoud's "I" of self-predication is subsumed by the implicit neuter "it" or "*il*" of closure, the pronoun that carries such a signal ambiguity for Maurice Blanchot. Narrative for Blanchot becomes the declension of the "I" of presence through various gender fictions of the plot to the depersonalized textual "it" of the neutered sign (see Chapter 3, n.10). Lying behind the virtual "*Il est fini*" of Conrad's French-speaking writer, then, is so complete and self-conscious an abdication from any "*Je suis*," so utter, and uttered, a surrender to the

literary rather than the lived moment, that the name Decoud is no longer available for denomination, only the deed that nullifies him in his own telling of "it."

5. Connective

1. From Hadrian Kornbleet, in "The Mailbag," *The New Yorker* (May 19, 1975), 35. Marshall Brickman's jabbing retort falls rather wide of the point: "We'll bet you didn't like Leonard's seduction of Helen in 'Howards End,' either. If surprises turn you off, better lay off the belles-lettres and get into something certain, like insurance."

2. Forster, ascribing the review to Will Beveridge, is quoted without a citation in Lawrence Brander, *E. M. Forster: A Critical Study* (London: Rupert Hart-Davis, 1968), p. 125. P. N. Furbank, in *E. M. Forster: A Life* (New York: Harcourt, Brace, Jovanovich, 1978), I, 149, also alludes to this early review from the *Morning Post*.

3. In *The Cave and the Mountain: A Study of E. M. Forster* (Stanford: Stanford University Press, 1966), Wilfred Stone's commentary on this passage seems to have dropped a stitch, for though he notices the tacit link of sex to extinction, and the metaphoric overtones of this death for Rickie, he does not distinguish the two "he's" as they signal the narrative's sly stress on that metaphoric overlap of corpse and protagonist, writing instead as if no pronominal liberty has been taken. " 'Before he went out to die'—it is a sexual death in the sense of the old pun, but it is also for Rickie . . . a spiritual dying" (p. 200).

4. This is an issue at the center of my essay "Forster's Epistemology of Dying," *The Missouri Review*, 2 (Spring 1979), 103–121. The feeling of being "only half alive," like his hero and surrogate, Rickie, was one that haunted Forster during his early manhood (see Furbank, I, 182), and led perhaps to the accusation leveled by another character at the protagonist of his first novel, *Where Angels Fear to Tread* (1905), where Philip Herriton is diagnosed as being emphatically "dead—dead—dead" (p. 150).

5. George H. Thomson, ed., *Albergo Empedocle and Other Writings by E. M. Forster* (New York: Liveright, 1971), lecture dated January–February 1907, p. 134.

6. Furbank, II, 310. Forster's distaste for anything more morbid than this "urbanity" of death goes back to his early reactions to Victorian literature. He was reading Pater's *Marius the Epicurean* just as he was completing his own first novel, before setting to work on *The Longest Journey* with its defiantly antivisionary deaths, and a contrast could not have helped

enter his mind between Pater's penchant and his own. Forster disliked especially the book's gravitation toward fatality, for "any death is wonderful: dead or wounded flesh gives Pater the thrill he can never get from its healthiness" (Furbank, I, 132).

7. Furbank, I, 26.

8. Furbank, I, 185.

9. Ascribed to Michelangelo by John Cohlmer, *E. M. Forster: The Personal Voice* (London: Routledge and Kegan Paul, 1975), p. 105, with the suggestion that Forster probably came across the paradox in Arthur Symons.

10. Forster, "Liberty in England," *Abinger Harvest* (New York: Harcourt, Brace, and World, 1936), p. 70.

11. Stevens, "Like Decorations in a Nigger Cemetery," *Collected Poems* (New York: Alfred A. Knopf, 1954), p. 151.

12. Forster, *The Manuscripts of "Howards End,"* Abinger edition, correlated with Forster's final version by Oliver Stallybrass (London: Edward Arnold, 1973), p. 85.

13. In *Style in Modern British Fiction* (Baltimore: The Johns Hopkins University Press, 1978), pp. 105–110, John Russell focuses his discussion of the welded antinomial structure in *Howards End* around this paragraph of reconciled antitheses. Treating the passage as a separable tour de force, Russell calls it "probably the greatest in the novel, certainly from the stylistic point of view . . . No paragraph in Forster better reveals his way of assaying his thoughts by ranging for boundaries to frame them" (p. 109). My interest in the paragraph requires that we recall it later, alongside the death scene of Leonard Bast and his transcendence of contradiction and antithesis.

14. The half-title illustration to this chapter is a version of the painting by George Frederic Watts that in Forster's day was hung in St. Paul's Cathedral, its allegory glossed by the artist as follows: "Time, represented as the type of unfailing youth and vigour, advances hand in hand with Death, while, poised in the clouds above their heads, follows the figure of Judgment, armed with the attributes of Eternal Law." See the catalogue to the posthumous Royal Academy Exhibition of Watts's work (London: William Clowes, 1905), p. 35.

15. Forster, *The Manuscripts of "Howards End,"* p. 336.

16. Henry David Thoreau, *Walden*, ed. H. Lyndon Shanley (Princeton: Princeton University Press, 1971), p. 98.

17. Forster, *The Manuscripts of "Howards End,"* p. 336.

18. Furbank, II, 10.

6. Rites of Trespass

1. Lawrence's famous letter to Edward Garnett, explaining his interest not in the "old stable *ego*" of a character but in its being, what it "*is*— inhumanly, physiologically, materially," is the basis of my stylistic study "Lawrence, 'Being,' and the Allotropic Style," *Novel*, 9 (Spring 1976), 217–244—reprinted in Mark Spilka, ed., *Towards a Poetics of Fiction* (Bloomington: Indiana University Press, 1977), pp. 221–356—where I discuss the rhetoric of predication and erotic reciprocity in several passages not treated in this chapter.

2. Lawrence, "Study of Thomas Hardy," in *Phoenix: The Posthumous Papers of D. H. Lawrence,* ed. Edward D. McDonald (New York: Viking Press, 1963), p. 497.

3. Ibid., p. 505.

4. In *D. H. Lawrence: His Life and Works*, rev. ed. (New York: Twayne, 1964), p. 89, Harry T. Moore nicely notes of this last subjective rather than objective adverb that it is "not intended to signify rapidly, but is rather used in Lawrence's favored way to mean livingly" (p. 89).

5. Though she does not stress in particular the metaphoric deaths of sexual annihilation and revival, Dorothy Van Ghent puts the case well: "Perhaps no other modern writer besides Rilke and Mann has tried so sincerely to bring death into relationship with life as Lawrence did, and each under the assumption that life, to know itself creatively, must know its relationship with death," an intimacy disclosed as "half the rhythm of life." See *The English Novel: Form and Function* (New York: Rinehart, 1952), p. 260.

6. Frank Kermode, "Critical Exchange," *Novel: A Forum on Fiction*, 5 (Fall 1971), 58.

7. Kermode, *D. H. Lawrence* (New York: Viking Press, 1973), p. 10.

8. Michael Ryan, *Marxism and Deconstruction: A Critical Articulation* (Baltimore: The Johns Hopkins University Press, 1982), p. 77. Commenting on Adorno's *The Jargon of Authenticity*, Ryan adds, "As if he were following Derrida's early program of undoing metaphysical oppositions, Adorno shows how, in Heidegger's text, *Dasein* and death pass into each other" (p. 78).

9. See Alan W. Friedman, "Narrative is to Death as Death is to the Dying: Funerals and Stories," *Mosaic*, 15 (Winter 1982) 76, n.19, where *Sons and Lovers* is one of his examples.

10. *Collected Poems of Thomas Hardy* (New York: Macmillan, 1927), pp. 202–203.

11. To reverse historical terms recently put forth by Julia Kristeva, this amounts to a resacralizing of the cadaver so as to rectify the "abjection"

of corporeality itself. In *Powers of Horror: An Essay on Abjection* (see Chapter 1, n.5), in a subsection marked "Abomination of Corpses Wards Off Death Wish. Taxonomy as Morals" (pp. 110–112), Kristeva explores the biblical demotion of corpse from sacred to abominated object. "Death drive, in such an adjustment, does not disappear," she argues, but is "checked" and rechanneled into a coercive logic of self-persecution. Linked to other prohibitions and taboos, this "abjection" of the corpse is party to a larger biblical scourging of the flesh, so that Kristeva later mentions "Sex and Corpse" (p. 160) as one of the constraining dichotomies with which Céline's revolutionary fiction attempts to break. In its own terms Lawrencian fiction serves to return the corpse at least halfway from abomination toward sacrificial totem—as part of his whole attempt to rehumanize the body in the name of desire.

12. Speculating about the transition of a mortal body from dying person to thing to pure image, and privileging death (as always in his work) for its analogies to the textual encounter, Maurice Blanchot in *The Gaze of Oprheus* (see Chapter 1, n.46) comments in rather Lawrencian fashion on the corpse as an incarnate image of itself as absence: "If we look at him again, this splendid being who radiates beauty: he is, I can see, perfectly like himself; he resembles *himself*. The cadaver is its own image. He no longer has any relations with this world, in which he still appears, except those of an image" (p. 83, author's italics)—or, in more Lawrencian terms yet, except as communicable tableau of its own separateness.

7. Effigy and Transfiguration

1. Stella McNichol, ed., *Mrs. Dalloway's Party: A Short Story Sequence by Virginia Woolf* (New York: Harcourt, Brace, Jovanovich, 1973), p. 23.

2. Woolf, *A Room of One's Own* (New York: Harcourt, Brace, and World, 1929), p. 84.

3. E. M. Forster, "The Early Novels of Virginia Woolf," *Abinger Harvest* (New York: Harcourt, Brace, and World, 1936; essay originally published 1932), p. 107.

4. Louise A. DeSalvo, in *Virginia Woolf's First Voyage: A Novel in the Making* (Totowa, N.J.: Rowman and Littlefield, 1980), a study of the manuscripts and later revisions, happens to quote this passage on p. 96 from the second major draft of the novel (Chapter 9, p. 7) at a stage still before the suggestive addition in the later typescript (in the Henry W. and Albert A. Berg Collection, The New York Public Library, Astor Lenox and Tilden Foundations). In her later chapter, "The Death of Rachel" (pp. 126–153), on the holograph and typescript variants of the prolonged death scene,

DeSalvo stresses those additions of water imagery and allusions to drowning in the 1912 redrafting of the novel that emphasize parallels to Mr. Dalloway's unwanted kiss (p. 135) and that connect with similar classical and mythological allusions at this stage of the rewriting (p. 137). Another reading of Rachel's drowning in connection with the *Comus* lines is offered by Sandra M. Gilbert and Susan Gubar in their chapter on "Milton's Bogey: Patriarchal Poetry and Women Readers," in *The Madwoman in the Attic: The Woman Writer and the Nineteenth-Century Literary Imagination* (New Haven: Yale University Press, 1979). Their analysis stresses Rachel's succumbing to the patriarchal animus against female voice when she "seems to drown in waves of Miltonic verse" (p. 193). My emphasis is on the metatextual rather than literary-historical thematization of this drowning, registering the dream of textual release as well as the nightmare of preempted expression.

5. In another illuminating manuscript variant not logged by DeSalvo, the unrevised draft records at this point in the death chapter that "death came and made no difference." Idiom here too manipulated, as with "nothing" in the final version, death is seen both to make no difference between the lovers and to remove any. The literature of death once more charges the linguistics of negation with ambiguity. This implied fusion of the lovers in a bonding absence is the kind of moment Avrom Fleishman has in mind in *Virginia Woolf: A Critical Reading* (Baltimore: The Johns Hopkins University Press, 1975): "In a way that strikingly resembles the use that Eliot in *The Waste Land* and Joyce in *Finnegans Wake* were later to make of the Tristan theme, Woolf manages to scorn the *Liebestod* motif and affirm it, too" (p. 16).

6. See Woolf, *A Writer's Diary*, ed. Leonard Woolf (London: Hogarth Press, 1975), p. 80, an entry which mentions, in connection with work in progress on *To the Lighthouse*, that "the sea is to be heard all through it," as if it were a sustained objective correlative of Woolf's own creative currents. Earlier, in the composition of the sketch for *Mrs. Dalloway*, Woolf describes "laboriously dredging my mind . . . and bringing up light buckets" (pp. 47—48). When committed to the full-length version of the story, she notes "how I dig out beautiful caves behind my characters," selves thus accessible to their "depth" (p. 60). In an entry six weeks further along in the drafting process, she describes "how it took me a year's groping to discover what I call my tunnelling process" (p. 61).

7. Woolf, "Professions for Women," in *Collected Essays*, ed. Leonard Woolf (London: Chatto and Windus, 1966, 1967), II, 287.

8. In a revealing glance, perhaps, at the homoerotic bonding of the two soldiers, subsequently much discussed by critics, Woolf had originally described the relationship as "a friendship . . . on the classic model" (see

the holograph, I, 107, in the British Library, London), probably in an allusion to Greek or Roman habits, before crossing out the last four words, probably for being unnecessarily coy. In the second volume of the holograph, Woolf happens to interrupt her draft to dash off, in the same notebook, a one-paragraph notice later printed in *The Nation* of a book published just that month, Stephen Graham's biography of a dead soldier with a literary turn, named Wilfred Ewart. What is noteworthy about this book when read alongside Woolf's own current work, and what must have intrigued her about it, is not just that its nonfictional plot resembles her own most recent novel, *Jacob's Room* (1922), about the wartime death of a gifted young man and the elegiac recollection of him by those who (so Woolf writes of Graham's story) would "adumbrate what he might have become." In this, notes Woolf, Graham's is the general "type of book" with which the "war has made us familiar" (p. 42). The more interesting parallels, though none of Graham's corresponding details are mentioned in Woolf's notice, are to the novel she was still in the process of drafting. In *The Life and Last Words of Wilfred Ewart* (London: Putnam's, 1924), Graham chronicles the wartime death of Ewart's friend (as Evans was to Septimus) and the survivor's grim meditation upon it: "And Wilfred Ewart lay in hospital in Hill Street and his friend was dead. Fate had removed him from the mud and ruin of the war to a hospital bed, and he lay and thought about it all" (p. 30). The mention of anything like actual mourning is as absent as in the case of Septimus. When Ewart returned to England after a furlough in Paris, disgusted with the painted flesh of courtesans (pp. 84–85), he "carried over into peace," among other transformations, a set of "shattered nerves," a certain "querulousness of mind" that it "took some years of peace to restore" (p. 87). When he is later killed by an accidental bullet in Mexico, without having achieved his literary promise any more than Septimus would achieve his as visionary poet, the elegiac tone rises to a pure, unappeasable subjunctive: "He might have writen novels, books of the age, plays" (p. 261). The slain friend, the neutral response, the nervous distress, the recoil from feminine flesh, the need for recuperation, the truncated aesthetic promise, the gruesome death delayed from the war but completed in a later act of violence, the encompassing attempt by the work of imagination to incorporate and memorialize the loss: these materials certainly must have struck chords in Woolf's composition of *Mrs. Dalloway*.

9. Septimus is described in Woolf's holograph draft, in any number of reiterated variations, as "the first man who had crossed from life to death." "Men who have leant over boats and fallen," Septimus thinks, "have woken [sic], when the drumming in their ears had ceased, but I go and come through those waters." In the next line Woolf crosses out the explanatory

phrase "without drowning" to sustain, no doubt, the sense of a dark miracle. These visions seem to continue a more general meditation on the "solitary traveller" in London earlier in the first draft, the wanderer who sees "flakes of the jellyfish which rise to the surface of the green sea waves and tempt the fishermen to flounder through the flood to embrace them"; always "tempted, haunted, and sung to," the "solitary traveller takes his way" (p. 27), unless, like Septimus later, he cannot help answering in his fantasies the siren call of watery death.

10. The image of rending and spilling does not occur in the draft either; we read instead that "impelled by some force, his tongue shaped the words of an Ode, a poem" (I, 64), a song whose burden the birds soon pick up, "making the words into a chant about death" (p. 65).

11. Lawrence, "The Ship of Death," *Complete Poems of D. H. Lawrence*, ed. Vivian de Sola Pinto and F. Warren Roberts (New York: Viking, 1964), II, 718.

12. Georges Bataille has approached this seeming paradox, as he finds it in Nietzsche, in terms of existential limits: "A fundamental principle is expressed as follows: 'communication' cannot take place from one full and intact being to another: it requires beings who have put the being within themselves *at stake*, have placed it at the limit of death, of nothingness." Quoted in Jacques Derrida, *Writing and Difference*, trans. Alan Bass (Chicago: University of Chicago Press, 1978), p. 263.

13. *Mrs. Dalloway* is certainly the chief victim of Spilka's thesis in *Virginia Woolf's Quarrel With Grieving* (Lincoln: University of Nebraska Press, 1980), where biographical evidence, shedding new light, also casts a number of shadows with it. Of *Mrs. Dalloway*: "It is—to put it bluntly— a psycho-literary copout, this vicarious refusal to mourn" (p. 73), and for Spilka it "spoils" the very close of the novel, with its "intended shared excitement." Confronting the resonant last line, "For there she was," Spilka insists that "she was not there, certainly, when the real grieving was blocked and the real dying and/or defying done, and so we may legitimately ask, at least of the closing lines—Where? Where? Where? Where?" (p. 74). I suggest that Woolf goes to great lengths to suggest that Clarissa was there in the only way one *could* be and still keep a breathing space between elegy and extinction.

14. See Quentin Bell, *Virginia Woolf: A Biography* (New York: Harvest, 1972), I, 90.

15. Holograph in the British Library, London, III, 21.

16. James, *Varieties of Religious Experience: A Study in Human Nature* (New York: Mentor, 1958), p. 121.

17. Rainer Maria Rilke, *Duino Elegies*, trans. David Young (New York: W. W. Norton, 1978), p. 35.

18. See J. W. Graham, ed., *The Waves: The Two Holograph Drafts* (Toronto: University of Toronto Press, 1976), p. 422, a transcription of holographs in the Berg Collection at the New York Public Library. In an essay that takes its title from Neville's germinal crisis, " 'Death Among the Apple Trees': *The Waves* and the World of Things," Frank McConnell sees Woolf's inescapable connection here to Wordsworth's "Tree, of many, one" in the *Intimations* ode, the natural relic of the knowledge of loss, and by extension of mortality itself. It is the archetypal tree that stands for the "doom . . . of consciousness-in-the-body, the 'dying animal' of Yeats or the 'ghost in the machine' of Gilbert Ryle." See C. Sprague, ed., *Virginia Woolf: A Collection of Critical Essays, Twentieth-Century Views* (Englewood Cliffs, N.J.: Prentice-Hall, 1970), p. 126.

19. See the Berg Collection transcripts.

20. In an explication, as it were, of his very title, Derrida in *Writing and Difference* posits as the relevant "difference" between script and its intervening "white spaces" a contrast as great as that between life and death—and otherwise analogous as well. Recalling Rhoda's metaphor throughout *The Waves* of temporality as the repeating leap of a "tiger," threatening to rend the self from moment to moment, Derrida, with his own ominous choppiness, has it that "writing proceeds by leaps alone. Which makes it perilous. Death strolls between letters" (p. 71). To align Rhoda's temporal alienation with French thought of her own era, we may note that in the year of her fictional suicide as an escape from time, the French existentialist Gabriel Marcel entered the passage dated March 22, 1931, in *Être et Avoir* (Paris: Aubier, 1935): "Time as open toward death—toward my doom. Time-abyss; vertigo in the presence of this time at the bottom of which is my death which sucks me in." Quoted in Jacques Choron, *Death and Western Thought* (New York: Macmillan, 1963), p. 255.

21. In "A Sketch of the Past," Woolf describes one of her "moments of being" in the language of epistemological collapse much like that to which the death of Percival drives Neville, as well as in an obvious foreshadowing of Rhoda's metaphor: "There was the moment of the puddle in the path; when for no reason I could discover, everything suddenly became unreal; I was suspended; I could not step across the puddle; I tried to touch something . . . the whole world became unreal." See Virginia Woolf, *Moments of Being: Unpublished Autobiographical Writings*, ed. Jeanne Schulkind (Brighton: Sussex University Press, 1976), p. 78.

22. Graham, p. 720.

23. J. Hillis Miller, *Fiction and Repetition: Seven English Novels* (Cambridge, Mass.: Harvard University Press, 1982), p. 217.

24. Graham, p. 723. It measures the distance between Miss La Trobe (see n.23 above) and Bernard as authorial surrogate for Woolf to note that during her mental exhaustion while finishing work on *Between the Acts*, Woolf's style of confiding this to her diary almost exactly echoes the language of authorial "death" and art's lost "echo" in Bernard's last soliloquy, both draft and final versions: "The writing 'I' had vanished. No audience. No echo. That's part of one's death." See Woolf, *A Writer's Diary*, p. 203.

25. Barthes, "The Death of the Author," in *Image—Music—Text*, trans. Stephen Heath (New York: Hill and Wang, 1977), p. 145. Hugh Kenner, in his memorial essay "Decoding Roland Barthes," *Harpers*, 261 (August 1980), returns this insight upon Barthes's own posthumous reputation as a generous irony: "Roland Barthes (1915–80), prolific and eclectic writer who was one of the most celebrated French intellectuals," was "a semiotician (meaning meaning-specialist) and would not have missed the semiotic import of his own *New York Times* obituary, where, as in all obits, Life is reduced to Text . . . What's entered our heads is a verbal construct called 'Barthes' " (p. 68).

26. Daniel Albright, *Personality and Impersonality: Lawrence, Woolf, and Mann* (Chicago: University of Chicago Press, 1978), p. 104.

27. *Oxford English Dictionary*, s.v. "do," B 17.

28. Bernard alludes to Byron more than to any other narrative predecessor, and it is perhaps from the convergence of narrator and character at the end of *Childe Harold's Pilgrimage* that Woolf got the idea for this pun, when the now unitary voice, in its apostrophe to the ocean's waves, "trusted to thy billow far and near / And laid my hand upon thy mane" (IV, 84). The whole narrative logic of Byron's poem looks forward to Bernard as a "man without a self," for the "I" of the poetic text addresses its invented alter ego, Harold, as follows: "What am I? Nothing; but not so art thou, / Soul of my thought" (II, 6), where the verb of fictional predication happens nicely to coincide with the noun of aesthetic generation in "art."

29. I am indebted here to the particular use of these terms in connection with the fictional death scene in David Lodge's *The Modes of Modern Writing: Metaphor, Metonymy, and the Typology of Modern Literature* (Ithaca, N.Y.: Cornell University Press, 1977). Analyzing a wartime story by Lawrence, "England, My England," Lodge concentrates on the linguistic shift at the exact moment of death. The imagery happens to resemble Woolf's in *The Waves* and elsewhere, for in death the "soul" of Lawrence's soldier hero is found "brooding on the face of the uncreated flux, as a bird on a dark sea." Lodge's theory is quick to take notice of this as a test case; the

metaphor *as metaphor* "signals the movement of the discourse into a new register, the extension of the author's imagination into a realm beyond the reach of empirical experience: death itself" (p. 175). We may think again of Dylan Thomas's "Death is all metaphors" (Chapter 1, n.17). We may also recall here Peter Brooks's sense of the "totalizing" metaphor that breaks with, and breaks down, the metonymic principle of plot itself (see Chapter 1, n.28).

30. This generic and ultimately formalist issue, in somewhat different terms, has been taken up with two of the texts important for this study by Steven Cohan in "Narrative Form and Death: *The Mill on the Floss* and *Mrs. Dalloway*," *Genre*, 11 (Spring 1978); 101–129. Cohan generalizes there from the example of Eliot and Woolf about the contrapuntal relation of life to death in fiction: "The English novel examines the temporal experience of its characters to achieve an imaginative effect similar to Woolf's, which splits life (Mrs. Dalloway) and death (Smith), and keeps them suspended in formal co-existence" (p. 127). A related line of discussion is followed through Austen, Eliot, and Stendhal by D. A. Miller in *Narrative and its Discontents* (Princeton: Princeton University Press, 1981), where the very idea of the "narratable" is at definitive odds with the closural.

31. Lawrence, "Why the Novel Matters," *Phoenix*, p. 535.

32. Woolf, *A Writer's Diary*, p. 354.

Afterwords: Death Bequeathed

1. In his own version of this by-now received notion about fiction's obsolescence in its conventional forms, Roland Barthes's comments on literature's "dangerous game with its own death" over the past century serve as an appropriate epigraph to the concluding chapter of Robert Alter's *Partial Magic: the Novel as a Self-Conscious Genre* (Berkeley: University of California Press, 1975), p. 218. For Barthes, as quoted by Alter from "Literature and Metalanguage," modern writing "is like that Racinean heroine who dies upon learning who she is but lives by seeking her identity." In the terms of the present study, literature has moved through centuries of self-realization toward its own "epitomizing" death, an art fully disclosed in its referential essence only when its traditional forms are no longer viable.

2. It must be suspected that the expatriates Beckett and Nabokov (the Irish writer translating his French prose back into English, the Russian never feeling quite native to the language of his English fictions) emerge together at the forefront of the contemporary mode of reflexive narrative because exile is the condition not only of their writing but of their words, a self-conscious linguistic estrangement (with all its defamiliarizing tricks

of idiom and polyglot puns) that compounds the inevitable alienation from reality of any text.

3. Barthes, "The Death of the Author," see Chapter 7, n.25.

4. Christopher Ricks, coining the phrase "corpsed metaphor" to account for the incomplete struggle for resuscitation in Beckett's idiomatic graveyard, explored the complexities of Beckett's mortuary word play in a lecture at the University of California, Santa Barbara, in April 1977, using examples from Beckett's fiction at large rather than the specific instances I adduce here from *Malone Dies*. Though Ricks did not develop the connection, Joyce, in the "Hades" section of *Ulysses*, indulges in many of the same embalmed, cosmeticized, and so artificially refreshed metaphors as Beckett, with an occupied coffin pondered upon as "so much dead weight" (p. 101), a mourner "talking gravely" (p. 115), or amours among the tombstones called "courting death" (p. 108). Earlier in Joyce's funeral chapter, the vernacular formula interred in "must be his deathday . . . many happy returns" (p. 93) allows "returns" to parody at once the myths of both resurrection and reincarnation in a deflationary gesture pointing straight toward Beckett's fiction.

5. John Fletcher, *The Novels of Samuel Beckett* (London: Chatto and Windus, 1964), for whom Beckett "tends to indulge in neologisms that are not always very successful, such as *defunger* for 'to die' (concocted from *defunct*)" (p. 164). To coin one portmanteau term for another, Beckett's is a *necrologism* at least as pertinent as Joyce's "funferall" in *Finnegans Wake* (p. 13), a novel whose own title catches that pun's same mix of grief and celebration in the double valence of mourning and new morning, wake and awakening.

6. Interview with Beckett by Israel Shenker, "Moody Man of Letters," *New York Times*, 6 May 1956, sec. 2, pp. 1, 3.

7. Beckett, *Stories & Texts for Nothing* (New York: Grove Press, 1967), p. 66. In the same vein Malone thinks of his avatar Macmann as all story, an existence of autonarration waiting patiently for closure: "This is the kind of story he has been telling himself all his life, saying, this cannot possibly last much longer" (p. 239).

8. Nabokov, "The Room," *Poems and Problems* (New York: McGraw-Hill, 1970), p. 165.

9. Peter Brooks concludes *The Melodramatic Imagination* (see Chapter 1, n.22) by exempting such modern and contemporary writers as Beckett and Robbe-Grillet, possibly Joyce and Kafka, from the tradition he has explored (p. 198). Though he does not mention Nabokov, it would seem clear that his fiction does fit closely the melodramatic model, with its conviction that "the surface of the world—the surfaces of manners, the signifiers

of the text—are indices pointing to hidden forces and truths, latent signifieds. The energy and excess . . . betrays an unwillingness to exclude occulted meanings from the systems operative in human life and its fictions" (p. 199).

10. A remark of Derrida's in *Writing and Difference* bears not only on this grammatological irony in Nabokov but further on Rhoda's fear in *The Waves* of overleaping the chasmlike white blanks between the inscribed steppingstones of her life: "But, primarily, the caesura makes meaning emerge . . . It proceeds by leaps alone. Which makes it perilous" (p. 71). Again, "Death strolls between letters" (p. 71). Like Gradus, death is found "breathing with the caesura"—"hiding," that is, "between two words," perhaps between such letters as *X* and *Y*, or in Beckett's sense within the coma of the comma.

11. Most critics tend to see Kinbote as an emanation of Shade, while Page Stegner in *Escape into Aesthetics: The Art of Vladimir Nabokov* (New York: Dial Press, 1966), seems at least as near the mark when he concludes, "If Shade blends into Grey-Degree-Gradus, and Gradus turns into a dictionary for poetry writing, then the suggestion that the entire story including the poem is a fabrication of the artist-madman is not too far-fetched" (p. 130).

12. "Interview with William Burroughs," *The Rolling Stone College Papers*, 1 (Fall 1979), 42.

13. John Donne, *Devotions*, Meditation XVII (London: William Pickering, 1840), p. 99.

14. Quoted by G. Thomas Couser, "The Shape of Death in American Autobiography," *Hudson Review*, 31 (Spring 1978), 57.

15. Robert Gittings, *John Keats* (Boston: Little, Brown, 1968), p. 425.

Credits

Index